D1443958

# SYNTACTIC ARGUMENTATION

Donna Jo Napoli
and Emily Norwood Rando

Georgetown University Press, Washington, D.C. 20057

Library of Congress Cataloging in Publication Data
Main entry under title:

Syntactic argumentation

Includes bibliographies.
1. Grammar, Comparative and general--Syntax
--Problems, exercises, etc. 2. Generative grammar
--Problems, exercises, etc. I. Napoli, Donna Jo, 1948-
II. Rando, Emily Norwood, 1946-
P291.S95      415      79-17605
ISBN 0-87840-180-6

# Contents

iii

# INTRODUCTION

Linguistics is primarily an academic discipline, which progresses via argumentation rather than experimentation. Because it is very much a publish-or-perish field, its battles are fought in the journals and anthologies where articles on linguistics appear. Aspiring linguists must be able to read these articles critically and evaluate the reasoning presented. They must acquire the habit of looking immediately for the data not covered, the alternative not considered. Only when these skills are mastered, along with a knowledge of the forms of syntactic arguments and an ability to apply these traditional arguments to untested data--only then are the students prepared to write persuasive, well-argued articles of their own (as they all eventually will have to do).

It is the purpose of our book to foster these critical habits of mind. By following articles with questions and criticism we want to lead students to regard the theories presented not as facts to be memorized but rather as possibilities to be considered, demolished, or improved, expanded, and strengthened. Making reading an active rather than a passive skill is one of the most important steps toward good writing. It is a skill which authors themselves seldom encourage.

This book is designed for use in a second or intermediate level transformational syntax course in colleges and universities. We assume that in their first syntax course, our readers have been familiarized with (1) the structure of a generative grammar and its rules, (2) the formalization of and justification for the basic transformations of English, and (3) the rudiments of syntactic argumentation.

Most of the articles included here either assume or argue that there is a level of deep structure where grammatical relations are defined and lexical insertion is complete, and that the syntactic transformations then apply cyclically to these structures to produce the surface structure--the input to the phonological component of the grammar. However, we would like our readers to use even these assumptions only as working

v

hypotheses, which must be tested and evaluated along with all the other details of the analyses presented.

Again, most of the articles take for granted the existence of the syntactic movement, deletion, and substitution rules that are used to relate active and passive sentences, statement and command, etc. In our questions we try to make the reader appreciate the economy that justifies such rules, and the care and thoroughness required in the formulation of alternative proposals. For readers who need to review the framework within which these articles were written, two particularly helpful sources are Marina K. Burt's *From Deep to Surface Structure* (Harper and Row, 1971), for an understanding of formalism and a presentation of the basic transformations of English; and Adrian Akmajian and Frank Heny's *An Introduction to the Principles of Transformational Syntax* (MIT Press, 1975), for an introduction to syntactic argumentation.

Finally, even the techniques and logic of syntactic argumentation can be questioned. Certainly the skill of a particular author in applying these techniques can be questioned. This is the one area, however, where we have tried to choose articles that are instructive as good examples, rather than simply further challenges to the readers' imagination and critical abilities.

This book consists of 12 articles, each prefaced by a short introduction which explains the historical context and importance of the article, each followed by questions, commentary, additional references (besides those given in the article itself), and homework problems. The questions of moderate difficulty are starred. Those of great difficulty are double starred. In this way the less well-prepared student can concentrate on the more basic questions while the more advanced student can seek out suitable challenges. The book can be used as the curriculum of either a quarter-long or a semester-long college course. We assume it will take approximately a week to cover each article.

Several factors have influenced our choice of articles. We have included some important articles from the 1960s in order to provide historical perspective. We have included some articles from the 1970s in order to introduce the student to current controversies. We have avoided recent articles which require a great deal of familiarity with formal logic (even though this excludes a large amount of the most interesting current work), because we feel intermediate students will not yet have the necessary background.

We have not organized the book around a few constructions, nor around a single school of thought, such as generative semantics, nor even a specific controversy, such as lexicalism vs. transformationalism. Rather, we have attempted to be somewhat catholic, introducing several past and present controversies, based on quite varied bodies of data. We do not claim that the resulting choice of articles is fairly balanced and perfectly impartial, but at least the student is led by our questions to criticize every position urged in the articles, and to compare it with other alternatives.

Given the purpose of the book, our main consideration has been the quality of argumentation in the articles. We looked for clear, well-written examples of both classic and innovative ways of establishing syntactic positions, applied to interesting sets of data.

We are indebted to all our many students who worked with us on earlier drafts of this text and whose questions and comments helped us in our revisions. Thanks are also due to our teachers, whose influence on our linguistic development led us to write this text in the first place.

We would like to acknowledge the assistance and cooperation of the original publishers, editors, and authors of the articles reprinted here.

We wish also to extend our heartfelt thanks to Georgia Greene for undertaking a critical reading of this book at a very late stage and to Stephen T. Moskey for help in editing the text. A special thanks goes to Mark Moses for help in typing the final draft of the manuscript.

And to Barry and Bob we are forever grateful.

To our families--near and far

# 1

## THE TWO VERBS *BEGIN*

David Perlmutter

Introduction. Perlmutter's 'The two verbs *begin*' is a good example of classic syntactic argumentation. He wishes to show that *begin* must occur in two sorts of deep structures, with two very different sorts of subject. Of course, there should be a difference in semantic interpretation correlated with this difference in deep structure, and for *begin* no such difference is ever discussed. We raise this issue in the questions following the article. If the article were to be rewritten today, semantic arguments would probably be much more prominent. When the article was written, however, it was believed that if syntax and semantics were not exactly independent of each other, still the drawing of a syntactic distinction should be supportable on syntactic evidence alone. Many people still believe that this is the proper approach.

The arguments Perlmutter uses, then, are mainly syntactic, and, in the section on intransitive *begin*, they are arguments that are universally accepted and very frequently used in transformational work. Every student of syntax should know how to use arguments based on selectional restrictions or distributional properties, *There*-Insertion, and the synonymy or nonsynonymy of active/passive pairs.

The organization of the syntactic arguments is very clear. There are two sections: five arguments that *begin* can appear as an intransitive V in the deep structure, followed by six arguments that *begin* can appear as a transitive V in the deep structure. Nowhere in the article, however, does Perlmutter consider a deep structure in which *begin* appears as an auxiliary verb to the following infinitive, all within one S, as shown here.

1

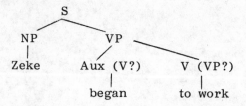

(Note that the details of the deep VP here need not be worked out as far as we are concerned, since we will see that this deep structure is untenable.)

The hypothesis that only one S node is involved even when two Vs are present in the surface could be called the 'null' hypothesis, since it is based on the assumption that the deep structure is essentially identical to the surface structure and that no significant structure-changing transformations have applied. In this hypothesis *begin* would be treated as something akin to an auxiliary. Undoubtedly, Perlmutter does not discuss the null hypothesis because he found it inadequate and assumed his reader could test it on his own and discard it for himself. But Perlmutter probably considered this as the very first hypothesis when first approaching the problems posed by *begin*. It is important that every student of syntax recognize the value and develop the habit of testing the null hypothesis for any given problem. Clearly, if the null hypothesis will account for all the data, it is the preferred hypothesis in that it is the simplest account we can give. Abstract deep structures should not be proposed unless the data make such proposals unavoidable. For this reason we suggest that the reader consider the 11 sets of data given in Perlmutter in light of the null hypothesis. The questions following the article also direct attention to this proposal.

# The Two Verbs *Begin*[1]

## DAVID M. PERLMUTTER

In the current theory of syntax[2] there are two ways available to represent the deep structure of sentences like

(1)  Zeke began to work.

*Begin* might be an intransitive verb like *seem* and *happen*, which take abstract (sentential) subjects in deep structure, so that the deep structure of (1) would be something like[3]

(2)

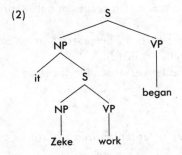

with the subject NP *Zeke* being substituted for *it* by *it*-replacement and the rest of the embedded S being moved to the right and brought under the domination of the matrix VP,[4] yielding the correct derived constituent structure of (1).

On the other hand, *begin* might be a verb like *try*, which takes object complements. Since there are no sentences like

(3)  * Zeke began for Oscar to work.

SOURCE: Revised version of a paper read at the annual meeting of the Linguistic Society of America, December 1967.

3

*Begin,* like *try, condescend,* and *refuse,* would manifest the like-subject constraint, requiring that the subject of the embedded S be identical to the subject of the matrix S in deep structure.[5] Under this analysis the deep structure of (1) would look something like

(4)

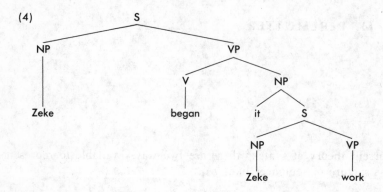

Equi-NP Deletion and other transformations which apply in the derivation of sentences with *try* and like verbs would apply here as well to produce the correct surface structure of sentences like (1).

In this paper evidence is presented to show that *begin* occurs in both types of structures in deep structure.

There is a variety of evidence that *begin* occurs in deep structure as an intransitive verb which takes abstract subjects, as in (2).

First, we note that it takes nominalized sentences as subject in such sentences as

(5) **The doling out of emergency rations began.**

*Begin* must occur in deep structures like (2) if sentences like (5) are to be accounted for.

The second piece of evidence that *begin* is an intransitive verb like *seem* comes from consideration of sentences like

(6) **There began to be a commotion.**

Sentences like (6) would be impossible if *begin* occurred only in structures like (4), for to generate them from such structures it would be necessary for *there* to be the subject of *begin* in deep structure, but there is independent evidence that *there* is not present in deep structures at all, but rather is introduced by a transformation.[6] If, on the other hand, *begin* occurs in deep structures like (2), sentences like (6) are easily accounted for. The *there*-insertion rule applies in the embedded sentence, producing a structure like

(7)
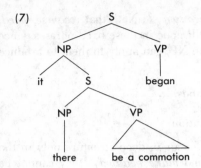

On the second cycle *it*-replacement substitutes *there* for *it* in the matrix sentence, bringing *be a commotion* to the right of *began* and under the domination of that VP.

A third piece of evidence for the existence of deep structures like (2) comes from sentences like

(8)   **It began to rain.**

in which the dummy subject *it* of weather verbs like *rain* occurs as the surface subject of *begin*. If *begin* occurred only in deep structures like (4), we would have to postulate this dummy *it* as the deep subject of *begin*. If *begin* occurs in deep structures like (2), the embedded subject will be the sentence *it rain* and the correct surface structure will result automatically from rules that are independently motivated.

Fourth, we note the synonymy of the sentences

(9)   a.  **The noise began to annoy Joe.**
      b.  **Joe began to be annoyed by the noise.**

If these sentences were derived from deep structures like (4), we would expect them to exhibit some difference in meaning, since the deep subject of (9a) would be *the noise*, while that of (9b) would be *Joe*. With a deep structure like (2), however, (9a) and (9b) have the same deep structure and differ only in that the passive transformation has applied in the embedded subject of (9b) but not in (9a). Their synonymy is thereby accounted for.

A stronger argument of this type for the existence of deep structures like (2) can be based on the distributional properties of lexical items like *recourse*, *heed*, and *headway*. These lexical items are not freely occurring nouns; we must exclude such sentences as

(10)   a.  * I like heed.
       b.  * Heed is nice.

and many others. The restriction on the occurrence of these nouns can be stated as follows: in deep structure they occur *only* in the fixed phrases *have recourse (to), pay heed (to),* and *make headway.*[7] Note that *recourse, heed,* and *headway* must be dominated by an NP node in these fixed phrases, since the passive transformation, which refers to NP, can apply to them to produce such sentences as[8]

(11)  Recourse was had to illegal methods.
(12)  Heed was paid to urban problems.
(13)  Headway was made toward a solution.

Now, since *recourse, heed,* and *headway* occur in deep structure only in the fixed phrases *have recourse, pay heed,* and *make headway,* they cannot be the subject of *begin* (or of any other verb) in deep structure. This being the case, if *begin* occurred exclusively in deep structures like (4), there would be no way to account for the grammaticality of sentences like

(14)  Recourse began to be had to illegal methods.
(15)  Heed began to be paid to urban problems.
(16)  Headway began to be made toward a solution.

If *begin* occurs in deep structures like (2), however, these sentences are automatically accounted for by rules that are independently motivated. The passive transformation, which applies to produce sentences like (11), will apply in the embedded sentence, yielding a derived structure like

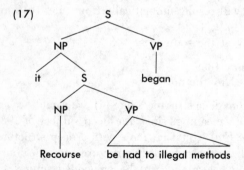

(17)

On the second cycle *it*-replacement substitutes the NP *recourse* for the *it* in the matrix sentence, bringing the rest of the embedded sentence to the right of *began* and under the domination of that VP. If *begin* occurs in deep structures like (2), the grammaticality of sentences like (14) through (16) is automatically accounted for.

There is abundant evidence, then, that *begin* occurs in deep structures like (2), in which it is an intransitive verb with an abstract (sentential) subject. We will now proceed to show that *begin* also occurs in deep structures like (4). The argument will proceed in several steps. First we will show that *begin* takes animate subjects in deep structure; this would be impossible if it occurred exclusively in deep structures like (2). Then we will see that *begin* occurs in sentences in whose deep structure it must have both an animate subject and a complement sentence, as it does in (4). Finally we will indicate the motivation for the NP node which dominates the complement sentence in (4).

That *begin* takes animate subjects in deep structure follows from the fact that it forms agentive nominalizations as in

(18)   Pete is a beginner.

Verbs like *seem* and *happen* which take only abstract subjects in deep structure do not occur in such nominalizations.

(19)   a. * Pete is a seemer.
       b. * Pete is a happener.

There is also evidence that *begin* occurs in deep structures with both an animate subject and a complement sentence, as in (4). As was mentioned above, verbs like *try, condescend,* and *refuse* manifest the like-subject constraint, requiring that the subject of a sentence embedded directly beneath them be identical to their own subject in deep structure. For this reason the deep structure of sentences like

(20)   I tried to begin to work.

must be something like

(21)

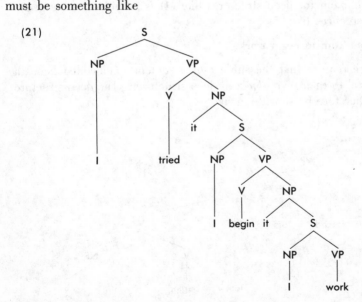

for the subject of the sentence beneath *try* must be identical to the subject of *try* in deep structure. If *begin* occurred exclusively in deep structures like (2), the deep structure of (20) would have to be something like

(22)

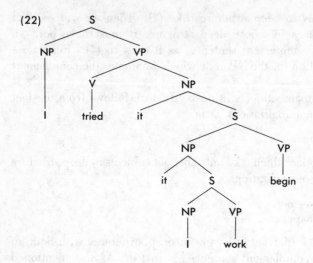

But in (22) the like-subject constraint is not satisfied, for the subject of the sentence beneath *try* is the entire NP containing an embedded sentence, and is therefore not identical to the subject of *try*. Since the like-subject constraint is not satisfied, an ungrammatical sentence must result. For this reason (21) rather than (22) must be the deep structure of (20). The grammaticality of (20) therefore shows that *begin* occurs in deep structures like (4).

A similar argument for deep structures like (4) is provided by the grammaticality of sentences like

(23) I forced Tom to begin work.

Verbs like *force* require that the subject of a sentence embedded beneath them be identical to their own *object* in deep structure.[9] The deep structure of (23) must therefore be something like

(24)

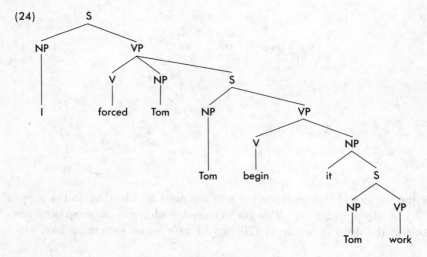

showing that *begin* occurs in deep structures with an animate subject and a complement sentence, as in (4).

Additional evidence for deep structures like (4) comes from imperative sentences like

(25)  Begin to work.

Since imperatives require a second-person subject in deep structure,[10] the grammaticality of sentences like (25) shows that *begin* takes animate subjects and complement sentences in deep structure, as in (4).

Let us now turn to the motivations for another aspect of deep structures like (4) — the NP node which dominates the embedded sentence. In this connection we notice that *begin* takes NP objects, as in

(26)  Sam began the job.

which predictably undergo the passive transformation:

(27)  The job was begun by Sam.

If these sentences are to be accounted for, *begin* must take objects in deep structure.[11]

A slightly more intricate argument for the transitivity of *begin* in deep structure comes from such sentences as

(28)  Mark began enthusiastically, but he got tired by noon.

Here, *begin* occurs without an overt object, and with a meaning like that of such verbs as *eat* and *read* when they have no overt object. If *begin* is a transitive verb, it can be marked for object deletion in the same way that *eat* and *read* are,[12] and this behavior is thereby accounted for in the same way in all such cases. If we are to achieve this parallelism, however, *begin* must take objects in deep structure.

To summarize briefly, we have seen that, on the one hand, *begin* occurs in deep structures like (2) and that, on the other, it takes animate subjects and object complements, as in (4).[13] We will call the former the intransitive *begin*, and the latter the transitive *begin*. No grammar of English can be considered adequate unless it provides for the occurrence of *begin* in both types of deep structures.[14]

This conclusion raises several questions which we will merely mention here without giving a satisfactory answer to them.

The first question concerns what restrictions each *begin* imposes on its subject, the kind of complements it takes, and so on. For example, all verbs which manifest the like-subject constraint require animate subjects. Since sentences like (3) must be ruled out as ungrammatical, the transitive *begin* must also manifest the like-subject constraint. We therefore expect the transitive *begin* to require animate subjects. This would mean that in all sentences in which the subject of *begin* in surface structure is inanimate we are dealing with the intransitive *begin*. That is, sentences like

(29) Oil began to gush from the well.

in which *begin* has an inanimate subject in surface structure must derive from a deep structure like (2) rather than from one like (4). While we will not fully test this hypothesis here, there is some evidence that it is correct. Note that in sentences which we have shown to contain the transitive *begin*, the verb phrase beginning with *begin* can be replaced by *do so*.[15]

(30) Warren tried to begin to work and Jerry tried to do so too.
(31) I forced Warren to begin to work and Paul forced Jerry to do so.
(32) Begin to work and do so at once.

In sentences which contain the intransitive *begin*, however, the verb phrase beginning with *begin* cannot be replaced by *do so:*

(33) * Heed began to be paid to urban problems and attention did so too.
(34) * There began to be a commotion and there did so at four o'clock.

This accords with a valid generalization about English: no verb which occurs in deep structures like (2) in which it takes abstract subjects can be replaced by *do so*. Now, if the transitive *begin* requires animate subjects, and all sentences like (29) in which *begin* has an inanimate subject in surface structure are consequently instances of the intransitive *begin*, it should be the case that in such sentences the verb phrase beginning with *begin* cannot be replaced by *do so*. This seems to be the case, since we do not get sentences like

(35) * Oil began to gush from the well and water did so too.[16]

While this is not conclusive, it can serve to illustrate the kinds of questions that need to be investigated in order to determine when we are dealing with the transitive *begin*, and when with the intransitive one.

The other major question that arises is that of the relation between the transitive and the intransitive *begin*. It has been the purpose of this paper to show that *begin* occurs in two distinct kinds of deep structures. The question will be left open here as to whether we are dealing with two distinct verbs, a single verb with two distinct sets of contextual features, or a single verb whose occurrence in these two kinds of deep structures is predictable in some way.

The properties of *begin* that have been pointed out here are shared by such verbs as *start, continue, keep,* and *stop*, as well as by verbs which appear to be quite different. The verb *threaten*, for example, must be an intransitive verb that occurs in deep structures like (2) because the following sentences are grammatical:

(36)   Thére threatened to be a riot.
(37)   It threatened to rain.

On the other hand, it must occur in deep structures like (4) because these sentences are grammatical:

(38)   I tried to threaten to resign.
(39)   I forced Tom to threaten to resign.
(40)   Threaten to resign.

The occurrence of *threaten* in both kinds of deep structures produces palpable ambiguities. For example, the sentence

(41)   The students threatened to take over the administration building.

has two quite different readings. With the transitive *threaten,* it means that the students made threatening statements to the effect that they would take over the administration building. With the intransitive *threaten* in deep structure, (41) might be used to describe a scene in which a mob of students surged toward the administration building; on this reading it does not entail anyone's making any threats at all.[17]

The question of the range of verbs which are like *begin* in occurring as both a transitive and intransitive verb in deep structure, like the question of how the two verbs are to be related, if at all, will be left open here. It appears, however, that the phenomenon of transitive–intransitive verb doublets is quite widespread, and extends into the modal system. It has been observed by grammarians that modals like *must,* for example, are systematically ambiguous.[18] A sentence like

(42)   Clyde must work hard.

can express some obligation on the part of Clyde to work hard, or it can be paraphrased as: It must be the case that Clyde works hard. This suggests that *must* is a transitive–intransitive verb doublet like *begin* in deep structure, occurring in deep structures like (4) on the former reading and in deep structures like (2) on the latter. Vetter (1967) has shown that this also is the case with *need.* If these analyses are correct, and it turns out that there are syntactic facts in English which can be accounted for only if modals are transitive–intransitive verb doublets in deep structure, this will constitute evidence for the hypothesis argued in Ross (1967) that there is no [auxiliary] constituent in deep structure, and that the so-called "auxiliary verbs" are real verbs in deep structure.

## NOTES

1. The subject of this paper is included in my doctoral dissertation *Deep and Surface Structure Constraints in Syntax* (MIT, 1968), where some of the issues raised here are discussed more fully. I am indebted to many friends and colleagues for their helpful

comments and criticism — particularly Stephen Anderson, George Bedell, Noam Chomsky, George Lakoff, and Haj Ross. Errors of course are my own. I am also indebted to the American Council of Learned Societies for support through a graduate fellowship in linguistics and to the National Science Foundation for support through grant GS-2005 to Brandeis University.

2. The theoretical framework presupposed here is basically that of Chomsky (1965) and Rosenbaum (1967). For more recent developments in this theory, see the other papers in this volume and the references cited there.

3. All tree diagrams given here are grossly oversimplified; I have omitted everything that is not relevant to the points under discussion.

4. For a justification of this formulation of *it*-replacement, see Lakoff (1966a).

5. For a discussion of the like-subject constraint and the evidence that it is a deep structure constraint, see Perlmutter (1968).

6. *There* behaves like an NP with respect to transformational rules in that it inverts in questions (*Was there a commotion?*), shows up in tag questions (*There was a commotion, wasn't there?*), shows up with *so* (*Joe said there would be a commotion, and so there was*), undergoes *it*-replacement (*We expected there to be a commotion*), and undergoes the passive transformation (*There was expected to be a commotion*). But *there* cannot occur everywhere that NPs occur in deep structure; we must be able to rule out as ungrammatical such sentences as * *I like there*, * *There is nice*, and many others. It is difficult to see how this could be done if *there* occurs in deep structures. If *there* is introduced by a transformation, on the other hand, we can correctly rule out such deviant sentences by stating the constraints on the distribution of *there* in the rule that introduces it. We will now show that these constraints *cannot* be stated in deep structure, and *must* be done by means of a transformational rule. *There* can occur only with a small number of intransitive verbs (such as *be*, in the examples already cited, and a few others, as in *There ensued a controversy*). *There* cannot occur with *kill*, for example, so alongside *A policeman killed a demonstrator* we do not get * *There killed a policeman a demonstrator*. Now, the passive transformation introduces *be*, which can co-occur with *there*. And if the structure underlying *A policeman killed a demonstrator* has been transformed by the passive transformation into the structure underlying *A demonstrator was killed by a policeman*, which contains *be*, then the corresponding sentence with *there* is grammatical: *There was a demonstrator killed by a policeman*. Whether or not *there* can occur in such sentences cannot be determined on the basis of their deep structures alone, for their deep structures do not contain a verb with which *there* can co-occur. It is only if the passive transformation has applied, introducing *be*, that these sentences can contain *there*. In other words, the question of whether or not *there* can appear in certain sentences cannot be decided on the basis of their deep structures, but only after the passive transformation has applied. For this reason the constraints on the distribution of *there* cannot be stated in deep structure. We must conclude that *there* is not present in deep structure, but rather is introduced by a transformation.

7. Some speakers also allow the fixed phrase *take heed (of)*. Note in passing that these fixed phrases can serve as indicators of environments in which particular verbs can be deleted. For example, Ray Dougherty has noted that although adverbials like *by tomorrow* cannot occur with verbs in the past tense (* *We ordered a bicycle by tomorrow*), sentences like *We needed a bicycle by tomorrow* are perfectly grammatical. This suggests that this sentence is derived from a deep structure with an additional

verb in it: *We needed to V a bicycle by tomorrow,* in which *by tomorrow* is not modifying *needed,* which is in the past tense, but rather the additional verb, which is not. On semantic grounds, the appropriate verb would seem to be *have,* so that the sentences in question would be derived from the structure underlying *We needed to have a bicycle by tomorrow,* by deletion of the verb *have.* Fixed phrases like *have recourse (to)* can be used to show that *have* is the correct choice here, since *have* must be able to undergo deletion in this environment anyway in order to account for the grammaticality of sentences like *We needed recourse to some higher authority.* This sentence must be derived from the structure underlying *We needed to have recourse to some higher authority,* since *recourse* can occur only as the object of *have.* The two motivations for an underlying *have* in this environment explain the grammaticality of *We needed recourse to some higher authority by tomorrow.*

8. This was pointed out by Chomsky to show the incorrectness of any analysis under which a passivized sentence like

(i)   The Mohawks were defeated by the Samoans.

has a deep structure like

(ii)

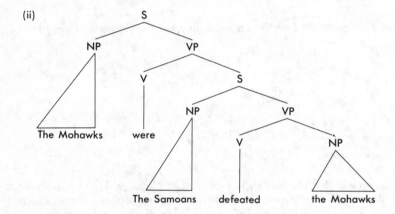

in which the surface subject of the passivized sentence (i) is the subject in deep structure of a higher sentence with the verb *be.* This analysis is incorrect, as (11) through (13) show, because *recourse, heed,* and *headway* occur in deep structure only in certain fixed phrases and therefore cannot be the subject of anything in deep structure. But the analysis of the passive under which (ii) is the deep structure of (i) would require *recourse, heed,* and *headway* to be the subject of *be* in the deep structures of (11) through (13). This analysis is therefore incorrect. Sentences (11) through (13) constitute extremely strong evidence that there is a passive transformation in English which takes deep structure objects and makes them into subjects in surface structure.

9. Evidence for this is to be found in Perlmutter (1968).

10. Evidence for this is to be found in Perlmutter (1968).

11. It might be argued that there are restrictions on the class of NPs that can be the objects of *begin* of a sort that make it necessary to derive these objects from more abstract underlying structures. Regardless of whether or not this is the case,

they must still be dominated by an NP node, as is shown by their ability to undergo the passive transformation in sentences like (27).

12. For some discussion of object deletion of this kind and its relevance to semantic interpretation, see Katz and Postal (1964, pp. 79–84) and Chomsky (1965, p. 87).

13. We have shown that *begin* takes objects in deep structure, but strictly speaking, we have not shown that its complement sentences are object complements. That is, we have not shown that a possible deep structure of (1) is not

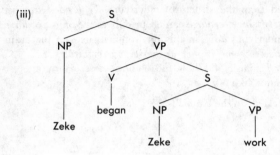

(iii)

rather than (4). Since we *have* shown *begin* to appear in deep structures like

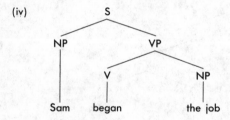

(iv)

however, it is clear that phrase structure rules of the kind justified by Rosenbaum (1967) will produce deep structures like (4) anyway, since these phrase structure rules provide for noun phrase complementation by means of a rule that introduces S under NP. The question therefore is whether *begin* occurs in deep structures like (iii) *in addition to* deep structures like (4) and (2). The answer to this question may well turn out to be negative, even though sentences with *begin* fail to satisfy Rosenbaum's criteria for noun phrase complementation. The fact that we do not get passive sentences like * *To work was begun by Zeke* is irrelevant, as Robin Lakoff has pointed out, since even with verbs which normally passivize we do not get passives when the subject of the embedded sentences is identical to the subject of the matrix sentence. Thus *expect*, for example, takes object complements and normally passivizes, yielding sentences like *For Mike to win was expected by everybody*. But if the matrix and embedded subjects are the same, no passive results: * *To win was expected by Mike*. Since the *begin* that appears in structures like (4) requires that the embedded subject be identical to the matrix subject, we will never get a passive like * *To work was begun by Zeke*. For this reason the lack of a grammatical passive here tells us nothing about whether *begin* takes object complements. George Lakoff has argued that the lack of grammatical pseudo-cleft sentences like * *What Zeke began was to work* is also not a valid argument against noun phrase complementation with such verbs, leading him to call into question the existence of intransitive verb phrase complementation, as in (iii). See Lakoff and Ross (in preparation) for these arguments. However this should turn out, it is only tangentially relevant to the point of this paper, which is to show that *begin* occurs both as a verb with abstract subjects, as in (2), and as a verb with animate subjects and complement sentences, as in (4) or (iii) or both.

14. Garcia (1967) points out that verbs like *begin* lack selectional restrictions on their subjects, and that sentences like (9a) and (9b) are synonymous. She concludes that on formal grounds *begin* should be treated as an intransitive verb that takes abstract (sentential) subjects, analogous to such verbs as *seem* and *happen*. She goes on to say that this solution does not accord with our intuitions about such sentences as *John began to read the book* and offers this as a case where the formally motivated solution and the intuitively correct solution are in conflict. In this paper evidence has been presented to show that no grammar of English is adequate if it does not allow *begin* to occur in two distinct kinds of deep structures. As a result the issue raised by Garcia does not present a problem.

15. For discussion of *do so*, see Lakoff and Ross (1966). This topic is explored in considerably greater depth in Anderson (1968).

16. Sentence (35) may be possible if *did so* is taken as having replaced *gushed from the well*, but *did so* cannot have replaced *began to gush from the well*, which is the reading that is of interest here. For this reason I have starred the sentence.

17. I am indebted to Wayles Browne for pointing out (41) to me. Note in passing that there must be some additional constraints on sentences with *threaten*, for we do not get sentences like * *Recourse threatened to be had to illegal methods*.

18. Within a generative framework, the remarks of Hofmann (1966) are very suggestive.

## REFERENCES FOR 'THE TWO VERBS *BEGIN*'

Anderson, S. 1968. Pro-sentential forms and their implications for sentence structure. In: Harvard Computation Laboratory Report to the National Science Foundation on mathematical linguistics and automatic translation, No. NSF-20. Cambridge, Mass.: Harvard University.

Chomsky, N. 1965. Aspects of the theory of syntax. Cambridge, Mass.: The MIT Press.

Garcia, E. 1967. Auxiliaries and the criterion of simplicity. Lg. 43.853-870.

Hofmann, R. 1966. Past tense replacement and the modal system. In: Harvard Computation Laboratory Report to the National Science Foundation on mathematical linguistics and automatic translation, No. NSF-17. Cambridge, Mass.: Harvard University.

Katz, J., and P. Postal. 1964. An integrated theory of linguistic descriptions. Cambridge, Mass.: The MIT Press.

Lakoff, G. 1966. Deep and surface grammar. [Published in 1968 in Linguistic Institute Packet of Papers, University of Illinois].

Lakoff, G., and J. R. Ross. 1966. Criterion for verb phrase constituency. In: Harvard Computation Laboratory Report to the National Science Foundation on mathematical linguistics and automatic translation, No. NSF-17. Cambridge, Mass.: Harvard University.

Perlmutter, D. 1968. Deep and surface structure constraints in syntax. MIT dissertation. [Published 1971, New York: Holt, Rinehart, and Winston].

Rosenbaum, P. 1967. The grammar of English predicate complement constructions. Cambridge, Mass.: The MIT Press.

Ross, J. R. 1967. Auxiliaries as main verbs. [In: Linguistic Institute Packet of Papers, 1968, University of Illinois. Also published in Studies in Philosophical Linguistics (1969) 1:1.77-102].

Vetter, D. 1967. Need. Unpublished honors thesis. MIT.

QUESTIONS

*Question 1. Perlmutter's first argument is based on the fact that *begin* can appear with a nominalization as its surface subject. He concludes that *begin* must be able to appear with a sentential subject in the deep structure. What assumption is Perlmutter making about the source of the subject NP in (i)?

(i) The doling out of emergency rations began.

(After you have read Chomsky's paper in this volume, come back to this question and test whether Perlmutter's assumption is justifiable. Consider Ss like (ii)-(iv), which Perlmutter does not mention.)

(ii) Then the hot weather began.
(iii) Then our troubles began.
(iv) Then the meal began.

Given Perlmutter's assumption, could the null hypothesis account for (i)?

**Question 2. The second argument rests on the fact that existential *there* can appear as the surface subject of *begin*. (Read footnote 6 carefully and try to reconstruct for yourself an argument that this *there* cannot appear in the deep structure. Note in particular the relevance of the fact that this *there* can appear in passives.) If *there* is inserted transformationally as Perlmutter argues, what is the simplest statement of the structural description of *There*-Insertion, considering only simple sentences? (By simple sentences we mean those with only one verb, with or without modals, perfective *have*, progressive *be*, and/or passive *be*.) How would the structural description of *There*-Insertion have to be changed in order to account for (i) if we assume the null hypothesis?

(i) There began to be a commotion.

Be sure you note the relevance of pairs such as:

(ii) a.   There was a commotion.
(ii) b.   There began to be a commotion.
(iii) a.   *There cried a little girl.
(iii) b.   *There began to cry a little girl.

Could the null hypothesis account for pairs such as (ii) and (iii) in an explanatory way? Does *begin* behave like modals, perfective *have*, progressive *be*, and/or passive *be* with respect to *There*-Insertion?

Considering only two possible deep structures for *begin*, one intransitive with a sentential subject, and one transitive with a sentential object, and noting that *there* cannot be present in the deep structure, Perlmutter concludes that Ss like (i) must have a sentential subject. Why can't (i) have a deep sentential object? (Try writing the deep tree for (i) with a sentential object and see what problem arises.) What assumption is Perlmutter making about deep structure nodes in general with respect to lexical items?

Note that Perlmutter refers to a rule of *It*-Replacement. This rule is known by various names, including Subject Raising and Raising into Subject Position. Basically, the rule moves the subject of a clause which is acting as a sentential subject of the next higher clause into subject position in that higher clause, and moves the remaining elements of the lower clause to the end of the higher clause. Some linguists have found it useful to separate this rule into two steps--a rule which extraposes sentential subjects (a rule which is needed independently) followed by a rule which moves the subject of the extraposed clause into subject position in the next higher clause. Since sentences with *begin* (such as (iv)) in which only Extraposition has applied are out, there is no evidence here that two rules have applied in (i).

(iv) *It began (that) there was a commotion.

**Question 3.** The third argument is based on the fact that the dummy subject *it* of weather Vs can appear with *begin* precisely when *begin* is followed by a weather V. How is this argument similar to that based on existential *there*? Could the null hypothesis handle these facts? What constraint on the distribution of dummy *it* will be violated if we propose for (i) a deep structure with a sentential object?

(i) It began to rain.

**\*Question 4.** The next argument is based on the fact that active and passive S pairs with *begin* are synonymous, as in (i).

(i) a. The noise began to annoy Joe.
(i) b. Joe began to be annoyed by the noise.

If *begin* is a main V, why can't (i-b) be directly derived from (i-a) by Passive? What is the environment for Passive according to (the assumption of) Perlmutter? What problem in the analysis of these active/passive pairs arises if *begin* is in a transitive structure underlyingly? If, instead, *begin* is an auxiliary, can (i-b) then be derived from (i-a) by Passive? (Compare *begin* to modals and other auxiliaries with respect to Passive.)

**\*Question 5.** The final argument that *begin* can be an intransitive V uses the fact that words like *recourse, heed,* and *headway* appear in simple active Ss only as the objects of the Vs *have*, *pay*, and *make*, respectively. They can appear as the subject of *begin* only when *begin* is followed by *be had, be paid,* or *be made*. Perlmutter says that if these NPs are generated in object position in a sentential subject of *begin* and if Passive then applies on the lower cycle, followed by Raising into Subject Position on the higher cycle, his sentences in (14)-(16) are accounted for.

If you were to consider only simple Ss, how could you describe the distribution of NPs like *recourse, heed,* and *headway*? (Consider both active and passive Ss.) Should the constraints on their distribution be stated at the deep structure level or at some derived level? If *begin* occurred only as a transitive V in the deep structure, in what way would the statement of distribution of these NPs have to be complicated? What does this argument have in common with the argument based on active/passive pairs? What does this argument have in common with that using existential *there* and that using dummy *it*?

**Question 6.** The foregoing five arguments can be grouped into two types. One type is of the form: a given element can appear in deep structure or can be inserted transformationally only in a particular environment. Thus, if that element appears in any other environment in the surface, it must have been moved there. The other type is of the form: certain structural phenomena are accounted for by particular transformations. Thus, whenever those structural phenomena occur, the given transformation(s) must have applied. Group Perlmutter's five arguments into these two types.

**Question 7.** The null hypothesis can account for the data on *there* Ss, dummy *it* Ss, active/passive pairs, and *recourse, heed,* and *headway* Ss by treating *begin* just like an Aux. But the null hypothesis cannot account for (i).

(i) The doling out of emergency rations began.

On the other hand, the hypothesis that *begin* is underlyingly transitive with a sentential object cannot account for any of the data mentioned earlier if we accept Perlmutter's unstated assumption (which you uncovered in answering Question 2) that deep structure subject nodes cannot be empty. If, however, we were to allow deep structure subject nodes to be empty, this hypothesis could account for all the data (*there* Ss, dummy *it* Ss, etc.) except (i) by giving *begin* an empty deep subject and a derived surface subject. Under this analysis we would have to propose a rule which raises the subject of a sentential object into the subject position in the next higher clause. But even with these modifications, (i) cannot be accounted for by this analysis.

Finally, the hypothesis that *begin* is underlyingly intransitive with a sentential subject can account for all the foregoing data

if we accept Perlmutter's assumption (which you uncovered in
Question 1) that nominalizations such as those in (i) come from
underlying sentences. However, even if it could be shown that
such nominalizations do not have their source in deep structure
sentences, (i) would only show that *begin* can also occur in an
intransitive deep structure with a *non*sentential subject NP.

Given the comparative explanatory powers of the three
analyses for the data discussed thus far, in which structure(s)
would you now say *begin* can appear in deep structure?

**Question 8.** The first argument that *begin* must also be
able to appear as a *transitive* verb in deep structure is based
on the fact that *begin* can form an agentive nominalization, as
in (i).

(i) Pete is a beginner.

Perlmutter claims that this is an argument that *begin* must be
able to take animate subjects in deep structure. Remember that
Perlmutter is considering only the two possibilities: that *begin*
takes either a sentential subject or a sentential object. How
does it, then, follow from (i) that *begin* can occur as a transitive V in deep structure? (Recall *\*seemer, \*happener.*) Is it
true that only Vs that can take animate subjects in deep structure can form agentive nominalizations? Consider the nominalization *mover* in (ii).

(ii) Pete's a real mover.

Here *mover* does not mean that Pete moves things, but only that
he himself moves in an especially skillful way. Thus *mover*
here corresponds semantically to the intransitive rather than the
transitive V *move*. If we find an agentive nominalization, then,
we can conclude that the corresponding V must allow animate
subjects in deep structure but not that that V need be transitive in deep structure. Thus Perlmutter's argument holds only
if the intransitive V *begin* can take sentential subjects but cannot take animate subjects in deep structure. None of the data
presented so far require the intransitive *begin* to allow non-
sentential deep subjects, according to Perlmutter. As you noted
in Question 7, however, if nominalizations such as that in (i) in
Question 7 do not have an underlying sentential source, we must
allow the intransitive *begin* to allow nonsentential deep subjects.
Can any of these nonsentential subjects be animate?

Can the null hypothesis account for *a beginner*? Try to form
agentives from other auxiliary elements.

Note that Perlmutter is claiming that there is a transformation
which turns the V *begin* into the agentive nominal *beginner*.
His argument does not rely on that claim, however. For even
if no such transformation exists, one can still use the fact that
any V which does have a corresponding agentive of this type

can take animate subjects in deep structure, when one is arguing about the types of deep subjects a verb may take, and hence what types of deep structures it may appear in.

In fact, there is a question as to whether there is indeed a transformation turning the V *begin* into the agentive *beginner*. Note that there is no straightforward semantic relationship between (iii) and an S with *John* as the surface subject of the V *begin*.

(iii) John is a beginner at skiing.

Probably the closest relationship is with Ss with progressive aspect, like (iv).

(iv) John is beginning skiing.

But here the relationship does not always go through: compare (v) and (vi).

(v) John is a beginner at love.
(vi) John is beginning??loving/*love.

Furthermore, some agentives lack corresponding V forms (*grocer*/*\*groce*), and many agentives do not have the *-er* ending (*cook, wastrel, repairman, typist*). In Chomsky's article in this volume you will see arguments that there is an idiosyncratic relationship of such nominalizations to the V. The transformational relatedness of *begin* and *beginner* cannot be used as an axiom, but the distributional properties of *beginner* itself are still relevant.

*Question 9. The next argument is based on the fact that Vs like *try, condescend,* and *refuse* can take *begin* in their complements, as in (i).

(i) I tried to begin to work.

Perlmutter claims, citing Perlmutter (1968) for arguments, that such Vs manifest the like-subject constraint, which requires that the subject of the S embedded immediately beneath them be identical to their own subject in deep structure. Thus in (i) the deep structure subjects of both *try* and *begin* must be *I*. Therefore, *to work* in (i) must come from a sentential object.

However, consider Ss like (ii).

(ii) Mary always tries to be seen in the most chic restaurants.

If Passive has applied on the lower cycle in this S, what aspect of the like-subject constraint does this example call into question? Now consider (iii) and (iv).

(iii) Mary usually tries to appear to understand, even when she misses the point entirely.
(iv) Mary always tries to be tough to convince, but Jack can win her over every time.

What rule has applied on the *appear* cycle in (iii)? What rule has applied on the *be tough* cycle in (iv)? Is the like-subject constraint a deep structure constraint, in light of (ii)-(iv)? How might we state it? If the like-subject constraint is not a deep structure constraint, does Perlmutter's argument about *begin* hold?

Question 10. The next argument uses the fact that *begin* can be embedded immediately under *force*. Perlmutter claims, again citing Perlmutter (1968) for arguments, that Vs like *force* require the subject of the S embedded immediately beneath them to be identical to their own subject in deep structure. Thus in (i), both the deep structure object of *force* and the deep structure subject of *begin* must be *Tom*.

(i) I forced Tom to begin to work.

Again, this argument rests on the claim that the constraint as Perlmutter states it is a deep structure constraint. What kinds of evidence would you look for in order to test whether or not this constraint is a deep structure constraint? Give some relevant examples.

*Question 11. The fourth argument is based on the fact that *begin* can be the matrix V of an imperative S, as in (i).

(i) Begin to work.

Perlmutter claims that imperative Ss require *you* as their subject in deep structure. If this is true, what problem arises in the analysis of the imperatives in (ii)-(iv)?

(ii) Don't be hurt by his rudeness.
(iii) This time at least appear to understand what she says.
(iv) This time be tough to convince.

Are the following imperative sentences? What are their deep structure subjects?

(v) Somebody turn off the light!
(vi) Nobody move!

If it is not the deep subject of an imperative but rather the subject at the time of Imperative Subject Deletion which must be animate, does Perlmutter's argument about *begin* hold?
Could the null hypothesis account for (i)?

**Question 12.** The next argument uses the fact that *begin* can take simple NP objects in the surface, as in (i).

(i) Sam began the job.

Perlmutter concludes that it can therefore be transitive in deep structure. Up to this point, the only transitive structure Perlmutter has argued for is that which has an underlying sentential object. Ss like (i) raise the question of whether or not transitive *begin* can also take nonsentential objects. Perlmutter assumes in his article that *begin* takes a nonsentential object in (i). He argues that if *begin* takes two kinds of objects, we have all the more reason to believe that it takes at least one kind of object. In footnote 11, however, Perlmutter suggests that it may be possible to argue that Ss such as (i) have a sentential object underlyingly and that the V of that sentential object for some reason does not appear in the surface. Note that (ii) can mean (iii) but not (iv).

(ii) I began dinner.
(iii) I began preparing/cooking/eating dinner.
(iv) I began throwing dinner on the floor/ruining dinner/
     cleaning up after dinner/digesting dinner, etc.

The way in which we understand *begin NP* then, is one of the strongest arguments for an analysis in which *begin* takes a full S object complement with an abstract (transitive) V, as in example (v).

$$(v) \quad _S[I \begin{bmatrix} V \\ +abstract \\ +typical \\ +agentive \\ \dots \end{bmatrix} dinner]_S$$

This abstract V would not be spelled out in the surface. After Equi and all spelling out rules, we would be left with *begin* followed by the NP object of the abstract V. The S complement of *begin*, however, need not have an NP dominating it in order for us to account for (vi).

(vi) The job was begun by Sam.

Can you find any syntactic arguments which offer evidence for choosing between Perlmutter's text analysis and the analysis of footnote 11 as expanded here? (See footnote 7, Newmeyer 1975, and Ross 1976 for relevant arguments.)
Can the null hypothesis account for (i) and (vi)?

*Question 13.** Another argument relies on the fact that *begin* can appear without an overt NP or verbal form after it in the surface, as in (i).

(i) Mark began enthusiastically, but he got tired by noon.

Perlmutter claims that there is a rule which deletes objects in Ss such as (ii) or (iii),

(ii) I usually eat late.
(iii) I read at night.

and that this rule can account for the lack of a complement after *begin* in (i) only if *begin* takes objects in deep structure. Can you think of any evidence that *eat* and *read* in these examples had objects in deep structure? Can the null hypothesis account for (i)?

**\*\*Question 14.** Perlmutter proposes that whenever *begin* has an inanimate subject in the surface, we are dealing with the intransitive *begin*. In support of this proposal, he gives an argument based on the fact that VPs beginning with *begin* can be replaced by *do so*, as in (i).

(i) I forced Warren to begin to work and Paul forced Jerry to do so.

He claims that Vs which take sentential subjects can never be replaced by *do so*. Thus (ii), in which *begin* takes a sentential subject by Perlmutter's analysis, cannot have *do so*.

(ii) \*Heed began to be paid to urban problems and attention did so too.

Likewise, (iii), in which we have a surface inanimate subject, cannot have *do so*.

(iii) ??Oil began to drip from the tanker and gasoline did so, too.

Sentences (i) through (iii) show the explanatory power of Perlmutter's analysis. Give other examples that would be ruled out by this constraint on *do so*. Now consider Ss such as (iv) with *continue*, noting that Perlmutter claims that *continue* shares all the properties of *begin* discussed in this article.

(iv) John replaced all the washers, but the kitchen faucet continued to leak and the bathroom faucet did so, too.

If this S is good for you with the reading in (v),

(v) The bathroom faucet continued to leak.

then for you the *do so* argument does not go through. What do you think is the crucial difference between (iii) and (iv)?

Certainly both Ss have inanimate subjects in the surface for *begin* and *continue*. But do you see any difference in the agentiveness of their subjects? If you do, try to salvage Perlmutter's argument.

Question 15. In terms of the form of the argument, what do the arguments mentioned in Questions 9, 10, 11, and 14 have in common? (Note that Perlmutter does not include the material of Question 14 as an argument per se, but rather as a proposal.)

Question 16. The null hypothesis meets some questions with the arguments mentioned in Questions 8, 9, and 10, since *begin* appears in the structures referred to in these arguments more readily than do the Aux's (*\*He's a haver, \*She's a muster; ??I tried to have understood; ?I forced John to be studying*). However, since Aux's certainly contribute to the semantics of an S, one might propose that these examples usually exclude most Aux's for semantic rather than structural reasons. Thus *begin* could still be argued to have the same status as an Aux in Questions 8, 9, and 10. Certainly Question 11 presents no problem for the null hypothesis. (Cf. *Mary, stop arguing! Just sit down and be studying when the curtain goes up.*) But the argument in Question 12 is more trouble. We never get Aux's followed immediately by NPs (*\*He has the problem* in the sense 'He has done the problem'). Thus we have no evidence that there is a rule deleting Vs between Aux's and direct objects. *Begin*, then, is quite different from the Aux's here--a fact the null hypothesis cannot account for. The argument in Question 13 is less of a problem, since we do have a VP deletion rule allowing Aux's to appear without following Vs, as in *Jack has been studying since noon and Paul has (been) since 1:30.* If *begin* were an Aux, we could try to say that VP deletion had applied in (i).

(i) Mark began enthusiastically, but he got tired by noon.

The problem is that VP deletion occurs in more restricted contexts than the deletion rule in (i). VP deletion requires that the deleted VP have an identical VP in either a preceding or a noncommanding clause, or in a preceding sentence in the discourse. The deletion in (i) does not observe this constraint. The null hypothesis, then, cannot account for (i).

If *begin* were to occur only in intransitive structures with a sentential subject, the data discussed in Questions 8, 12, and 13 could not be accounted for. In all these cases, *begin* behaves differently from Vs like *seem* and *happen*. (For the argument in Question 13, once more note the distinction between VP deletion and whatever deletion rule has applied in (i).) If Perlmutter is correct in holding that deep structure constraints are at work in the data of the arguments in Questions 9, 10, and 11, then this hypothesis also fails to account for these data.

However, if the constraints at issue are not deep structure constraints, these data present no problem for the intransitive-*begin* hypothesis.

Finally, the hypothesis that *begin* can occur in transitive deep structures (where the object may or may not be sentential) can account for all the data in Questions 8 through 13.

Considering all the data in Perlmutter's article, in what deep structures would you now say *begin* must be able to appear?

*Question 17. *Zeke began to work*, as Perlmutter shows, could be derived from either deep structure. Does it in fact have two readings? Consider (i) and (ii).

(i) Zeke made his decision and quickly began to work.
(ii) Unexpectedly the strike was over, and it turned out that Zeke began to work again Tuesday morning.

If you see a semantic distinction, what is it? If not, can one of the deep structures be ruled out in some way?

**Question 18. Consider Ss like *The sermon began*. What deep structure would you propose for this S? Is there any syntactic evidence for a raising rule from object position in an embedded S to subject position in the matrix S?

*Question 19. In both transitive and intransitive structures the complement V has a semantic restriction on it that accounts for the ungrammaticality of the bad Ss in (i)-(vi). What is this semantic restriction? Is this restriction shared by any other syntactic constructions?

(i) I began to understand the answer.
(ii) *I began to know the answer.
(iii) I began to be polite once in a while.
(iv) *I began to be tall once in a while.
(v) The sky began to turn red.
(vi) *The sky began to be red.

### HOMEWORK PROBLEMS

I. Classify each of the following sentences as to whether *begin* is transitive or intransitive in its deep structure.

(1) Finally some headway began to be made.
(2) Bill began the job.
(3) It began to thunder horribly.
(4) We all have something to do, so let's begin now.
(5) She went through a period in which everything irritated her; even his humming softly to himself began to annoy her.

Justify your answers if you can, or at least discuss the alternatives.

II. Perlmutter ends his article by suggesting that various Vs, including the modal Vs (*must, may, might, will, would, shall, should, can, could*), occur in both transitive and intransitive deep structures. Certainly, many modal Vs can be ambiguous, as shown in (1).

(1) John must wear those shoes every day;
    a.  the doctor ordered him to. (obligation--root reading)
    b.  just look at how worn out they are! (probability-- epistemic reading)

It has been claimed that the root reading of modals is transitive while the epistemic reading is intransitive. Consider the Ss in (2) and (3).

(2) These plants must be watered every day;
    a.  otherwise they'll die.
    b.  just look how green they are!

(3) There must be two doors on the second floor;
    a.  otherwise the building won't pass fire regulations.
    b.  how else could the thief have escaped?

How are (2) and (3) relevant to the proposal that root readings arise from transitive deep structures? (Review Perlmutter's arguments about the synonymy of active/passive S pairs and about *there* sentences before beginning this problem.) If modals were to occur only in one structure underlyingly, to what could we attribute the ambiguity of the Ss given here?

## SUGGESTED READINGS

Bresnan, J. 1972. Theory of complementation in English syntax. Unpublished doctoral dissertation. MIT. (See Chapter 3 for arguments for raising into subject position from a sentential object, as in Question 7.)

Gruber, J. 1965. Studies in lexical relations. Unpublished doctoral dissertation. MIT. (For Question 13.)

Hankamer, J., and I. Sag. 1976. Deep and surface anaphora. Linguistic Inquiry 7:3.391-428. (For VP Deletion, as in Question 13.)

Huddleston, R. 1974. Further remarks on the analysis of auxiliaries as main verbs. Foundations of Language 11.215-229. (For the analysis of modals.)

Lakoff, R. 1972. The pragmatics of modality. CLS 8.229-246. (For the analysis of modals.)

McCawley, J. D. 1974. On identifying the remains of deceased clauses. Mimeograph. Indiana University Linguistics Club. (For Perlmutter's footnotes 7 and 11 and for Question 12.)

Newmeyer, F. 1970a. On the alleged boundary between syntax and semantics. Foundations of Language 6.178-186. (This is relevant to the proposal of an abstract V in Ss such as Perlmutter's example (26); see Question 12.)

Newmeyer, F. 1970b. The 'root modal': Can it be transitive? Studies presented to Robert B. Lees by his students. Edmonton: Linguistic Research, Inc. (For Homework Problem II.)

Newmeyer, F. 1975. English aspectual verbs. The Hague: Mouton. (This book is relevant to the entire article.)

Pullum, G., and D. Wilson. 1977. Autonomous syntax and the analysis of auxiliaries. Lg. 53:4.741-788. (For arguments that Aux's, including modals, are intransitive main Vs.)

Ross, J. R. 1976. To have *have* and to not have *have*. In: Linguistic and literary studies in honor of Archibald Hill. Vol. 1: General and theoretical linguistics. Edited by E. Polome, W. Winter, and M. A. Jazayery. Lisse, The Netherlands: Peter de Ridder Press. 263-270. (For Perlmutter's footnotes 7 and 11 and for Question 12.)

# 2

## ON DECLARATIVE SENTENCES

John Robert Ross

Introduction. In this article Ross proposes that every S which does not have an overt performative V with a first person subject and, usually, a second person object of some kind is embedded in the deep structure in an S which does have a performative V and the requisite first person subject and second person object. In this proposal a rule called Performative Deletion (which is, perhaps, governed by the matrix V) optionally deletes all of the matrix S except the embedded S. Overt performatives result when Performative Deletion has not applied.

The proposal of deep performatives for every S regardless of whether such performatives appear in surface structure represents a giant step toward abstraction in syntax. In this proposal the transformational mechanisms are working on structures which are far removed from direct observation. Ross' movement toward such abstractions was one of the early forces leading linguists to consider proposing various kinds of abstract constructions which are never manifest in surface structure. For example, the proposal of higher abstract verbs has been used to account for many syntactic and semantic facts, such as the occurrence of subjunctives in independent clauses in Spanish by Lakoff (1968), a proposal reached independently and contemporaneously with Ross', and the association of presuppositions with certain sentences in English by Morgan (1969).

# On Declarative Sentences[1]

## JOHN ROBERT ROSS

1.1 In Austin (1962), the Oxford philosopher J. L. Austin pointed out that there is an important distinction between such sentences as those in (1)

(1) a. Prices slumped.
   b. I like you when you giggle.
   c. Even Rodney's best friends won't tell him.

which can be true or false, and sentences like those in (2)

(2) a. I promise you that I won't squeal.
   b. I sentence you to two weeks in The Bronx.
   c. I christen this ship *The U.S.S. Credibility Gap.*
   d. I pronounce you man and wife.

which have, instead of truth values, various conditions pertaining to appropriateness of use. Thus (2b) may be used appropriately only by a judge, or by one otherwise empowered to impose sentences, and (2d) only by someone with the authority to marry people. (2a) may be uttered by someone who intends to squeal, but it is not false, for all that: the uttering of (2a), whatever the intentions of the utterer, can *constitute* a promise,[2] whereas the action of uttering (1a) does not constitute a slump in prices.

Austin calls sentences like those in (1) *constative* sentences, and ones like those in (2) *performative* sentences. Performative sentences must have first person subjects and usually have second person direct or indirect objects[3] in deep structure.[4] They must be affirmative and nonnegative, they must be in the present tense, and their main verb must be one of the large class of true verbs which includes those in (3).

(3) advise, answer, appoint, ask, authorize, beg, bequeath, beseech, caution, cede, claim, close, command, condemn, counsel, dare, declare, demand,

> empower, enquire, entreat, excommunicate, grant, implore, inform, instruct, offer, order, pledge, pronounce, propose, request, require, say, sentence, vow, warn, write[5]

Since the sentences in (4), although their main verbs are [+ performative], do not conform to all the above conditions, they are not performative sentences. Therefore, the adverb *hereby*, which is characteristic of performative sentences,[6] produces strangeness or total unacceptability if inserted into these sentences:

(4)   a.   Bill (* hereby) promises you not to squeal.
      b.   I (? hereby) command Tom to pick up that wallet.
      c. * Do I (hereby) promise you to be faithful?
      d. * I don't (hereby) pronounce you man and wife.
      e.   I (* hereby) warned you that Bill would be shot.

Austin (1962, p. 32) makes the interesting claim that both sentences in (5) are performative, that the only difference is that in (5a) the performative verb is explicit, while in (5b) it is implicit:

(5)   a. I order you to go.
      b. Go!

1.2 It has long been argued by transformational grammarians[7] that imperative sentences like (5b), where no subject need appear in surface structure, but where a second person subject is understood, should be derived from structures which actually contain a noun phrase (NP) *you* as subject. This is but one of the many examples where a part of a sentence which has been called "understood" or "implicit" by traditional grammarians is present in deep structure, the abstract representation which is postulated by generative grammarians as underlying the more superficial constituent structure representations of traditional grammar.[8]

There are a number of facts which suggest that Austin's contention that sentences like (5b) contain implicit performatives is to be captured by postulating deep structures for them which are almost identical to the deep structure which has been assumed to underlie the superficially more complex (5a).[9] I will not discuss these arguments, for they are not central to the main thesis of this present paper.[10] This thesis is that declarative sentences, such as those in (1), must also be analyzed as being implicit performatives, and must be derived from deep structures containing an explicitly represented performative main verb. Thus, for example, the deep structure of (1a) will not be that shown schematically in (6), as has been generally assumed previously [in (6) and throughout this paper I will disregard problems connected with the deep structure representation of tenses and of the English verbal auxiliary, for I have discussed these elsewhere[11]].

(6)

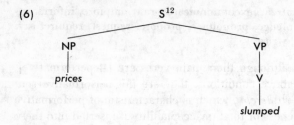

Rather, the deep structure of (1a) must be the more abstract structure shown in (7).[13]

(7)

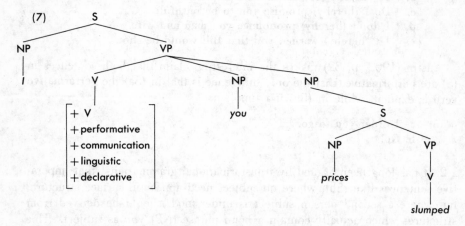

Thus every declarative sentence (but cf. Section 3.4 below) will be derived from a deep structure containing as an embedded clause what ends up in surface structure as an independent clause. Although most of the arguments which I will cite below in support of this analysis are drawn from English, analogs for some of them can be found in many languages, and I know of no evidence which contradicts the assumption that the analysis can be generalized to all languages of the world. Of course, the mere fact that no counterevidence is available in some particular language does not justify the postulation of more abstract deep structures like (7) for that language, unless positive evidence can be found. Nonetheless, the absence of direct counterevidence is at least encouraging.

1.3 The outline of this paper is as follows: In Section 2, fourteen arguments which support the analysis implicit in (7) are presented. In Section 3, the rule of *performative deletion,* which, among other things, converts (7) to (1a),[14] is stated, and various technical problems in the analysis are discussed. In Section 4, two alternative analyses for the facts presented in Section 2 are proposed, and each is compared with the analysis implicit in (7). Finally, in Section 5, some of the consequences which this analysis has for the theory of languages are examined.

2. The fourteen arguments below for assuming every declarative sentence to be derived from an embedded clause fall into three main groups. In Section 2.1 seven arguments suggesting the existence of a higher subject $I$ are presented. In Section 2.2, I discuss three further arguments which indicate that the main verb of the higher sentences must be a verb like *say,* and in Section 2.3 I discuss the three arguments I know of within English which suggest that the performative verb above must have an indirect object *you.* A final argument falling under none of these categories is discussed in Section 2.4.

2.1.1 In Lees and Klima (1963), it is shown that a large number of the cases in which reflexives cannot appear, such as the sentences in (8)

(8)   a.  I think that $\left\{\begin{array}{l} \text{I} \\ \text{* myself} \end{array}\right\}$ will win.

   b.  Have you ever wondered why Jill gave $\left\{\begin{array}{l} \text{you} \\ \text{* yourself} \end{array}\right\}$ that tie?

   c.  He resented Betty's having seduced $\left\{\begin{array}{l} \text{him} \\ \text{* himself} \end{array}\right\}$.

can be accounted for if the reflexive rule is stated (informally) as in (9):

(9)   One NP becomes the anaphoric reflexive pronoun of a preceding coreferential NP only if both NPs are in the same simplex sentence.[15]

Since (8a) has the deep structure shown in (10),

(10)

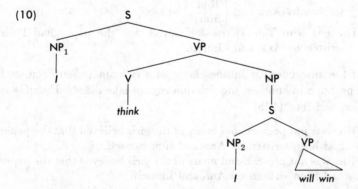

where the two occurrences of $I$ are not in the same simplex sentence (i.e., it is not the case that a node S dominates one occurrence of $I$ if and only if it also dominates the other), (9) will prevent the ungrammatical version of (8a) from arising. The same obtains for (8b) and (8c).

However, as sentence (11b) shows, there are grammatical sentences in which (9) appears to have been violated.[16]

(11) a. Tom believed that the paper had been written by Ann and him himself.
b. Tom believed that the paper had been written by Ann and himself.

I have only slight evidence (cf. Note 17) for this, but a plausible source for the reflexive pronoun in (11b) would be (11a), via a rule which deletes an anaphoric pronoun when this pronoun is followed by an emphatic reflexive, under certain further conditions. Whether this analysis is correct, or whether the reflexive in (11b) can be produced by modifying the rule given in Lees and Klima (1963), is of no relevance for the present discussion: I consider the question to be open. Let us assume, however, for the purpose of discussion, that the suggested analysis is correct. Then what are the conditions under which the proposed rule operates?

First of all, note that the pronoun *himself* in (11b) must be anaphoric — it can only refer to Tom. Therefore, sentences like (12), which contain a reflexive pronoun which can have no antecedent in the sentence, are ungrammatical:

(12) * Tom believed that the letter had been written by Ann and themselves.

Secondly, note that there are conditions on the location of the antecedent of the anaphoric pronoun to be deleted. The pronoun *him* in (11a) can be deleted, for its antecedent (*Tom*) is the subject of a higher sentence. But if the antecedent is embedded in a higher subject, as is the case in (13a), the deletion is impossible: (13b) is ungrammatical.

(13) a. The girl who Tom spurned believed that the paper had been written by Ann and $\left\{ \begin{matrix} \text{Tom} \\ \text{him}^{17} \end{matrix} \right\}$ himself.
b. * The girl who Tom spurned believed that the paper had been written by Ann and himself.

Similarly, if the antecedent is in one clause of a coordinate sentence, and the anaphoric pronoun in another, the deletion cannot take place. Thus (14a) cannot be converted into (14b):

(14) a. Tom was not present, and many of the girls believed that the paper had been written by Ann and him himself.
b. * Tom was not present, and many of the girls believed that the paper had been written by Ann and himself.

Note that it is not necessary for the NP *Tom* to be a higher subject, nor, in fact, for it to precede the emphatic reflexive. Thus (15a) and (16a) can be converted into (15b) and (16b), respectively:

(15) a. I told Tom that the entries should be designed by Ann and him himself.

b. I told Tom that the entries should be designed by Ann and himself.

(16) a. That the paper would have to be written by Ann and him himself was obvious to Tom.

b. That the paper would have to be written by Ann and himself was obvious to Tom.

Note also that the antecedent for the reflexive pronoun need not belong to the next sentence up the tree (in the obvious sense of this expression), as was the case in (11b), (15b), and (16b), for (17a) can be converted into (17b):

(17) a. Tom thinks that I tried to get Mary to make you say that the paper had been written by Ann and him himself.

b. Tom thinks that I tried to get Mary to make you say that the paper had been written by Ann and himself.

However, it can be seen that in all the cases where the emphatic reflexive is possible [namely, in (11b), (15b), (16b), and (17b)], it is the case that it belongs to a sentence lower than the sentence to which the antecedent NP belongs. This is not an accidental fact about the data, as is shown by the impossibility of converting (18a) to (18b), where this condition is not met:

(18) a. That the paper would have to be written by Ann and Tom was obvious to $\left\{ {\begin{matrix} \text{Tom} \\ {?\ *\ \text{him}} \end{matrix}} \right\}$ himself.

b. * That the paper would have to be written by Ann and Tom was obvious to himself.

The above facts lead to the formulation stated in (19):

(19) **If an anaphoric pronoun precedes an emphatic reflexive, the former may be deleted, if it is commanded by the NP with which it stands in an anaphoric relationship.**[18]

Inspection will reveal that (19) is satisfied only by (11b), (15b), (16b), and (17b). It can therefore be used to account for the ungrammaticality of (12), (13b), (14b), and (18b).

The restriction stated in (19) is the major one governing the rule that produces emphatic reflexives, but there are others, which have to do with the internal structure of the sentence to which the reflexive pronoun belongs. That this is so can be seen by the varying degrees of acceptability exhibited by the sentences in (20). [For convenience, I have repeated (11b) as (20a).]

(20) a. Tom believed that the paper had been written by Ann and himself.

b. ? ? Tom believed that the paper had been written by himself.

c. ? Tom believed that Ann and himself had written the paper.
d. * Tom believed that himself had written the paper.
e. ? Tom believed that the lioness might attack Ann and himself.
f. * Tom believed that the lioness might attack himself.

No doubt most readers would assign different degrees of acceptability to the sentences of (20) than I have, especially in the intermediate cases. But this will not concern us here. Nor will we be concerned with stating the rule which produces the sentences of (20) with the spectrum of acceptabilities I have assigned, or some other spectrum — far too little is known of the phrase structure configurations to which such a rule would be sensitive. Cursory inspection of the few facts shown in (20) shows that emphatic reflexives are invariably better if conjoined than if they occur alone, and that such reflexives are more acceptable as agent phrases than as subjects or direct objects. Doubtless there are many other conditions on this rule, which interrelate in a complex manner with those just stated, and which are of some intrinsic interest. But for my present purpose, which is to argue that (7) underlies (1a), they are beside the point. Whatever the rule is that produces the complex spectrum of acceptabilities in (20), it is obvious that the same rule is in operation in the case of such apparently simple sentences as those in (21):

(21) a. This paper was written by Ann and myself.
b. ?? This paper was written by myself.
c. ? Ann and myself wrote this paper.
d. * Myself wrote this paper.
e. ? The lioness may attack Ann and myself.
f. * The lioness may attack myself.

Notice that it is not the case that just any emphatic reflexive can occur in simple sentences like those of (21): the sentences lose all traces of acceptability if *myself* is replaced by *themselves*,[19] just as (12), whose reflexive pronoun cannot be anaphoric either, is unacceptable. That is, the pronoun *myself* in (21) is an anaphoric pronoun.

These facts are accounted for under my analysis, which assumes that just as (7) underlies (1a), so the deep structures of the sentences in (21) will contain a higher performative clause, which is obliterated by the rule of *performative deletion*, after the application of the rule stated in (19), with whatever additional constraints on this rule are necessary to produce the correct spectrum of acceptabilities in (20). Hereafter, I will refer to this analysis as *the performative analysis*, to distinguish it from the other two alternative analyses I will take up in Section 4.

Whether or not the performative analysis is correct, I submit that as a minimal precondition of adequacy for *any* analysis, the facts of (21) must be accounted for by *the same* rules or principles that account for the facts of (20). That is, it cannot be accidental that the two acceptability spectra match each other so exactly and, more importantly, that the configurations which seem to be producing the variations in acceptability, in both (20) and (21), do not, as far as I know, play a systematic role in any other grammatical phenomenon of English.

I do not want to be thought to be advocating something mystical because of my insistence that (20) and (21) be explained in the same way. Intuitions of similarity between phenomena, while they may prove to be mistaken, are the principal forces behind attempts to find explanations of these phenomena. In linguistics, as in other sciences, if phenomenon $A$ is intuitively felt to be similar to phenomenon $B$, but if the descriptions of these phenomena do not reflect the intuited similarity, the researcher is dissatisfied with the descriptions; he feels that while they may "work," they do not explain. Thus the fact that imperative sentences like *Kick that damn cat!* are felt to be binary predicates semantically, with a second person argument not being physically expressed, and the fact that the reflexive pronouns that show up in imperatives are second person pronouns (*Kick yourself!* not * *Kick themselves!*) are felt to be the same facts, and no theory of grammar which cannot reflect this sameness (e.g., no theory which provides only one level of syntactic representation) can be considered adequate.

Since the facts of (21) are felt to be the same as the facts of (20), they must be explained in the same way. The rule stated in (19), or its equivalent, must be stated in any adequate grammar of English so that (11b), (15b), (16b), and (17b) will be generated, and not (12), (13b), (14b), and (18b). Moreover, whatever conditions turn out to be appropriate to produce the acceptability spectrum of (20) must also be stated. Given those two pieces of grammatical apparatus, if the performative analysis is adopted, the facts of (21) follow. But it should be noted that the facts of (21) do not force one to accept the performative analysis in all its details: they provide no evidence for the existence of a higher *you,* nor for any higher verb, let alone one with the specific properties attributed to it in (7). Arguments for these stronger claims will be presented below.

2.1.2. The structure of the second argument is identical to that of the first, as are the conclusions that can be drawn from it. It has to do with *like*-phrases, such as the ones in (22).

(22)  a.  Physicists like $\left\{ \begin{array}{l} \text{Albert} \\ \text{him} \end{array} \right\}$ don't often make mistakes.

 b. * Physicists like himself don't often make mistakes.

While full NPs and pronouns can appear freely in *like*-phrases, the ungrammaticality of (22b) shows that this is not the case with reflexive pronouns. However, as the sentences in (23) show, if a pronoun in a *like*-phrase is commanded by the NP to which it refers, it may optionally become a reflexive pronoun:

(23) a. I told Albert that physicists like himself were a godsend.
b. Albert was never hostile to laymen who couldn't understand what physicists like himself were trying to prove.
c. That physicists like himself never got invited to horse shows didn't seem to faze Albert.

As (24) suggests, the reflexive pronoun can be indefinitely far away from the commanding NP:

(24) Albert accused me of having tried to get his secretary to tell you that physicists like himself were hard to get along with.

As was the case in Section 2.1.1, it is necessary that the reflexives in *like*-phrases stand in an anaphoric relationship with some other NP in the sentence. Thus if *himself* in the sentences of (23) and (24) is replaced by *themselves*, the sentences become ungrammatical.

The restriction that *like*-phrases containing reflexives be commanded by the NP to which they refer is necessary to exclude the ungrammatical sentences in (25), where this is not the case:

(25) a. * Physicists like himself always claim that Albert was hard to understand.
b. * That Albert's work wasn't comprehensible to high school science teachers worried physicists like himself.
c. * Albert was interested in astronomy, and physicists like himself should remember that.

Now note that in simple declarative sentences, the reflexive pronoun that occurs is *myself*:

(26) Physicists like myself were never too happy with the parity principle.

Once again, this fact can be accounted for by assuming a deep structure for all declaratives in which there is an NP *I* which commands what will end up as the main clause, and which will be deleted after the rule introducing reflexives into *like*-phrases has applied. As was the case in Section 2.1.1, the facts of sentences (22) through (26) do not support all facets of the performative analysis, but they are at least consonant with it, and they do support one facet of it.

2.1.3. The third set of facts which support the performative analysis has to do with *as for*-phrases, such as those that start the sentences in (27):

(27) a. As for the students, they're not going to sign.

b. * As for $\begin{Bmatrix} \text{them} \\ \text{themselves} \end{Bmatrix}$, the students aren't going to sign.

    c.  As for the students, adolescents almost never have any sense.

    d. * As for the students, hydrogen is the first element in the periodic table.

The requirement in such constructions seems to be that the NP which follows *as for* have some connection with the clause that follows. Thus (27a) is acceptable only if *they* is taken to refer back to *the students,* and (27c) presupposes that all students are adolescents. Since no reasonable connection can be imagined for (27d), it is deviant in some way.[20]

I have no idea as to the deep structure source of these *as for*-phrases, but for my present purposes this is irrelevant. It is sufficient to note that the NP in these phrases cannot be a pronoun which refers to some nonpronominal NP in the following clause, as the ungrammaticality of (27b) shows. In particular, reflexive pronouns are excluded, even if the NP to which they refer is itself a pronoun. Thus, though (28a) is grammatical, (28b) is not:[21]

(28)   a.  As for her, she won't be invited.

       b. *As for herself, she won't be invited.

However, there are cases where reflexive pronouns can appear in *as for*-phrases, as (29a) shows:

(29)   a.  Glinda knows that as for herself, she won't be invited.

       b. * Maxwell knows that as for herself, she won't be invited.

As the ungrammaticality of (29b) shows, it is not the case that just any reflexive pronoun can occur in an *as for*-phrase which has been prefixed to an embedded clause; this is only possible if the pronoun refers back to some NP in the upper clause. Furthermore, as the contrast between (29a) and the ungrammatical sentences of (30) indicates, it is only if the pronoun refers back to a higher subject NP that reflexives can appear in *as for*-phrases.

(30)   a.  Harry told Glinda that as for $\left\{ \begin{array}{l} \text{himself, he} \\ \text{* herself, she} \end{array} \right\}$ wouldn't be invited.

       b. * That as for herself, she wouldn't be invited enraged Glinda.

Finally, the ungrammatical sentences in (31) show that the subject NP to which the reflexive pronoun refers must be the subject of the sentence which immediately dominates the clause to which the *as for*-phrase is prefixed.

(31)   Harry believes that the students know that Glinda has been saying that

     as for $\left\{ \begin{array}{l} \text{herself, she} \\ \text{* themselves, they} \\ \text{* himself, he} \end{array} \right\}$ won't be be invited.

To sum up, these facts seem to require the postulation of a rule which optionally converts to a reflexive any pronoun appearing in an *as for*-phrase which is prefixed to an embedded clause, just in case this pronoun refers back to the subject of the next higher sentence. But if such a rule must be in the grammar in any event, the fact that *myself* can appear in the *as for*-phrase of an apparently unembedded main clause, as in (32)

(32) As for myself, I won't be invited.

suggests that in a more abstract representation of (32), it must itself appear as a clause embedded in a sentence whose subject is *I*.

Hence sentence (32) provides stronger evidence for the performative analysis than do the sentences in (21) and (26), which only suggest the existence of an NP *I* which commands all declarative clauses in deep structure. The grammaticality of (32) leads to the conclusion that the *I* cannot be indefinitely far above the embedded clause, but instead must be the next subject up, which is just what is asserted in the performative analysis.

2.1.4. The next argument, which is of the same structure as the one immediately preceding, was discovered by Jeffrey Gruber (1967). He pointed out that reflexive pronouns could be in a clause embedded in the one to which the full NP to which they refer belongs if the embedded clause contains certain constructions with picture-nouns,[22] like *picture, story, tale, photograph,* etc., as is the case in (33):

(33) a. Tad knew that it would be a story about himself.
b. Mike will not believe that this is a photograph of himself.
c. I promised Omar that it would be a poem about himself.

Whether it is possible for the reflexive pronoun to precede the NP to which it refers is not clear to me — the sentences in (34), where this is the case, are perhaps less acceptable than those in (33):

(34) a. ? That it was a portrait of himself worried Jasper.
b. ? That this is an article about himself has been emphatically denied by Dieter.

I will not investigate further the many problems related to such constructions, except to point out the obvious fact that these reflexive pronouns are anaphoric (thus if *himself* is replaced by *herself,* the sentences in (33) and (34) become ungrammatical), and the fact that the NP to which the reflexive pronoun bears an anaphoric relationship must belong to the first sentence above the one containing the picture-noun construction.[23] This is borne out by the contrast in grammaticality between the sentences in (33) and those in (35):

(35) a. * Tad knew that Sheila had claimed that it would be a story about himself.
b. * Mike will not believe that Jane found out that this is a photograph of himself.
c. * I promised Omar to tell Betty that it would be a poem about himself.

Of course, these latter sentences become grammatical if *herself* is substituted for *himself,* as is to be expected.

Once again, it is of no relevance to the present discussion whether the reflexives in (33) are to be generated by some extension of the normal reflexive rule, or by an extension of the rule of Section 2.1.1, which deletes an anaphoric pronoun before an emphatic reflexive under various conditions, or by some rule distinct from both of these. Some rule must be inferred to exist, and if the performative analysis is adopted, this rule will account for the fact that *myself* is the reflexive pronoun that appears when such clauses as those embedded in (33) appear as main clauses, as (36) shows:

(36)   This is a $\begin{Bmatrix} \text{picture of} \\ \text{story about} \\ \text{description of} \\ \text{joke about} \end{Bmatrix}$ myself.

Thus (36) is further evidence for the correctness of the performative analysis.

2.1.5.  The next argument is based on an observation made by Zellig Harris,[24] who pointed out that passive sentences with first person agents are generally not fully acceptable [compare (37a) with (37b)]:

(37)   a.    It was given by him to your sister.[25]
       b. ? ? It was given by me to your sister.

Note, however, that any formulation of the restriction on passives in terms of first person agents will be too narrow, for (38) is also ungrammatical:

(38)   ? ? $Tom_i$ thinks that it was given by $him_i$ to your sister.[26]

As the grammaticality of (39) shows, the restriction which is operative here does not exclude all passives in embedded clauses when the pronoun in the agent phrase refers to an NP in the matrix sentence:

(39)   That it had been given by $him_i$ to your sister was mentioned by $Tom_i$.

I am unable at present to state any restriction that will mark (38) as being less acceptable then (39), but it seems likely that however the restriction is finally stated, it will be instrumental in excluding (40b) as well as (38):

(40)   a.    $Max_i$ expected Sue to wash $him_i$.
       b. ? ? Sue was expected by $Max_i$ to wash $him_i$.

As a first approximation to a principle to account for these ungrammaticalities, I suggest (41):

(41)   If a deep structure subject NP and some other NP in the same deep
       structure are coreferential, then the former NP may not become a
       passive agent.

Rule (41) is obviously too strong, for (39) violates it twice and yet it is perfectly acceptable. But it cannot be assumed that all such double violations will result in grammatical sentences, for (42) is ungrammatical:

(42)    * Sue was expected by Max$_i$ to be washed by him$_i$.

But it does seem reasonable to assume that what is involved in accounting for the ungrammaticality of (38), (40b), and (42) will be some restriction which is like (41) in that it excludes certain types of deep structures *which contain two coreferential NPs* from participation in certain (types of) transformational operations. But if this assumption is correct, then it must be assumed that the deep structure of sentences like (37b) must contain two occurrences of the NP *I*, for it would seem natural to exclude this sentence by the same mechanism that excludes (38). Therefore, the ungrammaticality of (37b) may be taken as weak confirmation for one facet of the performative analysis.

2.1.6. The next argument for the performative analysis was called to my attention by David Perlmutter. He pointed out that the verb *lurk* is awkward with first person subjects, as (43) indicates:

(43)    a. ? * I am lurking in a culvert.[27]
        b. ? * I lurked near your house last night.

However, it is not always the case that *lurk* excludes first person subjects. In embedded clauses, such constructions are perfectly grammatical:

(44)    a. Max believes that I am lurking in a culvert — actually, of course,
           I'm here with you.
        b. Pat and Mike testified that I lurked near your house last night.

The true nature of the restriction on *lurk* can be seen in the ungrammatical sentences of (45), which differ from those of (44) only in having the subject of *lurk* identical to the subject of the verb in whose object the complement clause is embedded:

(45)    a. ? * Max$_i$ believes that he$_i$'s lurking in a culvert — actually, of course,
           he$_i$'s here with you.
        b. ? * [Pat and Mike]$_{NP_i}$ testified that they$_i$ lurked near your house
           last night.

As Perlmutter observed, *lurk* is a verb which one may predicate of others, but not of oneself. This suggests that *lurk* must be constrained    so that it does not appear in deep structures where its subject is identical to the subject of the next higher verb in the tree.[28] It seems to be necessary to state this restriction in terms of subjects of higher clauses, for the sentences of (46), in which the subject of *lurk* is identical to some other NP in the next sentence up, are more acceptable than those in (45):

(46)   a. ? Susan told $Max_i$ that $he_i$ should not lurk near her house any
          longer.
       b. ? Lurking near lakes is easy for Bobby.

Since some restriction on *lurk* must appear in the grammar in any case,
so that sentences such as those in (45) will be blocked, if the performative
analysis is adopted, the same restriction will automatically exclude the sentences of (43). Thus these latter sentences constitute further evidence for
the correctness of this analysis.[29]

2.1.7. The last argument I will adduce to show the existence of a higher
NP *I* in the deep structure of all declarative sentences has to do with sentences
containing *according to,* such as (47):

(47)   According to $\left\{ \begin{array}{l} \text{Indira Gandhi} \\ \textit{The Realist} \\ \text{Satchel Paige} \\ \text{you} \\ * \text{ me} \end{array} \right\}$ , food prices will skyrocket.

As far as I know, there are no restrictions obtaining between the clause
that follows the *according to*-phrase and the NP which appears in that phrase,
but there is a restriction to the effect that first person NPs may not appear
in these phrases in simple declarative sentences. However, as was the case
with *lurk,* first person NPs can appear in these phrases if they occur in an
embedded clause, as (48) shows

(48)   $Satchel\ Paige_i$ claimed that according to $\left\{ \begin{array}{l} \text{Indira Gandhi} \\ \textit{The Realist} \\ * \ him_i \\ \text{you} \\ \text{me} \end{array} \right\}$ , food
        prices would skyrocket.

It is evident that a situation similar to the case of *lurk* obtains here. But
there, although the restriction that was necessary was not clear in detail, it
seemed fairly certain that the restriction was to be stated in terms of the
deep structure subject of *lurk* and some higher NP. Here, because of the
present lack of knowledge as to the deep structure source of phrases containing
*according to,* it is not obvious as to whether the necessary restriction should
be stated in terms of deep structure or in terms of some lower level of
structure. I will assume, for the present discussion, that the former is true,
and that phrases containing *according to* are not to be derived from any more
complex source. In the absence of any evidence for or against these assumptions, they seem neutral enough, though I feel sure that the latter assumption
will prove wrong. However, if, for the sake of argument, we make these
assumptions, then the restriction which seems to be necessary to exclude such
sentences as the ungrammatical one in (48) can be stated as in (49):

(49) No well-formed deep structure may contain an embedded *according to*-phrase if the NP in that phrase is identical to any NP belonging to the first sentence above the one containing that phrase.

This condition will exclude the ungrammatical sentence in (48), but it is also strong enough to exclude the ungrammatical sentences of (50), though not (51):

(50) a. * That food prices, according to $him_i$, would skyrocket worried Satchel $Paige_i$.

b. * Indira $Gandhi_i$ told Satchel $Paige_i$ that according to $\begin{Bmatrix} her_i \\ him_i \end{Bmatrix}$, food prices would skyrocket.

(51) * Satchel $Paige_i$ stated that it was not true that according to $him_i$ food prices would skyrocket.

Unfortunately, condition (49) is not only too weak to exclude (51), but also too strong, for it will incorrectly block the grammatical (52):[30]

(52) Satchel $Paige_i$ drives a truck that gets, according to $him_i$, 37.8 miles per gallon.

While I am unable, at present, to improve on (49), I suspect that it is basically correct, for at least it is adequate to the task of excluding the ungrammatical sentences of (48) and (50). If this suspicion is correct, and if the performative analysis is adopted, whatever revised version of (49) is finally arrived at will explain why (47) is ungrammatical if *me* occurs following *according to*, for it will be identical to the higher NP *I* which is assumed in the performative analysis. Thus the sentences of (47) also provide indirect confirmation for this analysis.

2.1.8. I have avoided many complex issues in my brief discussions of the seven sets of phenomena above, in an attempt to present the basic evidence for the existence of a higher *I* as clearly as possible, without invalidating the arguments by oversimplification. In this section, I would like to mention, even more fragmentarily, three further constructions which I understand much too poorly to be able to argue from at present, but which seem to be likely candidates for future use as evidence for the performative analysis.

The first observation I owe to Joshua Waletzky. In his dialect, such sentences as (53a) are possible, and they are synonymous with sentences like (53b):

(53) a. Sid is coming with.
b. Sid is coming with me.

However, this stressed *with* is not always synonymous with *with me* — (54a) is synonymous with (54b), not (54c).

(54) a. $Abe_i$ mentioned that Sid was coming with.

b. $Abe_i$ mentioned that Sid was coming with $him_i$.
c. $Abe_i$ mentioned that Sid was coming with me.

The implications of these facts would appear to be the same as those of the other arguments presented above, but there are so many additional idiosyncratic restrictions on this construction that I do not understand that I will not pursue the matter further here.

The second construction was called to my attention by David Perlmutter and, independently, by Charles Elliott. They pointed out that there are relational nouns like *friend* which normally appear followed by an *of*-phrase, as in (55):

(55)  A friend of Tom's is going to drop by.

In simple declarative sentences, however, the *of*-phrase need not be present. If it is not present, as in (56a), the sentence is felt to be synonymous with an otherwise identical sentence which contains the phrase *of mine* after friend [cf. (56b)]:

(56)  a. A friend is going to drop by.
      b. A friend of mine is going to drop by.

Not surprisingly, when sentences like (56a) are embedded, the missing *of*-phrase is not always felt to be *of mine* — (57a) and (57b) are synonymous:

(57)  a. $Sheila_i$ whispered that a friend was in the trunk.
      b. $Sheila_i$ whispered that a friend of $hers_i$ was in the trunk.

Once again, the implications for the performative analysis seem clear — *of*-phrases after nouns like *friend* delete if the NP in the phrase is identical to some higher NP. But there are complications. In (58), the missing *of*-phrase is not *of mine*, but rather something like *of one's*:[31]

(58)  Friends are a great help in times of hardship.

At present, it is not clear to me how the rule which produces (58) is to be generalized so that it will also apply to (57a) and (56a) — if, in fact, it is even the same rule at work. I will leave this question unresolved in the present paper.

Lastly, there are certain types of vocatives which require first person pronouns in them. See, for example, (59):

(59)  Hoboken is a fine city, $\left\{ \begin{array}{l} \text{Peter} \\ \left\{ \begin{array}{l} \text{my} \\ \text{* her} \\ \text{* his} \\ \text{* Bill's} \end{array} \right\} \left\{ \begin{array}{l} \text{darling} \\ \text{boy} \\ \text{friend} \\ \text{son} \\ \text{* lawyer} \\ \text{* rival} \end{array} \right\} \end{array} \right\}$.

At present, I cannot explain why *my* is required in (59), but perhaps it can be shown to relate to the performative analysis somehow.[32]

Although these last three sets of facts are very unclear, it seems to me that those presented in Sections 2.1.1 through 2.1.7 more than amply support one facet of the performative analysis — the claim that deep structures of declarative sentences contain a higher subject NP *I*. The facts discussed in Section 2.1.1 (*by Ann and myself*), Section 2.1.2 (*like myself*), Section 2.1.5(? ? *It was given by me to your sister*), Section 2.1.6 (*lurk*), and Section 2.1.7 (* *according to me*) all show the need for postulating an NP *I* in deep structure which is somewhere above (and which commands) the embedded deep structure clause which will become the main clause in surface structure. The facts discussed in Section 2.1.4 (*a picture of myself*) show that the *I* cannot be indefinitely far away, but must rather belong to the first clause up in deep structure, and the argument in Section 2.1.3 (*as for myself*) indicates that the *I* must in fact be the subject of this first clause up. The remainder of the arguments in Section 2 will be aimed primarily at justifying other facets of the deep structure in (7), but several by-products of these arguments will offer further support for the claim that a higher subject *I* must be postulated to exist in all deep structures for declarative sentences.

2.2.1. The first of the three arguments I will advance in this section to show that the verb of the clause whose subject NP is *I* is a verb like *say* has to do with the verb *believe*. This verb can have a clausal object, but as Robin Lakoff, to whom this argument is due, pointed out, *believe* also can have a pronoun referring back to a human NP as its superficial object, under certain circumstances. Thus if one clause of a sentence contains a verb like *say* whose subject is some $NP_a$, a later clause can contain *believe* $NP_a$, as is the case in (60).

(60) Tom$_i$ told her$_j$ that Ann could swim, but nobody believed
$\left. \begin{array}{l} \text{a.} \\ \text{b.} \\ \text{c.} \end{array} \right.$
$\left\{ \begin{array}{l} \text{* them} \\ \text{* her}_j \\ \text{him}_i \end{array} \right\}$

As the ungrammaticality of (60a) shows, the pronoun that follows *believe* must stand in an anaphoric relationship to some other NP in the sentence. The contrast between (60b) and (60c) shows that the pronoun after *believe* cannot stand in an anaphoric relationship to just *any* NP in the rest of the sentence — in general, it must refer back to a subject of a particular class of verbs, whose precise specification I will now turn to.[33]

Compare the sentences in (61) with those in (62) and (63).

(61) a. $\text{Tom}_i$ $\left\{\begin{array}{l}\text{said} \\ \text{declared} \\ \text{asserted} \\ \text{shouted} \\ \text{whispered} \\ \text{told them} \\ \text{explained} \\ \text{wrote} \\ \text{cabled} \\ \text{wigwagged} \\ \text{? groaned} \\ \text{? ? snorted} \\ \text{? ? laughed}\end{array}\right\}$ that Ann could swim, but nobody believed $\text{him}_i$.

b. $\text{Tom}_i$ $\left\{\begin{array}{l}\text{told them} \\ \text{spoke to them} \\ \text{talked to them}\end{array}\right\}$ about $\left\{\begin{array}{l}\text{Ann's being able to swim} \\ \text{Ann's ability to swim}\end{array}\right\}$ ,

but nobody believed $\text{him}_i$.

(62) a. * $\text{Tom}_i$ frowned $\text{his}_i$ displeasure, but nobody believed $\text{him}_i$.
b. * $\text{Tom}_i$ smiled $\text{his}_i$ encouragement, but nobody believed $\text{him}_i$.
c. * $\text{Tom}_i$ shrugged $\text{his}_i$ resignation, but nobody believed $\text{him}_i$.
d. * $\text{Tom}_i$ roared $\text{his}_i$ amusement, but nobody believed $\text{him}_i$.

(63) a. * $\text{Tom}_i$ enquired whether Ann could swim, but nobody believed $\text{him}_i$.
b. * $\text{Tom}_i$ commanded them to leave, but nodody believed $\text{him}_i$.
c. * $\text{Tom}_i$ $\left\{\begin{array}{l}\text{knew} \\ \text{believed} \\ \text{felt} \\ \text{doubted} \\ \text{hoped}\end{array}\right\}$ that Ann could swim, but nobody believed $\text{him}_i$.

d. * $\text{Tom}_i$ forced Mary to leave, but nobody believed $\text{him}_i$.

The sentences in (61) all have main verbs denoting linguistic communication, as opposed to those in (62), whose main verbs denote nonverbal communication.[34] The ungrammaticality of the latter suggests that whether the restriction on *believe* is to be stated in terms of deep structure or as some condition on a transformational rule, there is need of some feature [±linguistic], so that (61) and (62) may be distinguished. I use the feature [±linguistic], instead of [±verbal], because of the fact that such verbs as *write, cable, wigwag,* and possibly *signal, buzz,* etc., can appear in sentences like (61a). The crucial feature of these verbs is not that they describe oral communication, but rather a kind of communication which is based on language, or, at least, on some kind of systematic code.

Since the sentences of (63c) and (63d) are ungrammatical, I propose to mark these main verbs with the feature [−communication], to distinguish them from the verbs in (61) and (62).

Presumably, all verbs that are [+linguistic] are redundantly [+communication] (unless verbs like *babble, gibber,* etc., are [+linguistic]), so the verbs *enquire* and *command* would not differ in their feature composition from the verbs of (61), as Mrs. M. A. K. Halliday has pointed out to me. But since the sentences of (61) are (almost) all grammatical, while (63a) and (63b) are not, some feature is necessary to distinguish these sets. I propose the feature [±declarative], to subcategorize verbs that are marked [+communication, +linguistic], and I assume that verbs like *enquire, ask, command, order, exclaim at, beseech,* etc., will be lexically marked [−declarative], while the verbs in (61) will be marked [+declarative].

Paul Kiparsky has pointed out[35] the need for distinguishing syntactically between such verbs as *groan, snort, laugh, quip, grumble,* etc., and verbs like *say, claim,* etc., and it appears that this same class of verbs will produce queer, though perhaps not totally unacceptable, sentences if their subjects serve as the antecedent for a pronominal object of *believe.*

I am at a loss to distinguish in any but an *ad hoc* manner among the verbs in (61b). All these verbs would seem to have the same feature composition, so I cannot explain the differences in their behavior with respect to *believe.* I will leave this question for future research.

To recapitulate briefly, it appears that a human anaphoric pronoun can appear only as the superficial object of *believe* if this NP stands in an anaphoric relationship to another NP which functions as the subject (but see Note 33) of a verb with the feature composition [+communication, +linguistic, +declarative]. No matter where in the grammar such a restriction is to be stated, the existence of such sentences as (64)

(64)   Ann *can* swim; but if you don't believe $\left\{{me \atop *\ them}\right\}$, just watch her.

strongly supports two conclusions: 1. in the deep structure of the first clause of (64), the NP *I* appears as the subject of a verb; and 2. this verb shares the features of a large class of verbs like *say, tell, scream, mumble,* etc., i.e., the features [+communication, +linguistic, +declarative]. This is precisely the claim made by postulating (7) as the deep structure of (1a) (see pages 222 and 224). Thus sentences like (64) provide further confirmation for the correctness of the performative analysis.

2.2.2. The second set of facts which indicates that the verb of the higher clause is a verb like *say* has to do with idiomatic expressions like *be damned if,* as exemplified by sentences like (65):

(65) $\begin{Bmatrix} \text{I'm} \\ \text{I'll be} \end{Bmatrix}$ damned if I'll have anything to do with her.

At first glance, it might seem as if this sentence were ambiguous, the first reading being roughly paraphrasable by "I am determined not to have anything to do with her," and the second by "People will damn me if I have anything to do with her." In my own speech, however, the second reading is impossible, because of the presence of the morpheme *will* in the *if*-clause.[36] If the *if*-clause is preposed, the first meaning is also excluded, and the result, (66), is ungrammatical:

(66)   * If I'll have anything to do with her, I'll be damned.

However, it is of no importance whether (65) is ambiguous for other speakers or not — as far as I know, it is grammatical for all speakers in the first meaning, and it is this meaning which the rest of the discussion will be concerned with.

There are a number of peculiarities connected with this idiomatic sense of *be damned if*. Notice first of all that it cannot appear with other modals than *will*, nor with any other sequence of auxiliary verbs; that it cannot appear in the negative or with various kinds of adverbs; and that it cannot be questioned:

(67)   a. * I $\left\{ \begin{Bmatrix} \text{must} \\ \text{may} \\ \text{should} \\ \text{would} \\ \text{am being, etc.} \end{Bmatrix} \text{be} \right\}$ damned if I'll have anything to do with her.

b. * I won't be damned if I'll have anything to do with her.

c. * I'll be damned $\begin{Bmatrix} \text{tomorrow at 8 A.M.} \\ \text{frequently} \\ \text{over at your place, etc.} \end{Bmatrix}$ if I'll have anything to do with her.

d. * Will I be damned if I'll have anything to do with her?

There are also indications that the embedded clause was a negative sentence in deep structure (in accordance with its meaning). Thus this clause can contain verbs like *budge*, which, as David Perlmutter has pointed out, occur only in negative environments (consider, for example, * *Harry budged*), and idioms like *lift a finger*, which are also restricted to negative environments[37] (for example, * *I'll lift a finger to help you*).

(68)   a. I'll be damned if I'll budge.
       b. I'll be damned if I'll lift a finger to help you.

The hypothesis that an originally present negative has been deleted receives further support from the fact that *any* can appear in (65), while this is not possible when the embedded clause appears as an independent sentence, unless it is in the negative:

(69)  I $\left\{ \begin{matrix} * \text{ will} \\ \text{won't} \end{matrix} \right\}$ have anything to do with her.

The most important restriction on *be damned if,* however, is that it requires a first person subject when it appears in a simple declarative sentence:

(70)  a. * Somebody will be damned if he'll have anything to do with her.
      b. * Your Uncle Frank will be damned if he'll have anything to do
          with her.[38]

But it is not the case that *be damned if* always requires a first person subject — when it appears in a clause embedded in the object of a verb like *say,* a subject cannot be *I* unless the subject of *say* is [cf. (71)]

(71)  $\left\{ \begin{matrix} \text{I} \\ * \text{ Ed} \end{matrix} \right\}$ said that I would be damned if I'd have anything to do with her.

The correct generalization becomes obvious upon considering the various sentences in (72).

(72)  a. $\text{Ed}_i$ said that Sally. $\left\{ \begin{matrix} * \text{ I} \\ * \text{ you} \\ \text{he}_i \\ * \text{ Ann} \\ * \text{ we} \\ * \text{ they} \end{matrix} \right\}$ would be damned if Bill would marry

      b. You said that Sally. $\left\{ \begin{matrix} * \text{ I} \\ \text{you} \\ * \text{ Ed} \\ * \text{ Ann} \\ * \text{ we} \\ * \text{ they} \end{matrix} \right\}$ would be damned if Bill would marry

      c. $\text{They}_i$ said that Sally. $\left\{ \begin{matrix} * \text{ I} \\ * \text{ you} \\ * \text{ Ed} \\ * \text{ Ann} \\ * \text{ we} \\ \text{they}_i \end{matrix} \right\}$ would be damned if Bill would marry

It appears that *be damned if* can appear only in a deep structure [assuming, in the absence of clear counterevidence (but see Note 38), that the restrictions in question are to be stated in terms of deep structure] if its subject is identical to the subject of a higher verb.

Furthermore, examples like (73) show that the higher verb must be the main verb of the first sentence up, in deep structure:

(73)    $Ed_i$ said that we had asserted that $Sheila_j$ had screamed that
$\begin{Bmatrix} * \; he_i \\ * \; we \\ she_j \end{Bmatrix}$ would be damned if $she_j$'d go.

That it is necessary for the subject of *be damned if* to be identical to the subject of the first clause up, rather than to just some NP which belongs to this clause, can be seen by the ungrammaticality of the sentences in (74).[39]

(74)    a. * I told $Ed_i$ that $he_i$'d be damned if $he_i$'d have anything to do with her.
        b. * That $he_i$'d be damned if $he_i$'d have anything to do with her worried $Ed_i$.

For some reason that I do not understand, the clause above *be damned if* cannot be passivized — (75b) is ungrammatical.

(75)    a. The Secretary of $State_i$ declared that $he_i$'d be damned if $he_i$'d let me travel in France.
        b. * It was declared by the Secretary of $State_i$ that $he_i$'d be damned if $he_i$'d let me travel in France.[40]

From the contrast in grammaticality between (76a) and (76b), it can be seen that there is a further restriction on deep structures containing *be damned if;* not only must its subject be identical to the subject of the next higher verb, but that verb must have the features [+ communication, + linguistic, + declarative]:[41]

(76)    a. $Ed_i$ $\begin{Bmatrix} said \\ stated \\ asserted \\ declared \\ claimed \\ screamed \\ whispered \\ told \; me \\ wrote \\ wigwagged \\ snorted \end{Bmatrix}$ that $he_i$'d be damned if Bill would marry Sally.

        b. * $Ed_i$ $\begin{Bmatrix} \begin{Bmatrix} knew \\ believed \\ hoped \\ expected \\ doubted \\ felt \end{Bmatrix} that \\ enquired \; whether \end{Bmatrix}$ $he_i$'d be damned if Bill would marry Sally.

Apparently, *be damned if* is impossible with *poss–ing* complementizers,[42] for (77) is ungrammatical, as opposed to the first sentence in (61b).

(77)   * $Ed_i$ told me about being damned if Bill would marry Sally.

The restrictions which so far have been imposed on the occurrence of *be damned if* actually are oversimplified, as the sentences in (78) show.

(78)   a. $Ed_i$ said that it was $\begin{Bmatrix} \text{* likely} \\ \text{? true} \end{Bmatrix}$ that $he_i$'d be damned if $he_i$'d go.

   b. $Ed_i$ said that the one thing that $he_i$'d be damned if $he_i$'d sell was this knife.

   c. $Ed_i$ claims that Betty $\begin{Bmatrix} \text{* feels} \\ \text{* says} \\ \text{? knows} \end{Bmatrix}$ that $he_i$'ll be damned if $he_i$'ll go.

I have not investigated such constructions as these in detail, but it is my impression that they can be accommodated if the restrictions on *be damned if* are not stated in terms of the subject and verb of the first clause up, but rather in terms of the subject of the first verb of saying above *be damned if* in deep structure. That is, I believe that the eventual restriction on this idiom will be a somewhat less permissive version of (79).[43]

(79)   No deep structure containing the VP *be damned if* S is well-formed unless the subject of this VP is identical to the subject of the first VP up the tree whose head verb has the features [+ communication, + linguistic, + declarative].

If this restriction, despite being inadequate to the task of distinguishing between *likely* and *true* in (78a), or *feel* and *know* in (78c), is basically correct, the grammaticality of such sentences as (65) and (68) provides compelling evidence for the performative analysis. For (79) says, in effect, that whenever the idiom *be damned if* occurs in a surface structure, the associated deep structure must contain a higher verb of saying, and that the subject of this higher verb must be identical to the subject of *be damned if.* Since the subject of the idiom is *I* in (65) and (68), (79) requires the presence of a higher sentence whose subject is *I* and whose verb is a verb like *say*, a requirement entirely in consonance with the performative analysis.

2.2.3. The last set of facts having to do with the nature of the verb in the higher clause was discovered by Michael Brame. In Arabic, there are three complementizers, which all start with highly similar phonetic sequences: ʔ*an*, which is used after verbs like ʔ*uriidu* "(I) want," ʔ*aʔmuru* "(I) command," and other verbs denoting expectation, command, or request; ʔ*inna*, which is used *only* after the verb *ʔaquulu* "(I) say"; and *ʔanna*, which is used after all other verbs [e.g., after *waswastu* "(I) whispered"]. Such a strange distribution would suggest an analysis which recognized only two basic complementizers, *ʔan* and *ʔanna*, whose distribution could hopefully be predicted largely on semantic grounds, and which postulated a low-level morphological (or even phonological) rule which replaced the expected *ʔanna* by *ʔinna* after the verb *ʔaquulu*.

However, if this rather plausible analysis is to be adopted, a rule deleting the verb *ʔaquulu* must be added to the grammar, and this rule must be ordered so as to follow the rule converting *ʔanna* to *ʔinna*, because of the rather startling fact that *ʔinna* occurs not only in sentences which contain forms of the verb *ʔaquulu* explicitly, but also optionally at the beginning of almost all declarative sentences. Thus the three sentences of (80) (*the boy left the house*) are synonymous and in free variation:

(80)  a. *ʔaquulu*       *ʔinna lwalada*        *qad*    *taraka lbayta*
   I say (indic.) that    the boy (acc.) (past)  leave   the house (acc.)

   b. *ʔinna lwalada qad taraka lbayta*.

   c. *ʔal walad u*        *qad    taraka lbayta*.
   the  boy      (nom.) (past) leave   the house (acc.)[44]

The consequences of these facts for the performative analysis need not be belabored. Even if no other evidence were available in Arabic,[45] one would be tempted to propose an analysis along the general lines of the performative analysis to account for them.[46] I might point out that Arabic is the only language I know of where strong evidence points to a rule deleting a particular verb, instead of a pro-verb specified only by an abstract bundle of features.[47] In English, it does not seem possible to identify the verb as being one particular member of the class of verbs designated by the feature bundle [+ communication, + linguistic, + declarative].

2.3.1. The first of the three arguments I know of within English for claiming that the deep structure for all declaratives contains an indirect object *you* was pointed out to me by David Perlmutter.

In sentences like those in (81), a possessive adjective referring back to the subject of the main verb must modify an NP in the object:

(81)  a. I craned $\left\{ \begin{array}{l} \text{my} \\ \text{* Suzie's} \end{array} \right\}$ neck.

   b. You hold $\left\{ \begin{array}{l} \text{your} \\ \text{* Bob's} \end{array} \right\}$ breath well.

   c. Ootek$_i$ went on $\left\{ \begin{array}{l} \text{his}_i \\ \text{* Farley's} \end{array} \right\}$ way.

When the verbal idiom *to hold one's breath* is embedded in the object of such verbs as *want, need, would like,* etc., as it is in (82)

(82) a. I want you to hold your breath for 2 minutes.
b. I want $Tom_i$ to hold $his_i$ breath for 2 minutes.

an optional rule can operate on the complements to convert (82a) to (83a):

(83) a. I want your breath (to be) held for 2 minutes.
b. * I want Tom's breath (to be) held for 2 minutes.[48]

As the strangeness of (83b) indicates, this rule would appear to be restricted to cases where the idiom has a second person subject.

I have suggested converting (82a) directly to (83a), instead of postulating a prior application of the passive on an earlier cycle, because the sentences in (84), which would result from such a derivation in isolation, are ungrammatical, for me at least:

(84) a. * Your breath was held by you for 2 minutes.
b. * $Tom's_i$ breath was held by $him_i$ for 2 minutes.

The ungrammaticality of the sentences in (85) shows that it is not the case that whatever rule effects the conversion of (82a) to (83a) works in the objects of all verbs:

(85) a. ?? I expect your breath to be held for 2 minutes.
b. * I $\left\{ \begin{array}{l} \text{believe} \\ \text{know} \\ \text{etc.} \end{array} \right\}$ your breath to have been held for 2 minutes.

Let us now return to the restriction as to the deep subject of the idiom in such sentences as those in (83). That it is wrong to insist that this subject must be second person can be seen from the sentences in (86):

(86) a. I told $Max_i$ that I wanted $\left\{ \begin{array}{l} his_i \\ * \text{ your} \end{array} \right\}$ breath (to be) held for 2 minutes.

b. They said to $us_i$ that they wanted $\left\{ \begin{array}{l} our_i \text{ breath} \\ * \text{ Max's breath} \end{array} \right\}$ (to be) held for 2 minutes.

c. We informed $them_i$ that we wanted $\left\{ \begin{array}{l} their_i \\ * \text{ your} \end{array} \right\}$ breath (to be) held for 4 minutes.

It is easy to see that the more general restriction to which this construction is subject is that the deep subject of the idiom must be identical to the indirect object of the second sentence up. Since any grammar must contain this restriction, so that the facts of (86) can be accounted for, if the performative analysis is adopted, the fact that only *your* is possible in (83) becomes a consequence of this independently motivated restriction.

2.3.2. The second argument for postulating a higher indirect object *you* was pointed out to me by Ray Jackendoff. He observed that the ungrammaticality of such sentences as those in (87)

(87)　　* You feel $\left\{ \begin{array}{l} \text{tired} \\ \text{bored} \\ \text{jaded} \\ \text{etc.} \end{array} \right\}$ .

is to be attributed to the more general restriction which must be postulated so that the ungrammatical sentences of (88) can be blocked:

(88)　　a. I told Mr. Feuerstein$_i$ that $\left\{ \begin{array}{l} \text{I} \\ \text{you} \\ \text{* he}_i \end{array} \right\}$ felt tired.

　　　　b. Blondie announced to Dagwood$_i$ that $\left\{ \begin{array}{l} \text{I} \\ \text{you} \\ \text{they} \\ \text{* he}_i \end{array} \right\}$ felt bored.

　　　　c. Jerry told Joyce$_i$ that $\left\{ \begin{array}{l} \text{Sam} \\ \text{Petrarca} \\ \text{we} \\ \text{* she}_i \end{array} \right\}$ felt jaded.

That is, the subject of such subjective predicates as *be tired, be bored, love,* etc., cannot be identical to the indirect object of the first verb up. In conjunction with the performative analysis, this restriction explains the ungrammaticality of (87), for this analysis postulates an indirect object *you* in the sentence which dominates all declarative sentences. Put in another way, (87) provides evidence for this facet of the performative analysis.

2.3.3. In addition to the fairly strong support for postulating a higher indirect object *you* which is provided by the arguments in Sections 2.3.1 and 2.3.2, there is some support from those dialects of English in which sentences like (89) are possible:

(89)　　? ? This paper was written by Ann and yourself.

To me, this sentence is highly dubious, but there are speakers who find no difference between it and (21a), while they would totally reject (89) with *themselves* in the place of *yourself.*

I have not investigated such dialects in detail, but it is my belief that in just those cases where *yourself* is possible in "simple" declaratives like (89), anaphoric reflexives like *himself* will be possible in sentences like (90):

(90) ?? Ted told Sarah$_i$ that the paper had been written by Ann and herself$_i$.

If this prediction holds true, then sentences like (89) will constitute further evidence for the performative analysis, by an argument exactly paralleling that in Section 2.3.1.

2.4. There is one final argument for the performative analysis which does not lend itself to grouping under Sections 2.1 through 2.3. It is based on such sentences as (91), which were called to my attention by Thomas Bever and, independently, by Edward Klima.

(91) Jenny$_i$ isn't here, for I don't see her$_i$.

It is clear that the *for*-clause in (91) does not provide a reason for Jenny's absence (indeed, Jenny may not in fact *be* absent), but rather a reason for the speaker to assert that she is absent. It is not clear to me how such a reading could be derived in a non-*ad hoc* way from any analysis of the sentence *Jenny isn't here* which did not derive it from a deep structure containing the main clause in surface structure as an object clause of some verb of saying.

2.5. To summarize briefly, in the fourteen arguments above, I have attempted to justify all facets of the performative analysis, which postulates (7) as the deep structure of (1a). Paradoxically, the one facet for which I have the least support is the claim that the verb of the deleted higher clause has the feature [+performative] and is in fact a performative in (7). Aside from the rather weak argument which is mentioned in Section 3.4 below, I have no syntactic justification for this claim. Nevertheless, the fact that the uttering of (1a) constitutes an assertion, just as the uttering of (2a) constitutes a promise, suggests that their deep structures should not differ markedly, so that there will be a uniform deep structural configuration on which to base the semantic notion *speech act*. And as Lakoff and I argue elsewhere [Lakoff and Ross (in preparation)], it is likely that all types of sentences have exactly one performative as their highest clause in deep structure, so the deep structures of declaratives should not differ from this general scheme. It should be quite clear, however, that this claim is highly speculative at present, so the facet of the performative analysis from which its name derives must for the time being be recognized as the most tentative claim of the whole analysis.

Finally, I would like to make two points which are perhaps too obvious to need emphasis. Firstly, the facts on which I have based the arguments given in Sections 2.1 through 2.4 are not logical truths. There is no reason why they should be consistent with one another. That is, it is logically possible that *myself* could appear in sentences like (21), but *himself* in sentences like (32), and that it could be only *Baxter* that was impossible in sentences like (47). Or *believe* [+human, +PRO]$_{NP}$ might require a verb of saying, while *be damned if* could only occur after a verb denoting fear. That these facts all *do* cohere requires an explanation, therefore, and the performative analysis is an attempt at one.

Secondly, the performative analysis makes a claim which transcends the fourteen sets of facts I have used in the arguments above. The claim is that if, in any language, other constructions are discovered in which there are restrictions on first or second person NPs, then these restrictions will prove to be special cases of more general restrictions which will be formulated in terms of properties of higher subjects and indirect objects, respectively.[49] And if peculiarities having to do with the allowable constructions in the objects of verbs of saying should turn up, then just these peculiarities should be observable in simple declaratives. Whether this strong claim is correct or not can only be decided by future research.

3.1. The rule which effects the conversion of (7) into (6) is stated in (92).[50]

(92)   **Performative Deletion**

$$[I]_{NP} \quad \begin{bmatrix} +V \\ +\text{performative} \\ +\text{communication} \\ +\text{linguistic} \\ +\text{declarative} \end{bmatrix} \quad [you]_{NP} \quad S_{VP}$$

$$\begin{array}{cccc} 1 & 2 & 3 & 4 \implies \\ 0 & 0 & 0 & 4 \end{array}$$

There are a number of problems with this rule. First of all, as was mentioned in Section 2.5, it appears that (92) must be made more general, so that not only verbs of saying will be deleted in generating declaratives, but also verbs of commanding, in generating imperatives. It also seems likely that it will be necessary to delete other types of verbs, so that exclamatory sentences, and optative sentences, and other sentence types, will arise from the same rule. At present, it is not clear to me how this rule is to be generalized sufficiently to handle this class of cases but still kept specific enough so that performative verbs like *authorize* and *grant* will not be deleted. Perhaps no general condition is statable, and verbs must be lexically marked as to whether or not they undergo this rule.

3.2. Secondly, is rule (92) optional or obligatory? McCawley (1968) has pointed out that while (93a) is possible, (93b) is not

(93) a. I tell you that prices slumped.
b. * I hereby tell you that prices slumped.

and has suggested that rule (92) be made sensitive to the presence of *hereby*, obligatorily converting (93b) into (la). This proposal seems highly plausible, and I will adopt it, in the hope that the (probably minor) difficulties mentioned in Note 47 can be avoided.

3.3. McCawley (1968) and Postal (1967a) have suggested that the pronouns *I* and *you* should be derived from underlying third person NPs. Under this proposal, the deep structure of (94)

(94) You nauseate me.

would be that shown in (95):

(95)

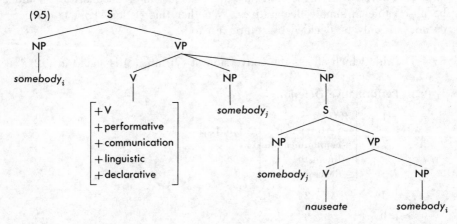

Prior to the application of rule (92), a rule of pronominalization would convert all NPs which were subjects of performative clauses, and all NPs identical to these subjects, to first person definite pronouns, and all indirect objects of performative clauses (but see Note 3), and NPs identical to these indirect objects, to second person pronouns.[51]

This proposal of McCawley's and Postal's also strikes me as correct. There are a number of facts which suggest that first and second person pronouns really derive from deeper third person NPs. Note, for instance, the possibility of using third person NPs to refer to the utterer, as in (96):

(96) a. The court is not amused, Mr. Nizer.

b. $\begin{Bmatrix} \text{The king} \\ \text{Your president} \end{Bmatrix}$ will announce his decision as soon as possible.

c. Yours truly better get himself a seven.[52]
d. Mrs. Ross's little boy needs to win himself a fat one.

Also, in German, appositive clauses which modify first or second person pronouns can either have the verb of the clause inflected for first person, as in (97a), or for third person, as in (97b), if the relativized NP is the subject of the appositive clause (*I, who am responsible*):

(97) a. *ich,   der        ich   verantwortlich   bin*
         I    (rel. pron.)  I    responsible      be (1st pers. sg. pres.)

     b. *ich,   der              verantwortlich   ist* (3rd pers. sg. pres.)

Finally, this proposal may provide a starting point for an explanation of the extremely puzzling facts of (98) and (99).

(98) a. It is I who $\left\{ \begin{array}{c} am \\ {}^*is \end{array} \right\}$ responsible.

     b. It is me who $\left\{ \begin{array}{c} {}^*am \\ is \end{array} \right\}$ responsible.

     c. It is you who $\left\{ \begin{array}{c} are \\ is \end{array} \right\}$ responsible.

     d. The one who $\left\{ \begin{array}{c} {}^*am \\ {}^*are \\ is \end{array} \right\}$ responsible is $\left\{ \begin{array}{c} I \\ me \\ you \end{array} \right\}$.

(99) a. I am the one who will have to protect $\left\{ \begin{array}{c} myself \\ himself \end{array} \right\}$.[53]

     b. The one who will have to protect $\left\{ \begin{array}{c} {}^*myself \\ himself \end{array} \right\}$ is $\left\{ \begin{array}{c} I \\ me \end{array} \right\}$.

While I agree with both of these proposals — that is, that rule (92) should be made to depend on the presence of *hereby*, and that *I* and *you* are to be derived from underlying third person NPs — I have postponed revising rule (92) until I understand better what other consequences the proposals will have. Thus (92) must be regarded as a very preliminary formulation.

3.4. A third problem connected with the operation of rule (92) is the following: if some syntactic rules can apply to their own output, as would seem necessary,[54] why can rule (92) not apply to its own output and produce infinite ambiguity? That is, why can (7) not be embedded again in the object of a higher performative verb of saying? Or doubly embedded? Or embedded an indefinitely large number of times?

The answer to this question is that there is an independently necessary constraint that prohibits any verb from having a performative interpretation when it is embedded as the complement of another verb. Thus while (100a), said in isolation, constitutes an admission, and (100b) a promise,

(100) a. I admit that I'll be late.
      b. I (hereby) promise that I'll be late.

when (100b) appears as the object of *admit*, as in (101)

(101)   I admit that I (* hereby) promise that I'll be late.

the result is an admission of having made frequent promises, but it is not a promise. This fact is also reflected in the inability of the adverb *hereby* to precede *promise* in (101). Thus, since performative verbs cannot be used performatively in complements, rule (92) will not produce infinitely ambiguous surface structures. This point provides some nonsemantic evidence for including the feature [+performative] in (7) and in (92).

3.5. One final point about the operation of rule (92): even granting that this rule operates in the derivation of sentences like (21), (26), (32), (64), (65), etc., where the superordinate sentence leaves traces in the surface structure, it might be argued that there is no superordinate sentence in the deep structure of sentences where no trace can be found of this higher clause. Thus (1a) would have (6), instead of (7), as its deep structure.

It seems to me that this line of argument is not tenable, for it would make the claim that while sentences like (21) are unambiguous (they can be derived only from deep structures containing a higher performative), sentences like (1a) are ambiguous, in that they can be derived from (6) *or from* (7). Since rule (92) must be in the grammar, it will convert (7) to (6) and then to (1a). But it is false that sentences like (1a) are ambiguous, so one of the two structures, (6) and (7), which were postulated to underlie (1a), must in fact not be a well-formed deep structure. It is obvious that (7) must be retained, and not (6), unless some non-*ad hoc* way can be found to block the conversion from (7) to (6). The only thing that suggests itself to me is some vastly more powerful convention on recoverability of deletion than is now available.[55] In the absence of such a convention, however, I will for the present assume that the only deep structure for (1a) is (7), or, more generally, that every declarative sentence has one and only one performative sentence as its highest clause, and that this highest clause is deleted by the rule of *performative deletion.*[56]

There is a class of true counterexamples to this claim, as was pointed out to me by Paul Kiparsky. The sentences which appear in an instruction manual, or in a newspaper article without a byline, obviously are not to be derived from a deep structure containing a superordinate clause. In fact, it is precisely in impersonal contexts like this that first person pronouns cannot occur. So my claim must be weakened somewhat, as has been done in (102).

(102)   All declarative sentences occurring in contexts where first person pronouns can appear derive from deep structures containing one and only one superordinate performative clause whose main verb is a verb of saying.

At present, I do not know of any reason to assume a more abstract underlying structure than (6) for (1a), if it is used in a newspaper article. Nor, more importantly, do I know how to give formal content to such terms as "occur" and "context," which Kiparsky's observation has forced me to use in stating (102). They seem to be definable only within a systematic theory of pragmatics, an area which up to now has been largely disregarded by generative grammarians. I will return to this topic, briefly, in Section 4.2 and in Section 5 below.

4. In this section, I will propose two alternative analyses of the facts in Section 2. While the first of these appears clearly inferior to the performative analysis, the second does seem to be equally satisfactory, and possibly superior.

4.1. The first alternative analysis I will refer to as *the quotative analysis*. The explanation it provides for the facts in Section 2 is the reverse of the explanation I have given. That is, while I have tried to account for the occurrence of *myself* in the *as for*-phrase of (32), which I repeat here for convenience

(32)   As for myself, I won't be invited.

by assuming a rule that optionally reflexivizes a pronoun in an *as for*-phrase if the pronoun refers back to the subject of the next higher verb, the quotative analysis assumes that (32) is basic — that an optional rule allows the *me* in an *as for*-phrase which starts an independent clause to become *myself*. Given this rule, and another, which converts direct quotes to indirect quotes, the fact that in embedded sentences other reflexives appear in *as for*-phrases is explained by the rule which changes pronouns in forming indirect quotations. That is, just as (103a) would be converted into (103b), so (104b), which has resulted from (104a) by the operation of the *as for* reflexivization rule, would be converted into (104c)

(103)   a. Harpo said to Greta, "I'll never forget you."
        b. Harpo said to Greta that he'd never forget her.

(104)   a. Harpo said to Greta, "As for me, I'll never forget you."
        b. Harpo said to Greta, "As for myself, I'll never forget you."
        c. Harpo said to Greta that as for himself, he'd never forget her.

It seems to me that there are insuperable difficulties with this analysis. First of all, since *as for*-phrases containing reflexives can appear after such verbs as *believe*, as in (105a), the objects of such verbs would have to be derived from direct quotes, as in (105b), which is hardly a plausible structure for semantic rules to work on:

(105)   a.   $Ed_i$ believed that as for $himself_i$, $he_i$'d be spared.
        b. * $Ed_i$ believed, "As for me, I'll be spared."

Further, since (105b) is ungrammatical, the indirect discourse rule would have to convert it to (105a) obligatorily.

Secondly, although it can perhaps be plausibly maintained that first person pronouns become third person pronouns which refer back to the subject of the matrix verb, by the operation of the indirect discourse rule, there is a problem concerning what should happen to second person pronouns. It might seem that they should become third person pronouns which refer back to the indirect object, but this proposal cannot be maintained, because there are verbs, like *determine,* which have no indirect objects for the second person pronouns to refer back to. So while (106a) could be converted to (106b), no "indirect quote" can be provided for (107a).

(106)  a.  * Tom determined, "As for myself, I won't eat anything Sarah cooks."
       b.  Tom determined that as for himself, he wouldn't eat anything that Sarah cooked.

(107)  a.  * Tom determined, "As for myself, I won't eat anything you cook."
       b.  Tom determined that as for himself, he wouldn't eat anything ?? cooked.

Finally, if *I* and *you* are obligatorily converted to third person anaphoric pronouns by the rule which produces indirect discourse, what is the source for the *I*'s and *you*'s which can appear in indirect discourse, as in (108)?

(108)  Philip$_i$ said to Mabel$_j$ that he$_i$ and I would go out with you and her$_j$ sometime.

Until these objections can be answered, the quotative analysis must be rejected as a possible explanation for the facts in Section 2.

4.2. The second alternative to the performative analysis I will refer to as *the pragmatic analysis.*

In this analysis, it is accepted that sentences like (32) are to be explained on the basis of sentences like (29a) by the same rule of optional reflexivization of the NP in the *as for*-phrase as was proposed for the performative analysis. What is different about the two analyses is that the pragmatic analysis postulates (6), and not (7), as the deep structure for (1a), and claims that certain elements are present in the context of a speech act, and that syntactic processes can refer to such elements. Thus, since the context provides an *I* which is "in the air," so to speak, and since the rule which produces reflexives in *as for*-phrases would be stated in such a way that the antecedents to the reflexive pronouns could either actually be present in deep structure or be "in the air," this rule would correctly produce the *myself* of such sentences as those in (21), (26), (32) and (36). Similarly, however, if the constraint preliminarily stated in (41) is to be revised, it would be stated in such a way as to take into consideration elements "in the air," so sentences like (37b) would be blocked. Furthermore, deep structure constraints would not only specify what interrelationships among elements of deep structure were permitted, but also what interrelationships were possible between elements of deep structure and elements "in the air." Thus the ungrammatical sentences in (43) and (47) would be blocked by the same mechanisms used to block the ungrammatical sentences in (45) and (48).

Note that in order to account for the facts in Sections 2.2 and 2.3 under the pragmatic analysis, it would have to be assumed not only that there was also a verb of saying and an NP *you* "in the air," but also that the *you* functioned as the indirect object of this verb [to account for the sentences of (83) and (87)]. Furthermore, the *I* that is "in the air" would have to function as the subject of this verb, for it will be recalled that the restrictions on *as for*-phrases and idioms like *be damned if* make use of the relation *subject of* in their formulations. Thus the elements that would have to be assumed to be "in the air" under the pragmatic analysis do not merely form an unstructured set. Rather, they must be assumed to be hierarchically grouped to form a structure which is exactly the same as that of a normal clause in deep structure.

Given this isomorphism, it may well be asked how the pragmatic analysis differs from the performative analysis: why are they not merely notational variants? Where the latter analysis has more abstract deep structures than the former, and needs a rule like (92), the former presupposes richer notions of analyzability [cf. Chomsky (1955)] and deep structure constraint, so there would not appear to be much to motivate a choice on the grounds of simplicity or elegance. Presumably, the two analyses would make different psychological claims, but exactly how these would differ is obscure to me.

The only argument I know of for distinguishing between these two analyses has to do with sentences like (109), which were called to my attention by François Dell:

(109)   As for myself, I promise you that I'll be there.

The problem is, how can the pronoun *myself* be generated? Since (109) can be a performative sentence, it cannot be argued that there is a higher performative verb of saying, for performative verbs cannot be embedded, as was pointed out in connection with (101). Furthermore, it is simply incorrect to claim that (109) is both a promise and an assertion, as the ungrammaticality of (110) shows:

(110)   * Fritz said to Ken, "As for myself, I promise you that I'll be there," which was a lie.

Thus sentence (109) poses real problems for the performative analysis.

In the pragmatic analysis, however, since there would presumably be elements "in the air" for promises, as well as for assertions, the regular rule which produces reflexives in *as for*-phrases could refer to the $I$ "in the air," and *myself* would be generated in such sentences as (109). This type of sentence, therefore, seems to constitute evidence for rejecting the performative analysis in favor of the pragmatic analysis.

However, there may still be a way to account for (109) in terms of the performative analysis. Paul Kiparsky has suggested to me that the *as for*-phrase which starts (109) may not modify *promise* in deep structure, but rather that it may be a constituent of the embedded clause. That is, (109) would be derived from (111), by means of a rule which preposes the embedded *as for*-phrase:

(111)   I promise that, as for myself, I'll be there.

In support of this derivation, Kiparsky points out that the strangeness of (112) is preserved when it is embedded in the object of *promise*, as shown by the contrast in acceptability between (113a) and (113b):

(112)   *?? As for me, Tom will be there.

(113)   a.      I promise you that Tom will be there.
        * b.   ?? I promise you that, as for me, Tom will be there.

If the normal rule which produces reflexives in *as for*-phrases applies to (113b), and then Kiparsky's proposed rule preposes this phrase, the resulting sentence, (114), retains the strangeness of (113b):

(114)   ?? As for myself, I promise you that Tom will be there.

Thus, Kiparsky proposes to explain the strangeness of (114) on the basis of the strangeness of (112).

It is obvious that the pragmatic analysis cannot explain the difference between (109) and (114), for if the $I$ "in the air" can occasion the conversion of *as for me* to *as for myself* in the former sentence, it should also be able to do so in the latter.

There is an assumption in the pragmatic analysis account of (109) that I have not challenged till now, namely, that *as for*-phrases can occur as constituents of performative clauses. That is, even if *myself* cannot occur in *as for*-phrases in sentences like (114), *me* should be able to, according to this analysis. However, I find (115) only slightly less strange than (114):

(115)   ? As for me, I promise that Tom will be there.

If (115) must be excluded, as well as (114), it is clear that only Kiparsky's account of (109) can be correct. However, my intuitions about (115) are not sharp enough to decide the issue.

If Kiparsky's proposal regarding the embedded origin of the *as for*-phrase in performative sentences is correct, we would predict that there could be no such *as for*-phrases in performative sentences containing no clause embedded as a direct object. The performative sentences in (116), which have this property, are certainly strange, but I am not sure enough in my judgments to state categorically that no such sentence would be grammatical.

(116)   As for myself,
$\left\{\begin{array}{l} \text{? * I authorize the purchase of a rodent.} \\ \text{? ? I sentence you to two years of TV dinners.} \\ \text{*\quad I christen this ship } \textit{The U.S.S. Intervention.} \\ \text{*\quad I pronounce you man and wife.} \\ \text{*\quad I grant you your freedom.} \\ \text{? * I dare you to leave.} \\ \text{? ? I condemn your intransigence.} \end{array}\right\}$

If even one such sentence is grammatical, the performative analysis must be rejected. However, even if they are all ungrammatical, the pragmatic analysis can be maintained, for their ungrammaticality would only confirm the correctness of Kiparsky's proposed rule to prepose embedded *as for*-phrases. Since such a rule is compatible with both analyses, performative sentences which start with *as for myself* do not provide crucial evidence for choosing either the performative analysis or the pragmatic analysis. However, if (115) is ungrammatical, this fact, in conjunction with the grammaticality of (109), does constitute counterevidence to the pragmatic analysis.

In conclusion, I must emphasize that neither the quotative analysis nor the pragmatic analysis has ever been worked out in detail. I have discussed them here merely as foils to the performative analysis.

However, even if they are only foils, certain qualitative differences between them remain. At present, the quotative analysis seems to be totally out of the question — not only would it occasion violent and otherwise unmotivated disruptions in fairly well established analyses, but it has a number of internal difficulties, which, as far as I can see, are irremediable.

The pragmatic analysis, by contrast, seems to me to be far less of a straw man. Since there are valid statements like (102) which seem to be linguistically significant, in an admittedly broad sense of "linguistic," somehow an extended theory of language, or a related theory of language use, must incorporate them. But it is clear that such a theory will have to be given a precise formulation, and that stylistic devices such as making use of colorful terms like "in the air" do not ensure that such a theory exists. A precise theory would have to specify formally what features of the infinite set of possible contexts can be of linguistic relevance. Furthermore, these features would have to be described with the same primes which are used for the description of syntactic elements, so that rules which range over syntactic elements will also range over them. While such a theory can be envisioned, and may even eventually prove to be necessary, it is obvious that it does not exist at present.

In fact, it seems to me that the only concrete information about the structure of contexts at present is that which can be inferred from the facts discussed in Section 2. These facts show that if the pragmatic analysis is to be carried through, contexts must be assumed to have the structure of clauses: They must have elements which share properties with subject NPs, elements which share properties with indirect object NPs, and elements which share properties with verbs of saying. Furthermore, if Lakoff and I are correct in our claim that questions are to be derived from structures roughly paraphrasable by *I request of you that you tell me S* (cf. Note 19), then contexts also exhibit properties of syntactic constructions with embedded clauses. However, while such observations may be interesting, they only serve to illustrate the enormous gap between what can now be said about contexts in fairly precise terms and what would have to be said in any theory which could provide a detailed understanding of language use.

Since no such theory exists, the pragmatic analysis does not exist. The performative analysis, on the other hand, can be said to exist: it fits naturally into a theoretical framework whose broad outlines are relatively clear, and it is for this reason that I have argued for its adoption in this paper. However, while the pragmatic theory, in the absence of a detailed theory of language use, is too vague to be testable, it does not seem to me to be impossible in principle, as the quotative analysis does. Therefore, while I would urge that the performative analysis be adopted now, given the vanishingly small amount of precise present knowledge about the interrelationship between context and language, I consider open the question as to whether the theory of language can be distinguished from the theory of language use. A pragmatic analysis implicitly claims that they cannot be distinguished, whereas the performative analysis makes the more conservative claim that they can be.

5. What consequences do the facts of Section 2 have for the theory of grammar?

First of all, regardless of whether the performative analysis, or the pragmatic analysis, or some third possibility I have not envisioned, turns out to be correct, it is obvious that English syntax in particular, but all syntax in general, will become more abstract than has previously been realized. If the performative analysis is chosen, the relationship between deep and surface structures will become slightly less direct than it formerly was. While rules which delete various grammatical morphemes or designated elements are well-known within generative grammar, I know of no rule which operates like rule (92) to delete a whole clause of deep structure. While no formal constraint precluded the existence of such a rule, no evidence had ever been discovered which suggested such rules might be necessary.

If, on the other hand, a precise theory of language use is developed, and the pragmatic analysis is chosen, the relationship between deep and surface structures will remain the same, but there will be an increase in the abstractness of the structures which must be assumed to be being manipulated by transformational rules. Thus, whether or not the superordinate *I, you*, and verb of saying are conceived of as being generated by the base rules, the constructs which must be postulated within generative grammar to explain features of surface structures will become even further removed from observable behavior than is now the case. Whatever analysis of the facts of Section 2 is finally decided upon, they will make generative grammar more mentalistic.

With this increase in the abstractness of the syntax of particular languages comes the possibility of making far stronger claims about universal grammar than have previously been tenable. It has often been observed that languages differ far less in their deep structures than they do in their surface structures. And as deep structures become more and more abstract, and get closer and closer to semantic representation,[57] it appears that differences between deep structural representations of widely disparate languages get smaller and smaller, which would follow, if semantic representations can be assumed to be universal.

As a case in point, it now seems likely that no matter whether the performative or the pragmatic analysis is adopted for English, the same analysis will hold universally. I would expect that arguments cognate to those in Sections 2.1.5 through 2.1.7, 2.2.1 and 2.2.2, and 2.3.2 will be discoverable in virtually all languages, so that rule (92), if it is a rule of English, will be a universal rule, when given a formulation abstract enough to allow for automatic reordering of its terms.[58]

But if it is correct to claim that this analysis is universal, not only will the deep structures of declaratives in all languages resemble each other in having a performative clause containing a verb of saying as their highest clause, but other apparent discrepancies in the base rules of various languages can be disposed of. Thus if we say, for the sake of argument, that one of the base rules for English is that given in (117)

(117)  S → NP   VP

then the base rules of Arabic would differ from those of English, without the performative or the pragmatic analysis, for one of the base rules for Arabic would presumably be (118):[59]

(118)  S → (ʔ*inna*) NP   VP

If we adopt the performative or the pragmatic analysis for Arabic, however, this apparent difference in deep structures disappears.

It might be argued that the ʔ*inna* at the beginning of (80b) need not be introduced in deep structure, but could be attached by a transformation. This appears to be possible for the Arabic example, but it would not be for the following facts from Thai.[60]

In this language, every sentence must end with the particle *khráp* or *kâ*.

The first particle signifies that a male has spoken the sentence; the second, that it was spoken by a female. Thus there are two sentences which translate the English sentence *he is coming* — both are given in (119):

(119) *khaw maa* $\begin{Bmatrix} khráp \\ kâ \end{Bmatrix}$.

     he   come

Since these utterer agreement particles (UAP) have meaning, and can be the cause of semantically anomalous sentences, I assume that they must appear in deep structure. That is, the base component for Thai would have to contain either the rule in (120) or those in (121):

(120)  S → NP     VP $\begin{Bmatrix} khráp \\ kâ \end{Bmatrix}$

(121)  a. S → NP     VP     UAP

      b. UAP → $\begin{Bmatrix} khráp \\ kâ \end{Bmatrix}$

But here once again the putative differences vanish if the performative or the pragmatic analysis is adopted — both English and Thai have rule (117) in their base components. The only difference will be that Thai will have a copying rule which precedes (92) and which places a morpheme which agrees in semantic gender with the superordinate *I* at the right end of the sentence.[61]

Rudolf de Rijk has informed me of a similar phenomenon in Basque. In this language, a morpheme in the verbal complex agrees with the semantic gender of the addressee. Once again, since this morpheme has semantic significance, it must find some reflection in the deep structures of Basque. However, Basque need not have a language-particular base rule introducing this morpheme, if the performative or the pragmatic analysis can be motivated for this language. A rule adjoining a copy of the semantic gender of the superordinate *you* in the appropriate place in the verbal complex can instead be used to account for the facts.

These three examples of the effects of more abstract syntactic representations on the theory of universal grammar are not atypical. Not only will the performative or the pragmatic analysis, if it can be internally motivated in Arabic, Thai, and Basque, *reduce* differences in the deep structure representations chosen for these languages, in this case it will *eliminate* them. This suggests that the hypothesis stated in (122) may be tenable:

(122)  THE UNIVERSAL BASE HYPOTHESIS
        The deep structures of all languages are identical, up to the ordering
        of constituents immediately dominated by the same node.

In Lakoff and Ross (in preparation), George Lakoff and I investigate a number of constructions in detail, attempting to show for each that underlying structures of far greater abstractness than have been proposed up to now must be assumed to underlie them. These abstract deep structures lead us to propose a concrete, albeit highly tentative, set of rules that generate an infinite set of deep structures that we hope may prove to be universal.

In conclusion, I want to emphasize that this investigation of declarative sentences cannot be viewed in isolation. The performative analysis of declaratives is only one fragment of a far more inclusive analysis which postulates that every deep structure contains one and only one performative sentence as its highest clause. The pragmatic analysis would have to be broadened in a similar way. Until an analysis with a scope broad enough to encompass all sentence types has been carried out, the conclusions I have reached in this paper must remain extremely tentative. In such a broader study, the interconnections between syntax and pragmatics should be investigated in detail. Possibly when they have been clarified, a reason for choosing either a performative analysis or a pragmatic analysis of all sentence types will emerge.

## NOTES

1. This work was supported by the National Institute of Health (Grant MH-13390-01).

I would like to thank Stephen Anderson, Michael Brame, Charles Fillmore, Bruce Fraser, Morris Halle, Ray Jackendoff, Paul and Carol Kiparsky, Edward Klima, Robin Lakoff, James McCawley, David Perlmutter, and Carlota Smith for many stimulating discussions and much criticism, which have greatly influenced the final shape of this paper. Far more than thanks goes to George Lakoff, with whom I am collaborating on a larger work on syntax and semantics, and to Paul Postal, whose ideas we are elaborating. Without their insights, the work would not have been possible.

2. I say "can constitute," because (2a), like all the sentences in (2), is ambiguous. It can be either a promise or a description of a habitual action of the utterer, as in *I make promise after promise to you that I won't squeal.* In this latter sense, the sentences in (2) are declaratives and do not differ in any significant way from those in (1). Henceforth I will disregard this sense of sentences like (2), and will concentrate instead on the usage which Austin was concerned with.

3. There are some performatives (I will use this term to refer to verbs which may appear in performative sentences), such as *move, question,* and *second,* and possibly *proclaim,* which exclude indirect objects, and some, such as *christen* and *name,* whose direct object can be second person, but need not be [cf. sentence (2c)]. For some performatives, such as *demand, order* and *promise,* the second person object need not appear in surface structure (cf. *I promise that I won't squeal*), but for others, it must (cf. * *I appoint captain,* * *I sentence to death,* ? *I warn that the trip will be difficult*). I assume that there is a rule which operates to delete the second person object in the former class of verbs, but I have no evidence to support this assumption.

4. This qualification is necessary because of the existence of passive performative sentences, such as *you are hereby authorized to commandeer sufficient bubblegum to supply a battalion for a week,* etc.

5. I will assume that such verbs as these are lexically marked with the feature [+performative], which will mean that they can be, but need not always be, used in performative sentences. They are thus distinct from such verbs as *divorce, insult, jump*, etc., which cannot be used as the main verb of a performative sentence, and will be marked [−performative].

6. At present it is not clear what the source for this adverb is. It would seem desirable to generate it and its related adverb *thereby* by the processes which produce such words as *thereafter, thereupon,* and possibly *therefore,* as well as other uses of *thereby.* I assume that the following sentences are all to be derived from the same underlying structure, by a sequence of optional rules:

**Mort fell down, and he broke his leg by falling down.**
**Mort fell down, and by it (OBL thereby) he broke his leg.**
$$\Rightarrow$$
**Mort fell down, thereby breaking his leg.**

*Hereby* might be derived from *by uttering this,* in a parallel fashion, but at present, such suggestions are only speculation. I am not aware of any research on such sentences as the above.

7. Cf., for example, Chomsky (1955, pp. 691–694).

8. For a discussion of this distinction, cf. Chomsky (1965).

9. A detailed analysis of a wide range of English complement constructions can be found in Rosenbaum (1967). In an important recent study [Kiparsky and Kiparsky (1967)], it is shown that semantic considerations play a much larger role in the grammar of these constructions than had previously been realized. Cf. also Robin Lakoff (in press).

10. A discussion of all the relevant evidence will be presented in Lakoff and Ross (in preparation).

11. Cf. Ross (1967*b*). A fuller treatment of this highly complex matter will appear in Lakoff and Ross (in preparation).

12. In (6), as elsewhere in the paper, I have drastically simplified the constituent structure representations, both deep and superficial, of the examples discussed, as long as the point at issue was not materially affected by such simplification.

13. The bundle of syntactic features [cf. Chomsky (1965, Chapter 2)] dominated by the highest V of (7) would appear in the lexical representation of such actually existing verbs as *assert, declare, say, state, tell,* etc.; but it need not be assumed that any of these occurs in the deep structure of (1a). The more abstract feature representation, which all these verbs have in common, is sufficient for my present purposes (but cf. Section 2.2.6). For some arguments that the stronger claim that a particular member of this class of verbs must be singled out as the performative verb for all English declarative sentences, cf. McCawley (1968). I assume that the preposition *to* which appears in surface structure before the indirect objects of most such verbs will be introduced transformationally, though nothing below depends on this assumption.

14. I will often use the locution "sentence *A* is transformed (converted, etc.) into sentence *B*" for the more correct but awkward phrase "the structure underlying sentence *A* is converted into one which more immediately underlies sentence *B*." No theoretical significance should be attached to this abbreviation.

15. For some suggestions as to the way Lees and Klima's notion "simplex sentence" should be captured within the theory of grammar, cf. Ross (1967a, Chapter 5).

16. I say "appears," because it is doubtful whether the reflexive pronoun in (11b) is produced by the same rule as the one that Lees and Klima were discussing. The reflexives in (11) are felt to be emphatic, as in the sentence *I myself thought I could vote against Goldwater.* This matter will be taken up again shortly.

Ray Jackendoff has recently called attention to a large number of interesting cases which seem to be true exceptions to the formulation proposed by Lees and Klima [cf. Jackendoff (1967)].

17. I am not sure whether (13a) can even have a pronoun replace *Tom* before *himself,* hence the question mark before *him.* When I wish to distinguish between more than two degrees of acceptability, I will use the following notation: if a sentence has no prefix, it is (for me) completely acceptable. If it is preceded by a single question mark, it is doubtful; by a double question mark, very doubtful; by an asterisk, completely unacceptable; and if it is preceded by a sequence of question mark and asterisk, it is very bad, but maybe not completely out: some vestiges of grammaticality may remain. It is to be expected that when such fine distinctions are drawn, disagreements as to the choice of prefix will be frequent. However, none of the arguments below depends crucially upon such fine distinctions, and only large differences will be critical.

It is of course totally irrelevant to the point at hand as to whether (13a) is possible at all with *him* referring back to Tom; if it is impossible, then some constraint must be imposed upon the pronominalization rule that produces *him.* In fact, if *him* is impossible, that fact would provide support for the analysis I have proposed, for it is only anaphoric pronouns that can be deleted by the rule I suggested, and if *him* cannot replace the second *Tom* in (13a), the ungrammaticality of (13b) is explained.

However, all this is beside the point under discussion, which is that emphatic reflexives, such as I assume the reflexive in (11b) to be, cannot occur in all environments (unless, of course, an NP immediately precedes). Exactly what rule accounts for the ungrammaticality of the bad cases is immaterial.

18. The important notion of *command* is defined and discussed in detail in Langacker (1966). Briefly, node *A commands* node *B* if neither dominates the other, and if the first S node above *A* dominates *B.* Or, in the informal usage of the text, *A* commands *B* if *A* "belongs to" a sentence which dominates *B.*

19. The attentive reader will have noticed that *yourself* appears, with the same spectrum of acceptabilities, in questions related to the sentences in (21). I suggest that this should be accounted for by deriving questions from deep structures whose two highest sentences are, roughly, *I request of you that you tell me S',* where S' eventually becomes the main clause of the question. This suggestion is explored at some length in Lakoff and Ross (in preparation).

20. I might remark in passing that it is not at all clear to me that sentences like (27d) can be excluded on purely linguistic grounds — I suspect that the requirement that there be some connection between the NP of the *as for*-phrase and the following clause can be satisfied if there is a real-world connection. Thus while the sentence *as for Paris, the Eiffel Tower is really spectacular* is acceptable, it becomes unacceptable if *Albuquerque* is substituted for *Paris.* And since the knowledge that the Eiffel Tower is not in Albuquerque is not represented in the semantics of English, I conclude that this unacceptability is not linguistic.

21. This fact, and its implications for the performative analysis, were pointed out to me by Edward S. Klima.

22. This terminology was suggested by Florence Warshawsky Harris in two extremely interesting unpublished papers, Warshawsky (1964a, 1964b).

23. This statement is adequate for my purposes, but it is an oversimplification, as can be seen from the grammaticality of such sentences as *Tad concedes that it is probable that it was not known that it would be a story about himself.* What differentiates this sentence from the ungrammatical ones in (35) is the fact that the sentences which separate the NP *Tad* and its anaphoric reflexive pronoun here do not contain any occurrences of other human NP. Some consequences of this difference, which was first noted by Ray Jackendoff, are discussed in Jackendoff (1967).

24. In a class at the University of Pennsylvania in the fall of 1962.

25. David Perlmutter has brought to my attention the fact that most passive sentences with definite pronouns as agents are somewhat unacceptable. Thus, though the sentence *the final exam was passed by everybody in my class* is unobjectionable, the sentence *?? the final exam was passed by them* is decidedly odd. However, in line with Harris's observation, the sentence *?* *The final exam was passed by me* is even worse. I suspect that the explanation for the phenomenon noted by Perlmutter will be connected to the solution of problems in the area of what the Prague linguist Vilem Mathesius called "functional sentence perspective" (*aktuální členění větné*). Mathesius's basic idea was that, normally, the order of constituents in a sentence was determined by the amount of new information they conveyed to the listener. Already known constituents would tend to come at the beginning of the sentence, and constituents conveying new information at the end. Thus definite noun phrases of all kinds, but definite pronouns in particular, would tend to occur early in a sentence, which could explain the fact noted by Perlmutter.

An excellent introductory exposition to these problems, and a review of work done on them by Czech linguists, can be found in Garvin (1963). For an attempt to deal with functional sentence perspective within the framework of generative grammar, cf. Heidelph (1965).

26. Of course, I mean the pronoun *him* in (38) to refer back to the subject NP *Tom*. I will use the device of subscripting nouns which are intended to be coreferential with the same index.

27. Some speakers appear not to find sentences like those in (43) at all out of the ordinary, but for me they are beyond redemption. Robert Wall has suggested the verb *purport* as a substitute for *lurk*, for it exhibits all the properties of *lurk*, but with clearer ungrammaticalities for most speakers. Thus while *he purports to be with it* is grammatical, *\* I purport to be with it* is not.

28. This restriction is actually not stated correctly, for in addition to such sentences as those in (43), sentences with factive verbs [cf. Kiparsky and Kiparsky (1967)] like *know, find out*, etc., cannot embed as objects sentences with *lurk* and a first person subject (cf. *?* *Did Merv find out that I am lurking in his car?*), and some intransitive adjectives, like *likely*, are also transparent to this restriction (cf. *?* *it's not likely that I'll lurk here much more than 40 hours a week now*). These last two examples suggest the complexity of the necessary revisions to the restriction stated above, which I will not attempt to specify more fully here, as the stated version is adequate to prove the point at hand.

For a detailed examination of various kinds of deep structure constraints, cf. Perlmutter (1968).

29. It has been called to my attention by Izumi Ushijima that a situation paralleling that with *lurk* exists in Japanese. The bound morpheme *–garu*, when added to any of a lexically designated set of adjectives, converts the adjective to a verb. Thus, *omosiroi* "interesting": *omorosirogaru* "to feel interested (in something)." These verbs in *–garu* differ from other verbs in that they may not occur with first person subjects — the following sentence (*I feel interested in this*) is ungrammatical:

> \* *watakusi   wa        kore   o        omosirogaru*
>
> I                (part.)   this   (part.)   feel interested.

As was the case with *lurk*, when such sentences as the above are embedded, it turns out that first person subjects are possible, as long as the first verb up does not have a first person subject. The general restriction, then, is that the subject of verbs in *–garu* not be identical to the subject of the first verb up. Thus, while the first two versions of the sentence below are grammatical, the third, where the subject was identical in deep structure and has been deleted by the general rule which deletes unstressed pronouns, is ungrammatical:

> *biru   wa* $\left\{\begin{array}{l} zyoozyi \\ watakusi \\ \ast\underline{\hspace{1cm}} \end{array}\right\}$ *ga        kore o        omosirogatta to        itta*
>
> Bill   (part.) $\left\{\begin{array}{l} \text{George} \\ \text{I}\underline{\hspace{1cm}} \end{array}\right\}$ (part.)   this (part.)   felt interested that said
>
> Bill$_i$ said that $\left\{\begin{array}{l} \text{George} \\ \text{I} \\ \text{he}_i \end{array}\right\}$ felt interested in this.

I have no reason to believe that when a more precise restriction on *lurk* can be formulated (See Note 28), it will differ in any way from the restriction that is necessary for verbs in *–garu*. Thus, just as the facts of (43) support the performative analysis for English, those with *–garu* support it for Japanese. Together, these arguments suggest that it may be universally valid.

I wish to thank Agnes Niyekawa Howard and Susumu Kuno for their help in clarifying the above facts.

30. Sentence (52) will be blocked by (49) only if relative clauses are deep structure constituents of the NP whose head noun they modify in surface structure, an assumption which has been widely assumed to be correct. However, recent studies by Postal (1967*b*) and Brame (1968) indicate the untenability of this hypothesis, and suggest that relative clauses are to be analyzed as deriving from conjoined clauses in deep structure. If this analysis is correct, (52) will not constitute counterevidence to (49).

31. I assume, of course, that the ungrammatical phrase \* *friends of one's* would be obligatorily converted into *one's friends* by the normally optional rule which changes phrases like *a friend of mine* into *my friend*.

32. Note that there are some titles which require *my* when used as vocatives, and some that require *your;* compare, for example, the following:

$$\text{Hoboken is a fine city,} \left\{ \begin{array}{l} \text{my} \left\{ \begin{array}{l} \text{lord} \\ \text{liege} \\ \text{Führer} \end{array} \right\} \\ \text{your} \left\{ \begin{array}{l} \text{worship} \\ \text{honor} \\ \text{lordship} \\ \text{majesty} \\ \text{excellency} \end{array} \right\} \end{array} \right\}.$$

Why this should be is a total mystery.

33. There is one verb, *hear,* whose indirect object can serve as an antecedent to a pronominal object of *believe* — cf. *they heard from Tom$_i$ that Ann could swim, but nobody believed him$_i$.* As far as I know, *hear (from)* is the only verb which can appear in sentences like this — near synonyms like *learn (from), find out (from)* cannot. This suggests that *hear (from)* may be derived from *say (to)* by an optional rule which interchanges the subject and object of certain verbs, adjoining prepositions like *from* to the deep subject in the process. This rule, which was first proposed by Postal. [cf. Rosenbaum (1967), where it was called *subject–object inversion*], relates such sentences as *your advice benefited me* and *I benefited from your advice.* One indication that *hear (from)* is not basic is the fact that its indirect object cannot be a reflexive pronoun, whereas this is possible in the case of *say (to), tell,* and other verbs whose subjects can be antecedents for a pronominal object of *believe.* (Compare *I said to myself that she couldn't hurt me* with * *I heard from myself that she couldn't hurt me,* paralleling *I taught myself that she couldn't hurt me* but * *I learned from myself that she couldn't hurt me.*) The restriction which appears to be operative here is a very general condition on all transformational rules which prevents moving one NP in such a way that it crosses over a coreferential NP, under various complicated conditions. One of the effects of this condition is to exclude passives of reflexives (e.g., *they understand themselves* but not * *they are understood by themselves*). Hopefully, this restriction, which is studied in great detail in Postal (1968), can be generalized to include (41) as a subcase.

34. Sentences like those in (62) have never been studied by generative grammarians, to the best of my knowledge. There are some strange restrictions on whatever rule it is that produces such sentences. First of all, note that the possessive pronoun modifying the abstract noun in the object must refer back to the subject (cf. * *Tom frowned* $\left\{ \begin{array}{l} Ann's \\ my \end{array} \right\}$ *displeasure*). Secondly, there appear to be restrictions between the main verb and the abstract noun in the object; such sentences as

$$? * \text{Tom}_i \text{ scowled his}_i \left\{ \begin{array}{l} \text{mirth} \\ \text{gaiety} \\ \text{willingness} \\ \text{eagerness} \\ \text{bonhomie} \end{array} \right\}.$$

are certainly odd, though probably only for semantic, if not extralinguistic reasons.

A stronger restriction on the abstract noun is that it denotes a certain kind of mental state. Thus the following sentences are all unacceptable:

$$* \text{Tom}_i \text{ frowned his}_i \begin{cases} \text{departure} \\ \text{perusal of the text} \\ \text{height} \\ \text{construction of a counterexample} \end{cases}.$$

Interestingly, it appears not to be the case that all nouns which denote mental states can appear in such constructions: only those nouns which denote mental states which can be behaviorally manifested can, it would seem. For me, at least, there are clear differences between the sentences below.

$$\text{Tom}_i \text{ frowned his}_i \text{ disbelief of the witness's story.}$$

$$? * \text{Tom}_i \begin{cases} \text{nodded} \\ \text{smiled} \\ \text{grinned} \\ \text{etc.} \end{cases} \text{his}_i \text{ belief in the witness's story.}$$

Other abstract nouns which cannot appear in this construction are: *recklessness, prejudice, greed, hope, kindness,* and many more.

Such considerations suggest a derivation like the following

$$\text{Tom}_i \text{ registered (his}_i) \text{ displeasure by} \begin{cases} \text{frowning} \\ \text{scowling} \\ \text{roaring} \\ \text{etc.} \end{cases} \rightarrow$$

$$\text{Tom}_i \begin{cases} \text{frowned} \\ \text{scowled} \\ \text{roared} \\ \text{etc.} \end{cases} (\text{his}_i) \text{ displeasure.}$$

for it is only those abstract nouns which can follow such verbs as *register* that can appear in sentences like those in (62). The proposed rule, which would substitute such basically intransitive verbs as *frown, scowl,* etc., for a pro-verb of the class of *register,* closely parallels the derivation of sentences like *Max beat his wife into submission* from a deeper *Max got his wife to submit by beating her,* which was suggested in Lakoff (1965). It seems not unlikely that the same rule is involved.

One final note on this construction: the transformational rule which copies the subject NP as a possessive pronoun on the abstract noun in the object must follow the very general rule which nominalizes such sentences as those in (62), for these possessive pronouns do not appear in the associated nominalizations. Thus,

$$\text{He} \begin{cases} \text{grimaced disgust} \\ \text{shrugged resignation} \\ \text{nodded approval} \end{cases} \rightarrow \text{his} \begin{cases} \text{grimace of (* his) disgust} \\ \text{shrug of (* his) resignation} \\ \text{nod of (* his) approval} \end{cases}$$

$$\downarrow$$

$$\text{He} \begin{cases} \text{grimaced his disgust} \\ \text{shrugged his resignation} \\ \text{nodded (his) approval} \end{cases}.$$

The productivity of this nominalization (* *his beam of pleasure* is the only counterexample I know of) would appear to constitute one counterexample to Chomsky's proposal [cf. Chomsky (1967b)] that all constructions he refers to as derived nominals should be lexically derived.

35. In several lectures at MIT in the spring of 1967. Cf. also Dean (1967).

36. Barbara Hall Partee has made a plausible case for postulating the existence of a rule which deletes *will* in all *if*-clauses which superficially resemble present tense clauses [cf. Hall (1964)]. Two facts support such an analysis: firstly, future tense adverbs, like *tomorrow*, can occur in *if*-clauses, but not in certain of the corresponding present tense clauses (cf. *if he knows the answer tomorrow, he should raise his hand,* but not * *he knows the answer tomorrow*); and secondly, the only cases where *will* can occur at all in *if*-clauses are cases where it means "persist in" or "agree to" (cf. *if your son will stay up too late, slip him a Mickey Finn* and *if you will meet me in Tokyo, we can conclude the deal there*). Thus sentences where such a meaning is impossible (e.g., *there will be an explosion tomorrow*) are decidedly strange in *if*-clauses (cf. ? *only if there will be an explosion tomorrow should you stay here*). Probably such sentences are only acceptable with a sense parallel to that of *if you're so smart, why aren't you rich?*, which, as Paul Kiparsky has observed, mean "If what you say is right, . . . ."

It can be seen that the matter is too complex to pursue further here, but it should be clear, nonetheless, that it is not normal for *will* to appear in *if*-clauses. Therefore, the *if*-clause in sentence (65) is not a normal one.

37. This fact was noted in Kiparsky and Kiparsky (1967).

38. Sentence (70b) is ungrammatical if it is uttered as an observation about the subject, as would be the case in a sentence like *your Uncle Frank will be 39 next year.* There are certain contexts, however, where (70b) can be uttered as a report of a speech act, so that it would be paraphrased by the sentence *your Uncle Frank says that he'll be damned if he'll have anything to do with her.* Although I have none at present, I would hope that evidence will be forthcoming which would support the derivation of the grammatical reading of (70b) from this latter sentence. I would suppose this rule to be responsible for the well-known phenomenon of stream-of-consciousness prose (or *discours indirect libre*), which is typical of the novels of Virginia Woolf, for instance. I would hope that the rule involved could be combined with rule (92), which is discussed in Section 3.1. I am grateful to Morris Halle for calling my attention to this phenomenon in connection with the performative analysis.

39. If my intuition that the following sentence is grammatical is correct,

? I heard from $Ed_i$ that $he_i$'d be damned if $he_i$'d go.

then this would further support an analysis under which this sentence is derived from something like the following:

$Ed_i$ told me that $he_i$'d be damned if $he_i$'d go.

40. The contrast in grammaticality between (75a) and (75b) seems to indicate that, counter to my previous assumption, the restrictions on *be damned if* cannot be stated in terms of deep structure, at least not if previous conceptions of the passive as an optional rule are correct. Of course, if the passive is not optional, but instead triggered by some element in deep structure, like the one suggested in Chomsky

(1965), or by some other property of deep structure, then it would be possible to make reference to this element or this property in stating the restriction on *be damned if*. But such a complication in an otherwise fairly straightforward restriction is highly unsatisfying, and I hope that some alternative to this solution will turn up, for it seems impossible to state the necessary restriction on *be damned if* in surface structure, for a number of reasons too complex to go into here.

Ray Jackendoff has suggested to me that pronominalization should be constrained so that the agent phrase in a passive sentence may never enter into an anaphoric relationship with any other NP. Such a constraint would then render (41) unnecessary, as well as explaining the ungrammaticality of (75b). However, it would also rule out such acceptable sentences as (39) and *that Sheriff Clarkson$_i$ has ever taken any bribes has been repeatedly denied by him$_i$*, both of which are acceptable to me. Therefore, I see no way out of the *ad hoc* "solution" sketched above at present, although Jackendoff's suggestion should certainly not be dismissed without further study.

41. William Watt has pointed out to me that there are at least three verbs, *be resolved* (*that*), *decide* (*that*), and *make up one's mind* (*that*), but not, for some unknown reason, such a near synonym as *be determined* (*that*), which can occur with *be damned if* but not with *believe*. Compare the following sentences;

$$\text{Ed}_i \left\{ \begin{array}{l} \text{is resolved} \\ \text{has} \left\{ \begin{array}{l} \text{decided} \\ \text{made up his}_i \text{ mind} \end{array} \right\} \end{array} \right\} \text{ that he}_i\text{'ll be damned if Bill will marry Sally.}$$

$$* \text{ Ed}_i \left\{ \begin{array}{l} \text{is resolved} \\ \text{has} \left\{ \begin{array}{l} \text{decided} \\ \text{made up his}_i \text{ mind} \end{array} \right\} \end{array} \right\} \text{ that Bill will marry Sally, but nobody believes him}_i.$$

I have no explanation for this fact.

42. Cf. Rosenbaum (1967) for an explanation of this term, which is roughly equivalent to the traditional term "gerund."

43. I have not mentioned the various restrictions on negatives, auxiliaries, adverbs, and questions in (79), for the sake of simplicity.

44. The phonetic sequence [ʔa] which begins this sentence is inserted by an automatic phonological rule which applies to prevent certain sequences from starting with two consonants. I will not be concerned here with this rule, nor with the regular rule accounting for the automatic alternation between nominative and accusative case markings on the subject NP of the embedded clause.

45. I should point out that there is an unsolved problem concerning the specification of which declarative sentences can start with *ʔinna*. Brame informs me, for example, that (80b) becomes less acceptable if the particle *qad* is not present. But the argument has force if there are any sentences at all which can start with *ʔinna*. Furthermore, in Brame (1967), several other arguments are discussed, and it would not surprise me if an argument cognate to the one in Section 2.2.1 (*believe me*) could be constructed in Arabic, or if verbs with the properties of *lurk* and *be damned if* could be found. It is my belief that such arguments will be discovered in a wide variety of languages.

46. James Harris has called my attention to a similar, but weaker, argument in Spanish. There, both of the following sentences are possible:

*Que   mi   gato   se   en   raton   ó.*
that   my   cat   itself   (pref.)   mouse   (3rd pers. sg.
                                                    pret. indic.)

*Mi   gato   se enratonó.*
My   cat   got sick from eating too many mice.

However, the complement structure *que* + indicative is not unique to *decir* "say," and furthermore, the sentences appear to differ slightly in meaning — the sentence with *que* is more emphatic and more insistent than the one without it.

47. In McCawley (1968), it is argued that the particular verb *tell* is deleted ·by the rule of *performative deletion,* on the basis of the fact that while *hereby* can appear with performatives like those in (2), it is odd to say:

? * *I hereby tell you that prices will skyrocket.*

I agree that it is odd, but this sentence seems equally odd with *say* (*to*) in the place of *tell.* Therefore, while McCawley's argument is suggestive, I do not regard it to be as compelling a one as exists in Arabic.

48. Sentence (83b) is perhaps grammatical if construed as a request to ask or force Tom to hold his breath. This interpretation is impossible, however, if an adverbial modifier such as *starting now* is appended. In the sense which this modifier forces, the sentence is totally impossible, and it is with this sense in mind that I have starred it.

49. This may not always be true, for a rather trivial reason. For example, although sentences like those below must be restricted to first person subjects

$$
\text{(Well,)} \left\{ \begin{array}{l} \text{I'll} \\ \text{* you'll} \\ \text{* Blake'll} \\ \text{* Mr. Wonton'll} \\ \text{etc.} \end{array} \right\} \text{ be } \left\{ \begin{array}{l} \text{a monkey's uncle} \\ \text{hornswoggled} \\ \text{blowed} \\ \text{goldurned} \\ \text{etc.} \end{array} \right\}.
$$

this restriction cannot be stated in terms of higher subjects, for the simple reason that such sentences cannot be embedded, as the ungrammaticality of the following sentence shows:

* Blake said he'd be hornswoggled.

Barring special circumstances like this, however, the claim should hold true.

50. I disregard here a number of minor problems, such as how the nodes VP and NP which dominate the embedded S in (7) are to be pruned [cf. Ross (1967b)], and how the complementizer *that,* which would presumably have been inserted by the time rule (92) applies, is to be deleted (in English).

51. This analysis thus *explains* why *I, you,* and *we* are pronouns (note that they must be analyzed as such in English to account for the fact that they behave like the anaphoric pronouns *he, she, it,* and *they* in not following particles in verb-particle constructions — * *I egged on you* is as bad as * *I egged on them*).

52. Edward S. Klima first called such sentences as (96c) to my attention.

53. Ray Jackendoff has pointed out that the two sentences of (99a) answer different questions. With *myself,* the sentence answers the question "Who will have to protect you?" while with *himself,* it answers the question "Who will have to protect himself?"

Correct though this observation is, it merely adds to my bafflement concerning the analysis of (98) and (99).

54. In phonology, the convention which appears to be necessary is that no rules apply to their own output within the same cycle [cf. Chomsky and Halle (1968)]. In syntax, however, it appears that while cyclic rules may not apply to their own output, post-cyclic rules must be able to. One clear case of a cyclic syntactic rule which must not be allowed to apply to its own output is the rule of *there-insertion*. As William Grossman has pointed out to me, if this constraint were not imposed, an infinite number of derivations of the form

> A man was standing in the surf.
> There was a man standing in the surf.
> * There was there a man standing in the surf.
> * There was there there a man standing in the surf.

would ensue, unless an otherwise unnecessary restriction were imposed on this rule. Similarly, if the *dative rule* converts (i) to (ii)

> (i) I gave John a book.
> (ii) I gave a book to John.

then unless cyclic rules cannot apply to their own output, or some *ad hoc* restriction is imposed on the *dative rule,* (ii) will be converted to (iii):

> (iii) * I gave to John to a book.

That post-cyclic rules must be able to apply to their own output can be seen by examining sentences (iv) through (vi):

> (iv) They all must have left.
> (v) They must all have left.
> (vi) They must have all left.

If, as seems likely, (vi) is to be derived not directly from (iv), but rather *via* (v), and if the same rule converts (iv) to (v), and (v) to (vi), then obviously some rules must be able to apply to their own output. I know of no argument against claiming that the rule in question is a post-cyclic one.

And if there is a post-cyclic rule that freely permutes elements of the same clause in free word-order languages like Latin, then this rule, which I have called *scrambling* [cf. Ross (1967a, Section 3.1.2)], must be able to apply to its own output, as long as only adjacent constituents can be permuted, for (vii) must somehow become (viii), and no single permutation of adjacent constituents can effect such a change:

> "The good man loves the beautiful girl."
>
> (vii) *Homō   bonus   amat   puellam   pulchram.*
>        man     good   loves   girl      beautiful
>
> (viii) *Pulchram homō amat bonus puellam.*

Finally, G. H. Matthews (1965) has proposed a late rule reordering nominal affixes in Hidatsa, and this rule must be able to apply to its own output.

Thus it seems likely that post-cyclic rules can apply to their own output, and since *performative deletion* is such a rule, some way must be found to block it from applying in this manner, if infinite ambiguity is to be avoided.

55. For some discussion of this notion, cf. Chomsky (1964) and Chomsky (1965, Chapter 4, Section 2).

56. There are some apparent counterexamples to this claim. Deictic sentences such as the following, which were pointed out to me by Paul Postal

*There's Judy, behind that boar.*

although they have the superficial form of declaratives, are really not declaratives. Note that such sentences cannot be negated, embedded, or put in the past tense. More importantly, they cannot appear in such contexts as the one below:

\* *Mike said, "There's Judy, behind that boar," which was a lie.*

Nor can such sentences as those mentioned in Note 49:

\* *Hiram said, "I'll be hornswoggled!" which was a lie.*

Since it seems to be possible for all other declaratives to be followed by the sentential relative clause *which* $\begin{Bmatrix} is \\ was \end{Bmatrix}$ *a lie*, I tentatively conclude that the sentences in direct quotes are not declaratives, despite their surface form, and that they therefore are not embedded in the object of a performative verb of saying (though they may be, and probably are, embedded as objects of some other performative verb).

57. That increases in the abstractness of syntactic representations decrease the distance between these representations and semantic representations is a fact which needs explanation, since it is not a logical necessity. One possible explanation, which Lakoff and I and others are now exploring, is that there may be no level of syntactic representation which is distinct from semantic representation, and which could be called "deep structure."

58. For some discussion of the notion of a convention for automatically reordering the terms of certain types of transformational rules, cf. Ross (1967a, Section 4.1).

59. I disregard here the differences between Arabic and English in the order of the main constituents of S.

60. I am grateful to Mr. Udom Warotamisikkhadit for furnishing the Thai examples.

61. A further bit of evidence for the correctness of this rule, which I am grateful to Samuel E. Martin for bringing to my attention, is the fact that among the twenty-six words Thai has for the first person singular pronoun, there are some for male speakers (e.g., *pôm*) and others for females (e.g., *chăn*).

## REFERENCES FOR 'ON DECLARATIVE SENTENCES'

Austin, J. 1962. How to do things with words. Cambridge, Mass.: Harvard University Press.

Brame, M. 1967. Evidence for performatives from Arabic. Paper. MIT.

Brame, M. 1968. On the nature of relative clauses. Paper. MIT.

Chomsky, N. 1955. The logical structure of linguistic theory. [Published in large part 1975, New York: Plenum Press.]

Chomsky, N. 1964. Current issues in linguistic theory. The Hague: Mouton.

Chomsky, N. 1965. Aspects of the theory of syntax. Cambridge, Mass.: MIT Press.

Chomsky, N. 1967. Remarks on nominalization. [Reprinted in this volume.]

Chomsky, N., and M. Halle. 1968. The sound pattern of English. New York: Harper and Row.

Dean, J. 1967. Noun phrase complementation in English and German. Paper. MIT.

Garvin, P. 1963. Linguistics in Czechoslovakia. Current trends in Soviet and East European linguistics. The Hague: Mouton.

Gruber, J. 1967. Unpublished, untitled paper on child language. MIT.

Hall, B. 1964. Adverbial subordinate clauses. Working Paper W-07241. Bedford, Mass.: MITRE Corp.

Harris, Z. 1951. Methods in structural linguistics. Chicago: University of Chicago Press.

Heidolph, K. 1965. Kontextbeziehungen zwischen Sätzen in einer generativen Grammatik. Unpublished mimeo. East Berlin: Deutsche Akademie der Wissenschaften.

Jackendoff, R. 1967. An interpretive theory of pronouns and reflexives. Paper. MIT.

Kiparsky, C., and P. Kiparsky. 1967. Fact. [Reprinted in M. Bierwisch and K. Heidolph, Progress in linguistics. The Hague: Mouton and in Chapter 11 of this volume.]

Lakoff, G. 1965. Irregularity in syntax. Doctoral dissertation. Indiana University. [Published 1970, New York: Holt, Rinehart, and Winston.]

Lakoff, G., and J. R. Ross. (in preparation) Abstract syntax.

Lakoff, R. (in press) Abstract syntax and Latin complementation. [Published 1968, Cambridge, Mass.: The MIT Press.]

Langacker, R. 1966. Pronominalization and the chain of command. In: Modern studies in English. Edited by D. Reibel and S. Schane. Englewood Cliffs, N.J.: Prentice-Hall.

Lees, R., and E. Klima. 1963. Rules for English pronominalization. Lg. 39:1.17-29.

Matthews, G. 1965. Hidatsa syntax. The Hague: Mouton.

McCawley, J. 1968. The role of semantics in grammar. In: Universals in linguistic theory. Edited by E. Bach and R. Harms. New York: Holt, Rinehart, and Winston.

Perlmutter, D. 1968. Deep and surface structure constraints in syntax. Doctoral dissertation, MIT. [Published 1971, New York: Holt, Rinehart, and Winston.]

Postal, P. 1967a. Performatives and person. Unpublished paper. Yorktown Heights, N.Y.: Thomas J. Watson Research Center, IBM.

Postal, P. 1967b. Crazy notes on restrictive relatives and other matters. Unpublished paper. Yorktown Heights, N.Y.: Thomas J. Watson Research Center, IBM.

Postal, P. 1968. Crossover phenomena: A study in the grammar of coreference. [Published 1971, New York: Holt, Rinehart, and Winston.]

Rosenbaum, P. 1967. The grammar of English predicate complement constructions. Cambridge, Mass.: The MIT Press.

Ross, J. R. 1967a. Constraints on variables in syntax. Doctoral dissertation, MIT.

Ross, J. R. 1967b. Auxiliaries as main verbs. [In: Linguistic Institute Packet of Papers 1968, University of Illinois. Also published in Studies in Philosophical Linguistics (1969) 1:1.77-102.]

Warshawsky, F. 1964a. Unpublished, untitled paper on English reflexives, MIT. [Published 1977, in: Syntax and Semantics 7, New York: Academic Press, with the title 'Reflexivization' and incorporating Warshawsky (1964b).]

Warshawsky, F. 1964b. Unpublished, untitled paper on English reflexives, MIT. [Published 1977, in: Syntax and Semantics 7, New York: Academic Press, with the title 'Reflexivization' and incorporating Warshawsky (1964a).]

## QUESTIONS

Ross' article gives 14 arguments for the existence of a performative matrix in the deep structure of all declarative sentences. The first seven arguments support the claim that *I* is the underlying subject of the performative; the next three, that the performative V is semantically similar to *say*; the next three, that there is an object *you* in the performative clause; and the final one, that the performative clause must exist since adverbials attached to it in the deep structure may surface. Ross proceeds to discuss two alternative analyses to some of the data: the quotative analysis and the pragmatic analysis. He ends with the Universal Base Hypothesis.

In the following questions some of the data Ross presents are examined. Then the quotative and pragmatic analyses are discussed. And, finally, the nature of the Universal Base Hypothesis is questioned.

**The arguments and the data**

Question 1. Consider the Ss in (i) and (ii).

(i) I hereby baptise these children in the name of our Lord.
(ii) I, as judge of this court, sentence Mr. Manson and all his followers to life imprisonment and I further order that Mr. Manson and his followers be informed of this sentence at noon today.

Given that *baptise* and *sentence* are overt performatives, what aspect of the performative clause is 'unusual' in these two Ss, according to Ross? Can you find any declarative Ss whose performative clause is not present in surface structure for which you would propose an underlying third person object instead of the usual second person one? (Consider Ss such as *Screw you!* [cf. *Screw yourself!*], *Damn it!*, *Let counsel approach the bench.*) If so, could Ross account for such sentences? How would the pragmatic analysis account for them?

*Question 2. Ross claims, following Lees and Klima (1963), that (i) is bad because *myself* is missing a clause-mate antecedent.

(i) *I think that myself will win.

Alternatively, one might try to account for *myself* being rejected from (i) by claiming that reflexive pronouns are always oblique in case and since subjects must be nominative, *myself* is out. Discuss how the following data help us to decide between the two explanations.

(ii) I expect myself to win.

(iii) I expect John to kiss me/*myself.
(iv) The president himself walked in.

**Question 3.** Consider the emphatic reflexive in (i).

(i) Tom believed that the paper had been written by Ann
and him himself.

How does it differ from other reflexives in terms of its role in
a clause and its position with respect to its antecedent?

**Question 4.** Draw the deep tree for (i) and show how Ross'
proposal in (ii) (which is his example (19)) accounts for the
ungrammaticality of (i).

(i) *That the paper would have to be written by Ann and
Tom was obvious to himself.
(ii) If an anaphoric pronoun precedes an emphatic reflexive,
the former may be deleted, if it is commanded by the NP
with which it stands in an anaphoric relationship.

**Question 5.** Ross observes (in the paragraph preceding his
example (21)) that emphatic reflexives are best when conjoined.
Can regular reflexives be conjoined?

**Question 6.** How would (i) be explained by Ross?

(i) Physicists like yourself are rare.

(Notice Section 2.1.2 in Ross' article.) Do such Ss support or
weaken the performative analysis?

*Question 7. Consider Ross' footnote 23. Why do you think
the antecedent for a reflexive in a picture-noun construction
(such as *a story about himself*) can be indefinitely far away
from the reflexive as long as no other human NP intervenes?

**Question 8.** Can you say (i)?

(i) This is a story about yourself.

In the light of Ss like (ii) (Ross' (33c)), does the performative
analysis predict that (i) will be good or bad?

(ii) I promised Omar that it would be a poem about himself.

*Question 9. Consider the constraint in (i) (Ross' example
(41)).

(i) If a deep structure subject NP and some other NP in the same deep structure are coreferential, then the former NP may not become a passive agent.

Will (i) along with the performative analysis account for the ungrammaticality of (ii)?

(ii) ?*It was given by you to my sister.

How would both (ii) and (iii) be explained in a functional sentence perspective framework?

(iii) ??It was given by me to your sister.

In Ross' footnote 25 there is an implicit assumption that definite NPs are always 'known' constituents conveying old information. Why should this be the case? Does looking at the data leading to the constraint in (i) with a functional sentence perspective affect his argument for the performative analysis?

**Question 10. Ross claims that an anaphoric human NP in the VP of the V *believe* must stand in an anaphoric relationship to the subject of some other V in the same overall S. Consider Ss such as (i).

(i) I don't believe him.

How must Ross' constraint be modified in view of such Ss? Now, considering only human NP objects of *believe* that are coreferential with some other NP in the same overall S, read Ross' footnote 33 carefully. State a semantic generalization about the NP that can be the antecedent of *believe*'s object, a generalization which will cover both the subjects of Vs like *say* and *declare*, as in (ii), as well as the object of *hear (from)* (as in footnote 33).

(ii) Tom said that Ann could swim, but nobody believed him.

(Consider such oppositions as agent/patient and speaker/hearer.) How will your generalization explain the data presented for *believe* in footnote 41? Now will your generalization cover (iii)?

(iii) John faked a pass but no one believed him.

[Sentence (iii) is due to Chuck Thomas.] Try to modify your generalization to account for such Ss.

Question 11. Ross claims there is only one performative per sentence in deep structure. How could you analyze Ss such as (i)?

(i) I hereby announce before my public and my God that
I solemnly swear to tell the whole truth.

Modify Ross' claim to allow for such Ss.

Question 12. There is a widely accepted assumption in generative syntax that only constituents can be moved or deleted.
This assumption has been questioned for deletion rules, such as
Gapping. How does Ross' Performative Deletion rule 92 bear on
this issue?

### The quotative analysis

The facts in Section 2.1.3 of 'On declarative sentences' are
accounted for according to Ross' performative analysis by 'a rule
which optionally converts to a reflexive any pronoun appearing
in an *as for-* phrase which is prefixed to an embedded clause,
just in case this pronoun refers back to the subject of the next
higher sentence'. (See the paragraph following (31)). Thus
the *as for-* clauses with *myself* which are prefixed to independent clauses are evidence that these clauses were, indeed, embedded in deep structure in a sentence whose subject was *I*.
The quotative analysis gives the 'opposite' explanation for the
same facts. By this analysis an *as for me-* phrase prefixed to
an independent clause optionally becomes *as for myself*. Then
an *as for himself* prefixed to an embedded clause, as in example
(104c), is derived from precisely such an *as for myself* clause
prefixed to a direct quote, as in example (104b). This analysis
has several flaws pointed out by Ross, such as the need to
posit a direct quote under *believe*, as in example (105). Its
most important shortcoming, however, is that it is not comprehensive. The quotative analysis has nothing to say about most
of the data presented in this article. Thus, even if it were a
feasible alternative explanation to the facts in Section 2.1.3,
we would still need to account for all the other data in the
article--by the performative analysis or some third alternative.

### The pragmatic analysis

The performative clause Ross proposes has three major parts
to it: a first person subject, a verb which is [+linguistic],
[+performative], and [+communication] (with other features
such as [+declarative] or [+command]), and a second person
object. While Ross' proposal of deep performatives for all declaratives is 'abstract' in the sense that he is proposing elements in deep structure which may not appear in the surface,
it is still an attempt to give purely syntactic reasons for syntactic facts. The pragmatic analysis Ross discusses does not so
restrict itself. In such an analysis all elements that are present
in the context of a speech act are 'available' to the syntactic
processes of language. Since a speech act involves a speaker,

a linguistic and communicative act (whether it be a declaration, a command, or whatever), and usually a listener, all the elements Ross claims are present in the performative clause are already, by definition, present in a speech act. Thus in the pragmatic analysis no syntactic mechanism such as a higher performative clause need be proposed to account for the availability of these three elements to the syntactic process.

Ross points out two arguments against the pragmatic analysis that are not merely terminological. One is that the speaker must be grouped together with subjects of Vs and the listener must be grouped together with objects of Vs in order to account for the data in which the relations 'subject of' (such as with *as for-* phrases and *be damned if* Ss) and 'object of' (as in Sections 2.3.1 and 2.3.2) are crucial. In the pragmatic analysis this grouping is totally unaccounted for. But the performative analysis, in which the speaker is the subject of the higher clause and the listener is the object, nicely predicts this grouping.

The second argument is that the pragmatic analysis cannot account for the difference in grammaticality between examples (114) and (109), since *myself* in *as for-* phrases would be conditioned by the ever present speaker. The performative analysis, however, derives the *as for myself* phrase from a position prefixed to the clause embedded under the performative V *promise*. In example (109), *as for myself* is fine since the embedded clause has *I* as its subject; but in (114) it is out since the embedded subject is *Tom*.

The important point is that neither of the two analyses is superior in any a priori sense. Rather we must choose between them on empirical grounds. The two foregoing arguments are empirical. The first shows that the pragmatic analysis makes an arbitrary grouping where the performative analysis captures a generalization. The second shows that the pragmatic analysis cannot account for data easily handled by the performative analysis.

### The Universal Base Hypothesis (UBH)

The UBH at first sight may appear to make predictions which could be empirically tested. Thus we might think that we could go out and start examining languages and arguing for deep structures and that each language we come upon would tend either to confirm or disprove the hypothesis. This, however, is a false impression. In fact, by virtue of the definitions of 'transformational grammar' the UBH is true, regardless of empirical data. That is, for a particular fixed base grammar as the base component to a transformational grammar, we can devise a transformational grammar which is compatible with whatever facts arise in any possible natural language. For reports on a mathematical proof to this effect see Peters and Ritchie

(1969). Thus the UBH is neither a logical consequence of the performative analysis nor a hypothesis subject to empirical testing.

## HOMEWORK PROBLEMS

Early in Ross' article he suggests (after Austin) that imperatives such as

(1) Go!

come from:

(2) I order you to go!

by the rule of Performative Deletion.

I. Consider the following Ss:

(3) For the last time, turn down that radio!
For the last time, I order you to turn down that radio!

(4) Go home, or else!
I order you to go home, or else!

(5) I know it's insane, but be blond! I hate brunettes!
I know it's insane, but I order you to be blond!
I hate brunettes!

(6) Go home! That's an order!
*I order you to go home! That's an order!

(7) Please go home!
*I order you to please go home!
*I order you please to go home!

(8) I order you to have finished it by six.
*Have finished it by six.

The skeleton of six arguments concerning the performative analysis are found in the foregoing examples. What are the arguments? Which support the performative analysis and which offer evidence against it?

II. Consider sentence (9).

(9) Stop being so skeptical and just believe him!
I order you to stop being so skeptical and just believe him!

How does (9) offer evidence against Ross' eighth argument (in Section 2.2.1)?

III. Consider sentences (10) and (11).

(10) *Take a picture of myself!
*I order you to take a picture of myself!

(11) I'm telling you that this is, indeed, a picture of myself.

How are (10) and (11) relevant to Ross' fourth argument (in Section 2.1.4)?

IV. Why can we get both (12) and (13)?

(12) Because I'm curious, why are roses red?

(13) If you're not sick of my questions, why are roses red?

Note that sometimes the deleted performative of one speaker can be questioned by another, as in (14) and (15).

(14) Are roses red?

(15) Who--me? (i.e. 'Who are you asking--me?')

What other WH-words can be used in this way and which ones cannot? How can the occurrence of some WH-words and not others be explained?

V. How would a pragmatic analysis handle sentences (1) through (15)?

SUGGESTED READINGS

Banfield, A. 1973. Narrative style and the grammar of direct and indirect speech. Foundations of Language 10.1-39.
(For arguments against the quotative analysis.)
Cole, P. 1974. Hebrew tense and the performative analysis. CLS 10.73-89.
Davison, A. 1973. Performatives, felicity conditions and adverbs. Unpublished doctoral dissertation. University of Chicago.
Davison, A. 1975. Indirect speech acts and what to do with them. In: Speech acts. (=Syntax and Semantics 3).
Edited by P. Cole and J. L. Morgan. New York: Academic Press. 143-185.
Fraser, B. 1971. An examination of the performative analysis. Bloomington: Indiana University Linguistics Club.

Fraser, B. 1973. On accounting for illocutionary forces. In: A festschrift for Morris Halle. Edited by S. A. Anderson and P. Kiparsky. New York: Holt, Rinehart, and Winston. 287-307.

Fraser, B. 1975. Hedged performatives. In: Speech acts. (=Syntax and Semantics 3). Edited by P. Cole and J. L. Morgan. New York: Academic Press. 187-210.

Lakoff, R. 1968. Abstract syntax and Latin complementation. Cambridge, Mass.: The MIT Press. (See Chapter 5.)

Lees, R., and E. Klima. 1969. Rules for English pronominalization. In: Modern studies in English. Edited by D. Reibel and S. A. Schane. Englewood Cliffs, N.J.: Prentice-Hall. 145-159. (This is relevant to Question 2.)

Mitchell, G. 1974. Obviously I concede...: Performatives and sentence adverbs. CLS 10.436-445.

Morgan, J. 1969. On the treatment of presupposition in transformational grammar. CLS 5.167-177. (This is relevant to the initial discussion about abstractness in syntax.)

Peters, S., and R. Ritchie. 1969. A note on the Universal Base Hypothesis. Journal of Linguistics 5:1.150-152.

Peters, S., and R. Ritchie. 1971. On restricting the base component of transformational grammars. Information and Control 18.483-501.

Phuc Dong, Quang. 1971. English sentences without overt grammatical subjects. In: Studies out in left field. Edited by A. Swicky, P. Salus, R. Binnick, and A. Vanek. Edmonton: Linguistic Research. 3-10.

Sadock, J. 1970. Whimperatives. In: Studies presented to Robert E. Lees by his students. Edited by J. Sadock and A. Vanek. Edmonton: Linguistic Research. 223-238.

Sadock, J. 1971. Queclaratives. CLS 7.223-231.

Schreiber, P. 1972. Style disjuncts and the performative analysis. Linguistic Inquiry 3:3.321-347.

# 3

## A SYNTACTIC ARGUMENT FOR NEGATIVE TRANSPORTATION

Robin Lakoff

Introduction. In this article Robin Lakoff reviews the semantic rationale previously given for a rule of Negative Transportation, and concludes that this rationale is weak. She shows,
furthermore, that the one syntactic argument previously offered
for this rule is also not without problems. Then she turns her
attention to building a new syntactic argument for Negative
Transportation based on tag questions. The skeleton of her
argument is that we can explain the polarity of tag questions
only if we assume (1) performative verbs (real or abstract)
meaning 'suppose' are an essential part of the structural description for Tag Question Formation, (2) Negative Transportation exists and operates only across certain (real) predicates
with special semantic characteristics (such as being nonfactive
and involving mental state), and (3) both Tag Question Formation and Negative Transportation are cyclic rules. While evidence for the cycle is continually being debated in the literature,
evidence for the cyclicity of Negative Transportation and Tag
Question Formation had not been presented prior to Lakoff's
article; and her arguments here for the cyclicity of each of the
two rules are mutually dependent. This is one of the weakest
points of the paper, although the claim of cyclicity may still
be correct. (See Horn 1971 for an independent argument that
Negative Raising--his name for the same phenomenon--is
cyclic.) Likewise, the proposal of abstract performative verbs
for those Ss having tag questions and no overt performative is
supported by data that rely crucially on her analysis of Negative Transportation and her assumptions about cyclicity. Again,
we would prefer independent syntactic arguments for the
existence of such an abstract performative.

But while the intricate argument for Negative Transportation
given here begs for independent justification of the various
claims crucial to it, the article has many strong points. First,

91

the article stresses the need for syntactic evidence to support syntactic transformations and not just semantic evidence. Second, the problem of transported negatives is an important one to resolve since without a satisfactory analysis of them much data on the distribution of negative polarity items, the polarity of tag questions, the choice of moods and the presence of negative particles in languages such as French (see Prince 1976), and various other data would remain an enigma. And third, the issues of abstract predicates, rule ordering, and the cycle are central to syntactic analysis in the 1960s and 1970s and may well remain important issues in the future.

# A SYNTACTIC ARGUMENT FOR NEGATIVE TRANSPORTATION

Robin Lakoff

In his article, 'The position of embedding transformations in a grammar', Charles Fillmore proposed a rule which he called negative transportation. He proposed it in order to account for the difference between the sentence pair (1a), (1b), and the pair (2a), (2b).

(1a) John thinks that Bill doesn't like Harriet.
(1b) John doesn't think that Bill likes Harriet.
(2a) John claims that Bill doesn't like Harriet.
(2b) John doesn't claim that Bill likes Harriet.

This difference is that the first two sentences are semantically equivalent to each other; there could never be a situation in which (1a) was true and (1b) false, or vice versa. But for sentences (2a) and (2b), this is not the case; it is perfectly possible for one to be true and the other false for a given situation. Further, Fillmore showed that for at least one interpretation of (1b), its meaning had to be that of (1a)--the negative *not* actually negated the verb of the lower sentence;[1] the speaker was not denying that John was thinking, but rather saying that John thought that it was not true that Bill liked Harriet. Fillmore had no syntactic motivation for his rule: the semantic grounds given above were the only ones linguists were aware of for some time, but still the rule seemed plausible, and the only reasonable way to account for the difference between the pair (1a), (1b) and (2a), (2b).

Negative-transportation, granted that it was a rule, was a minor rule[2] that applies to a relatively small number of a subclass of verbs--nonfactive verbs of mental state, and one or two intransitives. Thus, in English (the class of verbs within which the rule was applicable was the same in each language in which it is known to exist, but the set of verbs within this class that is subject to it varies from language to language), *think, believe, suppose, guess,* and *want* are some of the verbs subject to the rule, while, for example, *hope, feel, realize,* and many others are not. Thus, several things were known about

93

the way the rule had to operate, although there was as yet no proof that such a rule existed.

In fact, it has been claimed by Dwight Bolinger[3]--and I believe with considerable justification--that the semantic evidence for negative-transportation is not as strong as it had seemed. Bolinger suggests that there is a slight difference between the meaning of (1a) and (1b)--not nearly as glaring a difference as between (2a) and (2b), but a difference nonetheless. With the (1b) type, according to Bolinger, there is greater uncertainty in the speaker's mind about the negation in the lower sentence. So, for example, he says, comparing (3a) and (3b), both containing *expect*, a verb subject to this rule:

(3a) I expect it not to happen.
(3b) I don't expect it to happen.

The second, to me, signifies, 'I rather believe it won't happen'. The negative affects the main verb. The negation is milder. If Bolinger's claim is true (and it seems to me that it must be true in part at least), then positing the existence of a rule of negative transportation on the basis of semantic evidence alone becomes even shakier and more unsatisfactory than ever.

The one serious piece of syntactic evidence that I know of for this rule was suggested by Masaru Kajita[4] on the basis of facts true in some dialects of English. In these dialects (4a) and (4b) are grammatical, as is (4c), but (4d) is not.

(4a) I thought John wouldn't leave until tomorrow.
(4b) I didn't think John would leave until tomorrow.
(4c) I said John wouldn't leave until tomorrow.
(4d) *I didn't say John would leave until tomorrow.

Kajita's claim was that the grammaticality of these sentences--if it was as indicated--could be explained by making a number of assumptions.

First (a point first noted by Klima[5]), *until* occurs only in a very restricted class of sentences: either those extending over a broad time-span, as in (5a), or in sentences containing negatives (5b), and in no other types.

Hence the ungrammaticality of (5c).

(5a) The guests arrived until 5:00.
(5b) John didn't arrive until 5:00.
(5c) *John arrived until 5:00.

It has been suggested that the class of verbs which can precede *until* is actually the class of statives or verbs of duration of time, of which the abstract verb of negation whose superficial form is *not* is one.

It has further been suggested that the negated verb must be the one directly above *until* in the underlying structure if the sentence is to be grammatical. Thus, (4a) and (4c) are clearly grammatical for that reason; (4d) must be ungrammatical for the same reason. Therefore, the reason (4b) is grammatical is that in the underlying structure the negative was in the lower sentence, so that *until* could be used.

This would be a persuasive syntactic argument, but for two problems. The first is that, though many speakers do in fact find (4b) grammatical, equally as many do not. Since this is so, it calls the whole argument into question, though it does not discredit it, just as Bolinger's claim weakens but does not discredit the purely semantic justification of negative-transportation.

There is a second serious difficulty. Although (4b) is grammatical for many speakers, none to my knowledge accept sentences like those of (6a)-(6c), but given Kajita's claim, these should be equally as grammatical as (4b).

(6a) *I didn't ever think that John would leave until tomorrow.
(6b) *I never thought that John would leave until tomorrow.
(6c) *At no time did I think that John would leave until tomorrow.

There should be one interpretation of these sentences in which the negation is introduced from the lower sentence, though the indefinite modifies the upper sentence. With other negated indefinites, these sentences are acceptable to those people who find (4b) good.

(7a) No one thought that John would leave until tomorrow.
(7b) It wasn't thought by anyone that John would leave until tomorrow.

It is not clear why the sentences (6a)-(6b) are so bad. But whatever the reason, they cast additional doubt on Kajita's argument.

There was, then, neither strong semantic nor strong syntactic proof of the existence of this rule. Recently, however, certain facts have come to light that appear to provide fairly conclusive evidence that this rule must exist.

The argument revolves around the formation of tag questions. Tag questions have been discussed, in particular by Klima,[6] and their general behavior is well known. So, if a statement is positive, the tag question is formed by affixing to it the corresponding negative sentence, and vice versa,

(12a) John has left, hasn't he?
(12b) John hasn't left, has he?

while questions which match the main sentence in negativity are

either ungrammatical or quite different in meaning, generally
sarcastic.

(13a) (So) John has left, has he?
(13b) *John hasn't left, hasn't he?

It has been assumed that tag questions are formed from the
simple declarative, though unlike declaratives, they share some
of the properties of simple questions. Like simple questions,
they are subject to certain constraints: certain types of sentences do not occur either as tag questions or as simple yes-
no questions.

(14a) *Am I worried?
(14b) *I'm worried, aren't I?
(14c) *Do I suppose the Yankees will win the pennant?
(14d) *I suppose the Yankees will win the pennant, don't I?

That is, for verbs of mental state, it is impossible for the subject to ask whether they are true of him. The reason for the
ungrammaticality of (14c) and (14d) is that *suppose* is being
used as a performative verb, in Austin's sense, and therefore
cannot be questioned, since it describes an action that is performed in the act of description, and to question it would be
nonsensical. [7]
It is true, however, of tag questions that, though they share
certain constraints with simple questions, they are obviously
not synonymous with them. Therefore, that they clearly could
not share the same underlying structure. So, for example,
where a simple question like (15a) makes no presupposition
about the answer the speaker anticipates, a tag, like (15b)
definitely presupposes a positive answer: the speaker, receiving a 'no' answer to (15a), would probably not be surprised;
receiving a 'no' answer to (15b), he would.

(15a) Did John leave?
(15b) John left, didn't he?

In fact, (15b), rather than a simple request for information,
can be paraphrased as a statement of supposition of a positive
answer, with an implied request not for information, but for
reassurance that the supposition is really correct. (15b) can
be paraphrased as (16): [8]

(16) I suppose John left--I'm just asking you in order to be
absolutely certain.

Since this is true, we must look for an analysis of the tag question that will differentiate it, in underlying structure, from the
simple declarative. Perhaps we should bear in mind the paraphrase (16): a tag since their meanings are similar. We might

assume that a sentence like (15b) was related to one like (17).

(17) I suppose that John left.

Both would contain performative verbs meaning *suppose*. The difference is that in (17) the performative is a real verb; in (15b) it is an abstract verb, present in the underlying structure but deleted transformationally. [9] Now consider a sentence containing the real verb *suppose*, again a performative:

(18) I don't suppose the Yankees will win, will they?

compared with the ungrammatical

(19) *I don't suppose the Yankees will win, won't they?

as well as, of course,

(20) *I don't suppose the Yankees will win, do I?

The ungrammaticality of (20) has already been explained. But the grammaticality of (18), rather than (19), is at first glance very odd. In meaning, the sentence is a true tag question: it is not a sarcastic rejoinder like (13a); yet, the tag is positive, as is the sentence it is formed on. Another fact is that the tag is formed on the lower sentence, which clearly is not always possible. In fact, forming the tag on the lower sentence is possible only in case the verb of the higher sentence is a performative verb--and for this reason not able to be questioned. Both positive and negative tag questions may be formed on the lower sentence, if the above condition holds.

(21a) *I'm surprised that John left, didn't he?
(21b) *Bill supposes that Mary is here, isn't she?
(21c) I suppose you think you're real smart, don't you?
(21d) I suppose John isn't here, is he?

The oddness of the grammaticality of (18) must be explained. First of all, we have already said--and there should be no disagreement on this issue--that the verb *suppose* in (18) is used just as it is in (21c)--as a performative. (Otherwise, (18) would be just as ungrammatical as (21b).) But it is negated, and it is as much nonsense to think of a negated performative as a questioned performative, by the very nature of a performative verb. This is, of course, only true of the underlying structure, since it is in the underlying structure that meaning is determined. This fact suggests that the negative cannot be in the higher sentence originally, or we are faced with an impossible situation semantically. We are faced with one syntactically as well: the lower sentence must be negative at the time the rule of tag formation goes into effect, in order to produce a positive tag question. Only after tag-question formation can the negative be removed from the lower sentence, unless we are to deny that the tag-question transformation can be formulated generally at all.

Then, we have hypothesized that sentences like (15b) and those like (18) and (21c) are derived from similar sources. We suggest, that is, that tag-question formation occurs only if a performative verb with the meaning of *suppose* is present-- abstract or real. Further, strong reasons have been given for assuming that negative transportation is, in fact, a syntactic rule of English. Apparently it will operate after tag-question formation, in order to produce (18). But consider a sentence like (22):

(22) John doesn't think the Yankees will win, does he?

In this sentence, since *think* is not being used as a performative, tag-question formation must operate on it, if at all. But the tag is positive, indicating that the sentence tag-question formation worked on was negative at the time tag-question formation applied. Yet, this negative in the higher sentence has come there just as the negative came into the higher sentence in (18), by negative transportation--at least in one interpretation of this sentence. Therefore, to produce sentence (22), the order of application of these two rules must be, negative transportation first, and tag-question formation second. We are then faced with an ordering paradox, if we wish to be able to generate both (18) and (22).

This paradox can be avoided, however, if we make two further assumptions. First, that performative abstract verbs exist, and that one underlies (22), though not (18). Second, that these syntactic rules apply cyclically. With these assumptions, let us see how the derivations of (18) and (22) proceed. For (18), we assume the underlying structure (very approximate, of course), of (23):

(23) I suppose

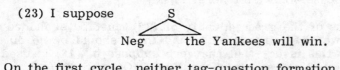

On the first cycle, neither tag-question formation nor negative transportation will operate. On the second, as suggested, tag-question formation operates first (producing the intermediate string *I suppose the Yankees won't win, will they?*) and then negative transportation applies, producing the superficial form of (18). So far, so good. But it was with (22) and this ordering that trouble arose. Let us, making the assumption of an underlying abstract performative verb [*suppose*], postulate the following, again approximate, underlying structure for (22).

(24) [I suppose]   S
           John thinks   S
                Neg The Yankees will win.

On the first cycle, again, neither rule can apply. On the second cycle, tag-question formation does not apply, since in the second sentence there is no performative verb meaning 'suppose'. Negative transportation can apply, since *think* is a verb of the correct class and is marked as undergoing the rule, and so it does apply. After the second cycle, the intermediate string looks like (25):

(25) [I suppose]   S
           John doesn't think   S
                The Yankees will win.

We now proceed to the third cycle, containing the abstract performative verb. Now tag-question formation can take place; in fact, since the verb is abstract, it must. Since the verb in the next sentence is negative, a positive tag is added. Since the verb is abstract, negative transportation cannot take place again; if it were a real verb, it might. Therefore, the order tag-question formation, then negative transportation, avoids the ordering paradox.

Thus, we have given evidence for the existence of three things: a rule of negative transportation, the presence of an abstract performative verb, and the syntactic cycle.

## NOTES

1. There is another interpretation, of course, with the higher verb itself being negated. Thus, 'John doesn't think Bill likes Harriet' might have two interpretations: (1) 'John thinks Bill doesn't like Harriet' (John has a definite opinion); (2) 'It isn't so that John thinks Bill likes Harriet' (John need not have any opinion; he might, in fact, not know anything about either Bill or Harriet or the feelings of the former for the latter.) In this case, of course, negative-transportation has not occurred.

2. For a discussion of minor rules, and an explanation of why negative transportation is one, see G. Lakoff (1965).

3. In two letters dated 12/5/67 and 12/7/67, to George Lakoff.

4. Oral communication to writer, winter 1966-1967.

5. In Klima (1964), pp. 288f.

6. Klima (1964).

7. For a discussion of performative verbs and their properties, see Austin (1955). The verb in (14c) and (14d) is to be interpreted here specifically in its performative sense, though other readings are possible.

8.   The contrast between negative simple yes-no questions and negative tag questions, as for example

(1) Didn't John leave?
(2) John didn't leave, did he?

is more complicated.  Sentence (1), unlike its positive counterpart, makes an assumption--namely, that the speaker had expected that John had left, but now has reasons to doubt his previous belief.  Sentence (2) does not oppose any new information to the speaker's previous beliefs.  Thus, (1) can be paraphrased, 'I thought John had left--but now I have been given information contradicting this belief, so I am asking you to tell me which of the two is correct, as I don't know--my belief or the new information'.  But (2) can be paraphrased as 'I thought John hadn't left, and in fact he apparently hasn't--but I'm asking you just to make sure I'm right'.  Thus, (1) asks the hearer to help the speaker choose between two conflicting beliefs; (2) merely asks the hearer to reinforce the speaker's single belief.

9.   For a discussion of the notion 'abstract performative verb' see R. Lakoff (1968) and J. R. Ross (1969).

## REFERENCES FOR 'A SYNTACTIC ARGUMENT FOR NEGATIVE TRANSPORTATION'

Austin, J. L. 1955. How to do things with words. Edited by J. O. Urmson. Oxford: Oxford University Press.

Fillmore, C. 1963. The position of embedding transformations in a grammar. Word 19.208-231.

Klima, E. S. 1964. Negation in English. In: The structure of language: Readings in the philosophy of language. Edited by J. A. Fodor and J. J. Katz. Englewood Cliffs, N.J.: Prentice-Hall.

Lakoff, G. 1965. On the nature of syntactic irregularity. In: Harvard Computation Laboratory Report to the National Science Foundation on mathematical linguistics and automatic translation, No. NSF-16. Cambridge, Mass.: Harvard University. [Published as Irregularity in syntax. 1970. New York: Holt, Rinehart and Winston.]

Lakoff, R. 1968. Abstract syntax and Latin complementation. Cambridge, Mass.: The MIT Press.

Ross, J. R. 1969. On declarative sentences. In: Readings in English transformational grammar. Edited by R. Jacobs and P. S. Rosenbaum. Waltham, Mass.: Ginn and Co.

QUESTIONS

Question 1. Lakoff credits Bolinger with the observation that a transported negative conveys a 'greater uncertainty in the speaker's mind about the negation in the lower sentence'. A rule such as Negative Transportation moves an element, yielding a sentence with a different word order. Consider the transformation Passive, which, like Negative Transportation, rearranges the word order of an S. Do you see any difference in meaning between pairs like the following?

(i) George Washington slept in that bed.
    That bed was slept in by George Washington.
(ii) Everyone in this room speaks two languages.
    Two languages are spoken by everyone in this room.

Find other Passive pairs of your own which exemplify such differences. Do other (all?) transformations that alter word order affect semantics in similar ways? (You might consider Dative Movement, *There* Insertion, *Each* Movement, Raising into Subject Position, and *Tough* Movement, among others.) Try to make a generalization about the kinds of semantic change that accompany such transformations.

Question 2. Reconstruct Kajita's argument for Negative Transportation based on *until*. In particular, what is the generalization you can draw from (i) about the distribution of *until*?

(i) a.   The guests arrived until 5:00.
(i) b.   John didn't arrive until 5:00.
(i) c.   *John arrived until 5:00.

How does this generalization offer evidence that Negative Transportation has applied in (ii) (Lakoff's example (4b))?

(ii) I didn't think John would leave until tomorrow.

What is wrong with (iii) (Lakoff's example (4d))?

(iii) *I didn't say John would leave until tomorrow.

*Question 3. Lakoff points out that many people reject the Ss in (i) (her example (6)) although those in (ii) (her example (7)) are accepted.

(i) a.   *I didn't ever think John would leave until tomorrow.
(i) b.   *I never thought that John would leave until tomorrow.
(i) c.   *At no time did I think that John would leave until tomorrow.
(ii) a.   No one thought that John would leave until tomorrow.
(ii) b.   It wasn't thought by anyone that John would leave until tomorrow.

What would be the source Ss for (i) and (ii) before Negative Transportation applies? Remember, Negative Transportation is supposed to be an optional rule. Is there a difference between the sources for (i) and those for (ii) that is relevant to the difference in their acceptability?

**Question 4.** Tag questions such as that in (i) have been called conducive, while ones like that in (ii) have been called belligerent.

(i) John has left, hasn't he?
(ii) (So) John has left, has he?

What is the constraint on conducive tag questions that is relevant to our study of Negative Transportation? If a tag question follows a complex S whose main V is not performative, with which of the Ss does this constraint hold, the main S or one of the embedded Ss, according to Lakoff? (Note Lakoff's discussion preceding example (21).)

Given the constraints on conducive tag questions, what is the problem with (iii)?

(iii) I don't suppose the Yankees will win, will they?

How does having a rule of Negative Transportation help solve that problem?

**Question 5.** Read carefully the paragraphs between Lakoff's examples (15) and (18). What is the underlying source Lakoff proposes for (i) before conducive tag-question formation?

(i) John left, didn't he?

What is her reason for proposing an abstract performative verb here? Does she give any syntactic evidence for her proposal?

**Question 6.** Review Lakoff's solution for the ordering paradox. In particular, be sure you understand the crucial use she makes of an abstract performative V and of the notion of the cycle. Why can't conducive tag-question formation apply on the first cycle in (i) and (ii)?

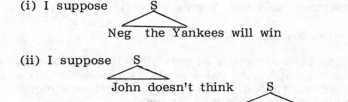

Why can't conducive tag-question formation apply on the second cycle in (ii)? (That is, what is the structural description for conducive tag-question formation?)

Question 7. Assuming both Negative Transportation and conducive tag-question formation have applied in (i) and (ii), in what order have they applied in each?

(i) I don't suppose the Yankees will win, will they?
(ii) John doesn't think the Yankees will win, does he?

Give the bad Ss that would result if the rules applied in the opposite order in each.

*Question 8. As we saw in Question 6, Lakoff's Tag Question Formation is triggered by *suppose* and does not apply until the cycle on the topmost S, but all the changes affect only the embedded S. Chomsky (1973) claims that rules with this power are not needed and can be eliminated from transformational grammars. Consider Equi NP Deletion. Is this rule of the type we are discussing? Is the matrix S any more crucially involved than it is in Tag Question Formation?

*Question 9. Lakoff's Tag Question Formation is optional if *suppose* is realized, because (i) is grammatical.

(i) I suppose the Yankees will win.

However, she says the rule is obligatory if *suppose* is abstract. This condition on the rule should make you suspicious. But the discussion in the next paragraph shows why Lakoff takes such a step.

Ross (1970, in this volume) proposes that the highest V of every S is a performative, whether abstract or realized. What deep structure does Ross give for (ii)?

(ii) Prices slumped.

Why is (iii) ungrammatical?

(iii) *I declare prices slumped, didn't they?

What deep structure would Lakoff give for (iv)?

(iv) Prices slumped, didn't they?

What S would the deep structure of (iv) yield if Tag Question Formation did not apply? Are (ii) and (iv) synonymous? If so, they should have the same deep structure. Is (ii) ambiguous? If not, it should have only one deep structure.

*Question 10. Consider an S such as (i).

(i) I see you have bought a new car, haven't you?

(Example (i) is due to Hooper and Thompson 1973.) What problem does this conducive tag question example raise for Lakoff? Can you find other matrix verbs that allow the same kind of conducive tags? If so, do these verbs have any semantic characteristic in common?

Question 11. Is *suppose* really a performative verb in the sense of Ross?

## HOMEWORK PROBLEMS

I. Consider the verb *budge*, which can appear in negative statements and yes/no questions (both positive and negative), but cannot appear in positive statements.

(1) He didn't budge an inch.
(2) Did he budge at all?
(3) Didn't he budge at all?
(4) *He budged (an inch).

Use *budge* to build an argument for Negative Transportation. Your argument will be very similar to that using *until* given in the article. Items like *budge* and *until* are called negative polarity items. Find examples of other negative polarity items. Does their behavior support a rule of Negative Transportation?

II. A positive polarity item cannot appear in a negative statement. Find a positive polarity item. Using this item, build an argument in favor of Negative Transportation. (If you cannot find a positive polarity item, use a form of *some*, as in *I didn't meet someone* but *I met someone*.)

III. With respect to negation, what are the important characteristics of the predicates *bother* (in the sense used in (1)) and *lift a finger*? What new question(s) do (1) and (2) now present?

(1) John didn't bother to lift a finger.
(2) *John didn't bother to meet someone.

Discuss possible explanations for these data. Consider Ss such as (3).

(3) I doubted that he would budge.

Will any of your explanations cover this example, as well? (See Klima 1964, cited in Lakoff's article, for further discussion.)

## SUGGESTED READINGS

Cattell, R. 1973. Negative transportation and tag questions. Lg. 49:3.612-639. (He gives an argument against Lakoff, proposing a different analysis for tag questions.)

Chomsky, N. 1971. Deep structure, surface structure, and semantic interpretation. In: Semantics. Edited by D. Steinberg and L. Jakobovits. Cambridge University Press. 183-216. (For Question 6.)

Chomsky, N. 1973. Conditions on transformations. In: A festschrift for Morris Halle. Edited by S. A. Anderson and P. Kiparksy. New York: Holt, Rinehart, and Winston. 232-286. (For Question 6.)

Hooper, J. 1975. On assertive predicates. In: Syntax and semantics 4. Edited by J. Kimball. New York: Academic Press. 91-124. (She gives a semantic reason for the un-grammaticality of the bad Ss in Question 3.)

Hooper, J., and S. Thompson. 1973. On the applicability of root transformations. Linguistic Inquiry 4:4.465-498. (For Question 10.)

Horn, L. 1971. Negative transportation: Unsafe at any speed? CLS 7.120-133.

Horn, L. 1975. Neg-raising predicates: Toward an expla-nation. CLS 11.279-294. (For an analysis of the semantic restrictions on neg-raising predicates and a bibliography of other works on the topic.)

Horn, L. 1978. Some aspects of negation. In: Universals of human language. Edited by S. Greenberg, C. Ferguson, and E. Moravscik. Stanford: Stanford University Press. 127-210.

Jackendoff, R. 1971. On some questionable arguments about quantifiers and negation. Lg. 42:2.282-297. (For a discus-sion of *until* as a negative polarity item and for a discussion of tag questions.)

McGloin, N. H. 1976. Negation. In: Japanese generative grammar. (=Syntax and semantics 5). Edited by M. Shibatani. New York: Academic Press. 387-388.

Oh, C.-K. 1971. On the negation of Korean. Language Research 7. (See especially p. 48.)

Pope, E. 1976. Questions and answers in English. The Hague: Mouton. (For an analysis of tag questions, see Chapter 2.)

Prince, E. 1976. The syntax and semantics of neg-raising, with evidence from French. Lg. 52:2.404-426.

Rivero, M. L. 1971. Mood and presupposition in Spanish. Foundations of Language 7.305-336. (See p. 307 and following.)

Shnukal, A. 1978. Syntactic indications of tentativeness in discourse. Presented at and to be published in the Proceed-ings of LSRL 8. University of Louisville, Kentucky. (For a discussion of the semantics and pragmatics of Ss having undergone negative transportation in French.)

# 4

## THE DEEP STRUCTURE OF RELATIVE CLAUSES

### Sandra Annear Thompson

**Introduction.** Thompson's article is an example of an argument that a certain analysis *could* work. Though she says she 'will suggest some facts which indicate that conjunctions *must* underlie relative clause sentences', she in fact offers no arguments to show that generating relative clauses in embedded position is impossible. In linguistics as elsewhere, one's initial assumption must always be that things are what they seem to be, and those who believe things are more complicated must first demolish this initial assumption.

Hale (1975) argued that the (putative) universal base must include two phrase structure rules which generate relative clauses. The first rule adjoins relative clauses to sentences, as in (i).

(i)

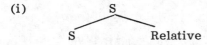

This is essentially the source Thompson is proposing, although she would not be able to go along with Hale's stipulation that this rule limits the number of relative clauses to one per S node. That is, although the relative clause may itself contain a relative clause, a single S node may not have a relative clause modifying its subject and another relative clause modifying its object in Hale's proposal.

The second rule embeds relative clauses under NPs (the order of NP and S is language particular), as in (ii).

(ii)

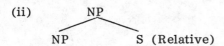

107

This rule may apply to any and every NP in a sentence.

Hale contends that languages start out with adjoined relatives, then over time develop a transformational attraction rule which moves the relative clause next to the NP it modifies, at first optionally, then obligatorily. Finally, the relative clauses are reanalyzed as embedded structures.

Hale also contends that some languages now have only the first base rule (with or without the attraction rule), some languages have only the second base rule, and some languages have both. Keep these three possibilities in mind while reading Thompson's article, and try to decide whether the second two possibilities for English relative clauses can be eliminated.

# THE
# DEEP STRUCTURE
# OF RELATIVE CLAUSES

**Sandra Annear Thompson**

A number of general studies in transformational grammar (including Chomsky (1965), Rosenbaum and Jacobs (1968), G. Lakoff (1966), Langendoen (1969), Ross (1967b)) have assumed that the appropriate underlying representation for a relative clause sentence involves a sentence embedded into a noun phrase. I would like to question this assumption, and to suggest that in fact the appropriate underlying representation for a relative clause sentence is a conjunction.

The argument will be developed in several stages. First, I will suggest some facts which indicate that conjunctions must underlie relative clause sentences. Next, I will show the general process of relative clause formation and some of the implications of my analysis. Finally, I will indicate in what respects the derivation of sentences containing nonrestrictive relative clauses is similar to that of sentences with restrictive relative clauses.

## 1. Indications That a Conjunction Source for Relative Clause Sentences Is Correct

**a.** To my knowledge, no arguments defending an embedding analysis against a conjunction analysis for relative clause sentences have ever been presented either in the literature or informally.

**b.** There is virtually no agreement among those who assume that relative clauses are underlying embedded as to what configuration of nodes is appropriate to represent the relationship between the two sentences. Stockwell *et al.* (1969) presents a summary of the various approaches which have been taken and the arguments given to support each.

**c.** There is a significant but generally overlooked set of structural distinctions between relative clause sentences and those complex sentences which are clearly realizations of structures containing embedded sentences, namely those containing sentential subjects or objects, such as:

(1) That Frieda likes to cook is obvious to me.
(2) I think that Frieda likes to cook.

For sentences like (1) and (2), an embedding analysis is well motivated since the contained sentence is required as an obligatory argument of the verb; it plays a role with respect to the verb which Fillmore (1968) has called the *objective* role and without which the verb cannot stand. Furthermore, the verb governs both the occurrence of clause and the type of clause which can occur. These conditions do not hold for relative clause sentences. A relative clause is always structurally superfluous; it plays no role whatever with respect to the main verb and no morphemes in the language are marked as requiring it. A relative clause sentence is equivalent to two independent predications on the same argument. These differences are captured by an analysis in which sentential subjects and objects are instances of underlying embedding, and relative clauses are only superficially embedded. If relative clause sentences are not underlyingly embedded structures this could account in part for the general disagreement, pointed out in **b** above, as to the underlying representation of the position of the embedded sentence.

## 2. The Derivation of Relative Clause Sentences

### A. Assumptions

In order to present the schematic outline for forming relative clause sentences, two assumptions must be made explicit.

**a.** The difference between parts of sentences such as the following:

(3) I know *a* student who plays the harmonica.
(4) I know *the* student who plays the harmonica.

will be assumed to be introduced at some level of derivation other than the one at which "content morphemes" and the relations among them are specified. I leave open the question of just where such a distinction must be made; for the present discussion, it suffices to point out that (3) and (4) must have identical representations insofar as the meanings of the nouns and verbs and the relations among them are concerned. I shall further assume that the choice of the definite determiner will in general correlate with certain presuppositions which the speaker makes about the extent of his listener's knowledge.

**b.** As pointed out by Bach (1968), numerals and quantifiers must be introduced outside the clause in which they ultimately appear. That this must be so is illustrated by the fact that the sentences of (5) are not matched by the respective pairs in (6):

(5) a. I have three students who are flunking.
    b. I know few people who smoke cigars.
    c. I saw no students who had short hair.

(6) a. $\begin{cases} \text{I have three students.} \\ \text{Three students are flunking.} \end{cases}$

    b. $\begin{cases} \text{I know few people.} \\ \text{Few people smoke cigars.} \end{cases}$

    c. $\begin{cases} \text{I saw no students.} \\ \text{No students had short hair.} \end{cases}$

### B. Derivation

Returning now to the proposal for deriving relative clause sentences from conjunctions, I suggest that underlying (7) is a structure like (8):

(7) I met the girl who speaks Basque.
(8) (I met girl) (girl speaks Basque).

The choice of the clause to become the relative clause correlates with certain suppositions on the part of the speaker about what the hearer knows, and accordingly with the choice of the determiner. Consider (8) again. If the speaker presupposes that the hearer knows neither about his meeting a girl nor about a girl's speaking Basque, then both of the following conjunction realizations of (8) are acceptable:

(9) I met a girl and she speaks Basque.
(10) There's a girl who speaks Basque and I met her.

as well as both of the following relative clause sentences with indefinite head nouns:

(11) I met a girl who speaks Basque.
(12) A girl I met speaks Basque.

If, on the other hand, the speaker presupposes that there is a girl such that it is known by the hearer that he met her, the relative clause sentence corresponding to this presupposition will have the conjunct containing *met* as the relative clause, and the head noun will be definite:

(13) The girl I met speaks Basque.

Similarly, if the speaker presupposes that his hearer knows about the girl who speaks Basque, the corresponding relative clause sentence will have the conjunct *speaks Basque* as the relative clause, and again the head noun will be definite:

(14) I met the girl who speaks Basque.

**C.** Implications

**a.** The distinction then, between the "matrix" and "constituent" sentences in a relative clause structure can be seen to be related to nothing in the structural portion of the representation of such sentences. The meaning difference between sentences (13) and (14), in other words, is not a function of the fact that the matrix and the constituent sentences have been interchanged; if it were, then we should expect the same meaning difference to characterize the pair (11)–(12). But (11) and (12) do not have different meanings in any usual sense of the word *meaning*. Instead, the semantic difference between (13) and (14) is a function of the presuppositions which the speaker has about the extent of his hearer's knowledge.

**b.** Similarly, the "restrictiveness" of a relative clause is also shown not to be a property best described in terms of an embedding underlying representation. Relative clauses with indefinite nouns do not "restrict" these nouns in the way that relative clauses with definite nouns seem to, and yet underlying embedding structures do not reveal a basis for this difference. Again, I think that the apparent "restricting" nature of relative clauses with definite head nouns is a function of the presuppositions discussed above.

**c.** Postal (1967) has shown that a certain ambiguity can be explained only if relative clauses are assumed to be derived from conjunctions. The sentence he gives is:

(15)  Charley assumed that the book which was burned was not burned.

On one reading, Charley assumed that a certain book had not been burned when in fact it had been. On the other reading, Charley assumed a contradiction. On the hypotheses that relative clause sentences are underlyingly embedding structures, there is no way to represent the ambiguity. This is because corresponding to (15), only one embedding structure can be constructed, namely:

(16)

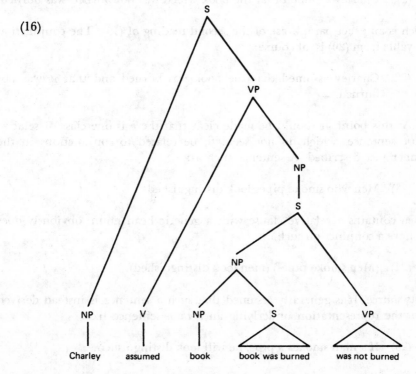

But there are two conjunction sources for (15). Underlying the first reading, in which Charley is merely mistaken, is the representation:

(17) (Charley assumed (book not burned)) (book burned).

Notice, that, as we would expect, (17) also underlies:

(18) The book which Charley assumed was not burned was burned.

which results from the first conjunct's becoming the relative clause, as well as the conjunction:

(19) Charley assumed that the book was not burned but it was burned.

Underlying the second reading, in which Charley assumes a contradiction, is:

(20) Charley assumed ((book burned) (book not burned)).

As with (19), (20) underlies two sentences besides (16). By selecting the second of the two conjuncts of (20) as the relative clause, we can derive:

(21) Charley assumed that the book which was not burned was burned.

which is an exact paraphrase of the second reading of (15). The conjunction derivable from (20) is, of course:

(22) Charley assumed that the book was burned and that it was not burned.

At this point, it should be made clear that there is one class of relative clause sentences which do not seem to be related to conjunctions in the manner just described. A sentence such as:

(23) Men who smoke pipes look distinguished.

which contains a relative clause with a generic head noun, obviously does not have a conjunction such as:

(24) (Men smoke pipes) (men look distinguished).

as its source. It is generally assumed that such a sentence is instead derived from the representation underlying an *if-then* sentence like:

(25) If a man smokes a pipe, he will look distinguished.

The extremely interesting semantic and syntactic issues raised by this assumption are unfortunately left unexplored here.

## 3. Nonrestrictive Relative Clauses

The similarities between nonrestrictive clause (=NR) sentences and conjunctions have been remarked upon by a number of linguists (see, for example, Thompson (1968), Drubig (1968), G. Lakoff (1966), Postal (1967), Ross (1967a)). I will not review these similarities, but I will assume that NR sentences must be derived from conjunctions. Again, as far as I know, no arguments have been advanced in favor of an embedded analysis for NR sentences; in those studies which present underlying embedding representations for NR's, the question of there being alternative analysis is not even raised.

At the outset, two types of NR sentences must be distinguished; I will refer to them as Type I and Type II NR sentences. Type I NR sentences are exemplified by:

(26) Jerry, who used to play football, now has a sedentary job.
(27) I had a date with the librarian, who read to me all evening.

Type II NR sentences are exemplified by:

(28) She took the children to the zoo, which was very helpful.
(29) Joe debated in high school, which Chuck did too.

In Type I NR sentences, the relative pronoun replaces a referring noun phrase; in Type II, it replaces an entity, the nature of which will be clarified later in this section. For the moment, we will consider only Type I.

### A. Type I NR's

Ross's proposal (1967b, p. 174) that all Type I NR's be derived from second conjuncts seems to be correct. That is, at some intermediate level before anaphoric pronominalization has applied, given a conjunction each of whose clauses contains an occurrence of a coreferential noun, the second conjunct can be moved to a position immediately following the noun in the first conjunct. Pronominalization can then apply, moving either backwards or forwards,[1] so that from the conjunction

---

[1] Ronald Langacker pointed out this fact to me.

(30) George noticed that Margie refused the candy, and George didn't take any candy.

any of the following can be derived:

(31) George, who didn't take any either, noticed that Margie refused the candy.
(32) George, who noticed that Margie refused the candy, didn't take any either.
(33) George, who didn't take any candy, noticed that Margie refused it too.
(34) George, who noticed that Margie refused it too, didn't take any candy.

One apparent counterexample to the claim that NR's are derived from second conjuncts is the following sentence:

(35) Is even Clarence, who is wearing mauve socks, a swinger?

As Ross (1967) points out, its conjunction counterpart does not exist:

(36) *Is even Clarence a swinger, and he is wearing mauve socks?

It seems to me that Ross's solution to this problem is not as radical as he indicates. As a source for (36) he proposes the structure underlying:

(37) Is even Clarence a swinger? Clarence is wearing mauve socks.

Instead of following Ross in his conclusion that all NR's must be derived from sequences of sentences, I claim instead that the connector is deleted between a question and a declarative.

Imperatives are similar to questions in this respect. The source of:

(38) Tell your father, who is outside, that supper is ready.

apparently cannot be:

(39) *Tell your father that supper is ready, and he is outside.

But if there is a rule deleting *and* between imperatives and declaratives, the problem disappears. Notice that it would not help to posit a conjunction source in which the declarative sentence came before the question or imperative; questions and imperatives simply cannot be connected to declaratives by *and,* either before them or after them.

(40)  *Clarence is wearing mauve socks, and is even he a swinger?
(41)  *Your father is outside, and tell him that supper is ready.

Finally, a restriction must be placed on the NR rule to the effect that questions and imperatives themselves cannot become NR's.

At this point two objections might be raised; I would like to consider these in slightly greater detail. First, it has often been suggested that an NR represents an assertion by the speaker, a comment injected into the sentence whose truth is being vouched for by the speaker independently of the content of the rest of the sentence. An example of the type of sentence which makes such an analysis seem likely is

(42)  The mayor, who is an old windbag, designated himself to give the speech.

An implication of this analysis is that NR sentences should be represented in such a way as to reflect that the NR is an independent assertion made by the speaker, perhaps by positing a separate superordinate declarative performative for it. However, it is not correct to assign the responsibility for the truth of every NR to the speaker of the sentence in which it occurs. Bach (1968, p. 95) points out that a sentence like

(43)  I dreamt that Rebecca, who is a friend of mine from college, was on the phone.

which might be thought to contain an NR asserted by the speaker, can be made ambiguous by changing *is* to *was*. The case is even clearer in a sentence in which the subject is different from the speaker. It seems to me that the following sentences are ambiguous as to whether the subject or the speaker is vouching for the truth of the NR:

(44)  Harold says that his girlfriend, who is a little bit crazy, wants to go to Hanoi.
(45)  The claims agent said that the paint job, which should have been done long ago, would cost $150.

In fact, each of the above sentences can be disambiguated by adding a clause which forces the interpretation in which it is the subject, rather than the speaker, who asserts the NR.

(46)  Harold says that his girlfriend, who is a little bit crazy, wants to go to Hanoi, but I think she's too rational to try it.
(47)  The claims agent said that the paint job, which should have been

done long ago, would cost $150, but he doesn't know that now is when it should be done.

The other possible objection to my thesis is that if both nonrestrictive and restrictive relative clause sentences are derived from conjunctions, then sentences of both types, which may have very different meanings, can be derived from identical sources. Arguments against having identical sources for the two types of sentences carry weight only for sentences with numerals in them, which I will discuss shortly. In other cases, it seems that once again, the differences between restrictive and nonrestrictive relative clause sentences are not of the sort that ought to be represented structurally; instead they are differences representing a speaker's decision about how to present to the hearer information present in the underlying representation. For example, consider the two sentences:

(48) The boy, who works at the library, is majoring in philosophy.
(49) The boy who works at the library is majoring in philosophy.

The representation underlying both of these is:

(50) (Boy works in library) (boy is majoring in philosophy).

For (48) the speaker has decided that the boy is already known to the hearer; the speaker is adding two pieces of information about the boy. For (49) the speaker assumes that the hearer knows about the boy who works at the library; *the* can be used with this NP, and the information which the speaker assumes to be new appears as the main predicate. I can see no way in which such a difference as that which exists between restrictives and nonrestrictives could be represented in a consistent way for all such sentences in terms of some underlying structural distinction.

Restrictive and nonrestrictive relative clause sentences with numeral associated with the head nouns do have different representations. Consider the sentences:

(51) Three boys who had beards were at the party.
(52) Three boys, who had beards, were at the party.

The assertions are quite different: (51) means not that three boys were at the party, but that there were three boys all of whom both attended the party and had beards. But (52) *does* mean that there were three boys at the party. Understanding very little about the representation of numerals, I can do no more now than to suggest that underlying (51), the numeral is associated with neither of the conjuncts, while underlying (52) it appears in both. This is confirmed by the fact that corresponding to (51) there is no two-clause conjunction, but corresponding to (52) we find:

(53) Three boys were at the party, and they had beards.

**B.** Type II NR's

Type II NR's are also derived from second conjuncts only. The examples given above of Type II NR's were

(28) She took the children to the zoo, which was very helpful.

(29) Joe debated in high school, which Chuck did too.

I suggest that these are immediately derived from the sentences.

(54) She took the children to the zoo, and that was very helpful.

(55) Joe debated in high school, and that Chuck did too.

Before outlining the process by which Type II NR's are formed, let us consider a derivation in reverse, with (28) as an example. Its immediate source is (54). The *that* of (54) is a pro-form for certain repeated portions of a sentence; directly underlying (54) would be

(56) She took the children to the zoo, and her taking the children to the zoo was very helpful.

Disregarding the tense of the first conjunct, we can see that the *that* in (54) has replaced the repeated portion of the second conjunct of (56). Let us take a derivation in reverse with another example:

(57) They said she could play the marimba, which she can.

The sentence containing *that* which immediately underlies (57) is

(58) They said she could play the marimba, and that she can.

Directly underlying (58) is the full form with the repeated portion preposed:

(59) They said she could play the marimba, and play the marimba she can.

The immediate source for (59) is

(60) They said she could play the marimba, and she can play the marimba.

In detail, the derivation of a Type II NR sentence proceeds as follows: Given a near-surface-level conjunction in which part of the surface VP of the first conjunct matches part of the VP of the second conjunct, (a) the repeated portion may be preposed;[2] (b) the preposed portion may be replaced by *that*;[3] and (c) the connector may drop, with concomitant change of *that* to *which*.

Notice that, as outlined by Chomsky (1957), when there is no auxiliary element to carry emphasis or negation, a *do* must be added, as in the following examples:

(61) She promised to dance for us, and she did dance for us.
    a. She promised to dance for us, and dance for us she did.
    b. She promised to dance for us, and that she did.
    c. She promised to dance for us, which she did.
(62) She dances well, and I don't dance well.
    a. She dances well, and dance well I don't.
    b. She dances well, and that I don't.
    c. She dances well, which I don't.

The following examples show the operation of an optional rule of "parenthesis":

(63) That Cornelius was pleased was to be expected, and he certainly seemed to be pleased.
    a. That Cornelius was pleased, and he certainly seemed to be pleased, was to be expected.
    b. That Cornelius was pleased, and pleased he certainly seemed to be, was to be expected.
    c. That Cornelius was pleased, and that he certainly seemed to be, was to be expected.
    d. That Cornelius was pleased, which he certainly seemed to be, was to be expected.

A special set of examples is the following, in which a *do* appears:

(64) She taught me to bake a cake, and I couldn't bake a cake before.
    a. She taught me to bake a cake, and bake a cake I couldn't do before.
    b. She taught me to bake a cake, and that I couldn't do before.
    c. She taught me to bake a cake, which I couldn't do before.
(65) We read *Tom Sawyer,* and we had never read *Tom Sawyer* as children.

[2] This formulation is slightly inaccurate. Exactly what gets preposed will be described more carefully below.

[3] The order of these two rules will be reviewed below.

    a. We read *Tom Sawyer,* and read *Tom Sawyer* we had never done as children.

    b. We read *Tom Sawyer,* and that we had never done as children.

    c. We read *Tom Sawyer,* which we had never done as children.

Sentences such as (64) and (65), when considered with certain other sentence types, provide evidence for two related hypotheses.

The first, advanced by Ross, is that activity verbs are associated at some level with the "primordial" action verb, *do.*[4] I understand him to be claiming that this *do* is present in the underlying representation of all activity sentences. Because its occurrence is entirely predictable, I would choose not to view it as present at this level, but as inserted into activity sentences early in their derivation.

The second hypothesis which sentences such as (64) and (65) provide evidence for is that the *do* in such sentences has as its object an NP. According to Ross, the NP in question is the underlying object of *do,* and it is an entire sentence:

(66) Frogs produce croaks.

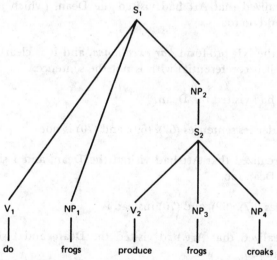

Aside from the fact that there seems to be no evidence for $NP_3$, that is a second underlying occurrence of the surface subject, the evidence which indicates that the *do* must take an NP object indicates that it is not an

---

[4] I cannot fully appreciate Ross's position since I have access to it only in the very sketchy form of a handout from his paper, "Act," presented at the July 1969 meeting of the Linguistic Society of America in Urbana, Illinois. From this handout, and from reports on the paper, I believe that the points which I have attributed to Ross are accurately stated here.

underlying NP that we are concerned with here at all, and that it is not a sentence. Let us consider this evidence. In a sentence like

(67) I realized that Art had visited the Dean, which I should do too.

we are tempted to declare that the *which* replaces an NP, since we know that in restrictive relative clause sentences and in Type I NR sentences, *which* always replaces an NP. However, this is not a very strong argument, since in questions, *which* can replace a demonstrative:

(68) Which book did you steal? I stole this book.

But the argument that *which* replaces an NP becomes more convincing when we consider the immediate source for (67), namely:

(69) I realized that Art had visited the Dean, and that I should too.

Beyond these NR sentences, no examples of *that* replacing anything but an NP come to mind. Further support comes from a paraphrase of (67):

(70) I realized that Art had visited the Dean, (which is) something I should do too.

*Something* is the NP pro-form *par excellence,* and it is clearly the object of *do.* But what it is coreferential with is not the sentence:

(71) Art had visited the Dean.

since what underlies sentences (67), (69), and (70) is not

(72) *I realized that Art had visited the Dean, and I should Art visit the Dean too.

What underlies (67), (69), and (70) instead is

(73) I realized that Art had visited the Dean, and I should visit the Dean too.

In other words, somehow the phrase *visit the Dean* must be an NP before the rules changing this phrase to *that* apply.

Ross has suggested that pseudo-cleft sentences provide additional support for the hypothesis that phrases like *visit the Dean* must be NP's:

(74) What I should do is visit the Dean.
(75) Art did what I should do: visit the Dean.

What examples (67) through (75) show is that the NP which the NR and pseudo-cleft rules, and certain other rules, must refer to need not be an S at any level.

Further evidence that the NP referred to by these rules is a surface NP rather than an underlying NP can be found in the fact that what follows surface *be* must also be an NP. A collection of relevant examples is

(76) Nick is tall, which I will never be.
(77) Nick is tall, (which is) something I will never be.
(78) What I will never be is tall.
(79) Nick is what I will never be: tall.

Ross (1969) has used examples like these to show that adjectives must be underlying NP's. However, examples like the following show that adjectives and other post-*be* expressions must be not underlying but superficial NP's.

(80) I saw that Irma was easy to please, which I should be too.
(81) I saw that Irma was easy to please, (which is) something I should be too.
(82) What I should be is easy to please.
(83) Irma is what I should be: easy to please.

The expression *easy to please* in (80)–(83) cannot be an underlying NP, since in deep structure *easy* and *please* are not even constituents of the same S:

(84) ((One please Irma) easy).

In the examples

(85) Chinese was easily mastered by Rich, which it was not by Claire.
(86) Chinese was easily mastered by Rich (which is) something it was not by Claire.
(87) What Chinese was was easily mastered by Rich.

We can see that the phrase *easily mastered* is not an underlying complement of *be* for there is no underlying *be*; moreover, since the verb *master* is an activity verb, at some intermediate level it would actually be the object of *do*.

My proposal, then, is the following: neither *do* nor *be* is present in underlying representations. *Be* may become the main verb by any of a variety of well-known obligatory transformations. *Do* is inserted preceding activity verbs. At the point at which *do* or *be* is inserted into a sentence, the part of the VP which follows becomes an NP; its NP status is then referred to by a number of optional rules, such as those which produce the sentences we have been considering here. If none of these rules applies to separate the *do* from its object, Ross's rule of "*do*-gobbling" applies, deleting *do*'s that are directly followed by their objects.

If this analysis is in general correct, we are ready to reformulate the steps by which Type II NR's may be formed. Rephrasing the set of three rules (a)–(c) given earlier, we arrive at the following statement: Given a near-surface-level conjunction in which part of the surface VP of the second conjunct is a repetition of part of the surface VP of the first conjunct, (a) the NP "complement" of *be* or *do* may be preposed; (b) this NP may be replaced by *that*; and (c) the connector may drop, with concomitant change of *that* to *which*. This reformulation corrects two inaccuracies in the previous (a)–(c). The earlier formulation said that the portion of the second conjunct involved in these rules was the "repeated portion." This is not quite accurate, since in

(83)   Nick is tall, and I shall never be tall.

*be* is part of the repeated portion of the second conjunct (with tense disregarded). But clearly the *be* is not part of what is changed to *that*, or preposed:

(89)   Nick is tall, which I shall never be.
(90)   Nick is tall, and that I shall never be.
(91)   Nick is tall, and I shall never be that.
(92)   *Nick is tall, which I shall never.
(93)   *Nick is tall, and that I shall never.
(94)   *Nick is tall, and I shall never that.

What does achieve the desired results is the requirement that what is preposed or changed to *that* be an NP.

Second, the order of rules (a) and (b) is irrelevant now, since *that* can appear either after *do* or *be* or in its preposed position. Beginning with the initial sentence of (64), we derive

(95)   She taught me to bake a cake, and bake a cake I couldn't do before.

by applying (a) alone,

(96)   She taught me to bake a cake, and I couldn't do that before.

by applying (b) alone, and:

(97)   She taught me to bake a cake, and that I couldn't do before.

by applying both rules. Similarly, beginning with (80), we derive

(98)  I saw that Irma was easy to please, and easy to please I should be too.

by applying (a) alone,

(99)  I saw that Irma was easy to please, and I should be that too.

by applying (b) alone, and:

(100)  I saw that Irma was easy to please, and that I should be too.

by applying both rules.

A final minor point: a *do* occurring right after a stressed modal may be dropped. Thus, sentences (57) and (65) have a variant form with final *do*:

(101)  They said she could play the marimba, which she can (do).

In this section I have considered two types of NR sentences, showing how both are related to near-surface conjunctions, and how NR sentences of Type II provide evidence for two hypotheses, one that activity sentences have at some level *do* as main verb, and the other that only at a fairly superficial level must the phrase following *do* or *be* be an NP.

## 4.  Summary

I have tried to present some heretofore unexamined evidence that both restrictive and nonrestrictive relative clauses must be derived from underlying conjunctions, and that this can be achieved in a grammar with certain well-motivated and fairly traditional restrictions on what aspects of the meaning of a sentence are to be represented in its underlying representation.[5]

---

[5] As this paper was going to press, Perlmutter and Ross (1970) appeared, in which it was proposed that sentences like

(i) A man entered the room and a woman went out who were quite similar.
"present the theory with a new paradox." In their words,

> Neither of these singular noun phrases can serve as the antecedent of a relative clause whose predicate (*similar*) requires an underlying plural subject, and whose verb (*were*) is inflected to agree with a plural subject in surface structure. The only possible antecedent of the relative clause in (i) would seem to be the discontinuous noun phrase *a man . . . (and) a woman*. But how can a discontinuous noun phrase be the antecedent of a relative clause? No analysis of relative clauses that has yet been proposed for the theory of generative grammar is able to account for sentences like (i).

I would like to point out that sentences such as (i) [which are indeed anomalous in a traditional embedding analysis of relative clause sentences] present no paradox at all if relative · clause sentences are viewed as underlying conjunctions; the conjunction source for (i) would simply be:

(ii) (Man entered room) (woman went out of room) (man and woman were similar).

## REFERENCES TO 'THE DEEP STRUCTURE OF RELATIVE CLAUSES'

Bach, E. 1968. Nouns and noun-phrases. In: Universals in linguistic theory. Edited by E. Bach and R. Harms. New York: Holt, Rinehart and Winston. 90-122.

Chomsky, N. 1957. Syntactic structures. The Hague: Mouton.

Chomsky, N. 1965. Aspects of the theory of syntax. Cambridge, Mass.: The MIT Press.

Drubig, B. 1968. Some remarks on relative clauses in English. Journal of English as a Second Language 3:2.23-40.

Fillmore, C. 1968. The case for case. In: Universals in linguistic theory. Edited by E. Bach and R. Harms. New York: Holt, Rinehart and Winston. 1-90.

Lakoff, G. 1966. Deep and surface grammar. Unpublished paper.

Langendoen, D. T. 1969. The study of syntax. New York: Holt, Rinehart and Winston.

Perlmutter, D., and J. R. Ross. 1970. Relative clauses with split antecedents. Linguistic Inquiry 1.350.

Postal, P. 1967. Restrictive relative clauses and other matters. Unpublished paper.

Rosenbaum, P., and R. Jacobs. 1968. English transformational grammar. Waltham, Mass.: Blaisdell.

Ross, J. R. 1967a. Auxiliaries as main verbs. [In: Linguistic Institute Packet of Papers 1968, University of Illinois. Also published 1969, in Studies in Philosophical Linguistics 1:1.77-102.]

Ross, J. R. 1967b. Constraints on variables in syntax. Unpublished doctoral dissertation. MIT.

Ross, J. R. 1969. Adjectives as noun phrases. Modern studies in English. Englewood Cliffs, N.J.: Prentice-Hall. 352-360.

Thompson, S. 1968. Relative clauses and conjunctions. The Ohio State University Working Papers in Linguistics 1.80-99.

## QUESTIONS

**Question 1.** One of Thompson's main arguments (Section 1C) for a conjoined source for relative clauses (henceforth RCs) is that RCs are 'structurally superfluous'--the sentences containing them would still be complete (and grammatical) if they were left out. Consider various adverbial clauses of purpose, reason, etc. A few examples are given in (i) through (v).

(i) I did it to make you happy.
(ii) I'll do it whether you want me to or not.
(iii) I did it because I wanted to.
(iv) I did it while standing on my head.
(v) I did it as if I were used to it.

Are these adverbial clauses structurally superfluous? Do all these examples (and those you may have added) have plausible sources with two independent conjoined or juxtaposed clauses?

**\*\*Question 2.** In Section 2A (Assumptions), Thompson forestalls any criticism of her analysis which centers on the problems of getting the proper determiners, numerals, and quantifiers in the conjoined source Ss, while maintaining the paraphrase relationship with the RC sentence. An alternative analysis (Smith 1964) of restrictive RCs has them modifying the determiner of the NP (rather than the N or the NP itself), while the determiner as a whole modifies the N. The Relativization transformation then extraposes the RC as shown in (i).

(i)

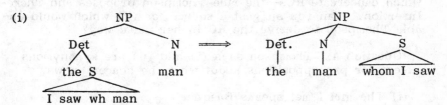

In this analysis, numerals and quantifiers are not generated 'outside the clause in which they ultimately appear'. Instead, their close structural connection with the relative clause naturally captures the semantic interdependence of the two.

This is similar to Bresnan's (1973) analysis of comparatives, shown in (ii), where the comparative clause modifies not the Adj but the determiner of the Adj.

(ii)

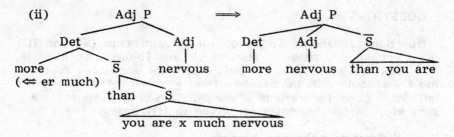

(iii) Though we are both quite calm, I'm more nervous than you are.

In (iii), is the comparative clause structurally superfluous? Can you suggest a source for (iii) which has independent conjoined clauses? If you can, is it synonymous with (iii)? If you can't, can you modify Thompson's suggestions in Section 2A for handling the determiners of NPs so that they will take care of the determiners of Adj Ps, too?

*Question 3. Thompson implies in Section 2B that (ii) is derived from (i).

(i) (A) girl speaks Basque.
(ii) There's a girl who speaks Basque.

Here, then, we have a main clause with a RC whose source is one unconjoined clause. Thus there are now two transformations which can create RCs--the rule Thompson proposes and *There*-Insertion. Can you suggest a source for (ii) which would enable Thompson to derive the RC in her usual way?

*Question 4. Thompson says (i) and (ii) are synonymous except for presuppositions about what the hearer knows.

(i) The girl I met speaks Basque.
(ii) I met the girl who speaks Basque.

This is clearly not the case for Ss with generic NPs (sentences (iii) and (iv) are not synonymous), which is why Thompson suggested a nonconjoined source for them in Section 2C.

(iii) A man who smokes a pipe looks distinguished.
(iv) A man who looks distinguished smokes a pipe.

What about predicates such as *look for*?

(v) I'm looking for a/the doctor who can cure boils.
(vi) A/The doctor who I'm looking for can cure boils.

Are (v) and (vi) synonymous? If not, is the difference in meaning the same as that between (i) and (ii)? (See Perlmutter 1970 for further discussion.)

**Question 5.** In Section 2C there is a somewhat confusing discussion of an ambiguous sentence--confusing partly because it is difficult to imagine a paradox to be true, but also because not all the readings are tracked down. Sentence (i) (Thompson's example (21)) is supposed to paraphrase the paradox reading of (ii) (Thompson's example (15)) and to have (iii) (Thompson's example (20)) as its source.

   (i) Charley assumed that the book which was not burned
       was burned.
  (ii) Charley assumed that the book which was burned
       was not burned.
 (iii) Charley assumed ((book burned) (book not burned))

But is (i) not itself ambiguous? If so, what would its other source be?

*Question 6.** Thompson says that (i) is generally assumed to be the source of (ii).

   (i) If a man smokes a pipe, he will look distinguished.
  (ii) Men who smoke pipes look distinguished.

Actually, it is more likely that (i) is the source of (iii), while (ii) has a slightly more complicated derivation.

  (iii) A man who smokes a pipe will look distinguished.

But Thompson's point about *if-then* sentences and restrictive RCs with generic head nouns remains, and there are good arguments to support the relationship. Two characteristics of *if-then* Ss are those in (A) and (B).

  (A) They allow negative polarity items like *any* in the *if*
     clause even when they contain no negation.
     (If a man has any brains, he goes far.)
  (B) They allow (in some dialects) subjunctives in the *if*
     clause.
     (If a man were to speak thus, he would be stoned.)

Do the corresponding restrictive RCs with generic head nouns have the same characteristics? What about *non*restrictive RCs with generic head nouns and restrictive RCs with *non*generic head nouns? Give examples.

**Question 7.** Thompson points out that (i) through (iii) are ambiguous as to whether the subject or the speaker is asserting the nonrestrictive RC, but she does not elaborate on this analysis.

(i) I dreamt that Rebecca, who was a friend of mine from college, was on the phone.
(ii) Harold says that his girlfriend, who is a little bit crazy, wants to go to Hanoi.
(iii) The claims agent said that the paint job, which should have been done long ago, would cost $150.

Ignoring noncrucial details, draw the two underlying structures (one for each reading) of each of these Ss.

*Question 8. Thompson says that (i) and (ii) are synonymous except for presuppositions about what the hearer knows, and that the difference between them should not be represented structurally.

(i) The boy, who works at the library, is majoring in philosophy.
(ii) The boy who works at the library is majoring in philosophy.

However, these examples work so well only because the class of boys is assumed to be large. Consider examples such as (iii) and (iv).

(iii) My son, who works at the library, is majoring in philosophy.
(iv) My son who works at the library is majoring in philosophy.

Do (iii) and (iv) introduce different assumptions about how many sons I have? Can Thompson's explanation of the difference between restrictive and nonrestrictive RCs handle all of the cases in (v) through (xi)?

(v) John, who is tall, arrived late.
  *John who is tall arrived late.
(vi) Earth's moon, which has a period of 28 days, influences the tides.
  ??Earth's moon which has a period of 28 days influences the tides.
(vii) *She greeted me with a warmth, which was surprising.
  She greeted me with a warmth which was surprising.
  She greeted me with a surprising warmth.
(viii) ??I'm accustomed to a lifestyle, which is debauched.
  I'm accustomed to a lifestyle which is debauched.
  I'm accustomed to a debauched lifestyle.

(ix) *The pains, which she took with my education, were heartening.
The pains which she took with my education were heartening.
(x) *The measures, to which he resorted, were unheard of.
The measures to which he resorted were unheard of.
(xi) *The headway, which we made, was encouraging.
The headway which we made was encouraging.

*Question 9. In deriving both restrictive and nonrestrictive RCs from conjunctions, Thompson runs into problems with numerals, as in (i) and (ii) (her examples (51) and (52)).

(i) Three boys who had beards were at the party.
(ii) Three boys, who had beards, were at the party.

Her analysis works in a straightforward way for (ii) but not (i). Would the analysis discussed in Question 2 (which generates RCs in the determiner) help here?

**Question 10. Thompson claims that Ss such as (i) are derived from Ss such as (ii).

(i) She dances well, which I don't/do, too.
(ii) She dances well, but I don't.
She dances well, and I do, too.

However, for some people at least, (iii) is ungrammatical, even though (iv), the putative sources of it, are fine.

(iii) *She doesn't dance well, which I do/don't either.
(iv) She doesn't dance well, but I do.
She doesn't dance well, and I don't either.

Notice also the ungrammaticality of (v) as opposed to (vi) and (vii).

(v) *Nothing which you did...
(vi) Nothing that you did...
(vii) Something which you did...

What could explain the ungrammaticality of (iii) and (v)? Is *which* in questions different from other WH words in the presuppositions it introduces, the kind of answer it expects? Could there be a restriction on *which* covering its use both in questions and in RCs? If so, try to formulate it in a way that accounts for both uses in one statement.

**Question 11. In Section 3B Thompson sidesteps a very interesting issue in saying that (i) cannot be the source of (ii), and so (iii) must be. Another possibility is that (iv) is the source of (ii).

(i) *I realized that Art had visited the Dean, and I should Art visit the Dean, too.
(ii) I realized that Art had visited the Dean, which I should do, too.
(iii) I realized that Art had visited the Dean, and I should visit the Dean, too.
(iv) [I realized that Art had visited the Dean, and I should I visit the Dean, too]

Sentence (iv) would call for an analysis of modals involving (obligatory) Equi NP Deletion, an analysis which was called into question in the homework problems for the Perlmutter article in this book. It is, however, instructive for us to consider (iv) here.

Another alternative which would be considered today as a source for (ii) is (v).

(v) [I realized that Art had visited the Dean, and I should $t$ visit the Dean, too]

In (v) the $t$ is the trace left behind after Raising into Subject Position, according to Chomsky's trace theory. (In trace theory every movement of an NP leaves behind a $t$ in the original position of the NP. See Chomsky 1976, among others. Note that Chomsky himself would not propose (v) as a source for anything, since he generates modals in the Aux.)

Notice that what (iv) and (v) have in common is that the clause embedded under *should* does not have a subject identical to that of *Art had visited the Dean*. Thus in deriving (ii) from either (iv) or (v), one might protest that the VP of the clause embedded under *should* cannot be deleted under identity with the VP of the clause *Art had visited the Dean* because the two VPs, being in clauses with different tenses and different subjects, are not identical. But apparently, the linguistic identity required for recovery of deletion is not always an exact one, as the following examples suggest. (Some of these examples require inexact ('sloppy') identity only on one reading of an ambiguity.)

(vi) Tom visited his father, which I should do, too.
(vii) Matilda got her arm broken in the accident, and I did, too.
(viii) Fern said she was tired and William did, too.
(ix) Vern didn't kill himself, nor will I.

Can you formulate a statement of what must and what need not be identical in order for VP Deletion to operate? Are other deletion rules constrained similarly?

Question 12. One of Thompson's major points is that both restrictive and nonrestrictive RCs come from conjoined sources. But note the following difference:

(i) a. Whales, which are mammals, are huge.
(i) b. *Whales, that are mammals, are huge.
(ii) a. Whales which live in the North Sea are vicious.
(ii) b. Whales that live in the North Sea are vicious.

Could we explain the distribution of *that* with Thompson's claims about the speaker's presuppositions or do we need to appeal to a structural difference between restrictive and nonrestrictive RCs?

**Question 13. Three proposed ways of generating relative clauses are: (1) as conjuncts to the clauses that end up containing them, (2) as embedded under an NP in the following way:

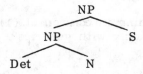

and (3) as embedded under the determiner node (as illustrated in Question 2). Consider the following examples of 'stacked' RCs.

(i) I want to buy a watch that keeps good time that's cheap.
(ii) The colt that our stallion sired that grew up in Indiana won the Derby.
(iii) The students who followed the march who evaded the police caused the trouble.

(These examples are from Stockwell, Schachter, and Partee 1973, Chapter 7.) Give the underlying structure and derivation for each of these examples in each of the three analyses. Discuss the problems which arise in each analysis and give arguments for which analysis can best handle stacked relatives.

HOMEWORK PROBLEMS

Answer Questions 5, 8, and 9 as homework problems along with the following problem.

I. In Section 2B Thompson argues that which conjoined clause becomes the relative is dependent on the speaker's presuppositions. In Section 2C Thompson says that relatives involving generic heads do not come from conjoined clauses. Consider example (1).

(1) A man smokes a pipe and he looks distinguished; a woman smokes a pipe and she looks silly.

Thompson must block Relativization from applying to (1) to give (2).

(2) A man who looks distinguished smokes a pipe; a woman who looks silly smokes a pipe.

Yet there is a reading of (1) which is synonymous with (3).

(3) A man who smokes a pipe looks distinguished; a woman who smokes a pipe looks silly.

Presumably Thompson would derive (3) from (4).

(4) If a man smokes a pipe, he looks distinguished; if a woman smokes a pipe, she looks silly.

How can Thompson account for the reading in common of (1), (3), and (4)? Does this problem arise only with generics? Consider (5).

(5) John lights a pipe and (suddenly) he looks the part of a professor.

In light of (5), must Thompson's analysis of RCs account for the identical readings of (1), (3), and (4), or is there something else interfering here? (You are not expected to give an elaborate analysis of (5) or (1), although some attempt at an analysis would be worthwhile. Rather, you should try to point out the general problem here.)

## SUGGESTED READINGS

Bresnan, J. 1973. Syntax of the comparative clause construction in English. Linguistic Inquiry 4:3.275-344. (For Question 2.)

Chomsky, N. 1976. Conditions on rules of grammar. Linguistic Analysis 2:4.303-351. (For Question 11.)

Dean, J. 1967. Determiners and relative clauses. Unpublished paper. MIT.

Green, G. 1973. Some remarks on split controller phenomena. CLS 9.123-138. (For more discussion of the kind of problem brought up in Thompson's footnote 5.)

Hale, K. 1975. Gaps in grammar and culture. In: Linguistics and anthropology: In honor of C. F. Voegelin. Lisse, The Netherlands: The Peter de Ridder Press. 295-317.

Hankamer, J., and I. Sag. 1976. Deep and surface anaphora. Linguistic Inquiry 7:3.391-428.

Jackendoff, R. 1968. Speculations on presentences and determiners. Unpublished paper. MIT.

Kuroda, S.-Y. 1968. English relativization and certain related problems. Lg. 44:2.244-266.

Perlmutter, D. 1970. On the article in English. Progress in linguistics. The Hague: Mouton. 233-248. (For Question 4.)

Pope, E. 1976. Questions and answers in English. The Hague: Mouton. (For Question 10, see pp. 63-65.)

Rando, E., and D. J. Napoli. 1978. Definites in *there*-sentences. Lg. 54:2.300-313.

Smith, C. 1964. Determiners and relative clauses in a generative grammar of English. Lg. 40:1.37-52. (For Question 2.)

Stockwell, R., P. Schachter, and B. H. Partee. 1973. The major syntactic structures of English. New York: Holt, Rinehart and Winston. (For Question 13, see Chapter 7.)

Ziv, Y. 1976. On the communicative function of relative clause extraposition in English. Unpublished doctoral dissertation. University of Illinois. Urbana, Illinois.

# 5

## REMARKS ON NOMINALIZATION

Noam Chomsky

Introduction. 'Remarks on Nominalization' is a dense, complex argument for one of the two positions taken in the first major divisive controversy within generative grammar--a controversy from which most subsequent ones have stemmed. Lexicalism has led, historically if not necessarily logically, to interpretive semantics and a fairly conservative approach to syntax, including adherence to the notion of deep structure. In the same way, transformationalism has led to generative semantics, global and transderivational rules, and the rejection of the notion of deep structure.

Chomsky's argument rests on four main points, and does not really stand or fall on the long though interesting discussions of how his proposals would be worked out in detail. Three of the points he groups together in what is now a classic form of syntactic argumentation. If a V with its surrounding S and a N with its surrounding NP are related transformationally, the relationship should be (1) productive--there should be a NP corresponding to nearly every sort of S, (2) meaning-preserving --the meanings of the two phrases should differ in only a limited, consistent, and easily specifiable way, and (3) structure-preserving--the NP should still look very much like a S, allowing few of the elements which occur only in NPs.

The fourth point is a sort of converse of the third. After showing that the base rules generating regular NP elements such as Det and Adj are needed to generate and properly place elements found in derived nominals, Chomsky shows that the base and transformational rules needed to generate and place the complements and possessive agents of derived nominals are also needed in regular NPs. For instance, while we need a transformation changing *John has left* into *John's having left*, we also need a base rule generating possessives like *John's*, as is,

136

in prenominal position. Chomsky's point here is that deriving from sentences all nominals that might be derived from sentences does not simplify the NP base rules. On the other hand, generating some of these nominals in the base does not complicate the NP base rules. At least two sources for possessives, etc., are needed independently. The only question is where the dividing line should fall.

Incidentally, the notion that transformationally derived structures echo base structures anticipates Emonds' structure-preserving hypothesis (see Emonds 1972, reprinted in Chapter 6 of this volume).

# Remarks on Nominalization[1]

## NOAM CHOMSKY

For the purposes of this paper, I will assume without question a certain framework of principles and will explore some of the problems that arise when they are applied in the study of a central area of the syntax of English, and, presumably, any human language.[2]

A person who has learned a language has acquired a system of rules that relate sound and meaning in a certain specific way. He has, in other words, acquired a certain competence that he puts to use in producing and understanding speech. The central task of descriptive linguistics is to construct grammars of specific languages, each of which seeks to characterize in a precise way the competence that has been acquired by a speaker of this language. The theory of grammar attempts to discover the formal conditions that must be satisfied by a system of rules that qualifies as the grammar of a human language, the principles that govern the empirical interpretation of such a system, and the factors that determine the selection of a system of the appropriate form on the basis of the data available to the language learner. Such a "universal grammar" (to modify slightly a traditional usage) prescribes a schema that defines implicitly the infinite class of "attainable grammars"; it formulates principles that determine how each such system relates sound and meaning; it provides a procedure of evaluation for grammars of the appropriate form. Abstractly, and under a radical but quite useful idealization, we may then think of language-learning as the process of selecting a grammar of the appropriate form that relates sound and meaning in a way consistent with the available data and that is valued as highly, in terms of the evaluation measure, as any grammar meeting these empirical conditions.

I will assume that a grammar contains a base consisting of a categorial component (which I will assume to be a context-free grammar) and a lexicon. The lexicon consists of lexical entries, each of which is a system of specified features. The nonterminal vocabulary of the context-free grammar is drawn from a universal and rather limited vocabulary, some aspects of which will be considered below. The context-free grammar generates phrase-markers, with a dummy symbol as one of the terminal elements. A general principle of lexical insertion permits lexical entries to replace the dummy symbol in ways determined by their feature content. The formal object constructed in this way is a *deep structure*. The grammar contains a system of transformations, each of which maps phrase-markers into phrase-markers. Application of a sequence of transformations to a deep structure, in accordance with certain universal conditions and certain particular constraints of the grammar in question, determines ultimately a phrase-marker which we call a *surface structure*. The base and the transformational rules constitute the syntax. The grammar contains phonological rules that assign to each surface structure a phonetic representation in a universal phonetic alphabet. Furthermore, it contains semantic rules that assign to each paired deep and surface structure generated by the syntax a semantic interpretation, presumably, in a universal semantics, concerning which little is known in any detail. I will assume, furthermore, that grammatical relations are defined in a general way in terms of configurations within phrase-markers and that semantic interpretation involves only those grammatical relations specified in deep structures (although it may also involve certain properties of surface structures). I will be concerned here with problems of syntax exclusively; it is clear, however, that phonetic and semantic considerations provide empirical conditions of adequacy that must be met by the syntactic rules.

As anyone who has studied grammatical structures in detail is well aware, a grammar is a tightly organized system; a modification of one part generally involves widespread modifications of other facets. I will make various tacit assumptions about the grammar of English, holding certain parts constant and dealing with questions that arise with regard to properties of other parts of the grammar.

In general, it is to be expected that enrichment of one component of the grammar will permit simplification in other parts. Thus certain descriptive problems can be handled by enriching the lexicon and simplifying the categorial component of the base, or conversely; or by simplifying the base at the cost of greater complexity of transformations, or conversely. The proper balance between various components of the grammar is entirely an empirical issue. We have no a priori insight into the "trading relation" between the various parts. There are no general considerations that settle this matter. In particular, it is senseless to look to the evaluation procedure for the correct answer. Rather, the evaluation procedure must itself be selected on empirical grounds so as to provide whatever answer it is that is correct. It would be pure dogmatism to maintain, without empirical evidence, that the categorial component, or the lexicon, or the transformational component must be narrowly constrained by universal conditions, the variety and complexity of language being attributed to the other components.

Crucial evidence is not easy to obtain, but there can be no doubt as to the empirical nature of the issue. Furthermore, it is often possible to obtain evidence that is relevant to the correct choice of an evaluation measure and hence, indirectly, to the correct decision as to the variety and complexity that universal grammar permits in the several components of the grammar.[3]

To illustrate the problem in an artificially isolated case, consider such words as *feel*, which, in surface structure, take predicate phrases as complements. Thus we have such sentences as:

(1)   John felt angry (sad, weak, courageous, above such things, inclined to agree to their request, sorry for what he did, etc.).

We might introduce such expressions into English grammar in various ways. We might extend the categorial component of the base, permitting structures of the form noun phrase–verb–predicate, and specifying *feel* in the lexicon as an item that can appear in prepredicate position in deep structures. Alternatively, we might exclude such structures from the base, and take the deep structures to be of the form noun phrase–verb–sentence, where the underlying structure *John felt* [$_S$*John be sad*]$_S$[4] is converted to *John felt sad* by a series of transformations. Restricting ourselves to these alternatives for the sake of the illustrative example, we see that one approach extends the base, treating *John felt angry* as a NP–V–Pred expression roughly analogous to *his hair turned gray* or *John felt anger* (NP–V–NP), while the second approach extends the transformational component, treating *John felt angry* as a NP–V–S expression roughly analogous to *John believed that he would win* or *John felt that he was angry*. A priori considerations give us no insight into which of these approaches is correct. There is, in particular, no a priori concept of "evaluation" that informs us whether it is "simpler," in an absolute sense, to complicate the base or the transformation.

There is, however, relevant empirical evidence, namely, regarding the semantic interpretation of these sentences.[5] To feel angry is not necessarily to feel that one is angry or to feel oneself to be angry; the same is true of most of the other predicate expressions that appear in such sentences as (1). If we are correct in assuming that it is the grammatical relations of the deep structure that determine the semantic interpretation, it follows that the deep structure of (1) must not be of the NP–V–S form, and that, in fact, the correct solution is to extend the base. Some supporting evidence from syntax is that many sentences of the form (1) appear with the progressive aspect (*John is feeling angry*, like *John is feeling anger*, etc.), but the corresponding sentences of the form NP–V–S do not (* *John is feeling that he is angry*). This small amount of syntactic and semantic evidence therefore suggests that the evaluation procedure must be selected in such a way as to prefer an elaboration of the base to an elaboration of the transformational component in such a case as this. Of course this empirical hypothesis is extremely strong; the evaluation procedure is a part of universal grammar, and when made precise, the proposal of the preceding sentence will have large-scale effects in the grammars of all languages, effects which must be tested against the empirical evidence exactly as in the single case just cited.

This paper will be devoted to another example of the same general sort, one that is much more crucial for the study of English structure and of linguistic theory as a whole.

Among the various types of nominal expressions in English there are two of particular importance, each roughly of propositional form. Thus corresponding to the sentences of (2) we have the gerundive nominals of (3) and the derived nominals of (4):[6]

(2)    a. John is eager to please.
       b. John has refused the offer.
       c. John criticized the book.

(3)    a. John's being eager to please
       b. John's refusing the offer
       c. John's criticizing the book

(4)    a. John's eagerness to please
       b. John's refusal of the offer
       c. John's criticism of the book

Many differences have been noted between these two types of nominalization. The most striking differences have to do with the productivity of the process in question, the generality of the relation between the nominal and the associated proposition, and the internal structure of the nominal phrase.

Gerundive nominals can be formed fairly freely from propositions of subject–predicate form, and the relation of meaning between the nominal and the proposition is quite regular. Furthermore, the nominal does not have the internal structure of a noun phrase; thus we cannot replace *John's* by any determiner (e.g., *that, the*) in (3), nor can we insert adjectives into the gerundive nominal. These are precisely the consequences that follow, without elaboration or qualifications, from the assumption that gerundive nominalization involves a grammatical transformation from an underlying sentencelike structure. We might assume that one of the forms of NP introduced by rules of the categorial component of the base is (5), and that general rules of affix placement give the freely generated surface forms of the gerundive nominal:[7]

(5)    $[_S NP \; nom \; (Aspect) \; VP]_S$

The semantic interpretation of a gerundive nominalization is straightforward in terms of the grammatical relations of the underlying proposition in the deep structure.

Derived nominals such as (4) are very different in all of these respects. Productivity is much more restricted, the semantic relations between the associated proposition and the derived nominal are quite varied and idiosyncratic, and the nominal has the internal structure of a noun phrase. I will comment on these matters directly. They raise the question of whether the derived nominals are, in fact, transformationally related to the associated propositions. The question, then, is analogous to that raised earlier concerning the status of verbs such as *feel*. We might extend the base rules to accommodate the derived nominal directly (I will refer to this as the "lexicalist position"), thus simplifying the transformational component; or, alternatively, we might simplify the base structures, excluding these forms, and derive them by some extension of the transformational apparatus (the "transformationalist position"). As in the illustrative example discussed earlier, there is no a priori insight into universal grammar — specifically, into the nature of an evaluation measure — that bears on this question, which is a purely empirical one. The problem is to find empirical evidence that supports one or the other of the alternatives. It is, furthermore, quite possible to imagine a compromise solution that adopts the lexicalist position for certain items and the transformationalist position for others. Again, this is entirely an empirical issue. We must fix the principles of universal grammar — in particular, the character of the evaluation measure — so that it provides the description that is factually correct, noting as before that any such hypothesis about universal grammar must also be tested against the evidence from other parts of English grammar and the grammars of other languages.

In the earliest work on transformational grammar [cf. Lees (1960)], the correctness of the transformationalist position was taken for granted; and, in fact, there was really no alternative as the theory of grammar was formulated at that time. However, the extension of grammatical theory to incorporate syntactic features [as in Chomsky (1965, Chapter 2)] permits a formulation of the lexicalist position, and therefore raises the issue of choice between the alternatives.[8] My purpose here is to investigate the lexicalist position and to explore some of the consequences that it suggests for the theory of syntax more generally.

Consider first the matter of productivity. As noted above, the transformation that gives gerundive nominals applies quite freely.[9] There are, however, many restrictions on the formation of derived nominals. The structures underlying (6), for example, are transformed to the gerundive nominals of (7) but not to the derived nominals of (8):

(6) a.  John is easy (difficult) to please.
    b.  John is certain (likely) to win the prize.
    c.  John amused (interested) the children with his stories.

(7) a.  John's being easy (difficult) to please
    b.  John's being certain (likely) to win the prize
    c.  John's amusing (interesting) the children with his stories

(8)  a. * John's easiness (difficulty) to please
     b. * John's certainty (likelihood) to win the prize
     c. * John's amusement (interest) of the children with his stories

There are, of course, derived nominals that superficially resemble those of (8), for example, those of (9), which pair with the gerundive nominals of (10):

(9)  a. John's eagerness to please [(2a), (4a)]
     b. John's certainty that Bill will win the prize
     c. John's amusement at (interest in) the children's antics

(10) a. John's being eager to please [(2a), (3a)]
     b. John's being certain that Bill will win the prize
     c. John's being amused at (interested in) the children's antics

These discrepancies between gerundive and derived nominals call for explanation. Specifically, we must determine why the examples of (8) are ruled out although those of (9) are permitted.[10]

The idiosyncratic character of the relation between the derived nominal and the associated verb has been so often remarked that discussion is superfluous. Consider, for example, such nominals as *laughter, marriage, construction, actions, activities, revolution, belief, doubt, conversion, permutation, trial, residence, qualifications, specifications,* and so on, with their individual ranges of meaning and varied semantic relations to the base forms. There are a few subregularities that have frequently been noted, but the range of variation and its rather accidental character are typical of lexical structure. To accommodate these facts within the transformational approach (assuming, as above, that it is the grammatical relations in the deep structure that determine meaning) it is necessary to resort to the artifice of assigning a range of meanings to the base form, stipulating that with certain semantic features the form must nominalize and with others it cannot. Furthermore, the appeal to this highly unsatisfactory device, which reduces the hypothesis that transformations do not have semantic content to near vacuity, would have to be quite extensive.[11]

The third major difference noted above between gerundive and derived nominals is that only the latter have the internal structure of noun phrases. Thus we can have such expressions as *the proof of the theorem* (* *the proving the theorem,* with a gerundive nominal), *John's unmotivated criticism of the book* (* *John's unmotivated criticizing the book*), and so on. Correspondingly, the derived nominals cannot contain aspect; there is no derived nominal analogous to *John's having criticized the book.* Furthermore, many derived nominals pluralize and occur with the full range of determiners (*John's three proofs of the theorem, several of John's proofs of the theorem,* etc.). And derived nominals, in fact, can appear freely in the full range of noun phrase structures. For example, the sentence *John gave Bill advice* is just like any other indirect object structure in that it has the double passive[*advice was* *given (to) Bill, Bill was given advice*]. It is difficult to see how a transformational approach to derived nominals can account for the fact that the structures in which they appear as well as their internal structure and, often, morphological properties, are those of ordinary noun phrases. None of these problems arises, as noted earlier, in the case of gerundive nominals.

These properties of derived nominals are quite consistent with a lexicalist approach and, in part, can even be explained from this point of view. Before going into this matter, let us elaborate the lexicalist position in slightly greater detail.

I noted earlier that the lexicalist position was not formulable within the framework of syntactic theory available at the time of Lees's work on nominalizations. The problem was that the obvious generalizations concerning the distributional properties of the base and derived forms were expressible, in that framework, only in terms of grammatical transformations. There was no other way to express the fact that the contexts in which *refuse* appears as a verb and *refusal* as a noun are closely related. However, when the lexicon is separated from the categorial component of the base and its entries are analyzed in terms of contextual features, this difficulty disappears. We can enter *refuse* in the lexicon as an item with certain fixed selectional and strict subcategorization features, which is free with respect to the categorial features [noun] and [verb]. Fairly idiosyncratic morphological rules will determine the phonological form of *refuse, destroy*, etc., when these items appear in the noun position. The fact that *refuse* takes a noun phrase complement or a reduced sentential complement and *destroy* only a noun phrase complement, either as a noun or as a verb, is expressed by the feature structure of the "neutral" lexical entry, as are selectional properties. Details aside, it is clear that syntactic features provide a great deal of flexibility for the expression of generalizations regarding distributional similarities. Hence what was a decisive objection to the lexicalist position no longer has any force.

Let us propose, then, as a tentative hypothesis, that a great many items appear in the lexicon with fixed selectional and strict subcategorization features, but with a choice as to the features associated with the lexical categories noun, verb, adjective. The lexical entry may specify that semantic features are in part dependent on the choice of one or another of these categorial features. This is, of course, the typical situation within the lexicon; in general, lexical entries involve certain Boolean conditions on features, expressing conditional dependencies of various sorts.[12] Insofar as there are regularities (cf. Note 11), these can be expressed by redundancy rules in the lexicon.

Consider now the problem of productivity noted above, specifically, the fact that we cannot form the derived nominals (8) corresponding to the sentences (6), although the structures underlying (6) can be transformed to the gerundive nominals (7), and we can form the derived nominals (9) associated with the gerundive nominals (10).

Consider first the examples *John is easy to please, John is eager to please,* only the second of which is associated with a derived nominal. This consequence follows immediately from the lexicalist hypothesis just formulated, when we take into account certain properties of the items *eager* and *easy.* Thus *eager* must be introduced into the lexicon with a strict subcategorization feature indicating that it can take a sentential complement, as in *John is eager (for us) to please.* In the simplest case, then, it follows that in the noun position, *eager* will appear in the contexts *John's eagerness (for us) to please,* etc., with no further comment necessary. But *easy* (or *difficult*) does not appear in the lexicon with such a feature. There is no structure of the form . . . *easy (difficult) S* generated by base rules. Rather, *easy* (*difficult*) appears in base phrase-markers as an adjective predicated of propositions as subject [(*for us*) *to please John is easy,* etc.]; forms such as *it is easy (for us) to please John* are derived by extraposition.[13] Consequently, *easy* (or *difficult*) cannot be introduced by lexical insertion into the noun position with sentential complements, and we cannot derive such forms as (8a), *John's easiness (difficulty) to please.* No such restriction holds for gerundive nominalization, which, being a transformation, is applicable to transforms as well as to base phrase-markers.

Consider next the examples *\*John's certainty to win the prize* [= (8b)], *John's certainty that Bill will win the prize* [= (9b)]. Again, the lexicalist hypothesis provides an explanation for this distinction between the two senses of *certain.* The sentence *John is certain to win the prize* is derived by extraposition and pronoun replacement from a deep structure in which *certain* is predicated of the proposition *John — to win the prize,* as is clear from the meaning.[14] In this sense, *certain* does not permit a propositional complement; it therefore follows from the lexicalist hypothesis that there cannot be a derived nominal *certainty to win the prize,* in this sense. But *John is certain that Bill will win the prize derives* from *John is certain* [s *Bill will win the prize*]s. In the sense of *certain* in which it is predicated of a person, a propositional complement can be adjoined in the base. Consequently, the lexicalist hypothesis permits the associated derived nominal *John's certainty that Bill will win the prize,* generated by lexical insertion of *certain* in the noun position before a sentential complement.

Consider now examples (6c) through (10c). If derived nominals are formed by transformation, there is no reason why *\*John's amusement of the children with his stories* [= (8c)] should not be formed from the proposition that underlies the gerundive nominal *John's amusing the children with his stories,* just as *John's amusement at the children's antics* [= (9c)] would, on these grounds, be derived from the proposition that underlies the gerundive nominal *John's being amused at the children's antics* [= (10c)]. The discrepancy would be accounted for if we were to adopt the lexicalist position and, furthermore, to postulate that such sentences as *John amused the children with his stories* are themselves derived from an underlying structure of a different sort. The latter assumption is not unreasonable. Thus it is well-known that among the properties of verbs of the category of *amuse, interest,* etc., is the fact that there are paired sentences such as (11):

(11) a. He was amused at the stories.
b. The stories amused him.

The facts regarding derived nominals suggest that (11b) is derived from a structure that involves (11a); this would account for the similarities in semantic interpretation and distributional properties of (11a) and (11b), and would also, on the lexicalist hypothesis, account for the occurrence and nonoccurrence of derived nominals.[15] Although independent motivation for the assumption that (11a) underlies (11b) is weak, there appears to be no counterevidence suggesting that (11b) underlies (11a). One might, for example, derive (11b) quite plausibly from a "causative" construction with roughly the form of (12):

(12) The stories [+cause] [$_S$he was amused at the stories]$_S$

I return to such structures briefly below. There is some evidence in support of the assumption that a causative construction exists in English [cf. Chomsky (1965, p. 180); Lakoff (1965, Section 9)],[16] and the operation that erases the repeated noun phrase in the embedded proposition of (12) is of a sort found elsewhere, for example, in the derivation of such sentences as *John used the table to write on, John used the pen to write (with), John used the wall to lean the table against,* etc., from *John used the table* [$_S$*John wrote on the table*]$_S$, and so on.

Other examples for which a causative analysis has been suggested fall into the same pattern, with respect to formation of derived nominals. Consider, for example, the transitive use of *grow* as in *John grows tomatoes,* which might plausibly be derived from a structure such as (12), with *the stories* replaced by *John* in the subject position and the embedded proposition being the intransitive *tomatoes grow.* But consider the nominal phrase *the growth of tomatoes.* This is unambiguous; it has the interpretation of *tomatoes grow* but not of *John grows tomatoes.* If the latter is taken as a base form, there should be an associated derived nominal *the growth of tomatoes* with the same interpretation, just as we have the derived nominal *the rejection of the offer* associated with the transitive verb phrase *reject the offer.* If, on the other hand, the sentence *John grows tomatoes* is derived from a causative construction, the corresponding derived nominal is excluded (though not, of course, the corresponding nominalization *the growing of tomatoes* — we return to nominalizations of this type on p. 214). Hence the lack of ambiguity offers empirical support for a combination of the lexicalist hypothesis with the causative analysis, though not for either of these assumptions taken in isolation.

Summarizing these observations, we see that the lexicalist hypothesis explains a variety of facts of the sort illustrated by examples (6) through (10) [in part, in conjunction with other assumptions about underlying structures, such as (12)]. The transformationalist hypothesis is no doubt consistent with these facts, but it derives no support from them, since it would also be consistent with the discovery, were it a fact, that derived nominals exist in all cases in which we have gerundive nominals. Hence the facts that have been cited give strong empirical support to the lexicalist hypothesis and no support to the transformationalist hypothesis. Other things being equal, then, they would lead us to accept the lexicalist hypothesis, from which these facts follow.

If the lexicalist hypothesis is correct, we should expect that derived nominals will correspond to base structures rather than transforms. I will return to some problems, which may or may not be real, that arise in connection with this consequence of the lexicalist hypothesis. Notice, however, that there is other corroborating evidence. For example, there are many verbs in English that must be listed in the lexicon as verb–particle constructions [*look up* (*the information*), *define away* (*the problem*), etc.]. These forms undergo gerundive nominalization freely (*his looking up the information, his looking the information up, his defining away the problem, his defining the problem away*). The derived nominals, in general, are rather marginal, and hence not very informative. However, it seems to me that the forms of (13) are somewhat preferable to those of (14.)[17]

(13)    a.    his looking up of the information
        b.    his defining away of the problem

(14)    a.    * his looking of the information up
        b.    * his defining of the problem away

This consequence follows from the lexicalist assumption, if the forms of (13) are regarded as derived nominals (see Note 17).

Notice also that although gerundive nominalization applies freely to sentences with verb phrase adjuncts, this is not true of the rules for forming derived nominals. Thus we have (15) but not (16):[18]

(15)    his criticizing the book before he read it (because of its failure to go deeply into the matter, etc.)

(16)    * his criticism of the book before he read it (because of its failure to go deeply into the matter, etc.)

This too would follow from the lexicalist assumption, since true verb phrase adjuncts such as *before*-clauses and *because*-clauses will not appear as noun complements in base noun phrases.

The examples (15) and (16) raise interesting questions relating to the matter of acceptability and grammaticalness.[19] If the lexicalist hypothesis is correct, then all dialects of English that share the analysis of adjuncts presupposed above should distinguish the expressions of (15), as directly generated by the grammar, from those of (16), as not directly generated by the grammar. Suppose that we discover, however, that some speakers find the expressions of (16) quite acceptable. On the lexicalist hypothesis, these sentences can only be derivatively generated. Therefore we should have to conclude that their acceptability to these speakers results from a failure to take note of a certain distinction of grammaticalness. We might propose that the expressions of (16) are formed by analogy to the gerundive nominals (15), say by a rule that converts $X$ $-ing$ to the noun $X$ $nom$ (where $nom$ is the element that determines the morphological form of the derived nominal) in certain cases. There is no doubt that such processes of derivative generation exist as part of grammar in the most general sense (for some discussion, see *Aspects*, Chapter IV, Section 1, and references cited there). The question is whether in this case it is correct to regard (16) as directly generated or as derivatively generated, for the speakers in question. There is empirical evidence bearing on this matter. Thus if the expressions of (16) are directly generated, we would expect them to show the full range of use and meaning of such derived nominals as *his criticism of the book*. If, on the other hand, they are derivatively generated in the manner just suggested, we would expect them to have only the more restricted range of use and meaning of the expressions of (15) that underlie them. Crucial evidence, then, is provided by the contexts (17) in which the derived nominal *his criticism of the book* can appear, but not the gerundive nominals (15) (with or without the adjunct):

(17)   a. — is to be found on page 15.
        b. I studied — very carefully.

The fact seems to be that speakers who accept (16) do not accept (18) though they do accept (19):

(18)   a. *His criticism of the book before he read it* is to be found on page 15.
        b. I studied *his criticism of the book before he read it* very carefully.

(19)   a. *His criticism of the book* is to be found on page 15.
        b. I studied *his criticism of the book* very carefully.

If correct, this indicates that speakers who fail to distinguish (16) from (15) are not aware of a property of their internalized grammar, namely, that it generates (16) only derivatively, by analogy to the gerundive nominal. It would not be in the least surprising to discover that some speakers fail to notice a distinction of this sort. As we see, it is an empirical issue, and there is relevant factual evidence. This is a general problem that must be borne in mind when acceptability judgments are used, as they must be, to discover the grammar that is internalized. In the present instance, the lexicalist hypothesis receives convincing support if it is true that there are fundamentally two types of acceptability judgment: the first, acceptance of (19) but neither

(16) nor (18); the second, acceptance of (19) and (16) but not (18). It is difficult to see how the transformationalist hypothesis could accommodate either of these cases.

Returning to the main theme, notice that aspect will of course not appear in noun phrases and therefore, on the lexicalist hypothesis, will be absent from derived nominals (though not gerundive nominals).

Consider next the adjectives that appear with derived nominals, as in *John's sudden refusal* or *John's obvious sincerity*. Two sources immediately suggest themselves: one, from relatives (as *John's aged mother* might be derived from *John's mother, who is aged*); another, from adverbial constructions such as *John refused suddenly, John is obviously sincere*. The latter assumption, however, would presuppose that derived nominals can be formed from such structures as *John refused in such-and-such a manner, John was sincere to such-and-such an extent*, etc. This is not the case, however. We cannot have * *John's refusal in that manner* (*in a manner that surprised me*) or * *John's sincerity to that extent*. Furthermore, adjectives that appear with derived nominals often cannot appear (as adverbs) with the associated verbs: for example, we have *John's uncanny* (*amazing, curious, striking*) *resemblance to Bill* but not * *John resembled Bill uncannily* (*amazingly, curiously, strikingly*). We might propose to account for this by deriving *John's uncanny resemblance to Bill* from something like *the degree to which John resembles Bill, which is uncanny*. But this proposal, apart from the difficulty that it provides no way to exclude such phrases as * *their amazing destruction of the city* from *the degree to which they destroyed the city, which was amazing*, also runs into the difficulties of Note 11. Though there remain quite a number of interesting problems concerning adjectives in derived nominal (and many other) constructions, I see nothing that conflicts with the lexicalist hypothesis in this regard.

Evidence in favor of the lexicalist position appears to be fairly substantial. It is important, therefore, to look into the further consequences of this position, and the difficulties that stand in the way of incorporating it into the theory of syntax.

Suppose that such phrases as *eagerness* (*for John*) *to please, refusal of the offer, belief in a supreme being*, etc., are base noun phrases. Clearly, if this approach is to be pursued, then the rules of the categorial component of the base must introduce an extensive range of complements within the noun phrase, as they do within the verb phrase and the adjective phrase. As a first approximation, to be revised later on, we might propose that the rules of the categorial component include the following:

(20)  a. NP $\rightarrow$ N Comp
     b. VP $\rightarrow$ V Comp
     c. AP $\rightarrow$ A Comp

(21)  Comp $\rightarrow$ NP, S, NP S, NP Prep-P, Prep-P Prep-P, etc.

Is there any independent support, apart from the phenomena of derived nominalization, for such rules? An investigation of noun phrases shows that there is a good deal of support for a system such as this.

Consider such phrases as the following:[20]

(22) a. the *weather* in England
b. the *weather* in 1965
c. the *story* of Bill's exploits
d. the *bottom* of the barrel
e. the *back* of the room
f. the *message* from Bill to Tom about the meeting
g. a *war* of aggression against France
h. *atrocities* against civilians
i. the *author* of the book
j. John's *attitude* of defiance towards Bill
k. his *advantage* over his rivals
l. his *anguish* over his crimes
m. his *mercy* toward the victims
n. a *man* to do the job
o. a *house* in the woods
p. his *habit* of interrupting
q. the *reason* for his refusal
r. the *question* whether John should leave
s. the *prospects* for peace
t. the *algebra* of revolution
u. *prolegomena* to any future metaphysics
v. my *candidate* for a trip to the moon
w. a *nation* of shopkeepers

In each of these, and many similar forms, it seems to me to make very good sense — in some cases, to be quite necessary — to regard the italicized form as the noun of a determiner–noun–complement construction which constitutes a simple base noun phrase. The only alternative would be to regard the whole expression as a transform with the italicized element being a nominalized verb or adjective, or to take the complement to be a reduced relative clause. In such cases as those of (22), neither alternative seems to be at all motivated, although each has been proposed for certain of these examples. Space prevents a detailed analysis of each case, but a few remarks may be useful.

The analysis of the head noun as a nominalized verb requires that we establish abstract verbs that are automatically subject to nominalization. This requires devices of great descriptive power which should, correspondingly, be very "costly" in terms of a reasonable evaluation measure.[21] Nevertheless, it is an interesting possibility. Perhaps the strongest case for such an approach is the class of examples of which (22i) is an example. It has been argued, quite plausibly, that such phrases as *the owner of the house* derive from

underlying structures such as *the one who owns the house;* correspondingly
(22i) might be derived from the structure *the one who * auths the book,*
* *auth* being postulated as a verb that is lexically marked as obligatorily
subject to nominalization. However, the plausibility of this approach dimin-
ishes when one recognizes that there is no more reason to give this analysis
for (22i) than there is for *the general secretary of the party, the assistant
vice-chancellor of the university,* and similarly for every function that can
be characterized by a nominal phrase. Another fact sometimes put forth in
support of the analysis of these phrases as nominalizations is the ambiguity
of such expressions as *good dentist (dentist who is a good man, man who
is good as a dentist).* But this argument is also quite weak. The ambiguity,
being characteristic of all expressions that refer to humans by virtue of some
function that they fulfill, can be handled by a general principle of semantic
interpretation; furthermore, it is hardly plausible that the ambiguity of *good
assistant vice-chancellor* should be explained in this way.

For some of the cases of (22), an analysis in terms of reduced relatives
is plausible; for example, (22o). But even for such cases there are difficulties
in this approach. Notice that there are narrow restrictions on the head noun
in (22o). Thus we have the phrase *John's house in the woods* meaning *the
house of John's which is in the woods;* but we cannot form *John's book
(dog, brother, . . .) in the woods (on the table, . . .).* If John and I each have
a house in the woods, I can refer to his, with contrastive stress on *John's,*
as *JOHN'S house in the woods;* if we each have a book on the table, I cannot,
analogously, refer to his as *JOHN'S book on the table.* Such observations
suggest that the surface structure of *John's house in the woods* is *John's
— house in the woods,* with *house in the woods* being some sort of nominal
expression. On the other hand, in a true reduced relative such as *that book
on the table,* there is, presumably, no main constituent break before *book.*

The analysis as a reduced relative is also possible in the case of (22r) and
(22s). Thus we have such sentences as (23), with the associated noun phrases
of (24):

(23)    a. The question is whether John should leave.
        b. The prospects are for peace.
        c. The plan is for John to leave.
        d. The excuse was that John had left.

(24)    a. the question whether John should leave
        b. the prospects for peace
        c. the plan for John to leave
        d. the excuse that John had left

Despite the unnaturalness of relative clauses formed in the usual way with
(23) as the embedded proposition, one might argue that these are the sources
of (24), as reduced relatives. Alternatively, one might argue that the sentences

of (23) are derived from structures incorporating (24). The latter assumption is far more plausible however. Thus there are no such sentences as (25):

(25) a. * The question whether John should leave is why Bill stayed.
b. * The prospects for peace are for a long delay.
c. * The plan for John to leave is that Bill should stay.
d. * The excuse that John had left was that Bill should stay.

Under the reduced relative assumption, there is no reason why (25) should be ruled out. This would be explained, however, if we assumed that such sentences as (23) are derived from structures incorporating the base noun phrases (24); for example, it might be proposed that (23) derives from (26) by replacement of the unspecified predicate $\Delta$ by the complement of the subject noun:

(26) $[_{NP} \text{ Det N Comp }]_{NP}$ be $[_{Pred} \Delta]_{Pred}{}^{22}$

Under this analysis, the copula serves as a kind of existential operator. Structures such as (26) are motivated by other data as well; for example, as the matrix structure for such sentences as *what John did was hurt himself,* which might be derived from $[_{NP} \textit{ it that John hurt John}]_{NP}$ be $[_{Pred} \Delta]_{Pred}$, through a series of operations to which we return below. In any event, there is an argument for taking the forms of (24) to underlie (23), rather than conversely.

The structures (22), and others like them, raise many problems; they do, however, suggest quite strongly that there are base noun phrases of the form determiner–noun–complement, quite apart from nominalizations. In fact, the range of noun complements seems almost as great as the range of verb complements, and the two sets are remarkably similar. There is also a wide range of adjective complements [*eager (for Bill) to leave, proud of John,* etc.]. Therefore, it is quite natural to suppose that the categorial component of the base contains rules with the effect of (20), (21), a conclusion which lends further support to the lexicalist assumption.

These observations, incidentally, considerably weaken the argument that verb and adjective are subcategories of a category "predicator," as has been suggested in recent syntactic work.[23] The argument based on distributional similarities of verbs and adjectives collapses when we recognize that nouns share the same distributional properties; thus the properties are simply properties of lexical categories. A number of other arguments that have appeared in support of this proposal fail for a similar reason. Thus it has been argued that verbs and adjectives can both be categorized as stative–active, so that we have such sentences as (27) in the case of actives, but not (28) in the case of statives:[24]

(27) a. Look at the picture.
b. Don't be noisy.

      c.    What I'm doing is looking at the picture.
      d.    What I'm doing is being noisy.
      e.    I'm looking at the picture.
      f.    I'm being noisy.

(28)  a.  * Know that Bill went there.
      b.  * Don't be tall.
      c.  * What I'm doing is knowing that Bill went there.
      d.  * What I'm doing is being tall.
      e.  * I'm knowing that Bill went there.
      f.  * I'm being tall.

At best, the logic of this argument is unclear. Suppose it were true that just verbs and adjectives crossclassify with respect to the feature active–stative. It would not follow that verbs and adjectives belong to a single category, predicator, with the feature [±adjectival] distinguishing verbs and adjectives. From the fact that a feature $[\pm F]$ is distinctive in the categories $X$, $Y$, it does not follow that there is a feature $G$ such that $X = [+G]$ and $Y = [-G]$, and a category $Z = [\pm G]$. What is more, nouns are subdivided in an exactly parallel way. Thus alongside (27) we have *be a hero, what he's doing is being a hero, he's being a hero;* alongside of (28) we must exclude * *be a person,* * *what he's doing is being a person,* * *he's being a person,* etc. Again, the property in question is a property of lexical categories; the fact that the lexical categories noun, verb, and adjective share this property does not imply that they belong to a super-category. In fact, there is, to my knowledge, no convincing argument for a category including just verbs and adjectives (or, to take another traditional view, nouns and adjectives), although it is not excluded that some such subdivision may be correct. It is quite possible that the categories noun, verb, adjective are the reflection of a deeper feature structure, each being a combination of features of a more abstract sort. In this way, the various relations among these categories might be expressible. For the moment, however, this is hardly clear enough even to be a speculation.

Returning to the main theme, a good case can be made that the lexical categories noun, adjective, and verb (whatever their further substructure may be) can appear in base forms with complements to form noun phrases, adjective phrases, and verb phrases. If this is correct, then it would be quite reasonable to expect that certain items might appear, with fixed contextual features, in more than one of these categories. The lexicalist analysis of derived nominals proposes that this expectation is fulfilled.

The lexicalist hypothesis faces additional problems, however. Consider the phrase *John's proof of the theorem,* as a typical illustration. According to the lexicalist hypothesis, the item *prove* appears in the lexicon with certain contexual features that indicate the range of complements it can accept and the choice of items that may appear in these associated phrases. Yet to be accounted for, however, is the possessive noun phrase *John's* and its relation to the head noun *proof.* It might be suggested that the possessive noun phrase derives from a relative clause with *have,* as *John's table* might derive from the structure underlying *the table* [$_S$*John has a table*]$_S$, along lines that have been frequently discussed. Thus the source of *John's proof of the theorem* would be, in this analysis, the structure underlying *the proof of the theorem that John has.* While not implausible in this case, this approach quickly runs into difficulties when extended. Thus to account for *John's refusal to leave, John's invention of a better mousetrap,* and many other forms, it would be necessary to postulate abstract verbs that obligatorily undergo certain transformations, a dubious move at best, as noted earlier.

An alternative would be simply to derive the possessive noun phrase itself as a base form. Suppose, tentatively, that the rules generating determiners in the base component are the following:[25]

(29)  a. Det → (Prearticle of ) Article (Postarticle)

  b. Article → $\left\{ \begin{array}{c} \pm \text{def} \\ \text{Poss} \end{array} \right\}$

The noun phrase *several of John's proofs of the theorem,* under this analysis, would have a structure of roughly the following form:

(30)

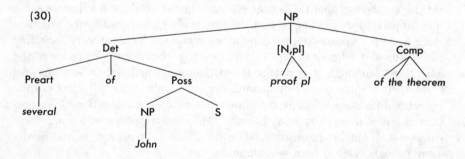

It would be analogous in structure, then, to the phrase *several of those proofs of the theorem.*

If this approach is correct, we would expect to find structures of the form NPs–N even where the N is not a derived nominal, and where the possessive construction in question does not derive from the corresponding structure: *N that NP has.* In fact, there is some evidence in support of this expectation. A number of people have noted that the distinction between alienable and inalienable possession, formally marked in certain languages, has a certain status in English as well. Thus the phrase *John's leg* is ambiguous: it can be used to refer either to the leg that John happens to have in his possession (alienable possession), that he is, say, holding under his arm; or to the leg

that is, in fact, part of John's body (inalienable possession). But the phrase
*the leg that John has* has only the sense of alienable possession. We cannot
say that the leg that John has hurts or that it is weak from the climb, though
we can make this statement of John's leg, in the inalienable sense of the
phrase *John's leg.*[26] These observations lend plausibility to the view that
*John's leg* has another source in addition to the structure underlying *the leg
that John has,* from which it can be derived (in the alienable sense) along
the same lines as *John's table* from the structure underlying *the table that
John has.* The second source, then, might be given by the base rules (29),
which are semantically interpreted as specifying inalienable possession. This
assumption would account for the facts just noted.

Within the framework that I am here presupposing, grammatical relations
are defined by configurations in the deep structure, and selectional features
relate the heads of phrases that are associated in specific grammatical relations. Then the words *John* and *proof* are the heads of the related phrases
*several of John's* and *proofs of the theorem* in *several of John's proofs of
the theorem,* and the same selectional feature that associates subject and verb
in *John proved the theorem* will relate these two items, despite the very
different syntactic origin of the relationship.[27] We return to this matter later
on. For the moment, it is sufficient to point out that by a suitable generalization of the interpretation of selectional features, we can account for the fact
that the selectional relation of the possessive noun phrase of the determiner
to the "verbal" head of the derived nominal is the same as that of the subject
to the verb of the associated verb phrase. Hence in the simplest case, all
of the contextual features of the items that appear as verbs in verb phrases
and as derived nouns in derived nominals will be common to the two types
of context.

It must be noted that only in the *simplest* case will exactly the same
contextual (and other) features be associated with an item as a verb and as
a noun. In general, lexical entries involve sets of shared features, organized
in complex and little understood ways, and we should expect to find the same
phenomenon in the case of derived nominals, given the lexicalist hypothesis.
Examples such as (31) and (32) illustrate the discrepancy of contextual features that may be found in the case of certain noun–verbs.

(31)   a.   our election of John (to the presidency)
       b.   our belief in God
       c.   our consideration of John for the job

(32)   a. * our election of John (to be) president
       b. * our belief in God (to be) omnipotent
       c. * our consideration of John (to be) a fool

Reactions to these sentences vary slightly; (31), (32) represent my judgments.
Given such data, lexical entries must indicate that embedded sentences are

not permitted in the complement to the nouns, although they are permitted in the complement to the associated verbs. Whatever generality there may be to this phenomenon can be extracted from individual lexical entries and presented in redundancy rules. This discrepancy in syntactic features between the noun and verb members of a noun–verb pair corresponds to the semantic discrepancies noted earlier (cf. p. 189) and like them, strengthens the lexicalist hypothesis. The appropriate device to rule out the sentences of (28) [while permitting (27)] is a lexical rule governing contextual features. To formulate such restrictions in the structure indices of transformations would be a rather complex matter.

Consider now some of the transformational rules that apply internally to complex noun phrases. Consider first such phrases as (33) through (36):

(33)  a.  that picture of John's
      b.  a picture of John's
      c.  several of those pictures of John's
      d.  several pictures of John's

(34)  a.  John's picture, several of John's pictures
      b.  the picture of John's that Bill painted

(35)  a. * the picture of John's
      b. * several of the pictures of John's

(36)     * John's picture that Bill painted

The expressions of (35), (36) illustrate a systematic gap in this set. In general, expressions of the form (*prearticle of*) the *N of NPs* and *NPs N that S* are unnatural. The gaps illustrated by (35) and (36) are filled by (34a) and (34b), respectively.

Alongside the examples of (33) there is a superficially similar set in which *John's* is replaced by *John*: thus, *that picture of John,* etc. In this case, the phrases are presumably complex noun phrases with a "relational" head noun, like the examples of (22). The status of the analogues to (35) (namely, *the picture of John, several of the pictures of John*) is unclear. It is clear, however, that such phrases as *John's picture* [ = (34a)] are ambiguous, meaning *the picture of John* or *the picture of John's.*

On just the evidence cited so far, one might propose various transformational analyses. Tentatively, let us suppose that there are three transformations, with roughly the effects of (37), (38), (39), applying in the order given:

(37)  *X–the–Y picture that John has* $\Rightarrow$ *X–John's–Y picture*
(38)  *X–John's–Y picture* $\Rightarrow$ *X–the–Y picture of John's*
(39)  *X–the–Y picture of John* $\Rightarrow$ *X–John's–picture*

$X$ and $Y$ are pre- and post-article (including the demonstrative element), respectively. There are problems in the formulation of such transformations to which we will return below. To account for the data presented above,

(38) will be obligatory when $Y$ contains a demonstrative element [giving (33a), (33c), for example] or when the phrase contains a relative clause [preventing (36)], and will be blocked when $Y$ is null, thus excluding (35).

Consider now such derived nominals as:

(40)  a. the destruction of the city
      b. the proof of it
      c. the murder of John

Rule (39) will apply, giving such transforms as *the city's destruction, its proof, John's murder.* The applicability of (39) to derived nominals varies in naturalness from case to case and from speaker to speaker, and must therefore be specified in part as an idiosyncratic property of lexical items, along the lines developed in Lakoff (1965). In part, the applicability of (39) is determined by the character of the noun phrase of the complement, there being certain noun phrases that do not possessivize. Whatever the detailed restrictions may be, it seems clear that the operation in question extends to derived nominals as well as to complex noun phrases with "relational" head nouns. For convenience of reference, I will refer to rule (39) as the rule of *NP-preposing.*

Let us suppose, as suggested in the references of Note 2, that the underlying structure for passives is roughly $NP-Aux-V-NP-by$ $\Delta$, where $by$ $\Delta$ is an agent phrase related, in ways that are still unclear in detail, to adverbials of means and manner. The passive operation, then, is an amalgam of two steps: the first replaces $\Delta$ by the subject noun phrase; the second inserts in the position vacated by the subject the noun phrase that is to the right of the verb. Let us refer to the first of these operations as *agent-postposing.* The second bears a close similarity to the operation of NP-preposing just discussed, and perhaps the two fall under a single generalization. If so, then the second component of the passive transformation can apply independently of the first, namely, as operation (39), internally to noun phrases. Whether or not this is so, we may inquire into the possibility that the operation of agent-postposing can apply independently of the second component of the passive transformation.

Pursuing this possibility, we note first that passivizability is a property of verbs — which is natural, given that V is the only lexical category mentioned in the structure index of the transformation. We can indicate this fact, along the lines of the references cited, by associating with certain verbs the contextual feature [ — $by$ $\Delta$] either as a lexical property (where it is idiosyncratic) or by a redundancy rule of the lexicon (where it is subject to some regularity). Assuming, as before, that the complements of nouns are the same in principle as those of verbs, we would expect to find in deep structures complex noun phrases of the form $Det-N-NP-by$ $\Delta$, for example, such phrases as *the enemy's-[destroy, +N]-the city-by* $\Delta$. The word *destroy* will be spelled out phonologically as *destruction* in this case, and the preposition *of* inserted by a general rule applying to N–NP constructions.[28] Agent-postposing will then apply, as in the passive, giving *the destruction of the city by the enemy*. To provide this result, we need only generalize the operation so that its domain may be a noun phrase as well as a sentence, a modification of the theory of transformations that is implicit in the lexicalist hypothesis; and we must somehow account for the appearance of the definite article in the transform, just as in the case of the transformation (38). A further generalization is required by such phrases as *the offer by John*, which indicate, as is quite natural, that of the two components of the passive transformation, only NP-preposing and not agent-postposing requires the presence of an object (more generally, a noun phrase, as in the "pseudo-passives" *John was laughed at, . . . approved of*, etc.) in the position following the verb.[29]

Notice that a verb which is not passivizable, such as *marry* (in one sense) or *resemble*, will not be subject to this operation as a derived nominal. Thus *John's marriage to Mary, John's resemblance to Bill* will not transform to *the marriage to Mary by John, the resemblance to Bill by John* [though *John's offer (of amnesty) to the prisoners* does transform to *the offer (of amnesty) to the prisoners by John*]. For additional related observations, see Lees (1960). This is a confused matter, however, and conclusions cannot be drawn with any confidence.

We have now discussed two transformations that apply to complex noun phrases: agent-postposing, which gives *the destruction of the city by the enemy*, and NP-preposing, which gives *the city's destruction*. Agent-postposing is simply a generalization of one of the components of the passive transformation. NP-preposing is similar to, and may fall under a generalization of, the other component. Suppose now that we have an underlying deep structure of the form *Det–N–Comp*, where the determiner is a noun phrase (ultimately possessive, if it remains in this position) and the complement is a noun phrase followed by the agent phrase *by* $\Delta$; for example, *the enemy–destruction–of the city–by* $\Delta$. Applying agent-postposing, we derive *the–destruction of the city–by the enemy*, as before. If we now extend NP-preposing so that it can apply not only in the cases given before, but also before agent phrases, we derive, from the last-formed structure, the phrase *the city's destruction by the enemy*. It is important to see, then, that the latter phrase is only apparently the nominalization of a passive; if it were really the nominalization of a passive, this fact would refute the lexicalist hypothesis, since, as was emphasized earlier, it follows from this hypothesis that transforms should not undergo the processes that give derived nominals. In fact, one major empirical justification offered for the lexicalist hypothesis was that, in a number of otherwise puzzling cases, it is precisely this state of affairs that we discover. But we now see that the crucial phrases need not be regarded as nominals derived transformationally from the passive (with the auxiliary mysteriously disappearing), but can rather be explained as, in effect, passives of base-generated derived nominals, by independently motivated transformations.

Notice that agent-postposing is obligatory for certain subject noun phrases that do not permit formation of possessives. Since agent-postposing is unspecifiable for gerundive nominals, there are certain derived nominals with no gerundive counterpart, as pointed out in Note 10. Under the transformationalist hypothesis, there would be no more reason to expect agent-postposing in derived than in gerundive nominals. Hence an additional argument in support of the lexicalist hypothesis is that it provides this distinction on independent grounds.

It is possible that such derived nominals as *the necessity for John to leave, the likelihood that John will leave,* and so on might be derived by obligatory agent-postposing from the underlying noun phrases [*for John to leave*]*'s necessity,* [*that John will leave*]*'s likelihood.*

A minor transformational rule will replace *by* by *of* under certain conditions, permitting *the refusal to leave of those men* (or *the refusal of those men to leave*) alternating with *the refusal to leave by those men* (or *the refusal by those men to leave*). Presumably, it is this rule that applies in the case of the nominals *the growling of the lion,* etc. Some speakers apparently accept expressions such as *John's likelihood of leaving,* though to me these are entirely unacceptable. Perhaps such expressions can be derived, by an extension of NP-preposing, from *the likelihood of John leaving.* Such expressions as * *John's likelihood to leave* apparently are acceptable to no one, exactly as is predicted by the lexicalist hypothesis.

Implicit in the rules given so far is the possibility that there will be base noun phrases of the form *Det–N–NP by* $\Delta$, where the head noun is not derived from an underlying stem that also appears as a verb, thus a case of the sort illustrated in (22). Of course, such a possibility will be realized as a well-formed surface structure only if the determiner is filled by a phrase which can ultimately appear in the agent position, replacing the symbol $\Delta$, which will otherwise, through the filtering effect of transformations, mark the structure as not well formed. If it is true, as suggested above, that some form of "inalienable possession" is expressed by base rules generating noun phrases in the determiner position, then the possibility just sketched can be realized. That there may be structures of this sort is suggested by a fuller analysis of such phrases as *John's picture,* discussed briefly above. We noted that there are two interpretations of this phrase, one derived from the structure underlying *the picture that John has* by rule (37), and the other derived by NP-preposing, rule (39), from the complex noun phrase that would otherwise be realized as *the picture of John.* There is, however, still a third interpretation, namely, with the same meaning as *the picture that John painted.* Conceivably, this is the interpretation given to the base structure [$_{Det}$ *John's*]$_{Det}$ [$_N$ *picture*]$_N$, with a generalization of the notion "inalienable possession" to a kind of "intrinsic connection." A similar triple ambiguity can be found in other cases, e.g., *John's story,* where John can be the subject of the story (*the story of John*), the writer (intrinsic connection), or an editor proposing the story for publication at a meeting (*the story that John has*). Notice that if *John's picture, John's story,* and so on are generated in the base with the sense of intrinsic connection, they will be subject to rule (38), giving *that picture of John's, those stories of John's, the story of John's that I told you about,* and so on, all with the meaning of intrinsic connection. The latter phrases will thus be two-way ambiguous, meaning *the picture that John has* or *the picture that John painted* (though not *the picture of John*), and so on. This is of course true, and gives some further support for the analysis proposed.

Now consider the base structure *Det–N–NP–by* $\Delta$, where the determiner is realized in the base as the noun phrase *John,* the head noun as *picture,* and the noun phrase complement as *Mary.* Without the agent phrase in the base structure, this will give *John's picture of Mary* (itself of course ambiguous, since another source could have been the structure underlying *the picture of Mary that John has*).[30] With the agent phrase generated in the base, the agent-postposing transformation must apply, giving *the picture of Mary by John.* Had the complement been omitted, we would derive *the picture by John.* Agent-postposing must precede the transformation of NP-preposing that gives *the city's destruction,* or we will derive *the destruction by the city* from *the–destroy–the city.* It therefore follows that *the picture (of Mary) by John* cannot be derived from the phrase *John's picture,* which is derived in turn from *the picture of John.* Hence *the picture of Mary by John* cannot have the latter meaning. Along these lines, a number of facts fall together in what seems a quite natural way.

Consider, finally, a slightly more complicated case, namely, a structure of the form: *Det–N–NP–by* $\Delta$*–that NP has,* where the determiner is a possessivized noun phrase. An example would be (41):

(41) Rembrandt's portrait of Aristotle by $\Delta$ that the Metropolitan Museum has.

Applying agent-postposing, we derive *the portrait of Aristotle by Rembrandt that the Metropolitan Museum has.* Rule (37) gives *the Metropolitan Museum's portrait of Aristotle by Rembrandt.* Rule (38) would then give the quite clumsy phrase *the portrait of Aristotle by Rembrandt of the Metropolitan Museum's.* This would be natural if the final phrase, *of the Metropolitan Museum's,* were omitted, in which case rule (39), NP-preposing, would then apply to give *Aristotle's portrait by Rembrandt.* Clearly, the rule of agent-postposing must be permitted to apply before rule (37), which forms *NP's N* from *the N that NP has.* Furthermore, the rule of agent-postposing cannot apply after rule (37). If this ordering were permitted, the underlying structure *the portrait of Aristotle by* Δ *that the Metropolitan has* would become, by (37), *the Metropolitan's portrait of Aristotle by* Δ, and then, by agent-postposing, *the portrait of Aristotle by the Metropolitan.* Therefore the ordering of the transformations we have been discussing must be: agent-postposing, (37), (38), (39).

So far we have been exploring the possibility that complex noun phrases, which ultimately will be possessivized if not removed from the determiner by a transformation, are derived directly by base rules such as (29). We have noted, however, that when the noun phrase is removed from the determiner, an article may appear in the position that it vacated. Thus we can have *the picture of Mary by John, a picture of Mary by John, several pictures of Mary by John, one of the pictures of Mary by John,* etc. These facts suggest that rule (29b) is incorrect, and that it be replaced by something like (42):

(42)   Article → [±def, (NP)]

The article, then, can be either definite or indefinite, or can be a full noun phrase with the associated feature [+definite] or [−definite]. When the noun phrase is removed from the determiner by a transformation, the feature [±definite] will remain, much as the feature [+PRO] remains in certain positions when a noun phrase is removed. [Continuing with such an analysis, we would have to stipulate that a rule that applies automatically after (37) and after (39) — hence also to NPs generated in the article position by base rules — assigns the possessive formative to the final word of the noun phrase in question.] A similar analysis would hold for derived nominals, giving such phrases as *(several of) the proofs of the theorem by John, several proofs of the theorem by John* [which is nondefinite, as we can see from the sentence *there were several proofs of the theorem (by John) in the most recent issue of the journal*], etc. When the noun phrase constitutes the full determiner in the surface structure, the feature in question must be interpreted as definite, as we can see from the impossibility of * *there were John's proofs of the theorem in the journal,* with the same interpretation.

Rule (42) is not formulable within the framework that we have so far presupposed (cf. Note 2), which takes feature complexes to be associated only with lexical categories, and permits complex symbols to dominate a sequence of elements only within the word [cf. Chomsky (1965, p. 188f.)]. It has been suggested a number of times that this restriction is too heavy and that certain features should also be associated with nonlexical phrase categories.[31] The present considerations lend further support to these proposals.

Such an extension of the theory of syntactic features suggests that the distinction between features and categories is a rather artificial one. In the earliest work in generative grammar it was assumed that the elements of the underlying base grammar are formatives and categories; each category corresponds to a class of strings of formatives. This assumption was carried over from structuralist syntactic theories, which regarded a grammar as a system of classes of elements derived by analytic procedures of segmentation and classification. For reasons discussed in Chomsky (1965, Chapter 2), it was soon found necessary to depart from this assumption in the case of lexical categories. The resulting "mixed theory" had a certain technical artificiality, in that lexical categories were interpreted both as categories of the base (N, V, etc.) and as features in the lexicon ($+N$, $+V$, etc.). In fact, when the reliance on analytic procedures of segmentation and classification is abandoned, there is no reason to retain the notion of category at all, even for the base. We might just as well eliminate the distinction of feature and category, and regard all symbols of the grammar as sets of features. If the elements NP, VP, and so on are treated as certain feature complexes, then there is no incoherence in supposing that there are complex symbols of the form [$+$ def, $+$ NP]. Of course, it is necessary to stipulate with care the precise conditions under which complex symbols can be formed, at each level, or else the system of grammar becomes so powerful as to lose empirical interest. A number of possible restrictions suggest themselves, but I will not explore this general question any further here.

The reanalysis of phrase categories as features permits the formulation of such base rules as (42) as well as the transformational rules that were introduced in our informal discussion of complex noun phrases. It also opens up other possibilities that should be considered. For example, with this reanalysis it becomes possible, under certain restricted circumstances, to introduce new phrase structure through transformations. To illustrate with a concrete example, consider such sentences as (43), (44):

(43)  A man is in the room.
(44)  There is a man in the room.

It is clear, in (44), that *there* is a noun phrase; (44) is subject to such rules, for example, as the interrogative transformation that presupposes this analysis. At the same time, there is some empirical support for the argument that (44) is derived from (43). However, these conclusions are difficult to reconcile within the theory of transformational grammar, since an item (such as *there*) introduced by a transformation can be assigned phrase structure only when it replaces some string which already has this phrase structure; and it requires some artificiality to generate (44) in this way. However, if [$+$ NP] is a feature (or a complex of features) that can be part of a complex symbol introduced by a transformation, the difficulty is easily removed. For example, if we give to the structure underlying (43) the proper analysis (*e, e, a man, is, in the room*)[32] and apply the elementary transformation that replaces the first term by the complex symbol [*there*, $+$ NP] (*there* standing for a feature matrix of the usual sort) and the second term by the fourth, which is then deleted, we derive a phrase-marker which is appropriate for further operations.

To take a slightly more complex example, consider such sentences as (45):

(45) a. What John did was read a book about himself.
     b. What John read was a book about himself.

As noted earlier (p. 198), we might explain many of the properties of these sentences by deriving them from a base structure of roughly the form (46):

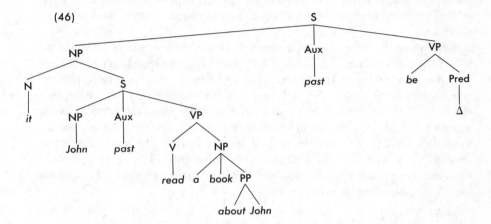

(46)

We might then derive (45b) in the following way: Familiar rules apply to the most deeply embedded S to give *John past read a book about himself.* A new substitution transformation replaces the unspecified predicate $\Delta$ of (46) by the object of the embedded sentence, *a book about himself,* leaving a "PRO-form" in its place. This gives: *it–John past read it–past be–a book about himself.* Relativization and other familiar rules, supplemented by a rule that replaces *it that* by *what,* give (45b).

But consider now (45a). Again, the most deeply embedded S is converted to *John read a book about himself.* But in this case, the new substitution transformation replaces the unspecified predicate not by the object of the embedded sentence but by its whole verb phrase, which is replaced by a "PRO-form," *do-it,* giving *it–John past do it–past be–read a book about himself.* The remaining rules give (45a). The problem, however, is that the element *do-it* must be specified as a structure of the form V–NP. This is straightforward in the case of the "PRO-verb" *do,* but in the earlier framework there was no way to specify that *it* is a NP in the derived structure. Observe that the embedded VP is replaced by *do-it* even when it contains no NP at all, as in *what John did was read.* The argument that the introduced element *do-it* is actually of the form V–NP is greatly strengthened by other forms, for example, the sentence (47),[33] in which case passivization applies to it:

(47)  John apologized more meekly than it had ever been done before.

Once again, if phrase categories are reinterpreted as features, there is no problem in formulating the required rules. The verb of the embedded VP can become *do* by an extension of the rule of *do*-insertion, and the complex symbol $[it, +\text{NP}]$ is introduced by the transformation in the appropriate position.

In short, there is some motivation for the limited extension of the mechanisms for assigning derived constituent structure that results from a decision to replace categories systematically by features that can enter into complex symbols.

Continuing to explore consequences of the lexicalist hypothesis, let us return to the rules (21) which expand NP, VP, and AP into expressions containing optional complements. The phrase category "complement" seems to play no role in transformations. We can easily abolish this category if we replace the rules (21) by a single schema, with a variable standing for the lexical categories N, A, V. To introduce a more uniform notation, let us use the symbol $\overline{X}$ for a phrase containing $X$ as its head. Then the base rules introducing N, A, and V will be replaced by a schema (48), where in place of . . . there appears the full range of structures that serve as complements and $X$ can be any one of N, A, or V:

(48)  $\overline{X} \rightarrow X \ldots$

Continuing with the same notation, the phrases immediately dominating $\overline{N}$, $\overline{A}$ and $\overline{V}$ will be designated $\overline{\overline{N}}$, $\overline{\overline{A}}$, $\overline{\overline{V}}$ respectively. To introduce further terminological uniformity, let us refer to the phrase associated with $\overline{N}$, $\overline{A}$, $\overline{V}$ in the base structure as the "specifier" of these elements. Then the elements $\overline{N}, \overline{A}, \overline{V}$ might themselves be introduced in the base component by the schema (49):

(49)  $\overline{\overline{X}} \rightarrow [\text{Spec}, \overline{X}] \; \overline{X}$

where $[\text{Spec}, \overline{N}]$ will be analyzed as the determiner, $[\text{Spec}, \overline{V}]$ as the auxiliary (perhaps with time adverbials associated), and $[\text{Spec}, \overline{A}]$ perhaps as the system of qualifying elements associated with adjective phrases (comparative structures, *very*, etc.). The initial rule of the base grammar would then be (50) (with possible optional elements added):

(50)  $S \rightarrow \overline{\overline{N}} \; \overline{\overline{V}}.$

Thus a skeletal form of the base is induced by the "primitive" categories N, A, V (which, as noted earlier, may themselves be the reflection of an underlying feature structure).

In other respects, the primitive categories might differ, for example, if V is analyzed into a copula–predicate construction. Furthermore, it can be expected that the base rules for any language will contain language-specific modifications of the general pattern. If this line of thought is correct, the structure of derived nominals would be something like (51), and the structure of a related sentence, like (52) (omitting much detail):

(51)

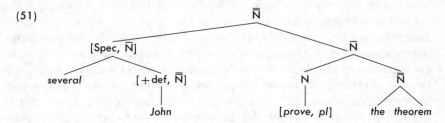

(several of John's proofs of the theorem)

(52)

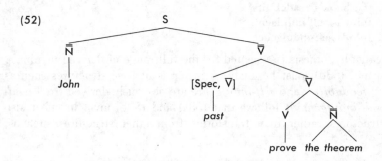

(John proved the theorem)

The internal structure of the nominal (51) mirrors that of the sentence (52). The strict subcategorization features of the lexical item *prove* take account of the phrases $\bar{V}$ and $\bar{N}$ dominating the category to which it is assigned in (51), (52), respectively. Its selectional features refer to the heads of the associated phrases, which are the same in both cases. The category $\bar{\bar{N}}$, like S, is a recursive element of the base.[34] Correspondingly, it would be natural to suppose that in the cyclic application of transformations, the phrases of the form $\bar{\bar{N}}$ play the same role as the phrases of the form S in specifying the domain of transformations.

A structure of the sort just outlined is reminiscent of the system of phrase structure analysis developed by Harris in the 1940's.[35] In Harris' system, statements applying to categories represented in the form $X^n$ ($n$ a numeral) applied also to categories represented in the form $X^m$ ($m < n$). One might seek analogous properties of the system just analyzed.

So far, we have surveyed some evidence in support of the lexicalist hypothesis and explored its consequences for grammatical theory and the analysis of English structure. As was noted, the central objection to any form of the lexicalist hypothesis in earlier work such as Lees (1960) was eliminated by later elaborations of syntactic theory to incorporate syntactic features and a separate lexicon. Other objections remain, however. The strongest and most interesting conclusion that follows from the lexicalist hypothesis is that derived nominals should have the form of base sentences, whereas gerundive nominals may in general have the form of transforms. We have indicated that in many cases this conclusion is confirmed, and that at least some apparent counterexamples (e.g., *the city's destruction by the enemy*) can be satisfactorily explained in terms of independently motivated rules. There remain, however, certain more difficult cases. As is well-known, processes of derivational morphology are applicable in sequence — they may even be recursive.[36] But consider such expressions as (53):

(53) a. The book is readable.
 b. the book's readability
 c. John is self-indulgent.
 d. John's self-indulgence

If the lexicalist hypothesis is accepted for the full range of derived nominals, then (53b) and (53d) must be analyzed in terms of base structures such as (51). Since *readability* and *self-indulgence* are obviously derived from *readable* and *self-indulgent*, it follows that (53a) and (53c) must in effect also be base structures rather than transforms from other structures such as, perhaps (54):

(54) a. the book is able [$_S$for the book to be read]$_S$
 b. John is indulgent to John.

However, a case can be made for transformational derivation of (53a) and (53c) from something like (54a) and (54b), contradicting the lexicalist hypothesis, in this instance.

The seriousness of this objection to the lexicalist hypothesis depends on the strength of the case for the transformational derivation in question. It seems to me that the case is far from persuasive. Notice, for one thing, that the proposed transformation is not "meaning-preserving" (except in the trivialized sense discussed on p. 188), as Chapin observes. In fact, the remarks of Note 11 can be extended to these cases as well. Thus, *readable* is much more sharply restricted in meaning than *able to be read*. In a wide range of other cases the meaning is restricted or based on a very different subregularity (consider *commendable, abominable, irreplaceable, incomparable, despicable, decidable, laudable, insufferable, noticeable, changeable, pitiable, enviable, preferable, insufferable, inviolable, admirable, deplorable, adorable, irritable, lamentable, quotable, detestable, lovable, admissible, livable, laughable, honorable, valuable,* and so on).[37] It follows that any argument for the transformational analysis that is based on semantic grounds or on grounds of selectional relations will be very weak.

In fact, even in the best of cases such arguments are weak; correspondingly,

since the earliest work in transformational generative grammar, the attempt
has been made to support them by independent syntactic arguments. The
reason is that an alternative, nontransformational approach can be envisaged
if the support for transformations is simply meaning equivalence or sameness
of selectional relations. Where the grounds are semantic, an alternative is
an enrichment of the rules of semantic interpretation;[38] and regularities
involving only selectional features might in principle be stated as redundancy
rules of the lexicon.[39] For example, insofar as a subregularity exists regarding
selectional rules in the case of $-able$, it can be formulated as a lexical rule
that assigns the feature $[X - ]$ to a lexical item $[V-able]$ where V has the
intrinsic selectional feature $[ - X]$. It would follow, then, that where the
embedded passive in (54a) has as its grammatical subject a noun phrase that
is not the underlying object (or, in the case of "pseudo-passives" such as
*he can be relied on,* the "pseudo-object"), the corresponding form (53a) will
be excluded. In fact, there is evidence in support of this conclusion. Thus
we cannot derive *John is believable (imaginable, expectable,* etc.) *to have
left* from *NP believes (imagines, expects) John to have left,* although a deep
object such as *this claim* can appear in the context — *is believable.* There
are many open questions regarding such constructions, but it seems to me
that the argument for a transformational analysis of (53a) is not compelling.

What is more, the argument for a transformational analysis of (53b) from
(53a) is weak on independent grounds. Thus it is difficult to see how such
an analysis could account for the fact that *readability* may refer not to a
fact, event, process, etc., but rather to a property; thus the phrase *the readability of the book is its only redeeming feature* does not mean (*the fact*)
*that the book is readable is its only redeeming feature.* Although perhaps
such difficulties can be overcome, as matters now stand, examples such as
(53a), (53b) do not seem to me to offer a serious argument against the lexicalist
hypothesis.

The situation seems to me similar in the case of (53c) and (53d). Examples
such as (53c) seem to provide the strongest case for transformational analysis
of derived forms, but even here, the matter is far from clear. Consider, for
example, the sentences in (55):

(55)   a. John sent a self-addressed envelope.
       b. This is clearly a self-inflicted wound.
       c. The prophecy is self-fulfilling.
       d. Confrontations between students and administration are self-generat-
          ing.
       e. John is self-educated.
       f. John's remarks are self-congratulatory.
       g. John's actions are self-destructive.

Sentence (55a) does not mean that the envelope was addressed to itself; the
phrase *self-addressed envelope* can appear in sentences where there is no

syntactic source for *self* at all (*self-addressed envelopes are barred by law from the mails*). The same is true of (55b), (55f), (55g). Sentence (55c) does not, strictly speaking, mean that the prophecy fulfilled the prophecy, which is senseless, but rather that it led to a state of affairs that fulfilled the prophecy. In the case of (55d), what is meant is that certain confrontations generate other confrontations of the same sort; confrontations do not generate themselves. (55e) cannot be derived by a rule analogous to one that purportedly forms (53c) from (54b), since the postulated underlying form, *John was educated by himself,* is ruled out by the principle, whatever it may be, that makes passives incompatible with reflexivization. A similar argument applies to (55g); the postulated underlying form, *John's actions destroy himself,* is ruled out by general conditions on reflexivization. Furthermore, a consideration of forms such as *self-conscious, self-proclaimed* (*enemy*), *self-contained, self-evident, self-esteem, self-explanatory* (i.e., needs no explanation), *self-important, self-seeking,* and so on makes one search for a general transformational analysis of such structures seem ill-conceived. The variety and idiosyncrasy of such items seem to be of the sort that is characteristic of the lexicon; it is difficult to see how they can be accounted for by syntactic rules of any generality. Furthermore, the difficulties in deriving (53b) from (53a) carry over to the pair (53c), (53d).

The discussion so far has been restricted to gerundive and derived nominals, and has barely touched on a third category with some peculiar properties, namely, nominals of the sort illustrated in (56):

(56)   a. John's refusing of the offer
       b. John's proving of the theorem
       c. the growing of tomatoes

These forms are curious in a number of respects, and it is not at all clear whether the lexicalist hypothesis can be extended to cover them. That it should be so extended is suggested by the fact that these forms, like derived nominals, appear to have the internal structure of noun phrases; thus the possessive subject can be replaced by a determiner, as in (56c). On the other hand, adjective insertion seems quite unnatural in this construction. In fact, there is an artificiality to the whole construction that makes it quite resistant to systematic investigation. Furthermore, the construction is quite limited. Thus we cannot have *the feeling sad, the trying to win, the arguing about money, the leaving,* etc.

In apparent conflict with an extension of the lexicalist hypothesis is the fact that these constructions exist in the case of certain verbs that we have tentatively derived from underlying intransitives, as in the case of (56c), which is structurally ambiguous, as contrasted with the derived nominal (57), discussed on p. 192, which is unambiguous:

(57)   the growth of tomatoes

If the lexicalist hypothesis is extended to the forms (56), then we must suppose that both *tomatoes grow* and *NP grows tomatoes* are base forms. However, to account for the interpretation of (57) as well as for the relation of transitive and intransitive *grow* we were led to regard *NP grows tomatoes* as the causative of the underlying structure *tomatoes grow*.[40] These various assumptions are mutually consistent only if we reject the analysis of the causative discussed on p. 192, which postulated the base structure (58) for *John grows tomatoes*, and assume instead that the base structure is (59):

(58)   John [+cause] [$_S$tomatoes grow]$_S$
(59)   John [+cause, grow] tomatoes

In other words, we postulate that there is a feature [+cause] which can be assigned to certain verbs as a lexical property. Associated with this feature are certain redundancy rules which are, in this case, universal, hence not part of the grammar of English but rather among the principles by which any grammar is interpreted. These principles specify that an intransitive with the feature [+cause] becomes transitive and that its selectional features are systematically revised so that the former subject becomes the object. Similar principles of redundancy apply to the associated rules of semantic interpretation. To account for the distinction between (56c) and (57), we must restrict the feature [+cause] with respect to the feature that distinguishes derived nominals such as *growth* from forms such as *growing*, limiting it to the latter case. Unless there are some general grounds for the hierarchy thus established, the explanation offered earlier for the nonambiguity of (57) is weakened, since it involves an *ad hoc* step. There is, nevertheless, a partial explanation and a natural way of stating a complex of facts.

To summarize, three types of nominalizations have been considered in this discussion: the gerundive nominals such as (60), the derived nominals such as (61), and the "mixed" forms (62), which to me seem rather clumsy, though quite comprehensible, when a derived nominal also exists:

(60)   John's refusing the offer
(61)   John's refusal of the offer
(62)   John's refusing of the offer

On the basis of the evidence surveyed here, it seems that the transformationalist hypothesis is correct for the gerundive nominals and the lexicalist hypothesis for the derived nominals and perhaps, though much less clearly so, for the mixed forms. This conclusion has a variety of consequences for general linguistic theory and for the analysis of English structure. Such material provides a case study of the complex of problems that arise when linguistic theory is elaborated so as to incorporate both grammatical transformations and lexical features.

## NOTES

1. This work was supported in part by the U. S. Air Force [ESD Contract AF19(628)-2487] and the National Institutes of Health (Grant MH-13390-01).

2. The presupposed framework is discussed in greater detail in a number of recent publications, specifically, J. Katz and P. Postal (1964); Chomsky (1965); and references cited there.

3. Needless to say, any specific bit of evidence must be interpreted within a fixed framework of assumptions, themselves subject to question. But in this respect the study of language is no different from any other empirical investigation.

4. Henceforth I shall use labeled brackets to indicate structures in phrase-markers; an expression of the form $X[_A Y]_A Z$ signifies that the string Y is assigned to the category A in the string XYZ.

5. There are a number of suggestive remarks on this matter in Kenny (1963).

6. The fullest discussion of this and related topics is in Lees (1960), from which I will draw freely.

7. I follow here the proposal in Chomsky (1965, p. 222) that the base rules give structures of the form NP–Aux–VP, with Aux analyzed as $Aux_1$ (Aspect), $Aux_1$ being further analyzed as either Tense (Modal) or as various nominalization elements and Aspect as (perfect) (progressive). Forms such as * *John's being reading the book* (but not *John's having been reading the book*) are blocked by a restriction against certain *–ing –ing* sequences (compare * *John's stopping reading, John's having stopped reading,* etc.). Tense and Modal are thus excluded from the gerundive nominal, but not Aspect. Nothing that follows depends on the exact form of the rules for gerundive nominalization, but I think that a good case can be made for this analysis.

8. The transformationalist position is adopted in much recent work, for example, Lakoff (1965). It is argued in some detail in Chapin (1967). The lexicalist position is proposed in Chomsky (1965, pp. 219–220), but with the analysis of possessive subjects that is rejected here on p. 189; it is implicitly rejected, incorrectly, as I now believe, in Chomsky (1965, p. 184). A compromise position of the sort noted above is developed in detail by Langendoen (1967a). It is also discussed in Annear and Elliot (1965). Langendoen presents an analysis very much like the one that I will propose directly, and cites a good deal of evidence in support of it. He refrains from adopting a full lexicalist position because of such ambiguities as that of *proof* in *John's proof of the theorem* (*took him a long time, is reproduced in the new text*). However, this objection to the full lexicalist hypothesis, for which I am responsible, seems to me very weak. One might just as well suppose that a lexical ambiguity is involved, analogous to the ambiguity of such words as *book, pamphlet,* etc., which can be either concrete or abstract (*the book weighs five pounds, . . . was written in a hurry*), as was noted by Postal (1966b). See Note 12 in this connection.

9. There are certain restrictions. For example, the transformation is inapplicable when the subject is of a type that does not permit possessives (e.g., * *that John was here's surprising me*), and it often is very unnatural with verbs that involve extraposition (* *it's surprising me that John was here,* * *John's happening to be a good friend of mine*), although *it's having surprised me that John was here* and *John's happening to be there* seem tolerable.

10. There is also at least one class of cases where the derived nominals are permitted but not the gerundive nominals, namely, examples where the gerundive is blocked

because the subject does not possessivize (cf. Note 9). Thus the gerundive nominal *his negative attitude toward the proposal's disrupting our plans* is clumsy and *his bringing up of that objection's disrupting our plans* is impossible, but we can form the associated derived nominals: *the disruption of our plans by his negative attitude toward the proposal, . . . by his bringing up of that objection.* We return to these cases directly.

11. The artificiality might be reduced by deriving nominals from underlying nouns with some kind of sentential element included, where the meaning can be expressed in this way: for example, *John's intelligence* from *the fact that John is intelligent* (in *John's intelligence is undeniable*), and from *the extent to which John is intelligent* (in *John's intelligence exceeds his foresight*). It is difficult to find a natural source for the nominal, however, in such sentences as *John's intelligence is his most remarkable quality.* This idea runs into other difficulties. Thus we can say *John's intelligence, which is his most remarkable quality, exceeds his foresight*; but the appositive clause, on this analysis, would have to derive from * *the extent to which John is intelligent is his most remarkable quality,* since in general the identity of structure required for appositive clause formation to take place goes even beyond identity of the given phrase-markers, as was pointed out by Lees (1960, p. 76). Many open questions regarding recoverability of deletion in erasure transformations arise as this problem is pursued. For some discussion, see Chomsky (1965, pp. 145f., 179f.), Ross (1967*a*); and Chomsky (1968). Ross (1967*a*) suggests (Chapter 3, *n.* 19) that identity of base structures is required for erasure.

The scope of the existing subregularities, I believe, has been considerably exaggerated in work that takes the transformationalist position. For example, Lakoff (1965) gives what are probably the strongest cases for this position, but even of these very few are acceptable on the semantic grounds that he proposes as justifying them. Thus *John's deeds* does not have the same meaning as *things which John did* (p. IV-2), but rather, *fairly significant things which John did* (we would not say that one of John's first deeds this morning was to brush his teeth). We cannot derive *John's beliefs* from *what John believes* (p. V-23), because of such sentences as *John's beliefs are not mutually consistent, . . . are numerous,* etc., or *John's beliefs, some of which are amazing, . . .* ; nor can we derive it from *the things that John believes,* since the semantic interpretation will then be incorrect in such expressions as *I respect John's beliefs* or *John's beliefs are intense.* It is difficult to see how one can transformationally relate *I read all of John's writings* to *I read all of what John wrote,* in view of such expressions as *I read all of John's critical writings,* etc. And if one is to postulate an abstract verb *poetize* underlying *John's poems,* then what about *John's book reviews, dialogues, sonnets, limericks, Alexandrines,* etc.? In general, there are few cases where problems of this sort do not arise. Correspondingly, the transformationalist position is impossible to support, and difficult even to maintain, on semantic grounds.

12. It is immaterial for present purposes whether a lexical entry is regarded as a Boolean function of specified features or is to be replaced by a set of lexical entries, each of which consists of a set of specified features. It is unclear whether these approaches to problems of range of meaning and range of function are terminological variants, or are empirically distinguishable. Some of the matters touched on in Note 11 may be relevant. Consider, for example, the ambiguity of *book* and *proof* mentioned

in Note 8. Certain conditions on recoverability of deletion would lead to the conclusion that a single lexical entry is involved when two senses of the word can be combined in apposition. Under this assumption, the choice between the alternatives just mentioned in the case of *book* and *proof* would be determined by the status of such sentences as *this book, which weighs five pounds, was written in a hurry* and *John's proof of the theorem, which took him a long time, is reproduced in the new text.*

13. For discussion, see Rosenbaum (1967), and Kiparsky and Kiparsky (1967).

14. See references of Note 13.

15. This solution is proposed by Lakoff (1965, p. A-15f.), but on the transformationalist grounds that he adopts, there is no motivation for it.

16. There are many problems to be explored here. Notice, for example, that *John interested me in his ideas* is very different from *John interested me with his ideas* (both types of prepositional phrases occur in *John interested me in politics with his novel approach*); only the latter is similar in meaning to *John's ideas interested me.* A full analysis of these expressions will have to take into account instrumental phrases, concerning which there are numerous problems that have been discussed in a number of stimulating papers by Fillmore, Lakoff, and others.

The brief mention of causatives in Chomsky (1965) takes the main verb of (12) to be the verb *cause*, but the distinction between direct and indirect causation suggests that this cannot be correct. Lakoff (1966b) argues that the distinction between direct and indirect causation is a matter of use, not underlying structure; thus he argues that *a breeze stiffened John's arm* and *a breeze caused John's arm to stiffen* are generally used to indicate direct causation, while *a breeze brought it about that John's arm stiffened* and *a breeze made John's arm stiffen* are generally used to indicate indirect causation, but that actually either interpretation is possible, from which it would follow that the underlying verb could be taken to be *cause* in causative constructions. However, it does not seem correct to regard this simply as a distinction of use. Thus we can say *John's clumsiness caused the door to open* (*the window to break*) but not *John's clumsiness opened the door* (*broke the window*). For some discussion of this matter, see Barbara Hall (1965).

17. It is not obvious that such forms as *the reading of the book* are ordinary derived nominals. I return to this matter briefly below.

18. This was pointed out to me by M. Kajita. Notice that *his criticism of the book for its failure . . .* is grammatical. Presumably, *for*-phrases of this sort are part of the complement system for verbs and nouns.

19. I refer here to the distinction drawn in Chomsky (1965, p. 11f.). For the distinction between direct and derivative generation, see Chomsky (1965, p. 227, *n.* 2).

20. Langendoen (1967a) discusses a number of examples of this sort.

21. For example, such a device could be used to establish, say, that all verbs are derived from underlying prepositions. If one wishes to pursue this line of reasoning, he might begin with the traditional view that all verbs contain the copula, then arguing that *John visited England* is of the same form as *John is in England* (i.e., * *John is visit England*), where *visit* is a preposition of the category of *in* that obligatorily transforms to a verb incorporating the copula. Thus we are left with only one "relational" category, prepositions. To rule out such absurdities, it is necessary to exclude the devices that permit them to be formulated or to assign a high cost to the use of such devices.

22. Still another possibility would be to take the underlying form to be $[_{NP}Det$ $N]_{NP}$ be $[_{NP}Det\ N\ Comp]_{NP}$ (e.g., *the question is the question whether John should leave*), with the second occurrence of the repeated noun deleted, but this too presupposes that the Det–N–Comp structures are base forms, not reduced relatives.

23. Cf., for example, Lakoff (1966b), Appendix A.

24. Examples from Lakoff, (1966b).

25. It is immaterial for the present discussion whether the structures to the right of the arrow are, indeed, base structures, or whether certain of them are derived from "deeper" or different structures. It is sufficient, for present purposes, to note that (30), or something sufficiently like it, is the general form of the determiner at some stage of derivation. What is crucial, for the present, is that the possessive noun phrase is being assigned the status of the article $\pm$def, whatever this may be in the base structure.

26. These examples are due to John Ross.

27. If we take the structure in question to be, rather, (*several of* [(*John's*) (*proofs of the theorem*)]), the same conclusion follows, with respect now to the embedded phrase *John's proofs of the theorem*.

28. Alternatively, it has been proposed that the preposition is an obligatory part of the underlying noun phrase, and is deleted in certain contexts, for example, the context: verb — . This seems to me dubious, however. Notice that the preposition is not invariably deleted in the context verb — NP, for example, in such cases as *approve of John.* Hence we would have to postulate an idiosyncratic feature $F$ that subdivides verbs into those that do and those that do not undergo *of*-deletion. An arbitrary bifurcation of the lexicon is the worst possible case, of course. No such arbitrary feature is needed if we suppose the *of* to be introduced in the context N — NP. Of course *approve* will be distinguished from *read* by the strict subcategorization features [ — PP], [ — NP] (or whatever variants of these are employed), exactly as *laugh* (*at John*) is distinguished from *see* (*John*); this, however, is not a new classification, but rather one that is necessary however the matter of *of* is handled. To make matters worse for the theory of *of*-deletion, the new, idiosyncratic feature $F$ will have to cut across related senses of a single item, since we have *approve–the proposal* alongside of *approve–of the proposal.* Furthermore, there is a possibility, which should be explored, of combining the proposed rule of *of*-insertion with the rule governing placement of *of* in prenominal constructions such as *lots of work, several of the boys, a group of men*, etc. Such considerations suggest that the preposition is an inherent part of the prepositional phrase, but not of the object.

29. Such an analysis of the phrases in question is proposed by Kinsuke Hasegawa, "The Passive Construction in English," forthcoming in *Language.* Hasegawa suggests, furthermore, that the passive derives from a matrix structure containing the grammatical subject as object: thus *Bill was seen by John* would derive from something like *Bill is: John saw Bill.* Despite his arguments, I am skeptical about this proposal. A serious objection, it seems to me, is that there are phrases which can appear as grammatical subject only in the passive construction. Thus we can have *a man to do the job was found by John* from *John found a man to do the job* [cf. (22n)], but such expressions as *a man to do the job came to see me* seem highly unnatural. Similarly, there are certain idioms that undergo passivization (cf. *Aspects*, p. 190f.) although the phrase that appears as grammatical subject cannot normally appear as a deep subject (*I didn't expect that offense would be taken at that remark, advantage was*

*taken of John,* etc.). Such facts are difficult to reconcile with the proposal that the passive derives from a matrix proposition with an embedded complement.

30. Notice, then, that the transformation (37) that gives *John's picture* from *the picture that John has* will also give *John's picture of Mary* from *the picture of Mary that John has.* The transformation therefore applies not to a structure of the form *Det-N-that NP has* but rather *Det-$\overline{N}$-that NP has,* where $\overline{N}$ represents the expression *picture of Mary* (in *the picture of Mary that John has*) or the expression *picture* (in *the picture that John has*). We return to the status of $\overline{N}$ below. On p. 197 we noted another situation in which the noun and its complement appear to form a single unit.

31. See Weinreich (1966), and McCawley (1967). Several of the arguments presented in these papers seem to me very weak, however. For example, McCawley argues that indices must be assigned to full noun phrases rather than to nouns, as suggested in *Aspects.* But this argument follows from an assumption which I see no reason to accept, namely, that in the theory outlined by Chomsky (1965), an index must be assigned to the noun *hat* in such sentences as *John bought a red hat and Bill bought a brown one.* This assumption in turn follows from a theory of indices as referents which I find unintelligible, since it provides no interpretation, so far as I can see, for the case in which nouns are used with no specific intended reference, or for plurals of indefinite or infinite reference, and so on. Until these matters are cleared up, I see no force to McCawley's contention.

32. Where $e$ is the identity element. To be more precise, the structural description of the transformation would have to provide further information, but this goes beyond the detail necessary to clarify the point at issue. One might extend this operation of *there*-insertion, introducing the complex symbol [*there,* $+$NP, $\alpha$ *plural*] ($\alpha = +$ or $\alpha = -$), where the third term in the proper analysis (*a man,* in the cited example) is [$\alpha$ *plural*], plurality now being regarded as a feature that ascends from a head noun to the NP node dominating it. This would make it possible for the rule of *there*-insertion to precede the rule of number agreement. It would also make possible the derivation of *there are believed to be CIA agents in the university* from *it is believed [there to be CIA agents in the university]* just as *CIA agents are believed to be in the university* might derive from *it is believed [CIA agents to be in the university]*, along lines described in Rosenbaum (1967).

33. Brought to my attention by John Ross.

34. The same conclusion is argued on different grounds by Lakoff and Peters (1966). Further evidence that transformations apply to the domain $\overline{N}$ is provided by the fact (pointed out to me by John Ross) that extraposition from the determiner takes place inside a noun phrase, as in: *one of the boys who are here who is a friend of mine.*

35. Harris (1951, Chapter 16).

36. Some examples are discussed by Chapin (1967), which presents the case for the transformationalist hypothesis on the grounds to which we now briefly turn.

37. There are also, of course, many cases where there is no possible base form such as (54a), e.g., *probable, feasible, (im)practicable, formidable, peaceable, knowledgeable, perishable, appreciable, sociable, flexible, amiable, variable, actionable, amenable, reasonable, seasonable, personable, miserable, venerable, inexorable, favorable, pleasurable, palatable, tractable, delectable, ineluctable, salable, habitable,*

*creditable, profitable, hospitable, charitable, comfortable, reputable, irascible, incredible, audible, legible, eligible, negligible, intelligible, indelible, horrible, visible, sensible, responsible, accessible, possible, plausible, compatible.*

38. Such an alternative is of course programmatic insofar as semantic interpretation remains obscure. But the necessity for rules that relate deep structures to (absolute) semantic interpretations seems clear, and it is dangerous to base any argument on the fact that we know little about such rules. If we knew nothing about phonology, it would be tempting to try to account for phonetic form by much more elaborate syntactic processes. Knowing something about phonology, we can see why this step is ill-advised.

39. As was pointed out to me by E. Klima.

40. An alternative analysis that derives *tomatoes grow* from *NP grows tomatoes* is implausible, since it would imply that *children grow* derives from * *NP grows children.* See Chomsky (1965, p. 214).

## REFERENCES FOR 'REMARKS ON NOMINALIZATION'

Annear, S., and D. Elliot. 1965. Derivational morphology in generative grammar. Paper presented to the LSA winter meeting.

Chapin, P. 1967. On the syntax of word derivation in English. Doctoral dissertation. MIT. [Also in MITRE Technical Paper No. 68. Bedford, Mass.: MITRE Corporation. September, 1967.]

Chomsky, N. 1965. Aspects of the theory of syntax. Cambridge, Mass.: The MIT Press.

Chomsky, N. 1968. Problems of explanation in linguistics. In: Explanations in the behavioural sciences. Edited by Borger and Cioffi. Cambridge, Mass.: The MIT Press.

Hall, B. 1965. Subject and object in modern English. Doctoral dissertation. MIT.

Harris, Z. 1951. Methods in structural linguistics. Chicago: University of Chicago Press.

Katz, J., and P. Postal. 1964. An integrated theory of linguistic descriptions. Cambridge, Mass.: The MIT Press.

Kenny, A. 1963. Action, emotion, and will. London: Routledge and Kegan Paul.

Kiparsky, C., and P. Kiparsky. 1967. Fact. Paper. MIT. [Reprinted 1970, in N. Bierwisch and K. Heidolph, Progress in linguistics. The Hague: Mouton; and in Chapter 11 of this volume.]

Lakoff, G. 1965. Irregularity in syntax. Doctoral dissertation. Indiana University. [Published 1970, New York: Holt, Rinehart and Winston.]

Lakoff, G. 1966. Some verbs of change and causation. In: Harvard Computation Laboratory Report to the National Science Foundation on mathematical linguistics and automatic translation, No. NSF-20. Cambridge, Mass.: Harvard University.

Langendoen, D. T. 1967. The syntax of the English expletive *it*. In: Georgetown University Round Table on Languages and Linguistics 1966. Edited by F. P. Dinneen, S.J. Washington, D.C.: Georgetown University Press. 207-216.

Lees, R. 1960. The grammar of English nominalizations. The Hague: Mouton.

McCawley, J. 1967. How to find semantic universals in the event that there are any. Paper presented at the Texas Conference on Language Universals. [Also in the Linguistic Institute Packet of Papers. University of Illinois, 1968.]

Postal, P. 1966. Review of: R. M. W. Dixon, Linguistic science and logic. Lg. 42:1.84-93. (Footnote 16.)

Rosenbaum, P. 1967. The grammar of English predicate complement constructions. Cambridge, Mass.: The MIT Press.

Ross, J. R. 1967. Constraints on variables in syntax. Doctoral dissertation. MIT.

Weinreich, U. 1966. Explorations in semantic theory. In: Current trends in linguistics. Vol. III: Theoretical foundations. The Hague: Mouton.

QUESTIONS

Let us consider each of Chomsky's four main points (mentioned in our introduction to his article).

In making his first point, productivity, Chomsky shows that derived nominals correspond only to what are essentially deep structure Ss--Ss to which no optional transformations have applied. The exception is that there are nominals corresponding to passivized Ss. Chomsky handles these by having a cycle on NPs as well as Ss, and generalizing the passive transformation so that it applies, in two steps (separable in NPs but not Ss), to both NPs and Ss.

Question 1. Assuming Chomsky's claim of nonproductivity is correct, how might a transformationalist handle this problem? That is, if there is a transformational rule converting Ss to NPs, how might one explain the putative failure of Ss to nominalize, once optional transformations have applied to them?

Question 2. Chomsky shows that the following rules, for which we have given example sentences, do not apply in derived nominals:

Particle Movement

(i) He looked up the information.
He looked the information up.

Flip or Psych Movement

(ii) He was amused at the stories.
The stories amused him.

Tough Movement or Object-to-Subject Raising

(iii) To please John is easy.
John is easy to please.

Subject-to-Subject Raising

(iv) [John win the prize] is certain.
John is certain to win the prize.

What about Subject-to-Object Raising (I believe that John is a Russian--I believe John to be a Russian) (cf. the discussion of Chomsky's (31) and (32))?

Question 3. Do any of the following rules apply in derived nominals, as Passive does?

Reflexive

(i) John believes in John.
John believes in himself.

Dative-Movement

(ii) John sold the cow to Mary.
John sold Mary the cow.

Equi NP Deletion

(iii) John hopes he will win.
John hopes to win.

*There* Insertion

(iv) A woman arrived.
There arrived a woman.

**Question 4.** Look at your answers to Questions 2 and 3. Why should certain rules and not others apply in both Ss and NPs (assuming the lexicalist hypothesis), i.e. do the two sets of rules have different characteristics? (You might consider the role of the V in the formal statement of each rule. Why might this be relevant?

*Question 5.** Why are the two parts of the Passive rule not able to apply separately in Ss?

Question 6. Why does Chomsky suggest (in the discussion between his examples (40) and (41)) deriving *the necessity for John to leave* and *the likelihood that John will leave* by agent-postposing rather than by extraposition?

**Question 7.** The NP-preposing part of the Passive rule can apply to many prepositional objects in Ss, but only objects of *of* in NPs.

(i) John referred to Mary.
Mary was referred to by John.
(ii) John's reference to Mary.
*Mary's reference to by John.

cf: The floods' destruction of the city.
The city's destruction by the floods.

Passive is also blocked by prepositions (other than *of*) which appear only in the NP.

(iii) John prefers Mary.
Mary is preferred by John.
(iv) John's preference for Mary.
*Mary's preference (for) by John

Try to formulate this restriction on the NP-preposing part of the Passive rule in a maximally general, minimally complicated way. (Remember, the rule must apply to both Ss and NPs.)

Question 8. Try applying the Passive rules to examples (i) and (ii).

(i) Mary's gift of a book to John.
(ii) Mary's criticism/discussion of John.

Can you think of other examples such as these?

The second point is that the relation between the V and the associated derived nominal is idiosyncratic. Chomsky says that this has so often been remarked that discussion is superfluous, and gives us no detailed examples.

Question 9. Explain the difficulty in the relation to the V for a few of the nominals Chomsky lists under his example (10) (*laughter, marriage, construction, actions, activities, revolution, belief, doubt, conversion, permutation, trial, residence, qualifications, specifications*).

Question 10. Chomsky admits that there are subregularities that have frequently been noted, but again gives no examples. Give a list of Vs or Adj's and associated nominals where the relationship is regular. Try formulating a lexical redundancy rule which captures this relationship.

*Question 11. Suppose transformationalists were to say that the regular relationships are transformational, and the irregular ones are lexical, with the Vs marked to keep Nominalization from applying. Consider an acknowledged transformation like Passive. Are there 'pseudo-passives' which appear at first to be derived from corresponding actives, but show idiosyncratic meanings and syntactic peculiarities on closer examination? Discuss, for example, the relationship between *bear* and *born*. How could transformationalists use such examples in their argument?

The third point is that derived nominals have the internal structure of NPs, allowing Adj's, pluralization, and all determiners, but not aspect.

Question 12. Chomsky claims that a major difference between gerundives (which he derives from underlying Ss) and derived nominals (which he derives from underlying NPs) is that the latter have the internal structure of NPs while the former do not. Compare gerundives to Chomsky's third class, the mixed *ing + of* forms. Examples (i) through (v) are several pairs of Ss contrasting these two forms. For each pair tell what property of NPs is being tested. (Note: the pairs are not intended to be synonymous. Synonymy is irrelevant to this question.)

(i) a. John enjoyed reading *The Bald Soprano*.
(i) b. John enjoyed a reading of *The Bald Soprano*.
(ii) a. John's killing the deer brutally upset Mary.
(ii) b. John's brutal killing of the deer upset Mary.
(iii) a. I reported John's having milked the cows.
(iii) b. *I reported John's having milked of the cows.
(iv) a. Sighting UFOs makes Mary nervous.
(iv) b. Sightings of UFOs make Mary nervous.
(v) a. Not reading that book is preposterous.
(v) b. No reading of that book is preposterous.

(Examples (i) and (iv) are taken from Wasow and Roeper 1972.)

*Question 13. Try adding restrictive and nonrestrictive relative clauses to both derived and gerundive nominals. Does the occurrence of relative clauses have anything to do with determiners?

**Question 14. Derived nominals, unlike Ss, do not allow modals or aspect. How might a transformationalist handle this problem?

**Question 15. Infinitive clauses do allow aspect, but not modals or tense. On the assumption that these clauses are transformationally derived from structures which are generated by the base rules and dominated by S, what solutions can you suggest to account for the nonoccurrence of (a) tense, and (b) modals? (Note: derived nominals also do not allow tense. A transformationalist might use the same solution for this problem as for (a), and the same solution for Question 14 as for (b).) (Hint for Questions 14 and 15: Consider Chomsky's rule in *Syntactic Structures* 1957, Auxiliary → Tense (Modal) (Perfect) (Progressive) (Passive). Leaving the problem of passive voice aside, what is the big formal difference between tense on the one hand, and modals and the aspects (perfective and progressive) on the other?)

*Question 16. In Chomsky's discussion of the base rule schema ($\overline{\overline{X}}$ → Spec,$\overline{X}$ $\overline{X}$), he allows X to be N, A, or V. Subsequent researchers, such as Bresnan (1972), have argued that X can also be S, and that complementizers are the Specs of S, being obligatorily deleted in topmost Ss. If this is the case, then complementizers might be the source, for a transformationalist, of the determiners of derived nominals. Can you suggest any transformational source for pluralization?

The fourth point is that the base and transformational rules needed to generate derived nominals with their complements and possessive agents are also needed for ordinary NPs.

**Question 17.** In discussing his examples in (22), Chomsky argues that complements just like those occurring with derived nominals must be generated with ordinary Ns, and cannot be derived via Relative Clause Reduction from predicate complements. He has the most difficulty when the complement is a full S, as in (i).

(i) the question whether John should leave

His analysis of such constructions leads him (in the paragraph following his example (25)) to propose, essentially, deriving Ss from NPs. While his formulation of the rule does not exactly create structure (something transformations cannot do), he generates the structure ahead of time, leaving it empty until needed. Try working out an approach which generates (ii) and pseudo-clefts, but not (iii),

(ii) The question is whether John should leave.
(iii) *The question whether John should leave is why Bill stayed.

by deletion from structures juxtaposing a question and its answer, as in (iv).

(iv) [John saw what] is [John saw a giraffe]
    [John saw a giraffe] is [John saw what]

(See Pope 1976, Section 2.3 for further discussion.)

*Question 18. The same problem of transformations creating structure comes up in the discussion of pseudo-cleft sentences in the text following example (46). Chomsky suggests that the *do* in (i) is derived by 'an extension of the rule of *do*-insertion'.

(i) What John did was read a book about himself.

Ross (1975) has argued that this *do* differs from the *do* of *Do*-Insertion or *Do*-Support, and claims that instead it is a main V which takes a S complement, as in (ii).

(ii) [John do [John read a book about himself]]

It appears on the surface only when the lower V is moved away or deleted.

Try deriving (i) and (iii) using this suggestion and that given in Question 17.

(iii) What John read was a book about himself.

*Question 19. Chomsky argues that the fact that the base rules that would be needed to generate derived nominals under the lexicalist hypothesis are needed anyway for nonderived nominals 'lends further support to the lexicalist assumption'. However, Emonds (1976) has proposed a structure-preserving constraint (discussed in our introduction to Emonds' article in Chapter 6) which requires that the output of a transformation like Nominalization must be a structure which, except for words, is generable by the base rules. How would a transformationalist use this proposal to answer Chomsky?

*Question 20. Give the base rules and the transformations (Agent-Postposing, Chomsky's (37), (38), and/or (39), in that order) involved in the derivation of each of the following NPs. Do not worry about the details of features and exact labels or the deeper analysis of relatives such as *that John has*.

(i) Many of those struggles of the pastor's son's with his conscience
(ii) My father's recording of 'Roll on, Columbia', by Woodie Guthrie
(iii) This type of construction's explication by Chomsky

Question 21. Chomsky says (between his examples (40) and (41)) that Agent-Postposing is 'unspecifiable' for gerundive nominals, and indeed it cannot apply to them. What keeps it from applying?

Question 22. Look at your answers to the foregoing questions, especially Questions 1, 4, 11, 14, 15, 16, and 19. Which of the two analyses (lexical or transformational) seems more attractive to you? Why? (For a defense of the transformationalist position, see Newmeyer 1971.) If both analyses can generate the data, look for cases where one analysis is mechanical and ad hoc rather than explanatory.

HOMEWORK PROBLEMS

Answer Questions 3, 12, and 20 as homework problems.

## SUGGESTED READINGS

Bresnan, J. 1972. The theory of complementation in English syntax. Unpublished doctoral dissertation. MIT. (p. 13 for Question 16.)

Chomsky, N. 1957. Syntactic structures. The Hague: Mouton.

Chomsky, N. 1973. Conditions on transformations. In: A festschrift for Morris Halle. Edited by S. A. Anderson and R. P. Kiparsky. New York: Holt, Rinehart and Winston. 232-286. (See footnote 64 in relation to (ii) of Question 20.)

Emonds, J. 1976. A transformational approach to English syntax. New York: Academic Press.

Fraser, B. 1970. Some remarks on the action nominal in English. In: Readings in English transformational grammar. Edited by R. Jacobs and P. Rosenbaum. Waltham, Mass.: Ginn and Co. 83-98.

Levi, J. 1978. The syntax and semantics of complex nominals. New York: Academic Press.

Newmeyer, F. 1971. The source of derived nominals in English. Lg. 47:4.786-796. (For Questions 4, 22, and several others.)

Pope, E. N. 1976. Questions and answers in English. The Hague: Mouton. (Section 2.3 for Question 17.)

Ross, J. 1975. Act. In: Semantics of natural language. Edited by D. Davidson and G. Harman. Dordrecht: Reidel. 70-126. (For Question 18.)

Wasow, T., and T. Roeper. 1972. On the subject of gerunds. Foundations of Language 8:1.44-61. (For Question 12.)

# 6

## EVIDENCE THAT INDIRECT OBJECT MOVEMENT IS A STRUCTURE-PRESERVING RULE

### Joseph Emonds

Introduction. In his 1970 MIT dissertation, *Root and structure-preserving transformations,* Joseph Emonds proposed one of the most comprehensive constraints on the operation of syntactic rules in a generative model: the structure-preserving constraint. This constraint is even more elaborately investigated and defended in Emonds (1976). The proposals in these works are important to the student of syntax for two reasons. First, they spawned much research and the student needs a clear understanding of the structure-preserving constraint in order to evaluate the resultant literature. But more importantly, Emonds' constraint is a serious attempt to reduce the power of grammatical transformations and, therefore, is a major contribution to the theory of syntax. His proposals make predictions about all syntactic rules and are empirically significant. This very general theory could be disproved by the existence of one intractable rule. It is instructive to study Emonds' proposals, particularly in order to see clearly how all the possible interrelationships of two rules must be taken into account in the separate formulation of each. Consistency and comprehensiveness are two of the major strong points of Emonds' work.

The structure-preserving constraint basically states that all transformational processes except those involving deletion under identity will be of one of three types: root, structure-preserving, or local. Emonds further claims that the major grammatical transformational operations are restricted to only the first two types of rules. A root transformation is one which can apply only once and only in main clauses. (Subject-Auxiliary Inversion, Right and Left Dislocation, and various other preposing rules are root transformations.) Root transformations are not restricted in the way that structure-preserving transformations, which may apply on any and every cycle, must be. A structure-preserving transformation, simply put, is one that moves, copies, or inserts a constituent C into a position in the phrase marker in which a node C could have been generated by the PS rules. This constraint is designed to capture the fact, for which no previous explanation had been offered, that transformations generally do not produce anything wildly different from deep structures. Examples of structure-preserving rules given by Emonds include Passive, *There*-Insertion, and Complex NP Shift. A local transformation (previously called 'Minor Movement Transformation' in Emonds 1970 and in the article reprinted here) affects only two specified adjacent constituents (with no variable between them), one of which must be a nonphrase node (the phrase nodes being S, NP, AP, VP, PP). The operation may not be subject to any condition exterior to the two affected adjacent constituents. Local transformations are exemplified by Auxiliary *Do*-Insertion, Quantifier Postposition, and Det Incorporation.

We have included Emonds' article 'Evidence that Indirect Object Movement is a Structure-Preserving Rule' in this volume because it is representative of the kind of argumentation and the type of data that one must explore in testing the structure-preserving constraint. Indirect Object Movement is the rule responsible for deriving (2) from (1).

(1a) I gave the book to John.
(1b) I baked the cake for Mary.
(2a) I gave John the book.
(2b) I baked Mary the cake.

Since Indirect Object Movement can apply in embedded clauses, it cannot be a root transformation.

(3a) Everyone knows that I gave John the book.
(3b) Everyone knows that I baked Mary the cake.

Likewise, since Indirect Object Movement affects only phrase nodes, it cannot be a local transformation. Therefore it must be structure-preserving if Emonds' constraint is correct.

Emonds organizes the article into two major divisions. In the first part, he examines particle movement and argues that particles are intransitive prepositions. He shows that in five separate cases if particles are prepositions, generalizations can be captured which would otherwise be missed. Once he has concluded that particles must be prepositions, he has a defensible reason for generating them in the position following the direct object, since this is where PPs are generated. In the second part of the article, he examines Ss in which both Particle Movement and Indirect Object Movement have applied, arguing that the most straightforward way to account for the data is with a structure-preserving rule for Indirect Object Movement which interchanges the indirect object and the direct object, rather than moving one of them over the other. His conclusion is that Indirect Object Movement obeys the structure-preserving constraint.

# EVIDENCE THAT INDIRECT OBJECT MOVEMENT
# IS A STRUCTURE-PRESERVING RULE

In *The Verb-Particle Construction of English,* Fraser investigated in detail a class of post-verbal particles which may precede or follow non-pronominal direct objects; he distinguished three main usages for these particles:

(1) As directional adverbs:
>John carried the trunk *up*.
>John carried *up* the trunk.
>Mary threw a box *out*.
>Mary threw *out* a box.
>The teacher handed every paper *back* to the students.
>The teacher handed *back* every paper to the students.
>They should gather these books *together*.
>They should gather *together* these books.

(2) In idiomatic verb-particle combinations:
>John will turn that job *down*.
>John will turn *down* that job.
>His offer really took John *in*.
>His offer really took *in* John.
>You shouldn't put such tasks *off*.
>You shouldn't put *off* such tasks.
>He has taken the government *over*.
>He has taken *over* the government.

(3) In 'completive' verb-particle combinations (*up* only):
>John fixed a drink *up*.
>John fixed *up* a drink.
>We painted the house *up*.
>We painted *up* the house.
>Cut the meat *up*.
>Cut *up* the meat.

Fraser demonstrated that noun phrases which follow particles are not their direct objects. That is, *up the trunk* is not a constituent in *carry up the trunk!* Rather, this verb phrase exhibits the structure of (4):

187

[546]

(4)

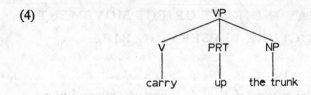

In the first half of this study, I will argue that these post-verbal particles should not be assigned to a category PRT distinct from the category preposition (P). In other words, I will argue that these particles should be regarded as intransitive prepositions.

I

We note first that post-verbal particles are almost all also transitive prepositions, and that when such a word is used as a directional adverb, it has the same intrinsic meaning whether or not it has an object. On the other hand, a non-productive syntactic caterory like modal (M) has no members in common with the other non-productive syntactic categories (particles, prepositions, determiners, or the 'degree' words which modify adjectives such as *too, enough, very, rather, quite, as, more, most, so, how, this, that,* etc.). Similarly, there are no determiners or degree words which are also particles or prepositions. The fact that some degree words are determiners might in fact be taken as evidence of an as yet unformalized syntactic relation between two categories, a suspicion strengthened by the existence of other properties common to the categories modified by determiners and degree words (nouns and adjectives, respectively). (For example, adjectives and nouns are declined in languages with declensions; only adjectives and nouns can be modified by *wh* words; neither category may have non-prepositional NP complements in surface structure.)

Thus, it appears that in general non-related, non-productive syntactic categories do not have members in common. In order to preserve this generalisation, we must formally relate the category of post-verbal particles to the category 'preposition', because these categories have *many* members in common.

Furthermore, if we postulate two distinct syntactic categories PRT and P, we are faced with the consequence that phrase structure rules such as PP →PRT–NP and PP→P would formally be just as possible as PP→P–NP and PP→PRT.

Basically, considering P and PRT as distinct categories leads to the same problems as those that early transformationalists faced when they proposed two verb classes, $V_T$ (transitive verb) and $V_I$ (intransitive verb). These two classes then shared many members whose only semantic differences in context seemed attributable to the presence or absence of an object and whose distribution was otherwise identical; furthermore, postulating two such distinct verb classes meant that phrase structure rules such as $VP \rightarrow V_I\text{-}NP$ and $VP \rightarrow V_T$ were formally possible. The solution to these difficulties was proposed in Chomsky (1965); he assumed that there was a single verbal category whose members were 'sub-categorized' to take or not take objects. That is, a lexical sub-categorization feature specifies for each verb whether it can or must be followed by a direct object.

In this way, it becomes formally impossible to have verb phrases whose transitive verbs have no objects in deep structure or whose intransitive verbs have objects. Furthermore, the rules which determine the distribution of verbs (including deletion rules) need only to mention the category V, and the intrinsic meanings of verbs which optionally appear with or without objects need be given only once for each verb.

If we analyze post-verbal particles as prepositions which are sub-categorized not to take objects, we explain in the same way why many prepositions are also particles, why the prepositions which are particles have the same meanings in both usages, and why prepositions and particles have similar distribution. (Of course, there are differences in distribution, but we will see as we proceed that these differences are less fundamental than might seem apparent.) And lastly, there is no formal possibility of particles with objects as distinct from prepositions with objects.

Thus, I propose that morphemes such as *with, in, apart* all be generated as prepositions by the phrase structure rule $PP \rightarrow P\text{-}(NP)$, and that these prepositions are associated in the lexicon with sub-categorization features as in (5):

(5)  with, $+P$, $+$_____NP (similarly for *at, for, toward,* etc.)
     in, $+P$, $+$_____(NP) (similarly for *out, down, around,* etc.)
     apart, $+P$, $+$_____(similarly for *away, back, together,* etc.)

II

This decision, for which I will continue to give independent justification in the following sections, implies that the deep structure position of particles should be the same as that of other prepositional phrases: they should follow the direct object. (That is, an advantage of analyzing particles as prepositions is that the symbol PRT is eliminated from the phrase structure rules, because particles are generated in the position of PP.) This means in turn that the pre-direct object position of particles is due to a particle movement transformation (6):

(6)  $X + V\text{-} NP \text{-}[P]\text{-} Y \Rightarrow 1\text{-}3\text{-}2\text{-}4$, where $1\text{-}2\text{-}3\text{-}4$ is a VP
         $-\text{PRO}$   PP

One might ask if the idiosyncratic verb-particle combinations such as those in (2) should not be contiguous in deep structure; this would have to be the case if lexical entries, viewed as insertion transformations, are constrained to insert only continuous sequences into trees generated by the phrase structure rules.

There are two answers to this question consistent with the decision that particles are moved next to the verb in surface structure only by virtue of the transformation (6). The first possibility is simply that there does not seem to be any convincing argument that in fact lexical entries must be sequences of contiguous elements. It may be that lexical entries (insertion transformations) may consist of verbs and other sister constituents which are not necessarily contiguous. If this were so, we would expect to find idioms of the form V–PP where direct objects obligatorily intervene between the two parts of the idiom. Such idioms do exist:

(7)     John *took* his students *to task.*
        *John *took to task* his students.
        His proposal will *bring* the crisis *to a head.*
        *His proposal will *bring to a head* the crisis.
        John wants to *put* that car *to the test.*
        *John wants to *put to the test* that car.
        The shopkeepers *took* some students *for a ride.*
        *The shopkeepers *took for a ride* some students.

On the other hand, if one insists in the face of idioms such as those in (7) that lexical entries should be continuous sequences of morphemes, it is clear that in order to account for the idioms in (7), there must be an obligatory transformation which applies to idioms of the form V–PP that moves the PP part of the idiom into the position after the direct object, as in (8):

(8)

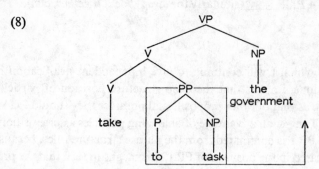

(Whether the PP in (8) is dominated by V or not is of no importance in this discussion.)

Given a deep structure configuration for V–PP idioms as in (8) and a rule which separates them, as indicated by the arrow in (8), it is clear that the same analysis and rule will produce (only) the discontinous idiomatic verb-particle combinations in (2). It then follows that the particle movement rule (6) should apply to idiomatic just as it does to directional adverb particles to produce the examples in (2) in which particles precede the direct object.

I conclude that the question of whether or not V–PP idioms are contiguous in deep structure is independent of the hypothesis that particles come to precede direct objects in surface structure only by virtue of the rule (6).

### III

Continuing with the justification for considering the post-verbal particles as prepositions, we next recall Fraser's point that certain verbs may or must have adverb complements of direction. For the sake of an example, consider the transitive verb *put,* the verb *sneak,* and the intransitive verbs *glance* and *dart.* These verbs must be followed by a directional adverb, but the directional adverb may be either a prepositional phrase or a post-verbal particle.

By analyzing particles as intransitive prepositions, we can account for this by simply assigning these verbs the sub-categorization feature $+\underline{\quad\quad}$ PP, where the head of PP has the feature DIR (directional). (How this condition is incorporated into the sub-categorization mechanism is of no importance; it is simply a fact that PP's whose heads are non-directional prepositions like *without, because, until, since, despite, for,* etc. do not fulfill the requirement of an obligatory directional complement after these verbs).

(9)     *John put some toys.
        John put some toys in the garage, downstairs, away, down, to-
        gether, back, out, etc.
        *John was sneaking (the food).
        John was sneaking (the food) into the theatre, out of the store, in,
        back, out, away, over, etc.
        *The children darted.
        The children darted outside, toward the door, in, back, off, apart,
        away, etc.
        *Why did you glance?
        Why did you glance at Mary, behind you, down, in, away, up,
        back, etc.

If post-verbal particles were not prepositions, we would have to sub-categorize such verbs as $+\underline{\quad\quad}\left\{\begin{array}{l}\text{PP}\\\text{PRT}\end{array}\right\}$, where the head of the PP has the feature "directional."

Similarly, for the very large number of verbs which take optional directional complements (*move, shove,* etc.), if we did not analyze particles as prepositions, we would have to always use the sub-categorization feature $+ -(\left\{\begin{array}{l} PP \\ PRT \end{array}\right\})$ Further, we note that no verbs of motion take directional adverb complements which must or must not be particles as opposed to prepositional phrases, as we might expect if these were distinct grammatical categories.

It is of course true that the directional adverb PP complements which follow certain verbs are subject to certain probably semantic restrictions, but these restrictions cut across (are independent of ) the distinction between particles and transitive prepositions, and so are not relevant to the discussion here.

(10)     John sewed the material together, into one piece, on, onto the coat, back, up, etc.

*John sewed the material apart, into shreds, off, out, out of the blanket, away, etc.

I conclude then that the sub-categorization of every verb which takes a directional adverb complement will be simplified if we analyze post-verbal particles as intransitive prepositions.

IV

In accepted American speech, the emphatic word *right* modifies only prepositions of space and time, but not other syntactic categories such as adjectives, adverbs, modals, etc.

(11)     *Bill visits Europe right often, frequently, etc.

*Fights happened right seldom in that town.

*Those girls were right attractive.

*A proposal of that sort seems right unjust, wise, etc.

*He ironed his shirt right wet.

*Some right ignorant students asked those questions.

(12)     Make yourself right at home.

We went right along that road.

Bill put the spices right on the meat.

He lives right up the street.

Some people can't work right before dinner.

It is also true that *right* modifies subordinating conjunctions of space and time, but this actually is only one among several indications that subordinating conjunctions are prepositions in underlying structure. Other arguments to this effect are given in Emonds (1970) and Geis (1970).

The word *right* also modifies post-verbal particles, which is a further similarity of this class of words to prepositions:

(13)    John came right in.
        He put the toys right back.
        Go right on to the stoplight.
        They looked it right up and left.
        John brought the bottles right down.

By analyzing the post-verbal particles as prepositions, we can simply state that *right* modifies only prepositions.

Another advantage of this analysis is that the particle movement rule (6) accounts for the fact that particles modified by *right* do not precede the direct object without the addition of any special conditions of the particle movement rule. On the other hand, if particles did not originate to the right of the direct object, we would have to add a condition on the rule moving them to that position: such a rule would ordinarily be optional, but it would have to be obligatory if the particles were modified by *right*, as shown by the examples of (14):

(14)    *He put right back the toys.
        *They looked right up the number.
        *John brought right down the bottles.

There are some idiomatic uses of particles which *right* can modify and some which it cannot, but the same is true of idiomatic prepositional phrases, so this irregular distribution is not an argument against the prepositional status of particles:

(15)    He put his life savings right on the line.
        He put his coat right on.
        *They put the enemy right to flight.
        *John put his vacation right off until Christmas.
        ?Bill should take those remarks right to heart.
        ?Bill should take the answer right down when it is given.
        *Bill should take his friends right to task.
        *Bill should take his friends right up on their offer.
        *The commitee took the suggestion right into account.
        *The storekeepers took the students right in. (idiomatic sense)

Given the validity of using *right* as a diagnostic for the syntactic category preposition, we can see that post-verbal particles (i.e., directional intransitive prepositions) are not the only intransitive prepositions in English, as is shown by (16):

(16)    John finished the task right before.
        John lives right outside.
        I heard something right overhead.
        They took the job right afterwards.
        You should do this right now.

V

There is an expletive construction in English which consists of a directional adverb plus a prepositional phrase introduced by *with*, as exemplified in (17).

(17)    Into the dungeon with that traitor!
        To the river with those sandbags!
        Out the door with it!
        To hell with this assignment!

If we consider the post-verbal particles as intransitive prepositions, the structure of this expletive is always of the form $\begin{smallmatrix} P \\ +DIR \end{smallmatrix}$ (NP)–with–NP. However, if we consider particles to be distinct from the category P, another sequence of the form PRT– with –NP is a possible example of this construction:

(18)    Off with his head!
        Down with the leadership!
        Out with what you know!
        Away with them!

This means that, whether such expletive constructions are to be accounted for by phrase structure rules or by deletion transformations, considering particles as instances of directional prepositions will simplify the analysis.

VI

There is a preposing rule for directional adverbs in sentences whose verbs are in the simple past or present. If the subject of such a sentence is not a pronoun, it may invert with the verb when such preposing occurs. Another difference between this preposing rule and other adverb preposing rules is that in this case there is no comma (breath pause) after the preposed adverb.

(19)    Into the house he ran!
        Down the street rolled the carriage!
        Out the window jumped the cat!
        Into the sink they go!

The directional adverb preposing rule applies not only to transitive prepositional phrases, but also to post-verbal particles:

(20)    In he ran!
        Down rolled the carriage!
        Out jumped the cat!
        Up she climbed!

By analysing particles as intransitive prepositions, we can simplify the statement of this preposing transformation by allowing it to apply only to constituents of the form $\left[ _{PP}\begin{smallmatrix} P \\ +DIR \end{smallmatrix} -X \right]$. Otherwise, we would have to state that it applies to two categories, directional prepositions and particles.

It should be remarked that this rule does not apply to particles or transitive prepositions which are part of V–PP idioms.

(21)    Bill ran into trouble.
        *Into trouble ran Bill.
        Bill went into detail.
        *Into detail went Bill.
        John jumped at the chance.
        *At the chance jumped John.
        Bill came to a conclusion.
        *To a conclusion came Bill.
        The gun went off.
        *Off went the gun.
        The battery ran down.
        *Down ran the battery.
        The meeting came off at six.
        *Off came the meeting.
        The kitten rolled up. (into a ball)
        *Up rolled the kitten.

VII

I think the advantages and simplifications in the phrase structure rules, in sub-categorization, in specifying the distribution of *right*, in analyzing the expletive construction mentioned above, and in stating the directional adverb preposing rule justify the claim that post-verbal particles are prepositions. (We have also seen that idiomatic post-verbal particles and other idiomatic prepositional phrases do not differ in syntactic behavior). However, there is one construction in which non-idiomatic particles do not act like prepositional phrases. As noted by Fraser, prepositional phrases but not single particles can appear in focus position in cleft sentences, and in other 'answers-to-questions' contexts:

(22)    It was into the house that John ran.
        *It was in that John ran.
        It was down the street that he pushed the cart.
        *It was away that he pushed the cart.
        Where did John run? *In. Into the house.
        Where did he push the cart? *Away. Down the street.
        Where he brought the radio was into the cellar.
        *Where he brought the radio was down.
        Where you should go is back home.
        *Where you should go is back.

I have no specific proposal as to where in the grammar the form of answers to questions is specified, but these facts, given the evidence that post-verbal particles are prepositions, suggest two possible analyses: (i) Wherever the syntactic form of appropriate answers to questions is specified, it is required that PP's are acceptable only if they contain, at some level of structure, an NP. (ii) In view of the unacceptability of answers like *In somewhere, *Down somewhere, and *Back somewhere in the contexts of (22), perhaps surface structure intransitive prepositions (particles) should be analyzed as transitive in deep structure with objects like somewhere, which would be deleted (optionally) in surface structure. Both of these analyses are compatible with the inclusion of post-verbal particles in the class of prepositions (P), and neither introduces any implausible complications into the grammar.

VIII

In the second half of this study, I will examine the relation between the particle movement rule, given as (6) above, and the indirect object movement rule or rules. The relevance of the first sections is that, once it is established that particles are always intransitive prepositions, it follows that particles follow the direct object NP in deep structure and that it is a transformation (6) which optionally moves them next to the verb.

Many verbs which take indirect objects also appear with particles. In sentences where the indirect object is not moved in front of the direct object (assuming these to be the deep structure configurations given by the rule VP → V–(NP)–(PP)–...), particles can precede or follow the direct object, as predicted by rule (6):

(23)    The secretary sent a schedule out to the stockholders.
        The secretary sent out a schedule to the stockholders.

Some student paid his loan back to the bank.
Some student paid back his loan to the bank.
John read the figures off to Mary.
John read off the figures to Mary.
A clerk will type a permit out for John.
A clerk will type out a permit for John.
Bill fixed a drink up for John.
Bill fixed up a drink for John.
He has brought some cigars down for Dad.
He has brought down some cigars for Dad.
The teacher put the trucks together for the children.
The teacher put together the trucks for the children.

According to the conclusions of the earlier sections, the first sentences of the pairs in (23) represent the deep structure order of constituents.

Let us now consider the possible positions for particles in sentences where the *to* or *for* indirect object movement rules have applied.

(24)    The secretary sent the stockholders out a schedule.
        Some student paid the bank back his loan.
        John read Mary off the figures.
        A clerk will type John out a permit.
        Bill fixed John up a drink.
        He has brought Dad down some cigars.
        ?The teacher put the children together the trucks.

(25)    *The secretary sent the stockholders a schedule out.
        *Some student paid the bank his loan back.
        *John read Mary the figures off.
        *A clerk will type John a permit out.
        *Bill fixed John a drink up.
        *He has brought Dad some cigars down.
        *The teacher put the children the trucks together.

(26)    ?The secretary sent out the stockholders a schedule.
        ?Some student paid back the bank his loan.
        ?John read off Mary the figures.
        ?A clerk will type out John a permit.
        ?Bill fixed up John a drink.
        ?He has brought down Dad some cigars.
        *The teacher put together the children the trucks.

In all the idiolects I have investigated, the most favored and natural position for particles in sentences with verb-indirect object-object order is *be-*

*tween* the two objects NP's, as in (24). Furthermore, in all idiolects, the position of the particle after the direct object, as in (25), is rejected. (There are differences in acceptability among the particles; *together* resists acceptance in sentences with two NP objects, while *back* sometimes is acceptable in sentences like (25). I am ignoring these differences which seem unsystematic and quite limited in number.)

Idiolects seem to differ with regard to the sentences like those in (26). In one dialect (dialect A), the sentences of (26) are acceptable. In another dialect (dialect B), they are not, although they are not rejected as firmly as are those in (25). (This may be due to the presence of other speakers in the speech community with dialect A). In a third dialect (dialect C), which I believe is my own, the sentences of (26) which derive from sentences with an underlying *to* indirect object are acceptable, while those which derive from sentences with an underlying *for* indirect object are not. Since in my own dialect underlying *to* indirect objects can be subjects of passives whereas underlying *for* indirect objects cannot, it is not surprising to see this difference reflected elsewhere in the transformational component, although it remains to be seen how these differences are to be formally related. I return to this point below.

I will now consider the interrelation of particle movement (6) and indirect object movement in all three dialects, A, B, and C. In dialects A and B, we can assume there is only one indirect object movement rule for the purposes of this paper. The structural description of this rule would be of the form (27). (In (27), I ignore conditions on the verb and on the animateness of the indirect object, which are irrelevant to the discussion in this paper).

$$(27) \qquad X + V - \underset{-PRO}{NP_1} - (P) - \left[ \underset{PP}{\begin{Bmatrix} to \\ for \end{Bmatrix}} - NP_2 \right] - Y \Rightarrow ?$$

(The subscripts in (27) are merely for reference in exposition.)

Before filling in the structural change of (27) for any of the three dialects, we can ask whether this indirect object movement rule moves $NP_1$ to the right over $NP_2$, $NP_2$ to the left over $NP_1$, or whether $NP_1$ and $NP_2$ exchange positions (both moving), or whether perhaps such a question has no possible empirical consequences so that the theory should be designed to make the question ill-formed.

If we move $NP_2$ to the left over $NP_1$, an optional position for particles will be after two object NP's, as in (25), no matter what order is used for particle movement and indirect object movement. To avoid this, an *ad hoc* condition must be added to particle movement (6) which states that the rule is obligatory in a second context, V–NP–NP–PRT. (It is also required that particle movement follow indirect object movement so that this condition and context can be stated. I use the symbol PRT here for expository purposes only.) But if particle movement is obligatory in sentences with two object NP's, a second undesirable consequence is that particle movement cannot be used to account for the two positions of particles in dialects A and C. This leads to complication in the indirect object movement rule. Thus, in all three dialects, assuming that $NP_2$ moves to the left over a stationary $NP_1$ introduces *ad hoc* complications in the contexts and conditions of the particle and indirect object movement rules.

If we move $NP_1$ to the right over $NP_2$, and if particle movement (6) follows indirect object movement, there is no principled way to obtain the favored order, $V-NP_2-PRT-NP_1$, since PRT precedes $NP_2$ in deep structure. If we move $NP_1$ to the right over $NP_2$ but order particle movement before indirect object movement, we can get the particles in the favored position between the two NP objects only by moving them to the right with $NP_1$, and thus complicating the context for the indirect object movement rule: the structural description would then be $V-(PRT)+NP-(PRT)-\begin{Bmatrix} to \\ for \end{Bmatrix}-NP$, and the structural change would be $1-3-\emptyset-5-2$. What is worse is that this is only a solution for dialect A; in dialect B and C no solution is possible under this set of assumptions. These complications lead me also to reject moving $NP_1$ over a stationary $NP_2$.

In contrast to the two types of indirect object movement just rejected, the third alternative, an interchange of $NP_1$ and $NP_2$ (terms 2 and 5 in (27)) leads to a perfect description of dialect A if we order this rule before particle movement.

$$(28) \qquad X + V- \underset{-PRO}{NP} -(P)- \left[ \underset{PP}{\begin{Bmatrix} to \\ for \end{Bmatrix}-NP} \right] -Y \Rightarrow 1-5-3-\emptyset-2-6$$

According to this analysis, the sentences of (25) are ungrammatical because the corresponding source sentences in which particles follow indirect objects in prepositional phrases are also ungrammatical:

(29)    *The secretary sent a schedule to the stockholders out.
        *Some student paid his loan to the bank back.
        *John read the figures to Mary off.
        *A clerk will type a permit for John out.
        *Bill fixed a drink for John up.
        *He has brought some cigars for Dad down.
        *The teacher put the trucks for the children together.
        (where "the trucks for the children" is not an NP)

Whether or not (28) applies, (6), which follows (28) in dialect A, can then optionally apply to place the particles next to the verb. If it does not apply, the particles appear in surface structure after the first NP after the verb.

We can account for dialect B by ordering particle movement *before* indirect object movement. If particle movement does not apply and indirect object movement does, the particle ends up between the indirect and direct object NP's. If particle movement does apply, the structural description for indirect object movement (28) is not met (since a particle intervenes between the verb and the direct object) and so the rule cannot apply, and the sequence V–PRT–NP–NP is correctly (for this dialect) excluded.

In dialect C, my own dialect, the *to* indirect object movement rule and the *for* indirect object movement rule are distinct, according to the analysis of Fillmore (1965). Furthermore, Fillmore postulates that *to* indirect object movement precedes *for* indirect object movement, thus allowing *to* indirect objects to become subjects of passives, but not *for* indirect objects.

By ordering particle movement (6) after *to* indirect object movement and before *for* indirect object movement, we can account for dialect C. That is, with regard to *to* indirect objects, dialect C is like dialect A, and the indirect object rule containing *to* precedes particle movement to account for this; but with regard to *for* indirect objects, dialect C is like dialect B, and the indirect object rule containing *for* follows particle movement to account for this.

IX

We have been able to account for the three different ways that post-verbal particles interact with indirect objects by formulating indirect object movement(s) as rules which interchange the positions of two NP's (making crucial use also of the fact that post-verbal particles are generated after direct object NP's in deep structure).

There is another formally different way to express the rule order (i) particle movement and (ii) indirect movement, which is worth mentioning as an alternative, although it does not affect any of the conclusions to be drawn in the next section. If rule (6) and rule (28) are simply collapsed as in (30), we also obtain the sentences of dialect B. ('e' stands for the identity element under concatenation in (30).)

$$(30) \quad X + V- \underset{-\text{PRO}}{NP} -(P)- \underset{PP}{\left[ \begin{Bmatrix} e \\ \begin{Bmatrix} to \\ for \end{Bmatrix} \end{Bmatrix} \begin{matrix} -P \\ \\ -NP \end{matrix} \right]} -Y \Rightarrow 1\text{–}5\text{–}3\text{–}\emptyset\text{–}2\text{–}6$$

Similarly, dialect C can be obtained by postulating a *to* indirect object movement rule and a following collapse of particle movement and *for* indirect object movement identical to (30) except for the absence of *to*.

There is actually a defect in (30) as it stands. According to (30), the second of two consecutive post-verbal particles should be interchangeable with a direct object. That this is not possible is easily seen from the example of (31):

(31)      John brought the radio back down.
           *John brought down back the radio.
           He pushed the shovel down in.
           *He pushed in down the shovel.

However, we will see below that the ungrammatical examples of (31) can be excluded on independent grounds if (30) is the correct way to account for dialect B.

Given this refinement, we see that there are two possible formal analyses for dialect B and C, provided that bracket notation is permissible in transformational notation. Which of these is correct is an open question; but in either case it remains true that the straightforward analyses of dialects A, B, and C which are free of *ad hoc* stipulations can be made only in terms of indirect object rules ((28) or (30)) which interchange two NP's rather than move one NP over another stationary NP.

x

The formulation of the indirect object movement rule as an interchange of two NP's, as in (28) or (30), is justified here because it correctly and simply accounts for the positions of particles in sentences containing indirect objects. It is interesting that this formulation is the *only* formulation of indirect object movement permitted by a general constraint on movement and insertion transformations which I proposed in my dissertation. This constraint limits movement and insertion transformations in embedded sentences to be either 'structure-preserving' rules or 'minor movement' rules.

Minor movement rules are defined by a number of very restrictive conditions, two of the most important being that (i) such rules interchange two adjacent specified constituents, and that (ii) one of these constituents must not be a phrase node (NP, S, VP, PP, AP). A typical minor movement rule is particle movement. However, it is clear that indirect object movement is not such a rule, since it violates condition (ii) and also condition (i) whenever a particle is present between the two interchanged NP's. This means that the constraint I proposed requires that indirect object movement be a 'structure-preserving' rule.

Before spelling out what this means, it should be remarked that the condition that the constituents interchanged by a minor movement rule be adjacent excludes the ungrammatical examples in (31) above, so I can see no principled way to choose between (28) and (30) at the moment.

A structure-preserving rule is one by which a node of category X is moved, inserted, or copied into a new position in a tree where nodes of category X can be generated by the phrase structure rules of the base. More precisely, the requirement that every node dominate a terminal symbol in deep structure is dropped and is replaced by the requirement that every node generated in deep structure must dominate a terminal symbol at some point in a transformational derivation. A structure-preserving rule is then one which substitutes a constituent of category X, by movement, insertion, or copying, for another constituent of that category which dominates either nothing or else recoverable material.

According to this definition, the indirect object movement rules (28) or (30) are structure-preserving, although the alternative formulations which would leave one NP stationary, rejected here on independent grounds, are not. For example, if $NP_1$ were moved to the right over $NP_2$ in structure-preserving fashion, it would have to substitute for an NP dominating nothing in deep structure. Such an NP could only be generated as the object of a prepositional phrase. But since the P of that PP would never dominate a terminal symbol in a transformational derivation, it is not a possible deep structure node, according to the condition on deep structure nodes given above.

In conclusion, we see that for reasons which have nothing to do with what I call the "structure-preserving constraint on transformations", we are led to formulate the indirect object movement rule or rules as structure-preserving. Since these were among the few rules in English for whose structure-preserving status I gave only weak evidence in my dissertation, such an independently justified formulation is an important step toward removing doubts about the validity of this constraint.

## BIBLIOGRAPHY

Chomsky, N.: 1965, *Aspects of the Theory of Syntax*, Massachusetts Institute of Technology Press, Cambridge, Mass.

Emonds, J.: 1970, *Root and Structure-Preserving Transformations*, unpublished Doctoral dissertation, Massachusetts Institute of Technology.

Fillmore, C. J.: 1965, *Indirect Object Constructions in English and the Ordering of Transformations*, Mouton, The Hague.

Fraser, B.: 1968, *The Verb-Particle Construction of English*, Massachusetts Institute of Technology Press, Cambridge, Mass.

Geis, M.: 1970, *Subordinating Conjunctions in English*, unpublished Doctoral dissertation, Massachusetts Institute of Technology.

QUESTIONS

**Question 1.** Consider the pairs in (i) through (iv).

(i) John peeked over the wall.
John looked over the problem set.
(ii) *John peeked the wall over.
John looked the problem set over.
(iii) Over the wall John peeked.
*Over the problem set John looked.
(iv) I sat on the wall over which John peeked.
*I worked on the problem set over which John looked.

Which VP involves a particle: *peek over the wall* or *look over the problem set*? What are (iii) and (iv) evidence for with regard to the internal structure of the VPs in question?

**Question 2.** Emonds says in Section I, 'It appears that in general nonrelated, nonproductive syntactic categories do not have members in common'. Does his statement allow for the fact that we have numerous words which can be either Vs or Ns, such as *walk, climb, cook, drink, drug, race, father, riddle,* etc.? Without resorting to saying Vs and Ns are members of some other larger syntactic category, how might you account for these pairs?

**Question 3.** State in words the restrictions embodied in (i).

(i) with, +P, + __ NP (similarly for *at, for, toward,* etc.)
in, +P, + __ (NP) (similarly for *out, down, around,* etc.)
apart, +P, + __ (similarly for *away, back, together,* etc.)

**Question 4.** Emonds proposes the following rule in Section II.

(i) X+V-NP-[P]-Y $\Rightarrow$ 1-3-2-4, where 1-2-3-4 is a VP
-Pro   PP

This rule optionally moves a particle from the position immediately following the direct object to the position immediately following the verb. Why does he generate the particle in deep structure following the direct object? What objections does he try to meet with examples such as (ii)?

(ii) John took his students to task.
*John took to task his students.

**Question 5.** Why is the NP in (i) of Question 4 specified as -Pro? (Rule (i) in Question 4 is Emonds' rule (6).)

**Question 6.** Emonds credits to Fraser the observation that Vs such as *put, sneak, glance,* and *dart* must be followed by a directional adverb which may be either a PP or a postverbal particle. How do such restrictions offer evidence for saying particles are (intransitive) prepositions?

Question 7. If Emonds is correct that *right* can occur only before PPs or particles, how is this fact evidence that particles are prepositions? Notice that if Emonds is right, words such as *now* in (i) must be analyzed as (intransitive) prepositions.

(i) You should do this right now.

Can you find any other evidence that *now, then, afterwards,* etc., are prepositions?

Question 8. How are (i) and (ii) evidence for Emonds' analysis?

(i) Into the dungeon with that traitor!
(ii) Off with his head!

What other argument(s) is this parallel to?

*Question 9. How are (i) and (ii) evidence for Emonds' analysis?

(i) Into the house he ran!
(ii) In he ran!

Is the outline of this argument parallel to any other(s)?
How would Emonds account for the ungrammaticality of (iii) and (iv)?

(iii) *Over he looked the problem set.
(iv) *In did John her.

Note that we cannot say that this fronting rule will not apply in transitive Ss because of examples like (v).

(v) Into the sink she dumped the dishes.

Why are (vi) and (vii) out while (viii) is good?

(vi) *Into the sink dumped Mary the dishes.
(vii) *Into the sink dumped the dishes Mary.
(viii) Into the sink jumped Mary.

*Question 10. Emonds' rule (6) (also given in Question 4 as (i)) predicts that a particle can appear before or after the direct object, as in (i).

(i) The secretary sent a schedule out to the stockholders.
The secretary sent out a schedule to the stockholders.

Consider the following Ss. (*Now* is a [-directional] intransitive preposition; *out* is a [+directional] intransitive preposition; and *in the mail* is a PP with a transitive preposition.)

(ii) I'll give the book to John now.
?*I'll give the book now to John.
*I'll give now the book to John.
(iii) I'll send a schedule to the stockholders in the mail.
I'll send a schedule in the mail to the stockholders.
?*I'll send in the mail a schedule to the stockholders.
(iv) *I'll send a schedule to the stockholders out.
I'll send a schedule out to the stockholders.
I'll send out a schedule to the stockholders.

What do the first sentences of each set tell us about the position after the indirect object with respect to particles and PPs? What do the second Ss of each set tell us about the position after the direct object? What do the third Ss tell us about immediately postverbal position? Do these examples raise any problems for Emonds?

Question 11. Emonds' argument in the first half of the paper is as follows:

(a) Particles are intransitive prepositions and should be generated under the node PP;
(b) PPs are generated between the direct object and the indirect object;
(c) therefore, particles are generated between the direct object and the indirect object.

Emonds gives many arguments for his first premise, and we see why his conclusion is important in the second half of the paper, but the second premise is completely taken for granted. Perhaps, to experienced syntacticians, it is so obvious that it does not need to be stated, much less justified, but the beginning student is often impressed by the great freedom of placement of PPs. Where, besides between direct object and indirect object, may the PP *in one fell swoop* occur in (i)?

(i) The tall woman with a white hat could have given a fatal blow, in one fell swoop, to all our hopes.

To be fair to Emonds, he may have meant to restrict the PPs of his premise to directional PPs, as in (ii).

(ii) He has brought some cigars down the stairs for Dad.

Perhaps one reason he did not wish to go into this matter is that when the directional PP is moved to the end, an irrelevant complication often arises in the form of an unwanted ambiguity. What is the other reading of (iii)?

(iii) He has brought some cigars for Dad down the stairs.

*Question 12. The argument in Section VIII of Emonds' article is elaborate and complex. Let us assume Emonds' data in this section are correct and review his argument. (The various possibilities are worked out in the homework problems.)

He says there are three logical possibilities for how Indirect Object Movement works: $NP_1$ can move to the right of $NP_2$, $NP_2$ can move to the left of $NP_1$, or $NP_1$ and $NP_2$ can both move and exchange positions.

If $NP_2$ moves to the left of $NP_1$, since Particle Movement is optional, examples like (i) (given in Emonds' (25)) will be generated unless ad hoc complications are added to one or both rules.

(i) *The secretary sent the stockholders a schedule out.

If $NP_1$ moves to the right of $NP_2$, examples such as (ii) (given in Emonds' (24)) cannot be generated without ad hoc complications to the Indirect Object Movement rule.

(ii) The secretary sent the stockholders out a schedule.

If $NP_1$ and $NP_2$ exchange positions, all the data can be explained by means of rule ordering. In dialect A (which accepts examples like (iii), given in Emonds' (26)),

(iii) ?The secretary sent out the stockholders a schedule.

Particle Movement follows Indirect Object Movement. In dialect B (which rejects examples like (iii)), Particle Movement precedes Indirect Object Movement. (Thus, if Particle Movement applies, the structural description for Indirect Object Movement is destroyed and examples like (iii) cannot be generated.) In dialect C (which accepts the underlyingly to Ss of example (26) but rejects the for ones; that is, accepts examples like (iii), but rejects ones like (iv)),

(iv) ?Bill fixed up John a drink.

to Indirect Object Movement precedes Particle Movement which precedes for Indirect Object Movement.

Are any or all of these formulations for Indirect Object Movement structure-preserving?

Question 13. In dialect C, to Indirect Object Movement precedes for Indirect Object Movement. In this dialect underlying *to* indirect objects can be subjects of passive sentences but underlying *for* ones cannot. Thus (i) is good but (ii) is bad for these speakers.

(i) John was given the ring by his grandmother.
The landlord was paid the rent by all but Tim.
The children will be read a book by the new librarian.
(ii) *John was baked a cake by his sister.
*The child was bought a pair of shoes by her guardian.
*John was made a drink by the bartender.

What ordering for the two Indirect Object Movement rules and Passive will account for these data? Is that ordering compatible with the ordering Emonds proposes for the two Indirect Object Movement rules and Particle Movement?

**Question 14.** Why does Emonds consider rule (30), repeated here as (i)?

$$\text{(i)} \quad X+V-NP-(P)- \left[ \begin{matrix} e & -P \\ \left\{ \begin{matrix} to \\ for \end{matrix} \right\} & -NP \end{matrix} \right] -Y \Rightarrow 1\text{-}5\text{-}3\text{-}\emptyset\text{-}2\text{-}6$$
$$\phantom{\text{(i)} \quad X+V-NP-(P)-} PP$$

(That is, what motivation would one have for wanting to collapse Emonds' rules (6) and (28)?) Although he sees no principled way to choose between (6)-(28) and (30), Emonds seems to prefer to keep (6) and (28) separate. What is behind this intuition and what sorts of circumstances might give it formal justification?

(Two notes on rule (30): (1) Emonds has assigned X+V the number 1 in the structural change; and (2), the optional P is needed only for the Indirect Object Movement half of the rule. It was assumed to be null for the Particle Movement half of the rule: i.e. there was to be only one P. It is only when a second P is present that the problem Emonds discusses in the next to the last paragraph of Section IX arises. Here we see an interaction between a rule that is too permissive because of formal problems that arise in collapsing rules and a compensating general constraint on the operation of rules.

*Question 15. If Prt (and PP) were generated in immediate postverbal position, could Indirect Object Movement be written as a structure preserving rule?

## HOMEWORK PROBLEMS

I. Consider the rule Passive which derives (2) from (1):

(1) Russia defeated Germany.
(2) Germany was defeated by Russia.

A. If all transformations are root, structure-preserving, or local movement transformations, why must Passive be a structure-preserving transformation?

B. Passive basically moves two NPs: the NP following the V gets preposed and the NP preceding the V gets postposed into a *by* phrase. In order for Passive to be structure-preserving, must one of these movements apply before the other? Discuss all the logical possibilities.

C. Emonds (1976) proposes that agentless passives (i.e. those passives lacking a *by* phrase) had no underlying subject. Thus he derives (4) from the underlying string in (3) where $\Delta$ stands for an empty node.

(3) $\Delta$ defeated Germany.
(4) Germany was defeated.

What problems for Emonds' analysis do the following examples present?

(5) The songs were sung in unison.
(6) The songs were sung with cheery faces.
(7) The songs were sung badly on purpose.

D. The more traditional view of agentless passives is that underlying (4) is a string with some indeterminate pronominal subject, then after Passive applies, a *by* phrase with such an indeterminate element is optionally deleted. If Emonds were forced to accept a *by* phrase deletion rule for Ss like (4), would his structure-preserving hypothesis be affected at all? That is, as far as you know from reading this article, is his analysis of agentless passives crucial to his overall thesis of how rules operate?

II. Let us assume Emonds' grammaticality judgments are correct. Consider the following sentences.

(1) Some student paid his loan back to the bank.
$\qquad$ $NP_1$ $\qquad$ $NP_2$
He has brought some cigars down for Dad.
(deep structure order)
(2) Some student paid back his loan to the bank.
He has brought down some cigars for Dad.
(3) Some student paid the bank back his loan.
He has brought Dad down some cigars.
(4) *Some student paid the bank his loan back.
*He has brought Dad some cigars down.
(5) ?Some student paid back the bank his loan.
?He has brought down Dad some cigars.

As you answer the following questions, assume the structural descriptions of Particle Movement and Indirect Object Movement are such that they allow the rules to apply as indicated. (You may at times have to use a structural description that differs from Emonds'.)

A. Assume $NP_2$ moves to the left over $NP_1$ (as Emonds discusses in Section VIII in the second paragraph following example (27)). What Ss result if the rules apply as follows? (DNA means 'does not apply'; Prt-Mvt, 'Particle Movement'; and IO-Mvt, 'Indirect Object Movement'.)

(a) Prt-Mvt  DNA         (b) Prt-Mvt  DNA
    IO-Mvt   DNA                IO-Mvt

(c) Prt-Mvt                 (d) Prt-Mvt
    IO-Mvt   DNA                IO-Mvt

(e) IO-Mvt   DNA          (f) IO-Mvt   DNA
    Prt-Mvt  DNA               Prt-Mvt

(g) IO-Mvt                (h) IO-Mvt
    Prt-Mvt  DNA               Prt-Mvt

Do you see why Emonds rejects this possibility?

B. Assume $NP_1$ moves to the right over $NP_2$ (as Emonds discusses in Section VIII in the paragraph following the discussion of the ordering examined in Homework Problem II.A). What Ss result if the rules apply as in (a) through (h)?

C. Assume $NP_1$ and $NP_2$ interchange positions. Applying the rules as in (a) through (d) should give the Ss of dialect B. Does it? Applying the rules as in (e) through (h) should give the Ss of dialect A. Does it? Now see if you get the Ss of dialect C by applying the rules as follows (still interchanging $NP_1$ and $NP_2$):

(i) to IO-Mvt  DNA       (j) to IO-Mvt DNA
    Prt-Mvt    DNA            Prt-Mvt
    for IO-Mvt DNA           for-IO-Mvt DNA

(k) to IO-Mvt           (l) to IO-Mvt
    Prt-Mvt DNA            Prt-Mvt
    for IO-Mvt               for IO-Mvt

(Of course, in any given example the structural description of only one of *to* IO-Mvt and *for* IO-Mvt can be met. Thus in (k) and (l) only one of the two indirect object movement rules will apply in any given example.)

## SUGGESTED READINGS

Aissen, J. 1975. Presentation-*there* insertion: A cyclic root transformation. CLS 11.1-14.

Emonds, J. 1976. A transformational approach to English syntax. New York: Academic Press.

Freidin, R. 1978. Review of: A transformational approach to English syntax, by J. Emonds. Lg. 54:2.407-416.

Green, G. 1974. Semantics and syntactic regularity. Bloomington: Indiana University Press.

Green, G. 1976. Main clause phenomena in subordinate clauses. Lg. 52.382-397.

Higgins, F. R. 1973. On J. Emonds' analysis of extraposition. In: Syntax and semantics 2. Edited by J. Kimball. New York: Seminar Press. 149-196.

Hooper, J. 1973. A critical look at the structure-preserving constraint. UCLA Papers in Syntax 4.34-72.

Hooper, J., and S. Thompson. 1973. On the applicability of root transformations. Linguistic Inquiry 4.465-498.

Jackendoff, R. The base rules for prepositional phrases. In: A festschrift for Morris Halle. Edited by S. A. Anderson and P. Kiparsky. New York: Holt, Rinehart and Winston. 345-356.

Subbarao, K. 1973. On the inadequacy of the structure-preserving constraint with reference to extraposition. CLS 9.639-651.

Shopen, T. 1972. A generative theory of ellipsis. Bloomington: Indiana University Linguistics Club. (See Chapter IV for Homework Problem I and agentless passives.)

# 7

## THREE REASONS FOR NOT DERIVING 'KILL' FROM 'CAUSE TO DIE'

J. A. Fodor

**Introduction.** In the late 1960s, that approach to syntax and semantics labelled 'Generative Semantics' really got underway. By the mid-1970s many linguists had moved on to other questions. (See Brame 1976 for a discussion of this development.) Still, in the decade in which Generative Semantics really flourished, many very interesting issues were raised.

Generative Semantics embraces the notion that there is no really clear dividing line between syntax and semantics, nor should there be. Instead, a series of rules operates on semantic structure and produces surface structure, with no intermediate level of deep structure. These rules include well-known transformations such as Passive, some new transformations, and prelexical transformations, applying to structures containing semantic elements before lexical insertion has applied. Prelexical transformations are supposed to conform to all the constraints, conditions, principles, etc., which regular transformations must meet. Lexicalization (any transformation which replaces semantic elements and the associated structure with words) can occur after such rules, or indeed at any point in the derivation. That is, lexicalization does not occur all at once and so cannot define a level of deep structure.

One of the initial reasons for allowing lexicalization to apply after various rules affecting the structure was to account for the phenomenon of paraphrases. For instance, we want to account for the fact that *The sky became red* can be paraphrased by *The sky reddened*. Lakoff (1965) proposed the same underlying source for the two sentences, with the difference that in one, the actual verb *become* appears, while in the other, there is an abstract verb which is [+inchoative]. In both derivations there is a sentential subject *(the sky be red)*.

In the first derivation, Subject Raising (or *It* Replacement, as Lakoff calls it) would be followed by *To be* Deletion, yielding *became red*. In the second derivation, Subject Raising occurs, and then some raising rule (called Inchoative, or more generally, Predicate Raising) applies and the items *[+inchoative] (to be) red* are finally spelled out as *reddened*, with the final structure being a simple rather than complex one.

This approach is clearly worth considering, since paraphrases must be accounted for by any syntactic/semantic theory. Unfortunately, lexical decomposition of this sort is riddled with problems. Fodor's article, "Three Reasons for not Deriving 'Kill' from 'Cause to Die'", points out one major flaw of lexical decomposition. Deriving a single word from a phrase raises the serious problem that a single word does not behave as a syntactically complex object, whereas a phrase does. Fodor offers three ways in which this contrast in syntactic behavior between words and phrases casts doubt on the viability of such lexicalization rules.

Other flaws of the theory involve problems in determining which paraphrases of a given surface structure are to be related in underlying structure. We have tried to point out some of these problems in the questions and homework problems which follow the article.

We have dealt here with only that aspect of Generative Semantics relevant to Fodor's article. For a more comprehensive discussion of the theory, we suggest that the student consult Lakoff (1965), McCawley (1973), Brame (1976), and Fodor (1977), as well as the relevant readings referred to in those works.

*J. A. Fodor*

# Three Reasons
# for Not Deriving "Kill"
# from "Cause to Die"[1]

**o.** Lakoff (1965) has suggested that sentences like (1) derive from deep structures like (2). Prima facie, there would appear to be a variety of types of facts which support this derivation. Notice, for example, that in many dialects one or more versions of (3) are ambiguous in just the way that the derivation of (1) from (2) would predict:

(1) Floyd melted the glass.
(2) (Floyd caused (the glass melt))

(3) Floyd melted the glass $\begin{cases} \text{and that} \\ \text{and it} \\ \text{which} \end{cases}$ surprised me.

namely, what is said to have surprised me can be either that Floyd melted the glass or that the glass melted. Now, if (2) is the deep structure of (1), these ambiguities are easily explained. On one reading of (3), the pro-forms have replaced the constituent (Floyd caused it (the glass melt)), and, on the other reading, they have replaced only the subordinated constituent (the glass melt). The ambiguity of (3) thus appears to provide strong evidence that (1) is not the simple sentence that it seems to be; in particular, that (1) has two sentoids in its deep structure.

Further arguments might be alleged for the same view; thus, the second *it* in (4),

(4) Floyd melted the glass though it surprised me that he was able to bring it about.

like the pro-forms in one reading of (3), appears to refer to the glass melting rather than to Floyd melting the glass, and this would follow naturally from the view that (the glass melt) is a constituent of the deep structure of (1). Finally, it may be noted that (1) has two associated "do so" forms, namely, (5) and (6):

(5) Floyd melted the glass though it surprised me that he would do so.
(6) Floyd melted the glass though it surprised me that it would do so.

Once again, the natural treatment would appear to require that (2) be the deep

---

[1] I am deeply indebted to Janet Dean Fodor for the discussions which went into planning this paper.

213

structure of (1) since, on that account, we could say that (5) is a case of "do so" replacing a matrix VP and (6) is a case of "do so" replacing a constituent VP.[2]

If (1) is derived from (2), the derivation presumably involves two transformations: *predicate raising* of the embedded predicate, which permits us to map (2) onto the intermediate form (7),

(7) (Floyd ((caused to melt) (the glass))

and *lexicalization,* which permits the transformational substitution of a word for a phrase (in the present case, "(cause to melt$_{Vitr}$) $\Rightarrow$ (melt$_{Vtr}$)."[3] If this analysis is correct, it follows, first, that there are transformations which derive words from underlying phrases, and, second, that at least one prima facie simple sentence containing a surface transitive main verb derives from a complex deep structure containing an intransitive embedded verb. The derivation of (1) from (2) thus provides a direct precedent for such derivations as "break$_{tr}$" from "cause to break$_{itr}$", "tear$_{tr}$" from "cause to tear$_{itr}$", etc. But, moreover, it indirectly supports such dramatic derivations as "kill$_{tr}$" from "cause to die", etc. The suggestion is that, from a semantic point of view, (8) is related to (9) and (10)

(8) John caused Mary to die.
(9) John killed Mary.
(10) Mary died.

in very much the same way that (i) is related to (1) and (11). On the proposed analysis the syntax mirrors these relations by deriving (9) from (12) in a way that strictly parallels the derivation of (1) from (2).

(11) The glass melted.
(12) (John caused (Mary die))

This argument is obviously appealing; no one could fail to be pleased if the theory of syntax were to support the theory of entailment in this surprising way. To suppose that word-to-phrase synonymies can, in any important class of cases, be handled as

---

[2] It is interesting to note that the ambiguity of (3) and the wellformedness of (4) and (6) constitute counterexamples to the claim that words are "anaphoric islands" since, on the present analysis, these sentences contain pro-forms which refer to deleted clauses in the transformational source of a word.

[3] Strictly speaking, *predicate raising* and *lexicalization* are supposed to operate not on phrases but on abstract semantic representations. Thus, we must imagine that what appears in the structural index of the rule just cited is not the word "cause", but a semantic feature bundle which will be transformed into "cause" in the derivation of such sentences as (i):

(i) Floyd caused the glass to melt.

This is, however, a refinement which we shall ignore. The arguments to be presented are indifferent to it so long as it is assumed that the feature bundle which underlies the English word "melt $_{tr}$" differs from the feature bundle which underlies the English word "cause" only by the addition of those features which underlie "melt $_{itr}$". If that assumption were to be abandoned, the theory would have failed to assign (i) and (1) the same base structures, thus providing a counterexample to the claim that synonymous sentences have identical transformational sources.

instances of *syntactic* relations is to suggest an answer for one of the deepest problems in semantics, since any semantic theory must provide a disciplined technique for representing such synonymies. (Notice, for example, that almost all dictionary entries report synonymies between (defined) words and (defining) phrases.) The present suggestion is that, for at least a wide variety of cases, words are related to their defining phrases in the sorts of ways in which surface structures are related to their transformational sources.

Nevertheless, it seems to be quite certain that the deep structure of (1) is not (2) and that (9) is not derived from (12). In the next three sections, I shall present arguments which seem to me to establish this conclusively. In the final section, I shall suggest a principle which apparently does explain the ambiguity of (3) and the wellformedness of (4)–(6).

1. I remarked above that part of the interest of the derivation of (1) from (2) is that it appears to provide a precedent for the derivation of (9) from (12). This appearance is, however, illusory; the distributional characteristics of "kill/cause to die" are, in fact, different from those of "melt/cause to melt" in ways that militate against handling these pairs symmetrically in the syntax.

To see why this is so, we must first consider the analysis of (9) which derives it from (12) (i.e. from the same deep structure that directly underlies (8)). It is noteworthy, to begin with, that corresponding to (8) we have both (13), in which "do so" replaces the matrix VP "caused Mary to die", and (14), in which "do so" replaces the VP in the constituent sentence "Mary die".

(13)  John caused Mary to die and it surprised me that he did so.
(14)  John caused Mary to die and it surprised me that she did so.

Now, if both "cause Mary to die" and "Mary die" are constituents in the deep structure of (9), we might expect that the *do–so* transformation should operate on (9) to produce both (15), which is in fact wellformed, and (16) which, however, is not.

(15)  John killed Mary and it surprised me that he did so.
(16)  *John killed Mary and it surprised me that she did so.

In short, it argues against the presence of a constituent "Mary die" in the deep structure of (9) that there is no wellformed sentence (16) in which that constituent has been replaced by "do so".

This argument is not, however, decisive against the analysis of "kill" as transformationally derived from "cause to die". For it might be argued either that there are special restrictions on the *do-so* transformation which prevent it from applying to (9) in such a way as to generate (16) or, more interestingly, that (16) is precluded by the nature of the ordering relations between the *do-so* transformation and *lexicalization*. The first line of reply leads to an ad hoc complication of the conditions upon the *do-so* transformation and so need not concern us. The second, however, merits discussion.

Suppose we assume that the transformation which introduces "do so" operates "post lexically" (i.e. *after* the transformation which collapses "cause to die" into "kill"). Since the latter transformation must be optional if we are to account for the wellformedness of (8), this way of ordering the rules permits either of two derivational routes. One possibility is that the *do-so* transformation operates under identity either with the matrix or with the embedded clause in (12) producing, respectively, sentences like (13) and sentences like (14). Alternatively, a lexicalizing transformation collapses (12) into (9) and *do-so* applies under identity with the resulting form to produce (15) but not (16). In short, ordering the *do-so* rule posterior to the transformation which converts "cause to die" into "kill" guarantees that we will never produce the ungrammatical form (16) in which it is *both* the case that "kill" has replaced (cause to die) *and* that *do so* has operated on the verb phrase of the embedded sentence.

So far so good. But, unfortunately, this solution, which works for the relation "kill/cause to die", fails for the relation "$melt_{tr}/melt_{itr}$". For as we have seen, there *are* two "do so" forms corresponding to sentences like (1), e.g. sentences like (5) and (6). If the base structure of (1) is assumed to be (2), then *do-so* must have replaced the matrix verb phrase "cause it = S" to produce (5) and it must have replaced the subordinated verb phrase "melt" to produce (6). However, it was precisely in order to avoid having *do-so* operate under identity with the subordinated verb phrase in (12) that we assumed that the *do-so* transformation must be ordered after *predicate raising* and *lexicalization*. In short, the transformational ordering required for the "cause to die/kill" case makes the wrong prediction for "$melt_{itr}/melt_{tr}$" and vice versa. The *do-so* transformation must be assumed to precede *lexicalization* if we are to account for one kind of case, but must be assumed to follow it if we are to account for the other.[4]

2. Thus far I have argued that the behavior of "do so" militates against assigning a deep structure containing an abstract causative verb to *both* "kill" sentences and "$melt_{tr}$" sentences. In this section and the following one, I want to argue that, for independent reasons, this sort of base structure ought not be assigned to *either* type of sentence.

The surface form (17) is clearly wellformed and surely derives from a deep structure like (18).

(17) (Floyd (caused (the glass to melt on Sunday))) (by (heating it on Saturday))

---

[4] This asymmetry between "$melt_{tr}$" and "kill" *vis à vis do-so* transformation has been independently noticed by Bouton (1969).

(18)

Floyd caused it                    by                    Adv

the glass melt on Sunday        Floyd heat the glass on Saturday

But now, if we are to recognize a transformation which reduces "cause to melt$_{itr}$" to "melt$_{tr}$", something will have to be done to prevent that transformation from acting on (18) to produce the ungrammatical (19).

(19) *Floyd melted the glass on Sunday by heating it on Saturday.

The point is, roughly, that one can cause an event by doing something at a time which is distinct from the time of the event. But if you melt something, then you melt it when it melts. If, despite this consideration, we wish to assume an abstract verb "cause" in the deep structure of sentences like (1), we will have to stipulate that *predicate raising* cannot apply to structures like (18) unless any time adverb on the embedded sentence matches any time adverb in the "by" phrase of the matrix sentence. While adverb matching of one sort or another may prove to be a general constraint upon embedding transformations, the particular condition just mentioned is, so far as I know, without precedent in the grammar. It appears to be an artifact of the decision to derive surface verbs like "melt", which are intrinsically constrained with respect to their time adverbs, from the same source that underlies surface verbs like "cause", which are intrinsically relatively free with respect to their time adverbs.[5]

It may be added that, though we have developed this argument in terms of "melt$_{tr}$/cause to melt$_{itr}$", the same points apply, mutatis mutandis, to "kill/cause to die". In particular, (20), but not (21), is wellformed.

(20) John caused Bill to die on Sunday by stabbing him on Saturday
(21) *John killed Bill on Sunday by stabbing him on Saturday.

3. The following argument, like the one in Section 2, purports to show that neither (1) nor (9) derive from complex base structures. Since it concerns "instrumental" (or "means") adverbials, and since such adverbials are, by and large, selectively restricted to verbs that take animate subjects, I shall develop the argument for "kill" rather than "melt$_{tr}$". The reader can check for himself, however, that, barring selectional restrictions, it works for the latter case as well as the former. Indeed, I think it provides a

---

[5] I say these constraints are "intrinsic" because they appear to vary from verb to verb. Thus a verb like "qualify" seems, for no very obvious reason, to operate on the same pattern as "cause", vide (ii).

(ii) Floyd qualified for his degree in March by submitting his thesis in December.

general argument against the existence of any transformation which derives structures of the form NP V (NP) from structures containing subordinated sentoids.

To begin with, notice that there are a variety of types of instrumental adverbial phrases which share NP with the verbs they modify, and that they invariably share the subjects of those verbs. Thus, (22) means that John (rather than Mary) used the telephone,

(22)  John contacted Mary by using the telephone.

and there is no surface structure corresponding to (23).[6]

(23)  *(John contacted Mary by (Mary use the telephone))

The generalization that instrumental adverbs NP share with the deep underlying *subjects* of *their* verbs holds, too, for instrumental adverbs on embedded verbs. Thus, in (24), as in (22), it is John who does the phoning.

(24)  I believe that John contacted Mary by using the telephone.

So, it appears that a necessary condition upon the wellformedness of sentences with NP-sharing instrumental adverbs is that the shared NP be the deep subject of the modified verb. Moreover, this appears to be a *sufficient* condition for this kind of NP sharing. That is, given that an NP is the deep subject of a verb, it can ipso facto be shared by an instrumental modifier of that verb (i.e. it can be the implicit subject of an instrumental modifier of that verb). This is apparently quite independent of the surface position that the NP comes to occupy.[7]

---

[6] Not all adverbial phrases that NP share work this way. For example, we have both (iii) and (iv) (compare (22) but *(23)).

(iii)  John bit Mary after Mary ate dinner.
(iv)  John bit Mary after John ate dinner.

What is striking about NP-sharing time adverbs is not only that they can NP share with deep objects, but also that *equi-NP* deletion seems to be governed by *surface* subjects. Thus, in (v) it was John who used the telephone, but in (vi) it was Mary.

(v)  John contacted Mary after using the telephone.
(vi)  Mary was contacted by John after using the telephone.

In both respects, NP-sharing time adverbials contrast sharply with noun-sharing instrumental adverbials. (Cf. fn. 7 et supra.) I am indebted to S. J. Keyser for having pointed out to me these curiosities in the behavior of time adverbs.

[7] Subject to the condition that in some dialects some such adverbial phrases cannot appear in full passives. Thus *(vii):

(vii)  *Mary was hit by John by using a hammer.

That this exception is unsystematic (possibly the consequence of a surface constraint against iterating "by"-phrases) is suggested by a variety of considerations. For example, (viii) is wellformed and follows the rule that it is the deep *subject* that is shared.

(viii)  Mary was hit with a hammer by John.

Similarly, in the short passive (ix),

(ix)  Mary was found by using radar.

although the deep subject of 'find' has been deleted, it is nevertheless the deep subject of 'find' (i.e. the unspecified someone who found Mary) who is understood to have used the radar. In short, it appears that the difference

If this is true it is important, since it provides us with a test for determining whether an NP has ever been the subject of a verb in the deep structure of a sentence. Namely, barring context restrictions, an NP is the deep subject of a verb in a sentence if and only if it can be shared with an instrumental adverbial phrase in that sentence.

We can validate this test by showing that it is in fact satisfied by NPs wherever we have independent motivation for assuming them to be deep subjects of some verb. Thus:

a. An NP which has been promoted from deep subject of an embedded verb to surface object of a higher verb can nevertheless be the implicit object of an instrumental adverbial on the embedded verb, as in (25).

(25) John expected Mary to treat her cold by taking aspirin.

b. An NP can be shared by an instrumental adverb despite nominalization of the sentoid of which the NP is subject, as in (26).

(26) John's breaking windows by using a hammer surprised us.

c. An NP can be shared with an instrumental adverbial on an embedded verb after having been promoted from deep subject of that verb to superficial subject of a higher verb, as in (27).

(27) John seems to break windows by using a hammer.

d. A subject NP can be shared with an instrumental adverb even after deletion of its verb by "gapping", as in (28).

(28) John breaks windows by using a hammer and Bill by using a brick.

e. Finally, an (implicit) subject NP can be shared with an instrumental adverbial even after the former has been deleted, as in (ix).

All this strongly suggests the correctness of the claim that a structurally necessary and sufficient condition for a NP being shared with an instrumental adverbial is that the NP be the deep subject of the verb that the instrumental modifies.[8] However, we will have to abandon this generalization if we permit derivations like (9) from (12) or, mutatis mutandis, (1) from (2).

Notice that there is a deep structure, (29), which transforms into the sentence (30).

(29) (John caused (Bill die)) (by (Bill swallows Bill's tongue))

(30) John caused Bill to die by swallowing his tongue.

(30) is ambiguous, just as the principle that any deep subject can be shared by an

---

between NP sharing time adverbs (see fn. 6 above) and NP sharing instrumentals is intrinsic; the former NP share with deep subjects *or* deep objects and *equi-NP* delete under identity with surface subjects. The latter NP share *only* with deep subjects.

[8] This formulation is used advisedly; for example, it is not satisfied by NPs that are subjects of predicate adjectives. Thus, (x) is wellformed if it is read as a short passive with deleted subject and main verb "break". But it is ungrammatical if it is read as *NP be Pred Adj*.

(x) The vase was broken by using a hammer.

instrumental adverbial requires. (That is, (30) has the source (31) as well as the source (29).)

(31)  (John caused (Bill die)) (by (John swallows Bill's tongue))

Now, if we suppose that *predicate raising* and *lexicalization* are transformations, we can derive not only (30), but also (32) from (29).

(32)  John killed Bill by swallowing his tongue.

But this will not do since (32), unlike (30), is clearly univocal and it is clearly John rather than Bill who does the swallowing.

In short, "Bill" cannot be shared with an instrumental adverbial in (32) despite the fact that "Bill" is the subject of a verb in (29) and, ex hypothesis, (29) is a deep structure source of (32). Hence, if we want to save *lexicalization* and *predicate raising* as transformations, we shall have to do so at the price of abandoning the generalization (which appears to be firmly supported by (ix) and (25)–(28)) that all deep subjects can be shared by instrumental adverbials. On the present evidence, then, it looks as though "Bill" is not the subject of any verb in the deep structure of (32) but simply the object of "kill"; an undramatic but thoroughly intuitive conclusion.

One further point. Suppose we (gratuitously) decide to save *lexicalization* and *predicate raising* at the cost of abandoning the generalization about NP sharing in instrumental adverbials. We can do this by accepting the constraint that *predicate raising* and/or *lexicalization* fails when the embedded verb is modified by an instrumental, or by any other kind of adverb that NP shares in the way that instrumentals do. What is worth noticing is that we *cannot* do it by a wholesale prohibition against *predicate raising* (or lexicalizing) modified embedded verbs. For, such a wholesale prohibition would block not only the derivation of (32) from (29), but also the derivation of (33) from (34),

(33)  John cooked the meat slowly.
(34)  (John caused (the meat cook slowly))

and that won't do since (33) *does* have a reading on which it means what (34) predicts. In short, any attempt to save *predicate raising* and *lexicalization* would have to include in one or the other of their structural indices an enumeration of the kinds of modifiers that let an embedded verb go through and the kind that require it to block. I think that the rational conclusion at this point is that the game's not worth the candle.

4. It is worth pausing to reflect upon the moral of the arguments in Sections 2 and 3. *Lexicalization* is a transformation which purports to derive words from phrases. But phrases are, ipso facto, syntactically complex objects in a way that words ipso facto are not. We might thus expect that phrases will exhibit distributional characteristics which differ from those even of words with which they are synonymous. That is, it is simply because they have internal syntactic structure that phrases can interact with

syntactic rules in ways that can prove embarassing for *lexicalization*. In the examples we have been investigating, the phrases offered as candidates for *lexicalization* permit of modifiers. The corresponding words resist some of these modifiers simply because they lack internal structures on which to hang them. We can have two time modifiers on (17) simply because there are two verbs capable of receiving them.[9] But there is only one verb available for modification in (1); hence either we must resist the temptation to lexicalize structures like (18) or we must specify ad hoc that *lexicalization* goes through only when certain identity conditions are satisfied by any time adverbs that the clauses in (18) may happen to have picked up.

Analogously, there are two instrumental adverb positions in (8) but only one in (9). This follows simply from the fact that (8) is a two verb sentence while (9) is a one verb sentence. But this formal difference between the structures produces an embarass-ment of adverbs if we attempt to lexicalize (8) into (9). In particular, *lexicalization* predicts surface structures in which instrumental adverbs are inherited from both the matrix and the embedded sentence in (8), and such structures do not exist.

In short, even where a phrase and a word are synonymous, the former will characteristically exhibit degrees of syntactic freedom unavailable to the latter; two verb sentences are, ipso facto, and independent of their meaning, different in their be-havior from one verb sentences. There is thus a dilemma. Either *lexicalization* carries these unwanted degrees of freedom over into surface structure, thereby predicting sentences which are in fact ungrammatical, or special, ad hoc constraints have to be instituted to insure that *lexicalization* does not apply to phrases in which these degrees of freedom have been exploited. This seems to me to be a principled reason for doubt-ing that there are transformations which map phrases onto words.

5. I think the arguments presented in Sections 2–4 are fairly decisive against the transformational analysis of verbs like "melt", and "kill". But it remains to try to find some alternative explanation of the fact that (3) is ambiguous and that we have the two "do so" forms (5) and (6). It was these facts that provided the strongest evi-dence for the transformational derivation of "melt$_{tr}$" from "cause to melt$_{itr}$".

It is tempting to argue that we are faced not with a fact about "causal" verbs but rather with a fact about "pro-" forms like "do so" and "it". In particular, I suspect that the widely held view that such forms enter into surface structure only as a result of deletion under identity (i.e. that they must invariably "refer back to" or "replace" material actually present in the base structure of a sentence) may be false. In certain cases, pro-forms may refer to material which is semantically and phonologically related to (but not identical with) material actually contained in the sentence in which the

---

[9] Only two because, I think, there is a context restriction which prohibits "cause" from accepting the sorts of time adverbs that "melt", "heat $_{vtr}$", "persuade", etc. accept. Compare (xi) and (xii):

(xi) *(What John did on Tuesday (caused on Wednesday (the glass melt on Thursday)))

(xii) What John said on Tuesday persuaded Bill on Wednesday to leave for Moscow on Thursday.

Roughly, "cause" names a relation between events, and relations have no dates.

pro-form occurs. Thus, given a verb V which, like "melt", "break", etc. (but unlike "kill", etc.) has the same phonological shape in its transitive and intransitive forms, and where "$x \, V \, y$" entails "$y \, V_{\text{itr}}$", it will generally be found that one or more of the pro-forms ("it", "do so", etc.) can "refer" to the intransitive form even when the pro-form occurs in transitive sentences like (3). It is this "loosening" of the conditions on the reference of pro-forms which explains why (3) is ambiguous and why both (5) and (6) are wellformed.

It may be maintained that this explanation requires an ad hoc exception to the otherwise tidy rule that pro-forms can refer only to material actually present in the sentences in which they occur. That *is* a nice rule, but, unfortunately, it has to be abandoned in any case. Sentences containing logically "symmetrical" verbs (i.e. where "$x \, V \, y$" entails "$y \, V \, x$") behave very much like "melt", "break", etc. in respect to pro-forms. Thus, we have not only (35) but also (36).

(35) John married Mary though we were surprised that he was willing to do it.

(36) John married Mary though we were surprised that she was willing to do it.

In the latter case, "it" refers to "Mary marries John", which surely is *not* a constituent of that sentence.[10]

In short, given a structure A, which is not present in, but which bears appropriate phonological and semantic relations to, items in the deep structure of sentence S, pro-forms in S may refer to A. It seems pretty likely that this is true, but how one goes about saying that it is in the framework of generative syntax is a problem I don't know how to solve.[11]

### References

Bouton, L. (1969) "Identity Constraints on the Do-so Rule," *Papers in Linguistics* 1, 231–247.

Lakoff, G. (1965) *On The Nature of Syntactic Irregularity*, in *Mathematical Linguistics and Automatic Translation, Report No. NSF-16*, the Computation Laboratory of Harvard University, Cambridge, Mass.

[10] I know of only one clear counterexample to this claim about symmetrical verbs, namely (xiii). The fact that (xiii) is ungrammatical, together with the fact that (36) is considerably better than (xiv) suggests that the generalization ought to be restricted to "volitional" symmetrical verbs. Why this should be the case, I have no idea.

(xiii) *John resembles Mary though it surprised us that she does.

(xiv) ?John married Mary though we were surprised that she did.

[11] Theorists who feel strongly about saving the theory that pro-forms invariably enter surface structure as the consequence of deletion might want to play with the possibility of liberalizing the deletion conventions. Thus, (6) might derive from (xv) under a deletion rule whch permits transitives to delete intransitives, and (36) might derive (xvi) under a deletion rule which permits $NP_1 \, V \, NP_2$ to delete the $V \, NP_1$ in $NP_2 \, V \, NP_1$.

(xv) Floyd melt the glass though that the glass would melt surprise me.

(xvi) John marry Mary though that Mary was willing for/to Mary marry John surprise me.

QUESTIONS

**Question 1.** In his introduction (Section 0), Fodor presents three types of data that have been taken to support the derivation of $melt_{tr}$ from *cause to* $melt_{int}$. These are exemplified here.

(i) Floyd melted the glass and that surprised me.
(ii) Floyd melted the glass though it surprised me that he was able to bring it about.
(iii) Floyd melted the glass though it surprised me that it would do so.

In (i) through (iii), the underlined words can be understood to refer to the glass melting. The argument goes as follows: we have a pro-form that refers to the glass melting, therefore *the glass melt* is a constituent of the deep structure of *Floyd melted the glass*. What assumptions about pronominalization and constituency are crucial to this argument? How can you challenge these assumptions? (Fodor discusses this in his Section 5, but you should try to see the assumption for yourself first.)

**Question 2.** In Section 1, Fodor shows that the *do so* construction behaves differently for *kill* from how it behaves for $melt_{tr}$. Specifically, the *do so* transformation must follow lexicalization, to prevent (i).

(i) *John killed Mary and it surprised me that she did so.

However, the *do so* transformation must precede lexicalization in the derivation of (ii).

(ii) Floyd melted the glass though it surprised me that it would do so.

Consider the alternative analysis of *kill* as *cause the death of* (instead of *cause to die*). Now does the *do so* construction present any evidence against this analysis?

**Question 3.** In Section 2, Fodor shows that *cause to* $V_{int}$ can have a time adverb in the embedded S that does not match a time adverb in an accompanying *by* adverbial phrase, as in (i).

(i) John caused Bill to die on Sunday by stabbing him on Saturday.

But $V_{tr}$ does not allow this mismatching of time adverbs:

(ii) *John killed Bill on Sunday by stabbing him on Saturday.

Does this same objection hold for deriving *kill* from *cause the death of*?

Consider the following S:

(iii) *John's vicious torture on Saturday evening eventually killed Bill on Sunday.

Certainly (iii) is very strange. But do you find it as strange as (ii)? If not, what possible explanations might there be?

**Question 4. In Section 3, Fodor claims that 'a structurally necessary and sufficient condition for a NP being shared with an instrumental adverbial is that the NP be the deep subject of the verb that the instrumental modifies'. If this claim is correct, then (i) should be ambiguous as to the subject of the instrumental (as, indeed, it is).

(i) John caused Bill to die by swallowing his tongue.

Furthermore, the fact that (ii) is not ambiguous (having, according to Fodor, only the reading in which *John* is the subject of the instrumental) is evidence that *Bill* in (ii) was never a deep subject, Fodor argues.

(ii) John killed Bill by swallowing his tongue.

But note that there is a possible ambiguity to verbs such as *die*.

(iii) a. On his own initiative, John died.
(iii) b. For no reason whatever involving himself, John died.

The subject of the verb *die* can be the initiator (or even the agent) of the verb, or it can be solely the experiencer, the one to whom the verb happens. In (iv), can *Bill* have an initiator reading?

(iv) John killed Bill.

Now consider Ss such as (v), which have been claimed to be derived from Ss such as (vi) by a rule called Flip in Lakoff (1965) and Psych Movement in Postal (1971).

(v) Mary amazed me.
(vi) I was amazed at Mary.

Note that (v), like (iii), is ambiguous as to whether or not *Mary* is the initiator or agent of the V. Is (vi) likewise ambiguous? (Compare to *I was amazed by Mary*.) Now if we add a *by* instrumental adverbial to (v), we find an acceptable S.

(vii) Mary amazed me by swallowing her tongue.

But this same adverbial cannot be added to (vi), as shown in (viii).

(viii) *I was amazed at Mary by swallowing her tongue.

Given (v) through (viii), can you propose a semantic restriction on these instrumental phrases that will account for these data? Note that Fodor's analysis of instrumentals cannot be correct if Flip exists. Why not? Will your restriction account for the lack of ambiguity in (ii) without militating against deriving *kill* from *cause to die?*

*Question 5. If we assume Fodor's analysis of instrumental adverbials is adequate, does his argument of Section 3 (discussed in Question 4) militate against deriving *kill* from *cause the death of?*

*Question 6. In Section 5, Fodor suggests that 'pro-forms may refer to material which is semantically and phonologically related to (but not [necessarily] identical with) material actually contained in the sentence in which the pro-form occurs'. Most relevant to the particular problems discussed in this article is that usually, when we find that if xVy is true then $yV_{int}$ must also be true (i.e. the first entails the second), then pro-forms can be found referring to the intransitive form even when occurring in transitive sentences. Thus, since (i) entails (ii) (as (iii) shows), (iv) is not at all surprising, according to Fodor.

(i) Floyd melted the glass.
(ii) The glass melted.
(iii) *Floyd melted the glass but it didn't melt.
(iv) Floyd melted the glass though it surprised me that he was able to bring it about.

Now consider the following data.

(v) Floyd tried to melt the glass.
(vi) Floyd tried to melt the glass but it didn't melt.
(vii) Floyd tried to melt the glass and it surprised me that he was unable to bring it about.

Do (v) through (vii) present evidence against Fodor's explanation of pro-forms, or do they merely point out that entailment is not necessary?
Consider (viii).

(viii) Mary goes to church regularly and John believes in all that, too.

What does *all that* refer to? How are such Ss relevant to Fodor's claim?

*Question 7. If Oedipus were an unfortunate enough fellow to marry a woman named Jocasta who was his mother although he was totally unaware of her blood relationship to him, we could say (i) but not (ii) even though (iii) is true.

(i) Oedipus didn't realize he had married his mother.
(ii) Oedipus didn't realize he had married Jocasta.
(iii) Jocasta was Oedipus' mother.

The context in which *his mother* appears in (i) is opaque, in that we cannot substitute *Jocasta* (or any other coreferential full NP) here and still ensure that the truth value of the S will not change. Consider (iv) and (v). Do opaque contexts present any problems for Generative Semantics? Should they if Fodor is correct?

(iv) John realized/believed Mary caused Sam to die.
(v) John realized/believed Mary killed Sam.

HOMEWORK PROBLEMS

I. If *kill* derives from *cause to die*, how could we prevent (1) from yielding (2)?

(1) John caused Mary to die a thousand deaths.
(2) *John killed Mary a thousand deaths.

II. One of the claims of Generative Semantics is that the rules applying to structures before lexical insertion and the lexical insertion operations themselves conform to the definition of possible transformations discussed in the literature (see McCawley 1973). Thus, for example, one of the conventions accepted by Generative Semantics will be that only a constituent can be deleted, moved, or substituted for. This convention is probably one of the major motivations for McCawley's proposal of a rule of Predicate Raising, which, indeed, forms a constituent *cause to die*, thus allowing lexical insertion to substitute *kill* for a single constituent.

If the word *assassinate* is understood as everything in (1) except X, what problem arises here for a lexical insertion operation?

(1) kill X by unlawful means and with malice aforethought, where X is human, reasonably important, etc.

(Sentence (1) is taken from Chomsky 1972:79.)

Consider next the Left Branch Condition of Ross (1967), which prohibits the extraction of the lower NP in the structure:

The LBC will block WH-Movement from applying to (2) to give (3); Topicalization from applying to (2) to give (4); and Passive from applying to (2) to give (5).

(2) You determined the weight of the box.
(3) *What did you determine of the box?
(4) *The weight you determined of the box.
(5) *The weight was determined of the box.

Now note that deriving *kill* from *cause the death of* avoids Fodor's objections to lexicalization given in Sections 1 and 3 of the article. Thus we might want to test further this possible derivation. In particular, let us test this derivation with respect to the convention on deletion/movement/substitution and with respect to the LBC. Give the underlying structure of (6).

(6) John caused the death of Bill.

If (6) underwent lexicalization to produce (7), would the convention, the LBC, both, or neither be violated?

(7) John killed Bill.

(See J. D. Fodor 1977:118-119 for further discussion of this point.)

III. Consider the Ss in (1) through (10).

(1) John waxed the floor.
(2) John caused the floor to shine.
(3) John caused the floor to become waxy.
(4) John caused the floor to become shiny.
(5) John used wax to cause the floor to shine.
(6) John used wax to cause the floor to become waxy.
(7) John used wax to cause the floor to become shiny.
(8) John rubbed the floor with wax (and it became shiny).
(9) John rubbed wax into the floor (making it become shiny).
(10) John rubbed wax on the floor (causing it to become shiny).

Which of these (and others) can be paraphrases under which (nonlinguistic) circumstances? What kinds of problems would arise if we tried to derive all the paraphrases from one or just a few very similar underlying structures?

IV.  Fodor says that instrumental adverbs 'share NP' with
the deep subject of the verbs they modify.  This is true even
for passive sentences, though the agent is usually deleted so
that there will not be two *by* phrases.

(1) Mary was found by using radar.

Thus (2) is out.  Why is (3) acceptable?

(2) *Mary was arrested by screaming obscene words at the
    top of her voice.
(3) Mary got (herself) arrested by screaming obscene words
    at the top of her voice.

Also, as we would expect, (4) is out.  However, (5) is not so
bad.  How would Fodor's statement have to be revised to account for (5)?

(4) ?*The whale was killed by bleeding to death.
(5) The whale was killed by being bled to death.

V.  In discussing modified embedded verbs in Section 3,
Fodor notes that (1) does have a reading in which it means
what (2) predicts.

(1) John cooked the meat slowly.
(2) John caused (the meat cook slowly)

That is, (1) is ambiguous, with at least two readings.  It may
mean that the meat cooked slowly; or it may mean that John was
slow in going about cooking the meat (with, perhaps, the concomitant result that the meat did, indeed, cook slowly).  Test
whether there is any syntactic evidence for deriving (1) from
(2).  Try the *do so* test, the ambiguous *it* test, and any others
that might apply to this example.  If these tests do not point
to a derivation of (1) from (2), try to give some other explanation for why (1) is ambiguous.

VI.  The problems Fodor deals with here for verbs are very
similar to a related set of problems for nouns, where terms
such as 'lexical decomposition', 'anaphoric island', and 'morphological relatedness' again arise.  Thus, while a generative
semanticist would derive the (b) sentences of (1) through (3)
from the (a) sentences, only the (a) sentences are fully grammatical.  (These examples are taken from Lakoff and Ross 1972.)

(1a) The person who lost his parents misses them.
(1b) *The orphan misses them.
(2a) The person who played the guitar thought that it was
     a beautiful instrument.

(2b) ?*The guitarist thought that it was a beautiful instrument.
(3a) John is a person who plays the guitar and he thinks that it's a beautiful instrument.
(3b) ?John is a guitarist and he thinks that it's a beautiful instrument.

As indicated here, (3b) is better than (2b). Why? And (2b) is better than (1b). Why? Is the difference between *guitarist* and *orphan* the same as that between *melt* and *kill* (see Section 5 of Fodor's article)? How might Fodor's statement of the conditions on the reference of pro-forms be even further 'loosened'?

## SUGGESTED READINGS

Brame, M. 1976. Conjectures and refutations in syntax and semantics. New York: American Elsevier.

Chomsky, N. 1972. Some empirical issues in the theory of transformational grammar. In: Goals of linguistic theory. Edited by S. Peters. Englewood Cliffs, N.J.: Prentice-Hall. 63-130.

Fodor, J. D. 1977. Semantics: Theories of meaning in generative grammar. New York: Thomas Y. Crowell.

Green, G. 1974. Semantics and syntactic regularity. Bloomington: Indiana University Press. (For Question 3.)

Lakoff, G. 1970. Natural logic and lexical decomposition. CLS 6.340-362.

Lakoff, G. 1971. On generative semantics. In: Semantics. Edited by D. Steinberg and L. Jakobovits. Cambridge: Cambridge University Press. 232-296.

Lakoff, G., and J. R. Ross. 1972. A note on anaphoric islands and causatives. Linguistic Inquiry 3:1.121-125. (For Homework Problem VI.)

McCawley, J. D. 1968. Lexical insertion in a transformational grammar without a deep structure. CLS 4.71-80.

McCawley, J. D. 1971. Interpretive semantics meets Frankenstein. Foundations of Language 7.285-296.

McCawley, J. D. 1973. Syntactic and logical arguments for semantic structures. In: Three dimensions of linguistic theory. Edited by O. Fujimura. Tokyo: TEC Co. (For Homework Problem II.)

McCawley, J. D. 1978. Conversational implicature and the lexicon. In: Pragmatics (=Syntax and Semantics 9). Edited by P. Cole. New York: Academic Press. 245-260.

Morreall, J. 1976. The nonsynonymy of *kill* and *cause to die*. Linguistic Inquiry 7:3.516-518.

Postal, P. 1969. Anaphoric islands. CLS 5.205-239.

Postal, P. 1971. Cross-over phenomena. New York: Holt, Rinehart and Winston. (For Question 4 and Flip/Psych Movement.)

Ross, J. R. 1967. Constraints on variables in syntax. Unpublished doctoral dissertation. MIT. (For Question 2 and LBC.)

Ross, J. R. 1971. The superficial nature of anaphoric island constraints. Linguistic Inquiry 2:4.599-600. (For Homework Problem VI.)

Shibatani, M., ed. 1976. The grammar of causative constructions. (=Syntax and Semantics 6). New York: Academic Press.

Thomason, R., and R. Stalnaker. 1973. A semantic theory of adverbs. Linguistic Inquiry 4:2.195-220. (For a discussion of the scope of adverbs relevant to Homework Problem IV.)

# 8

## SENTENCE STRESS
## AND SYNTACTIC TRANSFORMATIONS

Joan Bresnan

Introduction. Joan Bresnan's 'Sentence Stress and Syntactic Transformations' is without doubt one of the most important articles to appear in recent years, both because of the nature of the data involved and because of the conclusions that follow from her hypothesis. She proposes that the Nuclear Stress Rule (NSR), which is one of the rules responsible for the stress contour of major categories, applies on each cycle after all the syntactic rules have applied. The effect of this ordering hypothesis is that stress patterns will be preserved under syntactic transformations, thereby permitting the fundamental stress relations established in underlying structure and reflecting important semantic relations to survive throughout the derivation. Her hypothesis thus offers an explanation for various correlations of stress contour and semantics.

This hypothesis offers, as a by-product, evidence about many problems besides stress patterns. First, the ordering hypothesis, if correct, means that the syntactic and phonological components cannot be discrete. Rather, at least some rules of prosody are included in the syntactic component. An obvious question that follows is whether other types of phonological rules can apply on intermediate structures and whether one can characterize the kinds of phonological rules that are restricted to surface structures as opposed to those that are not so restricted. (Bresnan mentions external sandhi rules as examples of rules restricted to surface structure. These rules have been the subject of much recent research: see Selkirk 1974, among others.)

Second, Bresnan's proposal requires that VP nodes be generated in the base as complements to V. In particular, a sentence such as *John is hard (for me) to understand* would have a

231

simplex underlying structure. If she is correct, many structures which previously had been assumed to have a complex source need to be reexamined. Her proposal is a move away from distant and very abstract deep structures and toward deep structures that resemble more closely what we find in the surface. It is also a step away from the very free use of transformations that characterized syntactic work in the 1960s. Rather than have some transformation that reduces an embedded S, she starts with a VP in the base. It is no surprise that her proposal offers support for the lexicalist hypothesis (of Chomsky, in this volume), which likewise reduces the use of transformations.

Finally, she concludes that since word stress assignment precedes prosodic stress assignment and since prosodic stress assignment occurs at the end of each cycle, 'all lexical insertion must occur on or before the first transformational cycle'. By definition, then, deep structure, in the sense of Chomsky (1965), exists. Thus Bresnan's article offers evidence against generative semantics, which denies the existence of a significant level of deep structure.

Bresnan's hypothesis gave rise to a great deal of further research. Some of these articles are listed in the bibliography following the problems.

# SENTENCE STRESS AND SYNTACTIC TRANSFORMATIONS

## JOAN W. BRESNAN

If the Nuclear Stress Rule of English is ordered within the transformational cycle after all the syntactic transformations, many apparent exceptions to Chomsky & Halle 1968 are predictable, for the stress patterns of certain syntactically complex constructions reflect those of the simple sentences embedded within them in deep structure. This preservation of basic stress pattern through the syntactic derivation provides a new method for determining underlying grammatical representations and deciding questions of syntax. The consequences for linguistic theory, in particular regarding the lexical vs. transformational hypotheses, are discussed.

Perhaps the fundamental insight of generative phonology is that phonological phenomena are predictable from grammatical representations by a system of ordered rules. These grammatical representations are themselves 'predictable', i.e. generable, given the base and transformational components. In this paper I wish to advance a proposal, concerning the interaction of certain phonological and syntactic rules, which extends the predictive power of the phonology, and at the same time provides a new source of information about syntactic representations. If this proposal is correct, it has interesting and far-reaching consequences for linguistic theory. The phonological rule to be discussed is the Nuclear Stress Rule (NSR).

The NSR is a cyclic rule applying after all rules affecting the stress of individual lexical items. It is formulated as follows:[1]

$$(1)\ \text{NSR} \qquad \overset{1}{V} \to 1 / [_A X \overset{1}{V} Y \underline{\hspace{1em}} Z]$$
$$\phantom{(1)\ \text{NSR} \qquad} \underset{1}{\phantom{V}}$$

where Z contains no V, and where A ranges over major categories such as NP, VP, S. Given the convention that any application of 1-stress within a cycle reduces all other stress values by 1, the NSR has the effect shown in Figure 1.

There is a question whether the NSR should be allowed to cycle on VP: if it does not cycle on VP in Figure 1, the stress contour [221] will result. But there is another rule which alters [221] to [231].[2] Thus, instead of the derivation shown in Figure 1, that of Figure 2 may be correct.

For the moment I shall ignore this detail in the application of the NSR. It is clear that this rule' results in primary stress on the rightmost constituent in a sentence. This is, in general, the 'normal' intonation for an English sentence

---

[1] This is the preliminary formulation given by Chomsky & Halle (1968:17), though later they collapse the NSR with another rule. If the proposal of this paper is correct, the NSR should remain as first formulated. The statement of the rule by Chomsky & Halle omits the condition on Z which guarantees that only the rightmost primary-stressed vowel receives 1-stress by the NSR.

[2] This rule is tentatively stated by Chomsky & Halle (115-17) as a word-stress rule; they note that it could be generalized to such cases as I am considering here. I am assuming that the NSR may apply to any phrase node, including VP, in isolation.

$[_s$ [Mary] $[_{VP}$ [teaches] [engineering] $_{VP}]$ $_s]$

| 1 | 1 | 1 | (word stress) |
|---|---|---|---|
| | 2 | 1 | 1st cycle: NSR |
| 2 | 3 | 1 | 2nd cycle: NSR |

FIGURE 1

$[_s$ [Mary] [teaches] [engineering] $_s]$

| 1 | 1 | 1 | (word stress) |
|---|---|---|---|
| 2 | 2 | 1 | NSR |
| | 3 | | $[221] \rightarrow [231]$ |

FIGURE 2

There are, however, well-known classes of exceptions to this pattern. Final anaphoric pronouns do not normally receive primary stress:

(2)   Helen teaches it.
        *Helen teaches it.

('Normally' means 'excluding emphatic or contrastive stress'.) Nor do final indefinite pronouns normally receive primary stress:

(3)   The boy bought some.
        *The boy bought some.

Other anaphoric items, even when grammatically definite, receive no 1-stress:

(4)  John knows a woman who excels at karate, and he avoids the woman.

In what follows I will assume that, by some means or other, anaphoric and indefinite elements are not assigned primary stress, and generally I will ignore the stressing of items which are not relevant to the point at issue.

Now the stress patterns of certain syntactically complex constructions appear to violate the general prediction made by the NSR. I will be concerned with four cases here. The first is the type of contrast observed by Newman 1946:

(5)  a. George has plans to leave.

      b. George has plans to leave.

Roughly, the meaning of 5a is that George has plans which he intends to leave, while 5b means that George is planning to leave. The next pair of examples belongs to the same case:

(6)  a. Helen left directions for George to follow.

      b. Helen left directions for George to follow.

Ex. 6a means that Helen left directions which George is supposed to follow, while 6b means that Helen left directions to the effect that George should follow.

The second case I will consider is quite similar:

(7)  a. Mary liked the proposal that George left.

b. Mary liked the proposal that George leave. [1]

Here, as in 5–6, there is a syntactic difference corresponding to a difference in stress.

A third case involves questions, direct and indirect:

(8) a. John asked what Helen had written. [1]

b. John asked what books Helen had written. [1]

c. What has Helen written? [1]

d. What books has Helen written? [1]

e. You can't help noticing how he is. [1]

f. You can't help noticing how serene he is. [1]

g. Whose have I taken? [1]

h. Whose umbrella have I taken? [1]

It should be noted here that the interrogative *which* is inherently contrastive; in the sentence

(9) Which books has John read? [2] [1]

reading' is being implicitly contrasted with some other notion:

(10) He had READ SOME books but only SKIMMED OTHERS.

That such sentences with *which* do not have the intonation characteristic of 8a–h is therefore of no concern here.

The final case involves relative clauses again:

(11) a. George found someone he'd like you to meet. [1]

b. George found some friends he'd like you to meet. [1]

c. Let me tell you about something I saw. [1]

d. Let me tell you about something strange I saw. [1]

The interesting fact about the above apparent exceptions to the NSR is that they are all predictable without any special modifications in that rule, given one assumption: THE NUCLEAR STRESS RULE IS ORDERED AFTER ALL THE SYNTACTIC TRANSFORMATIONS ON EACH TRANSFORMATIONAL CYCLE.

Note first that if transformations cycle on the nodes NP and S (Chomsky 1970) but not on VP, then the above assumption entails that the NSR applies not on VP within S, but only on NP and S (and any other transformationally cycled nodes). Second, the above assumption entails that the NSR is cyclic. I will now verify the above claim.

First I will derive 6a–b (5a–b are similar, but involve an additional deletion), as shown in Figure 3. The grammatical representations that follow are only

$[_S$ Helen left $[_{NP}$ directions $[_S$ for George to follow directions $_S]$ $_{NP}]$ $_S]$

| | | | | | | |
|---|---|---|---|---|---|---|
| 1 | 1 | 1 | | 1 | 1 | 1 | (word stress) |
| | | | | 2 | 2 | 1 | 1st cycle: NSR |
| | | | | | | Ø | 2nd cycle: Syntax |
| 2 | 2 | 1 | | 3 | 3 | | 3rd cycle: NSR |

Derivation of 6a.

$[_S$ Helen left $[_{NP}$ directions $[_S$ for George to follow $_S]$ $_{NP}]$ $_S]$

| | | | | |
|---|---|---|---|---|
| 1 | 1 | 1 | 1 | 1 | (word stress) |
| | | | 2 | 1 | 1st cycle: NSR |
| | 2 | 3 | 1 | | 2nd cycle: NSR |
| 2 | 2 | 3 | 4 | 1 | 3rd cycle: NSR |

Derivation of 6b.

FIGURE 3

$[_S$ Mary liked $[_{NP}$ the proposal $[_S$ that George left the proposal $_S]$ $_{NP}]$ $_S]$

| | | | | | | |
|---|---|---|---|---|---|---|
| 1 | 1 | 1 | | 1 | 1 | 1 | (word stress) |
| | | | | 2 | 2 | 1 | 1st cycle: NSR |
| | | | | | | Ø | 2nd cycle: Syntax |
| 2 | 2 | 1 | | 3 | 3 | | 3rd cycle: NSR |

Derivation of 7a.

$[_S$ Mary liked $[_{NP}$ the proposal $[_S$ that George leave $_S]$ $_{NP}]$ $_S]$

| | | | | |
|---|---|---|---|---|
| 1 | 1 | 1 | 1 | 1 | (word stress) |
| | | | 2 | 1 | 1st cycle: NSR |
| | 2 | 3 | 1 | | 2nd cycle: NSR |
| 2 | 2 | 3 | 4 | 1 | 3rd cycle: NSR |

Derivation of 7b.

FIGURE 4

$[_S$ John asked $[_{\bar{S}}$ COMP $[_S$ Helen had written something $_S]$ $_{\bar{S}}]$ $_S]$
+WH +wh

| | | | | | |
|---|---|---|---|---|---|
| 1 | 1 | | 1 | 1 | | (word stress) |
| | | | 2 | 1 | | 1st cycle: NSR |
| | | something | | | | |
| | | +wh | | Ø | | 2nd cycle: Syntax |
| 2 | 2 | | 3 | 1 | | 3rd cycle: NSR |

FIGURE 5. Derivation of 8a.

approximate. As shown here, the stress difference in 6a–b is predictable from the fact that, in the deep structure of 6a, *follow* has a direct object, while in 6b *follow* has no direct object, and hence receives primary stress as the rightmost constituent. Examples 7a–b are parallel; see Figure 4.

In the derivations of 8a–h, I have bracketed the examples to reflect the phrase-structure rule

(12) $\bar{S} \to$ COMP S,

where [COMP, +WH] is Q, the interrogative morpheme (this rule is justified in Bresnan 1970b). I have omitted the corresponding bracketing from the preceding cases because it plays no role there. In Figure 5, I derive 8a. Here the object of *written* is the interrogative pronoun *what* (which I am assuming to be derived from *something*, though this is not a necessary assumption for the point at issue); pro-

[s John asked [s̄ COMP     [s Helen had written some books s] s̄] s]
        +WH                              +wh
    1     1                        1          1          1          (word stress)
                                   2          2          1          1st cycle: NSR

                  some books
                  +wh    1                                 Ø        2nd cycle: Syntax
    2     2              1          3          3                    3rd cycle: NSR

FIGURE 6. Derivation of 8b.

[s̄     COMP        [s Helen has written something s] s̄]
        +WH                                    +wh
                      1          1                        (word stress)
                      2          1                        1st cycle: NSR
                                                          2nd cycle, Syntax:
    something                         Ø                   Question Formation
    +wh
              has         Ø                               Subject-Verb Inversion
                                             2     1
Derivation of 8c: *What has Helen written?*

[s̄     COMP        [s Helen has written some books s] s̄]
        +WH                                    +wh
                      1          1          1             (word stress)
                      2          2          1             1st cycle: NSR
                                                          2nd cycle, Syntax:
    some books                            Ø              Question Formation
    +wh    1
              has         Ø                               Subject-Verb Inversion
                              1          2     2
Derivation of 8d: *What books has Helen written?*
FIGURE 7

nouns, it should be recalled, do not receive primary stress. Thus the verb retains primary stress.

In Figure 6, the full NP object of *written* is shown to receive primary stress, causing the stress on *written* to be lowered. The difference in stress between 8a and 8b reflects the stress difference between the simple sentences embedded in them:

(13) a. Helen had written something.

      b. Helen had written some books.

The same is true of 8c and 8d: see Figure 7.

The analysis given for 8 correctly predicts the existence of a stress difference associated with the two readings of sentences like *The parable shows what suffering men can create.* The readings may be indicated as follows:

(14) The parable shows what [suffering men] can create.

      The parable shows [what suffering] men can create.

These examples are exactly analogous to those of 8: the pronominal object *what* permits the verb to retain primary stress; the full object *what suffering* causes the verbal stress to be lowered. There are many similar examples, e.g. *I forgot how good bread smells.*

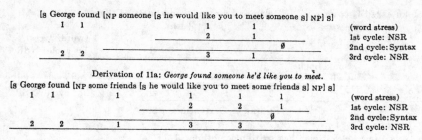

Derivation of 11a: *George found someone he'd like you to meet.*

Derivation of 11b: *George found some friends he'd like you to meet.*

FIGURE 8

In examples 6–7, the stress difference depends on whether there is an underlying object of the verb: if so, the verbal stress is lowered; if not, the verb retains primary stress throughout the derivation. In 8 the crucial factor is what KIND of object the verb has: if pronominal, the verb keeps primary stress; if a full object, the verbal stress is lowered. Now in 11 it appears that the kind of object—pronominal or full—affects the stress contours of relatives just as it does questions: see Figure 8. This fact would lead one to predict that the difference between *plans to leave* and *plans to leave* is neutralized when the head is pronominal. In other words, there should be a stress contrast between the relative clause construction of 5a—*George has plans to leave*—and the same type of construction with a pronominal head; this prediction is borne out by *George has something to leave.*

In general, where the simple sentence embedded in a relative would receive verbal primary stress by itself—

(15) I like a man (like that).

—the corresponding relative has verbal primary stress:

(16) He's a man I like.

In these two examples *a man* is predicative. If *a man* is specific, it can receive primary stress in the simple sentence:

(17) I like a (certain) man.

And correspondingly we find

(18) A (certain) man I like ...

There are sentences in which just this stress difference decides the reading, e.g., *A man I like believes in women's liberation.* When *man* has greater stress than *like*, the sentence is understood as being about a certain man; when *like* carries greater stress than *man*, the sentence is, in a sense, about the speaker.[3]

[3] Under the latter reading the sentence is generic, and may be paraphrased (approximately) as

A [= any] man I like $\left\{\begin{array}{c}\text{must}\\\text{would}\end{array}\right\}$ believe ...

All the cases discussed involve the movement or deletion of verbal objects rather than subjects. The reason is that since the NSR assigns primary stress to the rightmost element, only cases in which the underlying rightmost element has been affected by transformations can provide crucial evidence. Thus both the ordering hypothesis advanced here and the previously supposed ordering can account for the stress in

(19) a. I asked whose children bit Fído.

    b. the man whose children bit my dóg

    c. a desire to éat.

But only the new ordering hypothesis accounts for the stress in

(20) a. I asked whose children Fído bit.

    b. the man whose children my dóg bit

    c. fóod to eat.

In the latter examples the underlying objects have diverged from their original rightmost position, where they had caused the verbal stress to be lowered during cyclic application of the NSR.

The ordering hypothesis explains the fact that the stress patterns of certain syntactically complex constructions reflect those of the simple sentences embedded within them in deep structure. This preservation of basic stress pattern through the syntactic derivation provides a new method for determining underlying grammatical representations and deciding questions of syntax. To illustrate this method, I will consider the following question. It has been proposed (most recently by Emonds 1970, but earlier by Lees 1960) that certain infinitival complements should be derived from deep-structure VP's rather than S's. Suppose this proposal is applied to the analysis of certain adjective plus complement constructions. The question is whether, in a construction like *It is tough for students to solve this problem*, there is an underlying S = [*for students to solve this problem*] or an underlying PP + VP = [*for students*] [*to solve this problem*].[4]

---

Some examples of the general types I have been discussing are given in Bolinger 1958 as counter-examples to Newman's observations. As I have shown, these are only apparent counter-examples to the theory of generative phonology. A very few of Bolinger's examples —mostly idiomatic, e.g. *money to búrn*—remain unexplained.

[4] This is not an exhaustive alternative in that, if VP and S are both available as underlying complements, one would expect a full range of possible subcategorizations for Adjectives: VP, S, PP + VP, PP + S, etc. These possibilities are compactly expressed in the rule

$$VP \rightarrow \dots (PP)\left(\left\{{VP \atop S}\right\}\right).$$

In fact, as will become clear, all these possibilities are realized with various adjectives. But predicates do exist which clearly resist S complements, including PP + S complements: *For John to accept this view would be tough (for him)*; *It would be tough for John for him to accept this view*; *For us to solve that problem was a bear (for us)*; *It was a bear for us for us to solve that problem* (cf. *That problem was a bear for us to solve.*) In Appendix 1 I discuss the possibility of 'preserving' an S analysis for *tough, a bear*, and other predicates by deriving their PP + VP complements from PP + S.

Several facts argue against the sentential analysis: first, if there were an underlying sentence, one would normally expect a sentence-cyclic transformation such as *There*-Insertion to take place.[5] But though one can say *It will be tough for at least some students to be in class on time*, one cannot say *\*It will be tough for there to be at least some students in class on time*. Compare cases which are truly sentential:

(21) The administration is eager for there to be at least some students in class on time.

The commander left directions for there to be a soldier on duty at all times.

It wouldn't surprise me for there to be countless revolutionaries among the secretaries.

Second, the *for*-complementizer of a true sentential complement allows many types of objects which the preposition *for* after *tough* does not:

(22) Emmy was eager for that theorem on modules to become known.

\*It was tough for that theorem on modules to become known.

It would surprise me for a book on Hittite to please John.

\*It would be tough for a book on Hittite to please John.

Third, the complement of *hard, tough, a bear, a breeze*, and similar predicates does not behave as a sentential constituent under S Movement: compare a true sentential complement—

(23) It is surprising [for a woman to act that way $_s$]

[For a woman to act that way $_s$] is surprising

—with the complement of *hard* or *tough*:

(24) It is hard for a woman to act that way.

\*For a woman to act that way is hard.

It's tough for students to grasp this concept.

\*For students to grasp this concept is tough.

It is a difficult syntactic problem to determine the correct analyses of *for-*

---

Note that it is immaterial here whether the complement is conceived as originating in subject position or at the rightmost position in VP. See Emonds for a general argument in favor of the latter view.

[5] *There*-Insertion places the expletive *there* in subject position before certain indefinites: *There will be a son of the nobility present. There*-Insertion is cyclic, since it may both follow and precede Passive in a derivation. It follows Passive in this derivation:

While you watch, a pig will be roasted →
While you watch, there will be a pig roasted.

(The latter sentence must be carefully distinguished from

?While you watch, there will be a roasted pig.
?While you watch, there will be a pig that is roasted.

In these examples, Passive has not applied to the main sentence.)
*There*-Insertion precedes Passive in this derivation:

Δ proved that mercury was in the bottle →
Δ proved that there was mercury in the bottle →
There was proved to be mercury in the bottle.

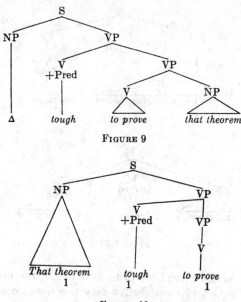

FIGURE 9

FIGURE 10

constructions.[6] The above ordering hypothesis provides new evidence bearing on this problem, for *tough, hard* and the other adjectives of this construction are subject to a transformation which affects the object of the complement to produce such sentences as *This theorem was a breeze for Emmy to prove.* Given that transformations do not cycle on VP, the hypothesis advanced above results in exactly the right stress contours for these sentences if the complement is represented as PP + VP. To illustrate, suppose that Figure 9 shows a permissible deep structure for *That theorem was tough to prove,* ignoring details. As noted, there is no cycle on VP, so not until S will any rules apply. At that point the object of *prove* is shifted, yielding the derived structure shown in Figure 10. Then the NSR will apply, giving the contour [221], which will eventually become [231] by the rule referred to in fn. 2.

On the other hand, suppose this example came from a deep structure with a sentential complement to *tough,* for example that shown in Figure 11. Again, the exact details of the representation are immaterial. The NSR would apply on the $S_1$ cycle, producing *prove that theorem*; on the $S_0$ cycle, *that theorem* would be moved into subject position and $S_1$ extraposed: see Figure 12. Again the NSR would apply, yielding the incorrect contour *[213].[7]

In this way one is led to conclude from both stress and syntax that VP as well

---

[6] The problem lies in determining the correct criteria to distinguish among the many possible analyses. The S-Movement criterion is probably the best type for determining simple sentencehood.

[7] The connection between this type of construction and the ordering hypothesis advanced here was brought to my attention by Joan Maling.

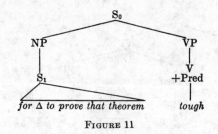

FIGURE 11

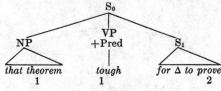

FIGURE 12

as S must be a possible adjectival complement in deep structure (see Appendix 1 for further discussion). A given adjective may therefore be subcategorized for VP or S (or both). If the Object Shift transformation applies only to adjectives with VP complements, there will be no need to resort to rule features to describe this phenomenon; that is, arbitrariness in the grammar may be reduced by stating Object Shift in such a way that it will apply only to VP complements.[8]

There is in fact a class of adjectives permitting both S and PP + VP complements—namely, the class including *good, bad, sweet, pleasant,* and *appropriate*; the ambiguity in such cases is noted by Lees. The sentence *It is good for John to leave*

[8] Object Shift may be (tentatively) stated as follows:

$$[_S \, \Delta \ \text{Pred (PP)} \ [_{VP} \ V^* \ (P) \ NP \ ] \ ]$$

where V* represents an arbitrarily long string of verbs. This formulation would permit derivation of

John is easy for Bill to please
John is hard for Bill to even try to please
John is hard for Bill to even begin to try to please

but not of

*You are tough for me to believe that Harry hates (Postal 1968a:103)
*Harriet is tough for me to stop Bill's looking at (Postal 1968a:109).

Postal (1968a:102) states that Object Shift (his 'Tough Movement') transports an NP into subject position only from an 'immediately lower clause'. This statement leads him to both awkward complications of the rule and ad hoc theoretical elaborations. While Postal's version states that Object Shift may not occur across MORE THAN ONE S-bracket, the version of the rule given here states, in effect, that Object Shift may not occur across ANY S-brackets. There is therefore an empirical difference between these two versions, and the crucial evidence is presented in paradigm 26 of this paper. The evidence there, as the reader will note, crucially favors an 'intra-sentence' version of the rule over any 'cross-sentence' version; that is, any version like Postal's will incorrectly predict that 26a is a grammatical sentence.

may mean either 'For John to leave is good = It is good (for John to leave)' or 'To leave is good for John = It is good for John (to leave.)' Lees maintains a clear distinction between the ambiguous class (*good*; his type 7) and the unambiguous class (*hard, tough*; his type 8). But some speakers may class certain of the latter with the former, permitting sentences like this:[9]

(25) For John to please Mary is $\begin{Bmatrix} \text{hard} \\ \text{easy} \\ \text{difficult} \end{Bmatrix}$.

The possibility of both VP and S complements for these adjectives accounts for the following paradigm:

(26) a. *Such things are not $\begin{Bmatrix} \text{good} \\ \text{appropriate} \end{Bmatrix}$ for there to be children involved in.

b. It is not $\begin{Bmatrix} \text{good} \\ \text{appropriate} \end{Bmatrix}$ for there to be children involved in such things.

c. Such things are not $\begin{Bmatrix} \text{good} \\ \text{appropriate} \end{Bmatrix}$ for children to be involved in.

d. It is not $\begin{Bmatrix} \text{good} \\ \text{appropriate} \end{Bmatrix}$ for children to be involved in such things.

The fact that 26a is ungrammatical is precisely what is predicted from the analysis given here, since *good* and *appropriate* may take both S and VP complements. Object Shift can apply only to VP complements, as shown in fn. 8, and *There*-Insertion can apply only to S complements. The presence of *there* in 26a and 26b forces the 'S interpretation' of the complement in both, and hence the shifted object in 26a is ungrammatical.[10]

[9] One such speaker is Postal (1968a:25) who writes:

one must observe that the whole construction involves a subtle structural ambiguity of a not understood type. A string like:

3.(8) It was difficult for Tony to rob the store

has two different Surface Structures:

3.(9) *a* it was difficult for Tony (to rob the store)

*b* it was difficult (for Tony to rob the store)

The difference in meaning is real though subtle. The first seems to associate the difficulty directly with Tony personally. The second allows for a more generic attribution of difficulty. The difference shows up clearly in two variant pronunciations.

[10] The sentence *John was good to leave* is itself ambiguous: John may be understood as the one leaving (*It was good of John to leave*) or the one left (*It was good to leave John*). Corresponding to these readings is a difference in stress:

John was good to leave (*John* is subject of *leave*).

John was good to leave (*John* is object of *leave*).

The former is probably transformationally derived from

It was good of John to leave.

*Of John* is probably a PP complement to *good*: the stress on *good of John* in isolation suggests that it is the Compound Rule which is applying. The Compound Rule (Chomsky &

I have discussed adjectives like *tough*, which take only (PP) + VP complements, as well as adjectives like *good*, which take both (PP) + VP and S. It should not be surprising to discover adjectives taking (PP) + S, and indeed that is just what we would expect if VP is, with S, a possible complement generated in phrase structure. The phrase-structure rules will then specify VP as an alternative choice wherever S is specified, as in the rule

(27) $\text{VP} \rightarrow \dots \text{(PP)} \left( \left\{ \begin{matrix} \text{VP} \\ \text{S} \end{matrix} \right\} \right).$

One adjective which displays the possibility PP + S is *good*:

(28) For Mary to learn karate would be good for her.

It would be good for Mary for her to learn karate.

In fact, one would predict that Object Shift cannot apply to these examples, since a full S follows *for Mary*. This prediction is borne out:

(29) *Karate would be good [for Mary $_\text{PP}$] [for her to learn $_\text{S}$].

Karate would be good [for Mary $_\text{PP}$] [to learn $_\text{VP}$].

The ungrammaticality of *Karate would be good for Mary for her to learn* is another crucial test in favor of the formulation of Object Shift given here.

To conclude, it is because both the *tough to prove* and the passive construction have rightward primary stress that I have ordered the NSR after all transformations on each cycle. This ordering guarantees that, on a given cycle, Object Shift or Passive may apply before the NSR:

$$\overset{1}{\text{(30) John was seen by Mary.}}$$

$$\overset{1}{\text{John was hard to see.}}$$

Note that the same applies to Noun Phrases: the passivization of nominals (Chomsky 1970) also precedes the NSR:

$$\overset{1}{\text{(31) the enemy's destruction of the city}}$$

$$\overset{1}{\text{the city's destruction by the enemy.}}$$

---

Halle, 17) results in the characteristic initial stress of English compounds: $\overset{1\quad 3}{blackbird}$ is produced by the Compound Rule, while $\overset{2\quad 1}{black\ bird}$ is produced by the NSR. Thus we have a derivation like the following:

| [It was [good [of John] ] [to leave] ] | | | | |
|---|---|---|---|---|
| 1 | 1 1 | 1 | (word stress) | |
| | 2 1 | | 1st cycle: NSR | |
| 1 | 3 2 · | | 2nd cycle: Compound Rule | |
| | | | 3rd cycle: | |
| 2 | ∅ ∅ | | Syntax | |
| John | | | | |
| 3 | 2 | 1 | NSR | |

Note that, to avoid the derivation of *Mary was good of John to leave* by Object Shift from *It was good of John to leave Mary*, either the prepositional phrase *for NP* must be distinguishable by the rule from *of NP*, or the infinitive must in these cases be an unreduced sentence at the point where Object Shift would apply.

Within a derivation, on the other hand, Question Formation and Relative Clause Formation must apply after the NSR has affected the simple S's embedded in nterrogative and relative structures:

(32) What books has Helen written?

I wonder what books Helen has written.

Here's a book for you to read.

This ordering follows automatically from the principle of the transformational cycle and the analysis given of syntactic structures, in which there is a simple S embedded within interrogatives as well as relatives (Bresnan 1970b). That Question Formation and Relative Clause Formation actually do apply on the transformational cycle is shown in Appendix 2, below, by independent syntactic arguments.

SOME CONSEQUENCES

The ordering of the NSR proposed here has interesting consequences for linguistic theory. The most immediate consequence is, of course, the inadequacy of a basic assumption of generative phonology: 'It is well known that English has complex prosodic contours involving many levels of stress . . . It is clear even from a superficial examination that these contours are determined in some manner by the surface structure of the utterance' (Chomsky & Halle, 15).

Instead, it appears that the stress contours of English sentences are determined in a simple and regular way by their underlying syntactic structures. Further, because prosodic stress rules like the NSR require prior assignment of word stress, the latter must occur either on deep structure or in the lexicon.[11] But if word stress is assigned prior to the syntactic transformations, then it follows automatically that transformationally attached affixes are stress-neutral.[12] For

[11] Since the ordering hypothesis entails that some phonological rules apply in deep structure or the lexicon, it is natural to ask whether all phonological rules so apply. It is clear that the rules of 'external sandhi' in some languages, affecting segments across word boundaries, must apply on surface structure, for two words which have separate locations in deep structure may be contiguous in surface structure and undergo sandhi. Such rules of 'external' phonological phenomena are analogous to the postcyclic or last-cyclic syntactic rules, in that both apply after the cyclic rules. Prosodic rules, such as the NSR, are analogous to cyclic transformations in a way that the ordering hypothesis makes clear. Word-internal rules affecting stress or segmental phonology (see Chomsky & Halle) are analogous to rules of derivational morphology and doubtless interact with them. Further research pursuing the parallel articulation of phonological and syntactic rules and their interactions may prove interesting.

[12] Arlene Berman first pointed out this consequence to me, and Noam Chomsky called to my attention the further consequence for the lexicalist hypothesis. Needless to say, it does not follow that stress-neutral affixes are transformationally attached, but only that a non-stress-neutral affix is not transformationally attached. This consequence raises a number of problems for further research. For example, inflectional morphology often involves radical phonological changes, yet the context for a passive vs. active verb or a nominative vs. accusative noun is determined transformationally. Since it is still an open question whether passive and active deep structures differ in some way (see Hasegawa 1968), it is possible that passive verbs are lexically inserted as such. Case-marking and number/gender agreement rules operate on derived structures. It is possible that these rules apply to already

example, the primary stress on the verb *derive* is unchanged by the affix *-ing*, but
shifts when *-ation* is affixed: *deriving*, but *derivation*. This would follow if *-ing*, but
not *-ation*, were attached to *derive* by a syntactic transformation; but that is
exactly what Chomsky 1970 argues on independent syntactic and semantic
grounds. His lexicalist hypothesis states that gerundive nominals like *Wanda's
deriving the answer*—which are productive and sentence-like—are created by
syntactic transformation, while derived nominals like *Wanda's derivation of the
answer*—which are restricted and noun-like—are created by lexical rules. Because
the NSR may apply on the first syntactic cycle, and because word-stress assignment precedes prosodic stress assignment, all lexical insertion must occur on or
before the first transformational cycle. If there is some level in derivations at
which all lexical insertion converges, then deep structure, in the sense of Chomsky
1965, exists. Now the assignment of word stress prior to prosodic stress simply
follows from the principle of the phonological cycle (Chomsky & Halle): in other
words, the stress of the whole is a function of the stress of the parts. Therefore,
IT IS A CONSEQUENCE OF THE ORDERING HYPOTHESIS PRESENTED HERE, TOGETHER
WITH THE PRINCIPLE OF THE PHONOLOGICAL CYCLE, THAT THE LEXICALIST HY-
POTHESIS IS CORRECT AND THAT DEEP STRUCTURE EXISTS.[12a]

Those grammarians who accept the transformational hypothesis (see Chomsky
1970, for references) must reject either the stress-ordering hypothesis presented
here, or else the principle of the phonological cycle. Let us see what is entailed in

---

inflected items, that is, that they are 'feature-checking' rather than 'feature-changing,'
in an obvious sense.

[12a] Deep structure is definable as the phrase marker $P_i$ of a derivation $\Sigma = (P_1, \ldots, P_n)$
such that (a) for $j < i$, $P_j$ is formed from $P_{j-1}$ by a lexical transformation, and (b) for
$j > i$, $P_j$ is formed from $P_{j-1}$ by a non-lexical, or syntactic, transformation. A lexical transformation inserts a lexical item into a phrase marker. (See Chomsky, MS, for further exposition.)

Strictly speaking, the phonological cycle and the ordering hypothesis imply that all
lexical insertion WITHIN THE DOMAIN OF CYCLE $C$ must occur on or before any transformation
on $C$. But in this case, all lexical insertion transformations can be re-ordered before all
cyclic and post-cyclic syntactic transformations without loss of any linguistically significant
generality. To see this, consider a hypothetical cyclic syntactic transformation which
precedes a lexical insertion transformation $L$. Our hypotheses imply that on a cycle $C$ at
which $T$ applies, all lexical insertion into the domain of $C$ had taken place prior to $T$'s
application. Therefore $L$ must occur on the 'next higher' cycle $C'$. But now, on $C'$, $L$ cannot
insert into the domain of the previous cycle $C$ without inserting a lexical item FOR OTHER
LEXICAL ITEMS, which is impossible. Therefore $L$ must insert into some sub-phrase-marker of
the domain of $C'$ not in the domain of $C$. Thus, $L$ is independent of the output of $T$, and
can be re-ordered prior to any application of $T$.

Concerning $L$, I am making the generally accepted assumptions (i) that lexical items are
not strictly subcategorized for syntactically transformed structures, and (ii) that lexical
items are not in general substitutable for lexical items. (i) is necessary since, otherwise, any
$L$ which inserted into $C'-C$ a lexical item subcategorized for a derived structure in $C$ which
is the output of $T$ obviously could not be re-ordered before $T$.

If one could display a well-motivated pre-cyclic syntactic transformation which preceded an $L$, then the above definition of deep structure would have to be given up. However,
a slightly weaker notion of deep structure would still be definable by omitting (a) from the
definition.

the latter course. One concrete way of rejecting the phonological cycle is to claim that the NSR assigns stress to non-terminal symbols only, and that word stress occurs subsequently.[13] This proposal implies that prosodic stress does not depend in any way on lexical information, but only on syntactic configurations. Yet, as we have seen, the NSR must 'know' whether it is applying to a pronoun or to a fully specified lexical noun phrase, if the systematic difference between such pairs of examples as these is to be explained:

$$\overset{1}{\text{Helen detests misogynists.}}$$

(33) Helen detests misogynists.

Helen detests them.

The parable shows [what suffering] men can create.

The parable shows what [suffering men] can create.

(Because the ordering hypothesis entails that pronouns are in deep structure, it is interesting to observe that recent work has shown independently that they are present there and not created transformationally: see, for example, Jackendoff 1969, Dougherty 1969, and Bresnan 1970a.) The same is true of semi-pronouns like *people, things*:

(34) I like people.

There are many people I like.

Similarly, the derived stress contours of sentences containing anaphoric and non-anaphoric noun phrases differ:

(35) John knows a woman.

John avoids the woman.

Different stress contours are produced by the NSR as a function of the difference in stress between anaphoric and non-anaphoric lexical items. It is hard to see how this dependency of stress contour on the stress level of individual lexical items can be explained if the phonological cycle is given up.

Another interesting consequence of the ordering hypothesis is that English is not a VSO (Verb Subject Object) language in the sense of McCawley 1970.[14] The reason is just this: McCawley proposes that English has underlying VSO word order throughout the transformational cycle, and converts to SVO (Subject Verb Object) only by a postcyclic verb-second rule. In McCawley's system, intransitive verbs would precede their subjects throughout the cycle, and thus get reduced stress by the cyclic application of the NSR. Instead of *Jesus wept*, the incorrect contour *\*Jesus wept* would result as the normal English intonation. On the other hand, if McCawley's verb-second rule were cyclic, his arguments for underlying VSO order in English would disappear.

[13] This formulation was suggested to me by James McCawley.
[14] This consequence was called to my attention by James McCawley.

We see that the stress-ordering hypothesis provides a kind of 'naturalness condition' on syntactic derivations: the formal properties of surface structures cannot diverge too greatly from those of deep structures without destroying the relationship between syntax and prosodic stress. In a sense, it is natural that a close relationship should exist between sound and syntactic structure; after all, languages, unlike the countless logics and 'logical languages' invented by philosophers, are spoken. It is not surprising that McCawley's system, explicitly modeled on one kind of notation used in symbolic logic, proves to be an inadequate syntactic basis for a description of English stress contours.

Having sketched these consequences for linguistic theory, I would like finally to consider three problems for further research. The first problem concerns sentences like *This theory was believed by George to have been thought by Paul to have been refuted by Jim.* It is possible that such sentences derive from an underlying form close to

(36) [$_s$ George believed [$_s$ that Paul thought [$_s$ that Jim refuted this theory $_s$] $_s$] $_s$]

by a sequence of operations indicated in Figure 13; note the derived stress contour.

Evidently, these syntactic processes can be repeated indefinitely:

(37) This theory was expected by Dave to have been believed by George to have been thought by Paul to have been refuted by Jim.

This theory was said by John to have been expected by Dave to have been believed by George to have been thought by Paul to have been refuted by Jim.

In such a way, the derived subject *this theory* may receive indefinitely weak stress compared to that of the verb. This result is clearly wrong. Therefore, if the syntactic derivation of such sentences is correct, it appears that some convention limiting iterated stress reduction is needed. Just this conclusion is argued independently in Bierwisch 1968. Further research on the form and scope of the stress reduction convention is necessary; if stress reduction is limited, the observed variation can be effected by 'rhythm' rules, e.g. [2221] → [2321].

A second problem may lie in the formulation of the Nuclear Stress Rule itself. The problem is seen when there is more material than one NP to the right of the verb. Compare the examples of 38 with those of 39:

(38) Peter used a knife.

Whose knife did Peter use?

(39) Peter sliced the salami with a knife.

Whose knife did Peter slice the salami with?

The first pair, but not the second, is explicable from what I have proposed so far. Here are further examples like 39:

(40) Mary found a car on Thursday evening.

```
                                          [George believed [Paul thought [Jim refuted this theory]]]
                                             1       1        1      1      1     1        1          (word stress)
                                                                        This theory was refuted by J.  Passive
                                                                              1          1       1
                                                                              2          2       1     NSR
                                             ____________________________________________________
                                            Paul thought this theory [Ø to have been refuted by J.]  Subject Raising
                                              1     1            2                        2      1
                                          This theory was thought by P. to have been refuted by J.  Passive
                                                  2             1     1                   2      1
                                                  3             2     2                   3      1     NSR
                                          ________________________________________________________
George believed this theory [Ø to have been thought by P. to have been refuted by J.]  Subject Raising
  1       1            3                     2     2                   3      1
This theory was believed by G. to have been thought by P. to have been refuted by J.  Passive
       3           1     1                   2     2                   3      1
       4           2     2                   3     3                   4      1     NSR
_________________________________________________________________________________
```

FIGURE 13

On what evening did Mary find a $\overset{1}{\text{car}}$?

Mary gave a book to Peter's $\overset{1}{\text{children}}$.

Whose children did Mary give a $\overset{1}{\text{book}}$ to?

What book did Mary give Peter's $\overset{1}{\text{children}}$?[15]

Recall that the effect of the NSR is to lower stress on every element to the left of the rightmost primary stress within the appropriate contexts. The above examples suggest that perhaps all primary-stressed items to the right of the verb—and not just the rightmost—should retain primary stress until the late application of a rhythm rule. This conjecture is illustrated in Figure 14.

The third problem is to account for the following contrast:[16]

(41) a. Peter had plans for $\overset{1}{\text{dinner}}$.

    b. Peter had clams for $\overset{1}{\text{dinner}}$.

As it stands, $\overset{1}{plans}$ *for dinner* is the predicted stress contour; the problem lies with 41b. Note that when a pronoun is used for *clams*, the stress shifts rightward: *Peter had them for* $\overset{1}{dinner}$. Further, *plans for dinner* but not *clams for dinner* is a constituent:

(42)   Plans for dinner were suggested by Peter.

      *Clams for dinner were suggested by Peter.

It appears that the formulation of the NSR may have to take into account certain kinds of prepositional phrases.

Although the problem posed by 41b is still unsolved, the basic principle that stress patterns are preserved through syntactic derivation still holds: compare 41 with the following:

(43) a. The plans Peter had for $\overset{2}{\text{dinner}}$ didn't come $\overset{1}{\text{off}}$.

    b. The clams Peter had for $\overset{2}{\text{dinner}}$ didn't come $\overset{1}{\text{off}}$.

Therefore, as in the preceding cases, this problem concerns the proper formulation of the NSR rather than the ordering hypothesis: once the principle for applying stress to 41b is found, the ordering hypothesis will predict 43b.

### Appendix 1

The existence of VP complements in deep structure is not a NECESSARY consequence of the ordering hypothesis presented here. It is possible to 'preserve sentences', so to speak, by deriving *John is tough to please* from

(44) John$_i$ is tough [$_s$ ... to please him$_i$ ].

The presence of the pronominal object of *please* will allow the verb to retain primary stress

---

15 The problem posed by the dative was pointed out to me by Frank Heny.
16 This problem was pointed out to me by Peter Culicover.

[s Peter sliced the salami with a knife ]

|   |   |   |   |   |   |   |   |
|---|---|---|---|---|---|---|---|
| 1 | 1 | 1 |   |   | 1 | 1 | (word stress) |
| 2 | 2 |   |   |   | 2 | 1 | revised NSR |
| 2 | 3 |   |   |   | 2 | 1 | rhythm rule |

[s Peter sliced the salami with someone's knife ] ]

+wh

| 1 | 1 | 1 |   | 1 | (word stress) |
| 2 | 2 | 1 |   | 1 | revised NSR |

[s̄ COMP   [s Peter sliced the salami with someone's knife ] ]
  +WH
  +wh

|   |   |   |   |   | ∅ | ∅ | Question Formation |

someone's knife   did Peter slice
+wh

whose   knife did Peter slice the salami with   Subject-Verb Inversion

| 1 | 2 | 2 | 1 |
| 2 | 3 | 3 | 1 | revised NSR |

FIGURE 14

on the innermost S-cycle, and the presence of a specified subject *John* prohibits a sentential subject: *\*For Mary to please John is tough*. However, this solution leaves unexplained several of the other non-sentential properties of such constructions:

(45) the absence of *There*-Insertion;

(46) the selectional properties of *for*;

(47) the generalization that Object Shift does not cross S-brackets.

Further, it would require some sort of special constraint to guarantee in the complement the presence of a pronominal object which would have the subject of *tough* as antecedent.

It is possible to amend the above solution to take account of 45–47, though the proposed amendment is ad hoc. Suppose that *Mary is tough for John to please* were derived from

(48) Mary$_i$ is tough [$_{PP}$ for John$_j$ ] [$_S$ he$_j$ please her$_i$ ]

by two obligatory deletions—Object Deletion, affecting *her$_i$*, and Equi-NP Deletion, affecting *he$_j$* (see Postal 1968a on the latter transformation). Object Deletion will be written almost exactly as Object Shift is stated in fn. 8:

(49) [$_S$ NP Pred (PP) [$_{VP}$ V* NP ] ]

    1    2   3      4  5      → 1 2 3 4 ∅.

Here the PP would account for 46; a new constraint that the subject of the complement must take the object of the preposition as antecedent will take care of 45, since *there* cannot be an underlying subject and cannot replace anaphoric pronouns; and 47 will follow from the pruning of the embedded S after Equi-NP Deletion. This solution requires, of course, that Equi-NP Deletion be cyclic (contra Postal 1968a): in order to derive *Mary is believed by everyone to be tough for John to please*, Object Deletion must take place before the cyclic Passive rule; and Equi-NP Deletion must precede Object Deletion so that S will prune to VP.

It is quite striking that this method of preserving a sentential complement for adjectives like *tough* uses only the bare verbal skeleton of the sentence: subject and object are obligatorily deleted pronouns, so that the postulated underlying S has no trace in any surface form derived from the proposed deep structure 48.

### APPENDIX 2

I have shown that it is possible for the NSR to be ordered within the transformational cycle; but I have not actually shown that it is necessary, since I have assumed without explicit justification that Relative Clause Formation and Question Formation are cyclic transformations. If these transformations were not cyclic, one might think of ordering the NSR after the entire transformational cycle but before the postcyclic transformations, taking the latter to include Relative Clause Formation and Question Formation.[17] There are two kinds of evidence against this alternative. First, all the stress evidence indicates that the NSR does not precede known postcyclic transformations; for example, we do not have 50, but 51:

        1      2

(50) *Away ran Fido.

        2      1

(51) Away ran Fido.

The former would result if the NSR preceded the postcyclic transformation which preposes *away*. Likewise, we do not have 52, but 53:

        1         2   3

(52) *Seldom does John sing.

        2         3   1.

(53) Seldom does John sing.

Yet the former would result if the NSR preceded the postcyclic transformation which fronts *seldom*.[18] (See Emonds on both of these transformations, Directional Adverb Preposing and Negative Adverb Preposing.)

---

[17] This alternative was suggested to me by James McCawley.

[18] I have excluded the transformation Topicalization from discussion because topicalized

Second, there is syntactic evidence that Relative Clause Formation and Question Formation are indeed cyclic transformations. Because of the consequences for linguistic theory of the cyclicity of the NSR, I will demonstrate here that Question Formation (QF) and Relative Clause Formation (RCF) are cyclic transformations. The matter is of some intrinsic interest as well.[19] From this demonstration and the fact that the NSR precedes these transformations while following other cyclic transformations, it can be concluded that the NSR is indeed cyclic, applying after all the transformations applying to each cycle.

As preparation, observe that there is a transformation which performs operations like the following:

(54) Mary has studied little and yet Mary has accomplished a great deal → Mary has studied little and yet accomplished a great deal.

This transformation, which I will refer to as Right Conjunct Reduction, may be thought of as deleting material in the right conjunct which repeats that in the left.[20] The conjuncts

---

sentences seem inherently emphatic or contrastive: *Jóhn I like*; *John I like*. It is likely that many postcyclic transformations, because they create so-called stylistic inversions, are closely connected with contrast and emphasis.

[19] Because relative and interrogative clauses have special properties which prevent certain kinds of interactions with many of the better-known cyclic transformations, it is difficult to prove from rule-ordering arguments that RCF and QF are cyclic. (See Ross 1967 for an exposition of some of these properties and a proposed explanation.) Postal (1968b:26–7) presents an argument that 'WH Q Movement' is not cyclic. Postal's argument is actually directed at a version of QF unlike that assumed here. Here, QF is a Complementizer-Substitution Transformation in the sense of Bresnan 1970b: QF scans a S on every S-cycle, but only applies when its structural description is met—that is, when the S is complementized by WH [= Q]—and then QF substitutes the first eligible question word for WH (see Bresnan, MS). For example, the structural description of QF is met only at $S_2$ in the following example, and so QF actually applies only on that cycle:

$[_{S_3}$ John asked me $[_{S_2}$ WH $[_{S_1}$ you thought $[_{S_0}$ he liked what ] ] ] ].

The derived sentence is *John asked me what you thought he liked*. Now the version of QF which Postal assumes permits the following kind of derivations:

John asked me WH you thought he liked what →
John asked me WH you thought what he liked →
John asked me what you thought he liked.

The question word (in this case, *what*) is brought to the front of every S until it reaches WH, or 'Q'. Postal notes that, since QF optionally preposes prepositional phrases—

Who did you speak to?
To whom did you speak?

—this version of QF would allow prepositions to be 'stranded', producing ungrammatical strings; for example, in addition to the grammatical sentences

Who did she think you spoke to?
To whom did she think you spoke?

an ungrammatical string like *Who did she think to you spoke?* would result optionally by fronting the entire phrase *to whom* on the first cycle, but fronting only *who* on the next cycle. Because QF, under the version I am assuming, moves question words only into (and never from) WH-complementizers, Postal's 'stranding' argument does not apply. But even the version of QF Postal assumes is not refuted by his argument, since the feature [+ wh] could be assigned either to NP or to PP, and whichever node carried the feature would be shifted by QF throughout the derivation. (This possibility was mentioned to me by Noam Chomsky.)

[20] If Right Conjunct Reduction MERELY deleted material, the derived constituent structure would be wrong. When *the news from France and the news from Italy* is reduced, *from France and from Italy* behaves as a prepositional-phrase constituent under the Post-

may be full sentences, as above, or noun phrases:

(55) The trees in Northern California and the trees in Oregon are similar → The trees in Northern California and (in) Oregon are similar.

The argument I will give consists in showing that there are derivations in which Right Conjunct Reduction may follow an application of QF, and derivations in which it may precede an application of QF. To show the latter, it will be necessary to use a transformation which I shall call Postposing. This is an optional rule which postposes certain complements to noun phrases, relating pairs like these:

(56) a. The news from Italy was the same → The news was the same from Italy.
b. The results on the virus were parallel → The results were parallel on the virus.
c. The stories about her are similar → The stories are similar about her.

Such a transformation is needed to explain certain peculiarities in the distribution of prepositional phrases. For example, the impossibility of 57a is explained by the ungrammaticality of 57b, its source under Postposing:

(57) a. *That was the same from Italy.
b. *That from Italy was the same.

Prepositional phrases which CAN be generated to the right of predicates are not excluded by such pronominal subjects:

(58) That is the same in France.
They were similar during the occupation.

Postposing 'preserves structure' (Emonds), so that if a prepositional phrase already occupies immediate post-predicate position, the rule does not apply (i.e., since a node is moved by a structure-preserving rule only into a place where the same node can be generated by the base, the transformation does not apply if the place is already filled):

(59) Some things about France are quite similar to those you mention about England.
*Some things are quite similar to those you mention about England about France.
*Some things are quite similar about France to those you mention about England.
(cf. Some things are quite similar about France.[21])
Their results on that virus were parallel to ours on the phage.
*Their results were parallel to ours on the phage on that virus.
*Their results were parallel on that virus to ours on the phage.

A second useful fact about Postposing may be inferred using the fact that it is structure-preserving. We have seen that the sentence

(60) Their results on that virus are similar to our results on the phage

cannot undergo Postposing, because there is already a prepositional phrase in immediate post-predicate position:

(61) *Their results are similar to our results on the phage on that virus.

Now suppose that the post-predicate phrase is removed by QF:

(62) To whose results on the phage are their results on that virus similar?

If it were in general possible for Postposing to follow QF, then these ungrammatical strings would result:

(63) *To whose results are their results on that virus similar on the phage?

---

posing rule, which will be discussed:

The news is similar from France and from Italy.
*The news from France is similar and from Italy.

For discussion distinguishing various kinds of conjunct reduction rules, see Kuno, MS, and the references cited there.

[21] This last sentence should be imagined in a conversational context, e.g. *Concerning what you have just observed about England, I can add that some things are quite similar about France.*

*To whose results on the phage are their results similar on that virus?

The conclusion is that Postposing precedes QF on any cycle.

A final fact needed for the ensuing argument is that Right Conjunct Reduction precedes Postposing on any cycle. Consider the following derivations, in which Right Conjunct Reduction precedes Postposing:

(64) The facts about him and the facts about her were virtually identical, but he got the job → The facts about him and (about) her were virtually identical, but he got the job → The facts were virtually identical about him and (about) her, but he got the job.

The wines from the eastern regions of France and the wines from the western regions of Germany are quite similar → The wines from the eastern regions of France and (from) the western regions of Germany are quite similar → The wines are quite similar from the eastern regions of France and (from) the western regions of Germany.

For Postposing to precede Right Conjunct Reduction in such cases, there would have to be a step like this in the derivation:

(65) The facts about him and the facts about her were virtually identical, but he got the job → *The facts and the facts were virtually identical about him and (about) her, but he got the job.

As shown, Postposing would have to separate the prepositional phrases from their conjoined subjects; but this operation is in general impossible:

(66) The rumors about Adele and the gossip concerning Jean were similar → *The rumors and the gossip were similar about Adele and concerning Jean.

Therefore, taking the second and third facts together, we have this ordering on any cycle:

Right Conjunct Reduction
Postposing
Question Formation

But note that two relevant situations may arise in deep structure: there may be a single interrogative S containing conjoined nodes embedded within it, or there may be two interrogative S's contained within a conjoined structure. In the latter case, we would expect Right Conjunct Reduction to follow QF, if QF were cyclic; and this is just what happens. To proceed with the argument, note that Right Conjunct Reduction must apply after QF in this derivation:

(67) a. I wonder what strange sights yòu'll see in mý country and what strange sights Ì'll see in yoúr country →

b. I wonder what strange sights yòu'll see in mý country and Ì'll see in yoúr country.

QF has already applied to 67a. If Right Conjunct Reduction preceded QF only in derivations, 67b would not be generable. To apply prior to QF, Right Conjunct Reduction would have to delete the material between the verb and prepositional phrase which has not yet been fronted by QF; but this operation is in general impossible, producing ungrammatical strings:

(68) *You'll hit some great spots in my country and I'll hit in your country.

Conjunct Reduction may delete repeated material only at the extreme of the conjunct. This establishes that Right Conjunct Reduction must follow QF to derive 67b.

On the other hand, Conjunct Reduction must also be able to precede QF within a derivation. Consider the following assertion and question:

(69) a. He said that some things about France and some things about Italy were similar.

b. What things did he say were similar about France and (about) Italy?

Ex. 69b cannot be taken as a base form for the same reasons that show Postposing to be a transformation. For example, the sentence *He said that they are similar about France and

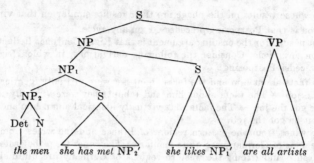

FIGURE 15

(about) Italy certainly has no reading like that of 69a. Therefore, 69b must have an application of Postposing in its derivation. Now we already know that Postposing cannot follow QF, so it must precede QF in the derivation of 69b. Right Conjunct Reduction must in turn precede Postposing in the derivation of 69b, for otherwise Postposing would have to detach prepositional phrases from conjoined subjects, an operation which has been shown to be impossible:

(70) He said that what things about France and what things about Italy were similar?
$\rightarrow$ *He said that what things and what things were similar about France and about Italy?

But this means that, in the derivation of 69b, Right Conjunct Reduction must precede QF:

(71) He said that what things about France and what things about Italy were similar?
$\rightarrow$ He said that what things about France and (about) Italy were similar?
$\rightarrow$ He said that what things were similar about France and (about) Italy?
$\rightarrow$ What things did he say were similar about France and (about) Italy?

We see that both 69b and the sentence *What things about France and (about) Italy did he say were similar?* are derived by applying Right Conjunct Reduction and then QF; the only difference is that in 69b the optional Postposing rule intervenes after Right Conjunct Reduction and before QF. We used Postposing merely as a means of 'forcing' Right Conjunct Reduction to apply before QF in this derivation.

From the demonstration that there is a derivation in which Right Conjunct Reduction must precede and a derivation in which it must follow QF, I conclude that both are cyclic transformations.

Let us turn now to Relative Clause Formation (RCF). We see at once that an argument exactly parallel to the last can be formulated, using a sentence analogous to 69b to show that Conjunct Reduction can precede RCF—

(72) The things that he said were quite similar about France and (about) Italy were these

—and a sentence analogous to 67b to show that Conjunct Reduction may follow RCF:

(73) There are many strange sights that yòu'll see in mý country and (that) Ì'll see in yoúr country.

Observe that RCF is not only cyclic, it is NP-cyclic. That is, its domain of application is NP rather than S, just as I have assumed in the stress derivations. This formulation is syntactically necessary to derive 'double relatives', such as *The men she has met that she likes are all artists*.

The only solution I've found that satisfies me is this. Each example contains two relatives, but only one head. For the first there would be an underlying representation (roughly) like that shown in Figure 15. (I take no stand here on whether relatives come from the Determiner in deep structure; if so, then the transformation which shifts them to the right of the head must be NP-cyclic to produce the configuration in Figure 15.) If RCF applies to NP, the derivation is easily accomplished by first applying RCF to $NP_1$ and then NP. Otherwise the sentence cannot be derived without letting cyclic transformations reapply on the same cycle.[22] See Bresnan, MS, for further discussion.

## REFERENCES

BIERWISCH, MANFRED. 1968. Two critical problems in accent rules. Journal of Linguistics 4.173–8.

BOLINGER, DWIGHT. 1958. Stress and information. American Speech 33.5–20. (Reprinted in Forms of English, ed. by Isamu Abe and Tetsuya Kanekiyo, 67–83. Cambridge, Mass.: Harvard University Press, 1965.)

BRESNAN, JOAN. 1970a. An argument against pronominalization. Linguistic Inquiry 1.122–3.

——. 1970b. On complementizers: toward a syntactic theory of complement types. Foundations of Language 6.297–321.

——. MS. The theory of complementation in English syntax.

CHOMSKY, NOAM. 1965. Aspects of the theory of syntax. Cambridge, Mass.: MIT Press.

——. 1970. Remarks on nominalization. Readings in English transformational grammar, ed. by R. Jacobs and P. Rosenbaum, 184–221. Waltham, Mass.: Ginn.

——, and MORRIS HALLE. 1968. The sound pattern of English. New York: Harper and Row.

DOUGHERTY, RAY. 1969. An interpretive theory of pronominal reference. Foundations of Language 5.488–519.

EMONDS, JOSEPH. 1970. Root and structure preserving transformations. MIT doctoral dissertation.

JACKENDOFF, RAY. 1969. Some rules of semantic interpretation for English. MIT doctoral dissertation.

KUNO, SUSUMU. 1970. Some properties of non-referential noun phrases. Studies in Oriental and general linguistics, ed. by Roman Jakobson and Shigeo Kawamoto, 348–73. Tokyo: TEC Co.

LEES, ROBERT. 1960. A multiply ambiguous adjectival construction in English. Lg. 36.207–21.

McCAWLEY, JAMES. 1970. English as a *VSO* language. Lg. 46.286–99.

NEWMAN, STANLEY. 1946. On the stress system of English. Word 2.171–87.

POSTAL, PAUL. 1968a. Crossover phenomena. Yorktown Heights, N.Y.: IBM. (Now published by Holt, Rinehart & Winston, New York, 1971.)

——. 1968b. On coreferential complement subject deletion. Yorktown Heights, N.Y.: IBM.

ROSS, JOHN. 1967. Constraints on variables in syntax. MIT doctoral dissertation.

[Received 22 June 1970]

[22] For suggestions for improving several earlier versions of this paper, I am very grateful to Noam Chomsky, Morris Halle, and James D. McCawley, who of course are not responsible for the defects remaining. This work was supported in part by the National Institutes of Mental Health (Grant MH-13390) and the National Institutes of Health (Grant 5 T01 HD00111).

## QUESTIONS

*Question 1. The NSR applies to major categories, according to Bresnan. Chomsky and Halle (1968) say that it applies to 'any phrase which is not a lexical category'. The bracket may have 'any label except N, A, or V'. What keeps the NSR from applying to Ps and Dets and Comps? What does it apply to besides NP, VP, and S, under Chomsky and Halle's formulation? Bresnan later excludes VP, saying the NSR applies only to cyclic nodes. From her work on comparative clauses (Bresnan 1973) we know she would mean this to include AP, as well as NP and S. Remember that it is for the most part only lexicalists who accept the notion of cycles on nodes other than S.

Can you think of any rules other than the NSR which have been proposed (in either syntax or phonology) that apply only to or make reference to major categories? What about conditions or constraints sensitive to major categories? How would you define 'major category'?

Question 2. Which of (i) and (ii) is an apparent exception to the NSR?

$$1$$
(i) George has plans to leave.

$$1$$
(ii) George has plans to leave.

Given the readings presented by Bresnan, draw deep trees for (i) and (ii). What is the major difference between the smallest VP containing *leave* in (i) and that containing *leave* in (ii), in the deep structure? Go through the derivations of (i) and (ii), applying the NSR as the last rule on each syntactic cycle.

Question 3. Why does the NSR stress *tough* and not *prove* on the $S_0$ cycle in the tree below (which is Bresnan's Figure 12)?

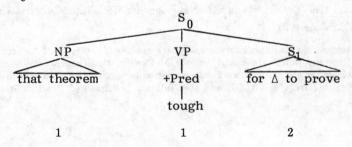

Consider an alternative analysis in which the S follows *tough* as shown here.

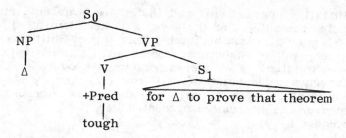

On the $S_1$ cycle the NSR would stress *theorem*. On the $S_0$ cycle *that theorem* would replace the first $\Delta$. What would the NSR stress on this cycle? Does this analysis give the correct stress contour?

*Question 4. How are the following Ss relevant to Bresnan's claim that adjectives like *tough* take PP + VP complements in the base, while predicates like *surprise* take S?

(i) *It will be tough for it to rain.
(ii) It wouldn't surprise me for it to rain.
(iii) For Mary it would be tough to quit.
(iv) *For Mary it wouldn't surprise me to quit.
(v) To quit would be tough for Mary.
(vi) *To quit wouldn't surprise me for Mary.

Why is it crucial to Bresnan's argument that Object Shift (also known as 'Tough Movement' and 'Object Raising') can apply only to VP complements?

**Question 5. Bresnan notes that certain predicates can take PP + S complements, as in

(i) It would be good $[_{PP}$ for Mary $_{PP}]$ $[_S$ for her to learn karate $_S]$

She claims that (ii), deriving from (i), is impossible, because Object Shift applies only to VPs.

(ii) *Karate would be good $[_{PP}$ for Mary $_{PP}]$ $[_S$ for her to learn $_S]$

Example (iii), however, is good. Bresnan derives it not from (i) but from (iv).

(iii) Karate would be good $[_{PP}$ for Mary $_{PP}]$ $[_{VP}$ to learn $_{VP}]$

(iv) It would be good $[_{PP}$ for Mary $_{PP}]$ $[_{VP}$ to learn karate $_{VP}]$

Assume that (i) underlies (iii) and that there is an Equi rule which deletes the subject of the lower S under identity with an NP in the higher S. Assume further that Object Shift can apply to the resultant structure. Go through this derivation of (iii) step by step. What stress contour is produced? Go through Bresnan's derivation of (iii) from (iv) step by step. What stress contour is produced? Why did Bresnan choose her derivation over the alternative presented here?

Now consider S (v).

(v) It would be good for Mary to be kissed by John.

Example (v) is ambiguous between 'For Mary to be kissed by John would be good' = 'It would be good (for Mary to be kissed by John)' and 'To be kissed by John would be good for Mary' = 'It would be good for Mary (to be kissed by John)'. In the second reading, *for Mary* is a PP. But an S must underlie *to be kissed by John*. Why? How is (v) evidence that an Equi rule of the sort discussed earlier must be able to apply to these structures? Can you say (vi)?

(vi) John would be good for Mary to be kissed by.

What does Bresnan's hypothesis predict about the grammaticality of (vi)? How is (vi) crucial to the formulation of Object Shift and, hence, to the thesis that the NSR applies at the end of each cycle?

Question 6. In Appendix 2 Bresnan gives the following examples:
$$\overset{2}{} \qquad \overset{1}{}$$
(i) Away ran Fido.
$$\overset{2}{} \qquad \qquad \overset{3}{} \quad \overset{1}{}$$
(ii) Seldom does John sing.

She notes that the stress here is that expected if the NSR follows the relevant postcyclic fronting rules. Do you think there is an inconsistency here? When is the NSR supposed to apply? If the NSR applies after all the syntactic rules on each cycle, does that mean it cannot follow postcyclic (or last cyclic) rules on the highest S?

**Question 7. Bresnan argues that the NSR applies cyclically because it cannot be precyclic or postcyclic. It cannot be precyclic, since it can follow the cyclic rules of Passive and Object Shift, as in:
$$\overset{1}{}$$
(i) John was seen by Mary.
$$\overset{1}{}$$
(ii) John was hard to see.

It cannot be postcyclic, since it can precede the cyclic rules of QF and RCF, as in (iii) and (iv).

(iii) What books has Helen written?

(iv) Here's a book that you should read.

This argument depends crucially on the assumed orderings of the rules Passive, Object Shift, QF, and RCF. Thus Bresnan devotes Appendix 2 to arguing that QF and RCF are, indeed, cyclic rules. But consider examples (v) and (vi) (from Berman and Szamosi 1972).

(v) John asked what books had arrived.

(vi) Mary likes the proposal that was made.

If the NSR is responsible for stress here, what stress contour does Bresnan's hypothesis predict in these cases? How would the NSR have to be ordered with respect to RCF to derive (v)? How would the NSR have to be ordered with respect to Passive and to RCF to derive (vi)?

We can see that (v) and (vi) present serious problems for Bresnan if the NSR is responsible for the stress contours of these sentences. But has the NSR applied in (v) and (vi)? Consider the stress of the embedded Ss in (v) and (vi) when they stand in independent clauses.

(vii) Some books had arrived.

(viii) A proposal was made.

Clearly, the NSR has not applied in (vii) and (viii), for if it had, the final word of each would receive 1 stress. Bresnan (1972) calls the stress pattern in (vii) and (viii) 'topical stress'. If topical stress applies, the NSR will not apply. Like the NSR, topical stress, according to Bresnan, applies on the cycle after all the syntactic rules on that cycle. Furthermore, it is ordered before the NSR. Bresnan's ordering hypothesis, then, would predict that whichever rule applies (the NSR or topical stress), stress patterns will be preserved under syntactic transformation. Is this prediction born out by (v) and (vi)?

*Question 8. Bresnan notes that anaphoric elements do not receive 1 stress, as in (i).

(i) John knows a woman who excels at karate, and he avoids the woman.

One of Bresnan's conclusions is that word stress is assigned in the deep structure. Thus, *the woman* in the deep structure of (i) would not receive 1 stress. It follows that anaphoricity is somehow marked in the deep structure. Consider the deep structure Bresnan presents for (ii), given in (iii).

(ii) Helen left directions for George to follow.

(iii) $[_S$ Helen left $[_{NP}$ directions $[_S$ for George to follow directions $_S]_{NP}]_S]$

Note that the second occurrence of *directions* in (iii) is anaphoric. Yet Bresnan assigns it 1 stress by the NSR. Of course, it is later deleted. (Deletion, like unstressed definiteness, is a common consequence of anaphoricity.) What is the difference between the situation of the anaphoric NP in (i) and that in (iii)? What would happen to the derivation of (iii) if the NSR never stressed anaphoric NPs?

**Question 9.** In footnote 10, Bresnan allows the NSR to apply to the PP *of John*. Does this accord with what she says elsewhere about the domain of the NSR? She then allows the Compound Rule to apply to *good of John*. Does *good of John* seem like the same sort of construction as *blackboard* (N), *whitewash* (V), or *mealy-mouthed* (A)? If not, another possibility is that *good* is stressed instead of *John* because *John* is anaphoric, in that it is assumed that he, as well as what he did, has already been mentioned in this discourse. Consider the strangeness in beginning a conversation with (i) or (ii).

(i) It was good of Thaddeus Kosciusko to help the Americans.

(ii) Helping the Americans was good of Thaddeus Kosciusko.

Why would these sentences be strange even if we had just been discussing Thaddeus Kosciusko helping the Americans? What change would improve the sentences?

Could this sort of discourse-anaphoricity help explain the lack of stress on *dinner* in (iii), Bresnan's unsolved problem sentence?

(iii) Peter had clams for dinner.

## HOMEWORK PROBLEM

Give the derivations of the following sentences, noting all applications of the NSR. Do any of these sentences present problems for the Ordering Hypothesis? If so, in what way?

(1) Mary wasn't $\overset{1}{\text{noticed}}$ by him.

(2) Mary wasn't $\overset{1}{\text{noticed}}$ by John.

(3) I'd like to meet the girl who's standing with $\overset{1}{\text{John}}$.

(4) I'd like to meet the girl $\overset{1}{\text{John's}}$ standing with.

(5) Who did you $\overset{1}{\text{say}}$ you'd like to meet?

(6) $\overset{1}{\text{How}}$ many girls did you say you'd like to meet?

(7) Now, which girl did you say you'd $\overset{1}{\text{hate}}$ to meet?

## SUGGESTED READINGS

Bach, E., and G. Horn. 1976. Remarks on 'Conditions on transformations'. Linguistic Inquiry 7:2.265-299. (For a discussion of the type of sentence found in the Homework Problem.)

Berman, A. 1974. Adjectives and adjective complement constructions in English. NSF-29. (For an analysis of *tough* adjectives and many other adjectives.)

Berman, A., and M. Szamosi. 1972. Observations on sentential stress. Lg. 48:2.304-325. (For arguments against the Ordering Hypothesis.)

Bolinger, D. 1972. Accent is predictable (if you're a mind-reader). Lg. 48:3.633-644. (For more arguments against the Ordering Hypothesis.)

Bolinger, D. 1977. Review of: Aspects of English sentence stress. American Journal of Computational Linguistics.

Bresnan, J. 1972. Stress and syntax: A reply. Lg. 48:2.326-342. (For a reply to Berman and Szamosi, and to Lakoff.)

Chomsky, N. 1973. Conditions on transformations. In: A festschrift for Morris Halle. Edited by S. A. Anderson and P. Kiparsky. New York: Holt, Rinehart and Winston. 232-286.

Lakoff, G. 1972. The global nature of the nuclear stress rule. Lg. 48:2.285-303. (For arguments against the Ordering Hypothesis.)

Lasnik, H., and R. Fiengo. 1974. Complement object deletion. Linguistic Inquiry 5:4.535-571. (For an analysis of *tough* adjective constructions.)

Pope, E. 1971. Answers to yes-no questions. Linguistic Inquiry 2:1.69-82. (For another argument that the syntactic and phonological components of the grammar cannot be discrete.)

Schmerling, S. 1976. Aspects of English sentence stress. Austin: University of Texas Press.

Selkirk, E. 1974. French liaison and the $\overline{\text{X}}$ notation. Linguistic Inquiry 5:4.573-590.

# 9

## ON THE REQUIREMENT THAT TRANSFORMATIONS PRESERVE MEANING

Barbara Hall Partee

Introduction. Partee's article, 'On the requirement that transformations preserve meaning', really gives its own introduction in that she carefully discusses the history of the question she is facing and the positions that were being taken at the time the article was written. Since that time proponents of the EST have gradually moved to the position that all the meaning of a sentence can be read off its surface structure enriched by traces. (See Chomsky 1976 and Chomsky and Lasnik 1977, in particular.) Thus the deep structure need not contribute to semantic interpretation at all. Suddenly we find that the very question Partee is addressing is theoretically irrelevant in the present state of EST. Still, even Chomsky would want to relate synonymous sentences but not arbitrarily relate non-synonymous ones. That is, the synonymy criterion is still reflected in all major approaches to syntax today, including the EST.

This article's value, however, lies perhaps as much in the examples discussed as in the theoretical question posed, for much of the data here still remain largely unexplained. We have tried to bring out some possible areas for research in our questions.

# ON THE REQUIREMENT THAT TRANSFORMATIONS PRESERVE MEANING

Barbara Hall Partee

## Introduction

Although the basic notions of semantics are about as little understood by generative linguists now as they were ten years ago, there has been a major shift in the general attitude of linguists toward semantics. Where once the claims made about the "semantic component" virtually ended with the statement that every complete grammar would have to have one, now questions about the relation of semantics to other parts of the grammar are receiving widespread attention and are central to some of the major current controversies. It is difficult to point to anything that might be called a substantive semantic result, but the most important step has been taken: we have stopped playing ostrich about semantics.

Among the important issues in the area of semantics and its relation to the rest of the grammar, the idea that transformations might be meaning-preserving is one that has an interesting history and one whose fate is still far from clear. In Part 1, I will review its history briefly; then in Part 2, I will discuss generally some important factors in disputes about it; and finally in Part 3, I will talk about some of the more interesting phenomena with respect to which the meaning-preservingness of transformations seems to be called into question.

## 1. Evolution of the Hypothesis 1957–1969

### 1.1 The Emergence of Deep Structure Semantics 1957–1965

In *Syntactic Structures* Chomsky presented quite emphatically the view that semantic considerations play no role in the linguist's analysis of syntactic structure. He suggested further that although the underlying syntactic structure might well be of considerable relevance to the description of meaning, it was probably not sufficient for it. The following quotation is from the summary chapter:

> The notion of "structural meaning" as opposed to "lexical meaning," however, appears to be quite suspect, and it is questionable that the grammatical devices available in language are used consistently enough so that meaning can be assigned to them directly. (Chomsky, 1957, p. 108)

A major change in this view was brought about through the pioneering efforts in exploring the semantic component of a transformational grammar made by Katz, Fodor, and Postal. In Katz and Fodor's original work (1963), there were two types of semantic "projection rules" envisaged: one type to build up the meaning of kernel sentences from the meanings of their lexical items, a specific semantic rule being correlated with each phrase-structure rule; and rules of another type associated with the transformations, designed to represent how the meaning of a sentence changed as it was transformed. A major theoretical innovation in Katz and Postal (1964) was the suggestion that the second type of rule might be dispensable because it might be the case that transformations never did change in meaning. They stress the empirical nature of the claim in the following words:

> This principle, it should be stressed, is not . . . a statement in linguistic theory, but rather it is a rule of thumb based on the general character of linguistic descriptions. The principle can be stated as follows: given a sentence for which a syntactic derivation is needed; look for simple paraphrases of the sentence which are not paraphrases by virtue of synonymous expressions; on finding them, construct grammatical rules that relate the original sentence and its paraphrases in such a way that each of these sentences has the same set of underlying P-markers. Of course, having constructed such rules, it is still necessary to find independent syntactic justification for them. (Katz and Postal, 1964, p. 157)

The principle presented by Katz and Postal as an empirical hypothesis gained support very quickly, to the point where it was widely accepted as one of the more solidly established generalizations in linguistic theory and used as a criterion for transformational rules. In Chomsky's writings from about 1964 to 1966 this is clearly the case. In *Aspects of the Theory of Syntax,* Chomsky puts it quite succinctly:

> . . . the syntactic component of a grammar must specify, for each sentence, a *deep structure* that determines its semantic interpretation and a *surface structure* that determines its phonetic interpretation. (Chomsky, 1965, p. 16)

Note that as long as the notion of a syntactically defined deep structure is accepted, the claim that semantic interpretation is entirely on deep structure is indeed equivalent to the claim that transformations preserve meaning.

### 1.2 Early Challenges to Deep Structure Semantics 1965–1967

An early challenge to the claim was made by Kuroda (1965), in the section called "Attachment transformation." There he noted that certain words, notably *even, only,* and *also,* were limited to one occurrence per sentence but that occurrence could be in any of a large number of positions in the sentence. He argued that the one-per-sentence limitation could be reasonably captured only by making such items constituents of the sentence under, for instance, a pre-sentence node, in which case their variety of surface positions would have to be assigned by a transformational rule (which he called an attachment rule).

One part of Kuroda's evidence is now widely rejected, namely the observation that such words are limited to one occurrence per sentence. It seems quite easy to get more than one *only* per sentence, and the difficulty in getting more than one *even* per sentence may just be a performance difficulty connected with the complexity of the semantic interpretation.[1]

(1) a. Only John danced with only one girl all evening.
   b. Most of the fellows either prefer blonds or don't care; only John will date only redheads.

But otherwise the analysis of words like *even* and *only* is still very much at issue, since the apparent generalization that they can have as semantic scope virtually any phrase which is a constituent at the level of surface structure does not seem to be naturally capturable at the level of deep structure.

Chapin (1967) suggests one important reservation that might be made to the claim that transformations preserve meaning, which is a necessary one in distinguishing the lexicalist-transformationalist controversy from the controversy over whether meaning is determined only at the deepest level of structure. Chapin suggests that some lexical transformations must follow some of the ordinary transformations—that, for example, the formation of words with the prefix *self* (*self-starting, self-defrosting,* and so forth) follows the reflexive transformation, and that of words with the suffix *-able* (*breakable, returnable,* and so forth) follows the passive transformation; but the lexical transformations which Chapin sets up to form such words are not meaning-preserving, since even where the basic meaning of a word is consistent with its phrasal source, additional unpredictable bits of meaning are usually associated with the word (compare *payable, admirable, self-reproducing*).

### 1.3 Current Positions

In the more recent past, Lakoff, McCawley, Postal, and others have accepted the hypothesis that transformations preserve meaning and extended it to the position that all and only sentences which are paraphrases of each other should have the same deep structures. They have shown that consistent adherence to such a principle requires much more abstract deep structures than were previously contemplated. Many of their analyses have independent support from purely syntactic arguments, and it is often not easy to determine how much of the weight of their arguments is borne by the criterion of meaning-preservingness of transformations. Chomsky and Jackendoff, on the other hand, have argued that the more abstract deep structures do not have sufficient independent syntactic motivation, and that a simpler overall grammar will be achieved by keeping a more conservative deep structure and allowing semantic interpretation to take into consideration

---

[1] Bruce Fraser (1971) has stated that more than one *even* could occur in a sentence. From the semantic interpretation he provides for *even* one would indeed predict difficulty in understanding such sentences.

some aspects of surface structure and perhaps of intermediate structures as well.

It would appear then that within the abstract-deep-structure or generative semantics camp, the principle of meaning-preservingness of transformations is a fundamental condition on most of the grammar, but not necessarily on those transformations which introduce lexical items. This exception would appear to be inconsistent with the strongest version of "generative semantics," which is that the deepest level of structure is prelexical but is the only level relevant to semantic interpretation—in some sense *is* the semantic interpretation. I am not certain whether anyone seriously holds such a view, but it is certainly the view suggested by the term "generative semantics."[2]

## 2. Basic Issues

### 2.1 The Notion of Synonymy

The question of meaning-preservingness is a difficult one to discuss in part because of difficulties with the notions of meaning and synonymy. Some philosophers have claimed that no two sentences are synonymous, including even pairs that would unanimously be claimed to be transformationally related. Another extreme is to call any two sentences synonymous if they have the same truth-value. A position which seems closer to what most linguists seem to have in mind is to call two sentences synonymous if they would have the same truth value in all possible worlds. However, this notion is useful only for declarative sentences, and furthermore doesn't seem to get at things like focus and presupposition very easily.

### 2.2 The Empirical Nature of Hypothesis

The various stands taken on synonymy all have to do with synonymy between *sentences,* and in talk about transformations preserving or changing meaning, the most common examples are transformations which can infor-

---

[2] McCawley in the discussion following this paper asserted that he does indeed hold the strong form of the generative semantics position; in his view, although at least some lexical insertion does indeed follow other transformations, the idiosyncratic details of meaning connected with individual lexical items must be present on the deepest level and constitute conditions on the insertion of the lexical items.

The independence of the lexicalist-transformationalist question from the question of meaning-preservingness can thus ·be illustrated by the following positions:

|  | Lexicalist/ transformationalist | All transformations meaning-preserving |
|---|---|---|
| Chomsky (1968) | Lexicalist | Yes (?) |
| Chomsky (1969) | Lexicalist | No |
| Chapin (1967) | Transformationalist | No |
| McCawley (1969b) | Transformationalist | Yes |

mally be thought of as relating sentences to other sentences. But transformations in fact operate not on sentences but on abstract phrase-markers, and it is not obvious that we have any direct semantic intuitions about these abstract structures, in particular any notion of synonymy between them. Failure to distinguish sentences from abstract P-markers is often harmless, as in discussion of very late optional "stylistic" transformations, where the abstract structures involved are very close to surface structures, that is, sentences. But for obligatory transformations the fact that abstract structures and not sentences are involved is significant. For obligatory rules, in fact, the question of meaning-preservingness does not even make sense, for the input to the rule is an abstract structure with which we have no independent acquaintance. This point can be illustrated by considering the affix-switching rule that moves -ing, -en, and so forth, into their surface positions: it makes no sense to ask whether the rule preserves meaning or not, because the question presupposes that we have some independent idea of the meaning of sentences whose affixes are not switched.

The question of whether transformations change meaning can therefore be meaningfully asked only of optional transformations. The clearest case is that in which two sentences are derived from the same deep structure, their derivations differing only in the application versus nonapplication of a certain optional rule. If the two sentences are synonymous, and if the same is true of all pairs related by the given rule, the rule is meaning-preserving; otherwise it is not. A slightly more complicated case is that in which pairs of sentences differ in derivation by one optional rule and one or more subsequent obligatory rules; it still seems reasonable in such cases to attribute any change in meaning to the optional rule. An example of this occurs further below: sentences (4)a and b differ by both that rule and the later obligatory any-no rule; however, all discussions of such sentences assume that the meaning change is due only to the some-any rule.

A case in which it would be much more difficult to assign responsibility for meaning change could arise in the following sort of situation:[3] Suppose a grammar contains the optional rules $T_1$ and $T_2$ and an obligatory rule $T_3$ whose structural conditions are met just when $T_1$ and $T_2$ are both applied. Then there might be four sentences with the same deep structures and the following differences in rules applied:

$S_0$: none of the rules applied
$S_1$: only $T_1$ applied
$S_2$: only $T_2$ applied
$S_3$: both $T_1$ and $T_2$, and hence also $T_3$, applied

Then supposing $S_0$, $S_1$, and $S_2$ were all synonymous but $S_3$ was not synonymous with the others, it would be rather difficult to decide nonarbitrarily

[3] I am indebted to Frank Heny for this observation.

what rule or rules were responsible for the change of meaning. I do not know of any actual cases of this sort, however.

To simplify the remainder of the discussion, we will ignore potential cases of the last-mentioned sort, and assume that the question of meaning-preservingness is meaningful for optional transformations and not for obligatory ones. There is then a corollary of this assumption, a corollary which was illustrated quite clearly in Katz and Postal (1964). Suppose it is observed that a certain optional transformation does change meaning significantly: it will often be possible to add some abstract element to the deep structure which serves as obligatory trigger to that transformational rule, thus exempting that rule from the requirement of meaning-preservingness. Unless such additional deep-structure elements are independently motivated (as they are in all the Katz and Postal examples), they reduce the claim of meaning-preservingness to near vacuity. Insofar as they can be shown necessary on syntactic grounds, they strengthen it. This issue is crucial in subsequent developments in syntax and semantics, although it is sometimes obscured. I will present below first some examples from Katz and Postal illustrating the independent syntactic justification of the introduction of deep-structure elements which make previously optional rules obligatory; then I will discuss a more recent example which seems to lack such justification.

Two of the classic examples discussed by Katz and Postal are the interrogative and negative transformations. In *Syntactic Structures* both were optional rules, so that (2)b had the same deep structure as (2)a, and (3)b the same as (3)a, but the rules were clearly not meaning-preserving under any definition of synonymy.

(2) a. John smokes pot.
   b. Does John smoke pot?
(3) a. John smokes pot.
   b. John doesn't smoke pot.

Katz and Postal cite Klima's arguments, which are purely syntactic and were given prior to the introduction of the meaning-preservingness hypothesis, that interrogative sentences must have an extra morpheme, which might be represented as WH, in their deep structures, and negative sentences must also contain a special morpheme, say NEG, in their deep structures. Then the *b* sentences are no longer optional variants of the *a* sentences but obligatory transforms of the *c* sentences below, so that they are no longer predicted to be synonymous with the *a* sentences.

(2) c. WH  John smokes pot.
(3) c. NEG  John smokes pot.

Katz and Postal did overlook one important violation of their hypothesis in Klima's analysis of negation, namely that for Klima the *some-any* suppletion rule was optional in most environments. For Klima, therefore, an optional transformation related sentences (4)a,b and (4)c,d.

(4) a. I couldn't answer some of the questions.
    b. I couldn't answer any of the questions.
    c. Some of the books were not on the shelf.
    d. None of the books were on the shelf.

The relation of *some* and *any* turns out to be a very interesting problem and has been one of the important factors in a number of recent proposals, including Fillmore's (1967) distinction between $+/-$ specific indefinite articles, George Lakoff's (1970d) proposal of quantifiers as predicates on higher sentences, and Robin Lakoff's (1969) suggestion that there can't be a *some-any* rule. All these proposals start from the position that Klima's *some-any* rule is inadequate insofar as it violates the Katz/Postal hypothesis of meaning-preservingness, thus elevating what started out as an empirical hypothesis to the position of a constraint built into the theory.

Katz and Postal took great pains to point out the need for independent syntactic justification for analyses, being fully aware that as soon as meaning-preservingness itself is taken as a criterion for transformational rules, it loses almost all empirical content (except for the empirical question of whether it is possible to write a grammar conforming to that principle; but the answer to that is almost certainly affirmative, given the present power of transformational grammar—see Peters and Ritchie's (1969) refutation of the empiricalness of the universal base hypothesis). An example which seems to me to illustrate this weakening of empirical content is the causative analysis of transitive/intransitive verbs like *break*.

In Partee (1965) it is argued that transitive *break* is not a causative of intransitive *break* in English, on the grounds that transitive *break* not only fails to be fully synonymous with *cause to break*, but differs from it in co-occurrence properties. Thus (5)a and (5)b are not alike in meaning, and (6)a and (6)b are not alike in well-formedness; the latter fact gives a syntactic argument against the causative analysis, the former showing that such an analysis does not even have strong semantic support.

(5) a. John broke the window.
    b. John caused the window to break.
(6) a. A change in temperature caused the window to break.
    b. *A change in temperature broke the window.

In Lakoff (1965), where a causative analysis is defended, it is claimed that the above argument is irrelevant, because his causative analysis involves not the lexical item *cause* but a dummy verb CAUSE which presumably differs semantically from *cause* in just whatever ways will account for the meaning difference between (5)a and (5)b, and differs from it in co-occurrence restrictions in just the right ways to account for the impossibility of sentences like (6)b. Since this dummy verb has no lexical realization, the causative transformation must be obligatory and is therefore exempted from the criterion of meaning-preservingness. But since no independent reasons are given for this dummy trigger element being analyzed as a verb, let alone for its being related in any principled way to the verb *cause,* the empirical claim that seems to be made by the statement that English has a causative transformation is greatly weakened, and in particular the analysis offers no support to the Katz/Postal hypothesis.

In short, I am suggesting that the hypothesis that all transformations preserve meaning, so long as it remains an empirical hypothesis, is interesting, debatable, and important. But although it is a plausible hypothesis with a considerable amount of evidence in its favor, it seems to me a mistake to prematurely shut the door on its investigation by accepting it as a criterion for transformations.

### 2.3  Alternative Hypotheses

The position that transformational rules *don't* preserve meaning is of much less inherent interest than the contrary position, since it amounts simply to the position that a certain strong hypothesis is false. It may of course turn out to be the correct position, but it doesn't seem like anything one could rationally *want* to champion—it is analogous to the position that synchronic rules don't reflect historical development, or that not all languages use the same stock of phonological features, and so forth, the sum of all such positions being that "languages can differ from each other without limit and in unpredictable ways" (Joos, 1957, p. 76). Of course, just being strong doesn't make a hypothesis right; in fact it increases its chances of being wrong—but it does make it interesting, in the sense that it increases our stock of generalizations about the structure of language if it is right.

So for the position that transformational rules can change meaning to be comparable in interest to the position that they can't, it would have to be coupled with some alternative claims of comparable strength, such as the following:

(a) Most transformational rules preserve meaning; those of such-and-such a form, however, do not, and their effect on meaning is predictable in such-and-such a way from their form. (This is a very rough generalization of Kuroda's position as described above.)

(b) All meaning is determinable at the surface-structure level. (This position is certainly strong enough to be of interest, but is unfortunately extremely easy to falsify.)

(c) All meaning connected with the basic grammatical relations between major lexical categories is determined at the deep-structure level, but that connected with reference and with logical relations such as quantification and negation is determined at the surface level. (This bears some resemblance to the Chomsky/Jackendoff position, but for pronominalization, at least, they need to let rules of semantic interpretation apply cyclically, which weakens the position considerably.)

(d) All those parts of meaning that have to do with truth-value (in all possible worlds) are determined at the deep structure level and preserved by transformational rules; what can change in the course of a transformational derivation are just those subtler aspects of "meaning" which are suggested by terms such as "topicalization," "focus/presupposition," or other equally ill-understood notions. (This is the position I tend toward but it is not a well-defined one because of the vagueness of the distinction between the different sorts of meaning.)

### 2.4 Possible Counterevidence

The last general matter that I want to bring up in this section is the question of counterevidence to the hypothesis that transformations preserve meaning. Just as no empirical support is gained for it by those analyses for which the assumption of its truth lay behind a major part of the evidence, no valid empirical counterargument can be made simply by showing that there exists for a given phenomenon one possible analysis violating the hypothesis. Counterevidence must rather take the form of showing that the best available analysis based on syntactic evidence alone is one which violates the hypothesis. One cannot expect there to be a final word in such arguments, of course, since presumably no analysis will ever be immune from overthrow by a better one.

## 3. Relevant Phenomena

### 3.1 Quantifiers

A good bit of the current interest in quantifiers stems from the fact that there are a number of transformations which, as traditionally formulated, preserve meaning except when quantifiers are involved. This is particularly true of those transformations which delete or pronominalize an NP when it is identical to some other NP in the sentence: when identity of NP's is taken to include quantifiers as part of the NP, a change of meaning generally results. The pairs of examples in (7), (8), and (9) illustrate such a change with reflexivization, equi-NP deletion, and relativization, respectively.

(7) a. Every man voted for himself.
   b. Every man voted for every man.
(8) a. Every contestant expected to come in first.
   b. Every contestant expected every contestant to come in first.
(9) a. Every Democrat who voted for a Republican was sorry.
   b. Every Democrat [every Democrat voted for a Republican] was sorry.

Since there are so many transformations which change meaning only when quantifiers are present, it is natural that suspicion should fall on the analysis of quantifiers. So far the choices seem to be among syntactically simple analyses for which the rules of semantic interpretation have to be applied throughout the transformational cycle in rather complex ways, and analyses with semantically more plausible deep structures but some rather unnatural-looking syntactic rules (insofar as the syntactic rules have been made explicit). If an analysis which is elegant in both respects should be found, it ought to have considerable effect on the outcome of the general theoretical dispute.

3.1.1 *Each*-hopping: a surfacist argument and the rebuttal. In Chomsky (1969) a number of interesting phenomena are discussed. Most of them purport to illustrate the need to have some semantic interpretation rules be sensitive to surface structure, but to me it seems questionable whether any of them actually do so. I will single out for discussion one which seems particularly vulnerable, in that there are purely syntactic counterarguments which lead one to a solution which supports the meaning-preservingness hypothesis. The phenomenon in question is *each*-hopping, typically illustrated by sentence pairs like (10)a and b.

(10) a. Each of the men is involved in this.
    b. The men are each involved in this.

Chomsky's argument, attributed to Dougherty (1968, 1969),[4] is that since it is possible to make a syntactically simple statement of *each*-hopping without concern for any constituents to the right of the Aux, the rule will have to be allowed to derive (11)b from (11)a, with subsequent adjustments to the semantic interpretation.

(11) a. Each of the men hates his brothers.
    b. The men each hate his brothers.

___

[4] Since I have not seen Dougherty (1968, 1969), it is possible that my objections apply only to Chomsky's representation of his arguments.

But such a derivation is questionable on syntactic grounds alone, since purely syntactic arguments can be found for changing *his* to *their* when applying *each*-hopping to a sentence like (11)a. Consider first some facts about conjunction. The distributional facts illustrated in (12) support the intermediate stages shown in (13), which have been independently proposed by a number of people.[5]

(12) a. John hates himself and Bill hates himself.
    b. *John hates themselves and Bill hates themselves.
    c. John and Bill hate themselves.
    d. *John and Bill hate himself.
(13) a. John and Bill hate $himself_1$ and $himself_2$ respectively.
    b. $himself_1$ and $himself_2$ respectively $\Rightarrow$ themselves

That is, we can take all conjunction-reduction as derivative from *respectively*-conjunction, with the generalization that formally identical conjuncts may be collapsed (each collapse accompanied by deletion of *respectively*), the collapsed nouns keeping their number intact if they are coreferential, but becoming plural otherwise. Thus (14)a has two reduced forms, the difference depending on whether the two occurrences of *book* are coreferential or not.

(14) a. John read a book and Bill read a book.
    b. John and Bill read a book and a book respectively.
    c. $\begin{cases} \text{a } book_1 \text{ and a } book_1 \Rightarrow \text{a book} \\ \text{a } book_1 \text{ and a } book_2 \Rightarrow \text{books} \end{cases}$
    d. John and Bill read $\begin{cases} \text{a book} \\ \text{books} \end{cases}$

The same process can be seen to apply twice in a case like the following:

(15) a. $John_1$ hates $his_1$ $brother_3$ and $Bill_2$ hates $his_2$ $brother_4$.
    b. John and Bill hate $his_1$ $brother_3$ and $his_2$ $brother_4$ respectively.
    c. John and Bill hate $his_1$ and $his_2$ $brother_3$ and $brother_4$ respectively.
    d. John and Bill hate their brothers.

That *each*-hopping has a good bit in common with conjunction-reduction appears from examination of sentences containing *each* and a reflexive pronoun. The distribution shown below is parallel to that in (12).

[5] See the reference to Postal (personal communication) in McCawley (1968, p. 166); also Schacter in the conjunction section of Stockwell *et al.* (1969).

(16)  a.  Each of the men shaves himself.
       b.  *Each of the men shaves themselves.[6]
       c.  The men each shave themselves.
       d.  *The men each shave himself.

Exactly the same kind of distribution appears for sentences like (11)a and b if we add *own*; this case was noted by Chomsky, who proposed handling it by a surface filtering rule.

(17)  a.  Each of the men hates his own brothers.
       b.  *Each of the men hates their own brothers.
       c.  The men each hate their own brothers.
       d.  *The men each hate his own brothers.

Chomsky explicitly suggests deriving (17)d from (17)a and then filtering out (17)d; he does not point out that (17)c would then have to be derived from (17)b and (17)b also filtered out; nor does he point out that the same kind of problems would arise for (16). Although I don't know how to state the pluralization rule so as to make it apply "in the same way" to conjunction-reduction and *each*-hopping, it seems to be that this is clearly what's going on. Otherwise it must be counted as a coincidence that the derivation which would preserve meaning (namely from the *a* to the *c* cases) in both conjunction-reduction, (12), and *each*-hopping, (16) and (17), is also the derivation that eliminates all the ungrammatical sentences without appeal to filtering devices. Thus it seems to me that the example Chomsky offers in support of the need for surface structure interpretation plus filtering devices in fact provides an argument against them.

**3.1.2  Conjunction-reduction: a problem for everyone.**  Another case where a rule as traditionally stated is meaning-preserving most of the time but not so when quantifiers are involved is the case of conjunction-reduction, noted in Partee (1970) and discussed further in G. Lakoff (1968b). The rules for conjunction-reduction as proposed by Chomsky (1957) and subsequently refined by a number of writers would allow the derivation of (18)b from (18)a, but the two sentences are clearly not synonymous.[7]

---

[6] A commonly accepted form is *each of the men shave themselves* where the verb as well as the reflexive pronoun is pluralized. The existence of such a dialect, together with the absence (as far as I know) of any dialect which accepts (16)b, simply lends support to the claim that pronouns as well as verbs can change number transformationally.

[7] For those speakers who can understand "few students" as referring to a *specific* few in both sentences, the resulting readings will be synonymous; however, for all speakers "few students" can be taken as nonspecific, and the two sentences are nonsynonymous on the resulting readings.

(18)  a.  Few students are popular and few students are likely to succeed.
      b.  Few students are both popular and likely to succeed.

A priori there is no way to choose between a complication of the syntactic rules for conjunction-reduction and a complication of the semantic rules of interpretation; the choice must depend on how one can make the greatest generalizations with the least amount of extra apparatus, taking both syntax and semantics into account.

One suggestion made by Lakoff (1968b) has considerable initial attractiveness but runs into some serious problems. The analysis of quantifiers suggested in G. Lakoff (1965) would lead to deriving (18)b from something like the synonymous (18)c,

(18)  c.  Students who are both popular and likely to succeed are few.

but nothing suggested in that analysis would block the derivation of (18)b from (18)a, so that there would be two derivations of the unambiguous[8] (18)b. What Lakoff (1968b) suggested was that the derivation from (18)a to (18)b could be blocked by a quite general and plausible condition, namely that conjunction-reduction should not take place on nonreferential NP's: this would correctly allow reduction of cases like (18)a and b with subjects like *those three students, John,* and so forth, and with *few students* for those speakers who can interpret it as referring to a specific few. It would block the cases which make the problem, namely those with indefinite quantified subjects. However, it would also block reduction of nonreferential NP's in cases where such reduction does not lead to any change in meaning, and therefore it seems to be too strong a restriction. For example, the phrase "few questions" in (19)a and b does not appear to differ in any significant regard with respect to referentiality from the phrase "few students" in (18)a and b, and yet the application of conjunction-reduction to (19)a to yield (19)b is perfectly meaning-preserving.

(19)  a.  Mary will answer few questions and Susan will answer few questions and Joan will answer few questions.
      b.  Mary, Susan, and Joan will answer few questions.

There appear to be many complicating factors. One significant factor seems to be the relative order of the quantifier and the conjoined phrase, or perhaps the subject position of the quantifier, since the passives of (19)a and b are not synonymous.

---

8 There would presumably be four derivations if (18)b can be understood two ways, as either specific or nonspecific; in either case, that is, there are too many derivations.

(19) c. Few questions will be answered by Mary and few questions will be answered by Susan and few questions will be answered by Joan.
   d. Few questions will be answered by Mary, Susan, and Joan.

It seems that (19)d is ambiguous for many speakers (apparently more so than (19)b, so that on one reading it is indeed synonymous with (19)c, but on the other reading it is not. Another complication is the apparent alternation of *and* and *or*. Thus (19)e below is much closer in meaning to (19)g than to (19)f.

(19) e. Many airplanes stop at Dallas and many airplanes stop at Chicago.
   f. Many airplanes stop at Dallas and Chicago.
   g. Many airplanes stop at Dallas or Chicago.

The first and third sentences are not fully synonymous, however, since (19)g asserts only that the total number of airplanes stopping at the cities is many, and that not necessarily many airplanes stop at each, as is asserted in (19)e. Although (19)g does not appear to involve phrasal conjunction, it has no obvious sentential source with either an *and* or an *or*.

Still another complicating factor is the behavior of words like *both*, *each*, and *apiece* with conjunction and quantification. Despite considerable attention, these words are still very poorly understood, and they are obviously of crucial importance in relating conjoined full sentences to sentences with phrasal conjuncts. Thus it is still not at all obvious whether the eventual solution to the problem of (18)a and b will involve reanalyzing the syntax in such a way that all the rules are meaning-preserving or alternatively allowing the semantic component to take into account certain aspects of derived structure or of the derivations themselves.

**3.1.3 Q-magic: a generative-semantics argument and a rebuttal.** Another interesting problem with meaning-preservation in the area of conjunction and quantifiers arises with the Lakoff/Carden rule of quantifier-lowering ("Q-magic"; see G. Lakoff (1968b), Carden (1967)). Lakoff (1968b) suggests that sentence (20)a shows that quantifier lowering cannot apply into conjoined structures, that is, obeys the Ross (1967) coordinate structure constraint, because (20)a cannot have as one of its readings anything like (20)b.

(20) a. Abdul believes that few men and many women like baba ganouze.
   b. There are few men such that Abdul believes that they and many women like baba ganouze.

But if there is indeed such a rule as quantifier-lowering, the relation between it and conjunction is more complicated than Lakoff noticed, and in a way which seems very peculiar indeed within the framework that Lakoff proposes.

Recall first of all the ambiguities noted by G. Lakoff (1965) for sentences such as (21)a.

(21) a. 100 soldiers shot two students.
  b. A group of 100 soldiers shot a total of two students.
  c. 100 soldiers each shot two students.
  d. Two students were each shot by 100 soldiers.

Virtually all speakers can interpret (21)a as either (21)b or (21)c; some can also interpret it as (21)d while others have that reading only for the passive of (21)a. What is significant here is not how many readings one obtains, but the fact that exactly the *same* number of readings (for any given speaker) will be obtained for (22)a, namely (22)b, (22)c, and perhaps (22)d. One does not, however, get any "mixed" readings, such as (22)e below.

(22) a. On that safari, five hunters shot three lions and two tigers.
  b. On that safari, a group of five hunters shot three lions and two tigers.
  c. On that safari, five hunters each shot three lions and two tigers.
  d. On that safari, three lions and two tigers were each shot by five hunters.
  e. On that safari, a group of five hunters shot three lions and five hunters each shot two tigers.

What makes this set of data interesting is that starting with a sentential conjunction like (23),

(23) On that safari, five hunters shot three lions and five hunters shot two tigers.

one has, assuming coreferentiality of the hunters, either $2 \times 2 = 4$ or $3 \times 3 = 9$ readings for the unreduced sentence; but when (23) is reduced to (22)a one has

  i. not, as blind conjunction-reduction would predict, four or nine readings,
  ii. not, as Lakoff would predict, only one reading (namely (22)b, since the quantifiers supposedly could not be lowered from higher sentences),
  iii. but rather either two or three readings, corresponding exactly to the two or three readings for an unconjoined sentence like (21)a.

This would appear to be prima facie evidence in favor of treating conjunction-reduction as one formal operation, letting semantic interpretation depend in part on the output, since the generalization indicated by iii above is that in conjoined NP's containing quantifiers, the quantifiers must have the same scope. The transformationalist position must have two different rules for conjunction-reduction, one for specific and one for nonspecific NP's. Otherwise, if conjunction-reduction is to be treated as a single rule followed by quantifier-lowering, as Lakoff appeared to regard it, then quantifier-lowering must be allowed to violate the coordinate structure constraint just in case it violates it equally for all conjuncts.

The facts when stated informally do not after all seem terribly peculiar; they are obviously related to the fact noted by Chomsky (1966) that (24)a is only two ways ambiguous, like (24)b, not four ways ambiguous as one might have expected.

(24)   a.   John likes Mary better than Susan, and so does Bill.
      b.   John likes Mary better than Susan.

But these facts are nevertheless not explained within any of the current frameworks, and until an explanation is found it can only be a question of plausibility of what sort of framework is most likely to harbor a satisfactory explanation. It is the fact that the reduction of ambiguity accompanies the transformational processes of conjunction-reduction, (23) to (22)a, and verb-phrase ellipsis, (24)a, that suggests that semantic interpretation must take into account either the processes involved or the outputs thereof.[9]

### 3.2   Subject and Object: the Problematical Relation of Surface Structure to Semantic Interpretation

The last four sets of examples I want to discuss all concern the semantic significance of subject and object position, particularly of what appears to be derived subject and object position.

**3.2.1   *Easy.*** Firstly, classical syntactic arguments[10] have favored assigning a single deep structure to the sentences of (26), and hence presumably to those of (27).

---

[9] Lakoff's most recent suggestions (G. Lakoff 1969a,b) seem to present a new alternative, namely that aspects of the semantic interpretation—dependent only on or perhaps equated with deep structure—may be carried along in some manner through a derivation and may determine constraints on the operation of syntactic rules. Lakoff claimed in the discussion following this paper that his suggestion makes the question of meaning-preservingness quite vacuous and offers a framework in which examples like (22) might indeed be able to be handled. However, unless it can be shown that there are some empirical claims connected with the introduction of such a powerful new device (and particularly some possibility of falsification), it would appear to be a matter of making the meaning-preservingness question vacuous by begging it.

[10] See Chomsky (1964), Partee (1968).

(26) a. It is easy to please John.
    b. John is easy to please.
(27) a. It is particularly easy to get this baby into these overalls.
    b. This baby is particularly easy to get into these overalls.
    c. These overalls are particularly easy to get this baby into.

It is clear from co-occurrence restrictions that the surface subjects *John, this baby,* and *these overalls* must each occur in deep structure in the clause which ends up as an infinitive phrase, but it is not out of the question that they *also* occur as deep structure subjects of *easy,* after the manner of (28):

(28) This baby is $_{ADJP}$[particularly easy $_S$[NP gets this baby into these overalls]]

If a structure something like (28) could be justified on independent (that is, nonsemantic) grounds[11] as underlying (27)b, and analogous deep structures for (26)b and (27)c, then there would not necessarily be a violation of the meaning-preservingness condition in deriving those sentences. But there is certainly a violation by the classical analysis, since the raising of a constituent sentence NP into matrix subject position has always been treated as an optional transformation.

Note, incidentally, that even if (28) could be syntactically justified as the deep structure for (27)b, there would remain a significant unexplained correlation. Sentence (27)a with heavy stress on *these overalls* seems synonymous with (27)c. It would seem that adding stress and raising to subject are two ways of accomplishing the same result, namely the bringing into focus (speaking vaguely) of one of the NP's. Without some way of relating (28) to the corresponding stressed version of (27)a, then, (28) is only half a solution to the problem for representing the differences between (27)a, b, c.[12]

**3.2.2** *Appears.* The second set of examples exhibits a similar pattern with even less semantic difference but still not quite total synonymy.

(28) a. It appears that John is shooting at Bill.
    b. John appears to be shooting at Bill.
    c. Bill appears to be being shot at by John.

Whereas the difference among the sentences of (27) seems to involve attribution of different properties to the derived subjects, the difference here seems

---

[11] Tentative but unpublished suggestions along these lines have been made by R. P. V. Kiparsky and David Perlmutter.

[12] Probably of relevance here is the discussion of clefting and stress in Postal (1968).

to be a difference in point of view of the speaker—in *a* he is taking in the whole situation, in *b* and *c* focussing on John and Bill respectively. Following the direction taken by Postal (1971) for the verb "remind," we might look for a relation between the sentences of (29) and those of (30) below:

(30)   a.   I see that John is shooting at Bill.
   b.   I see John shooting at Bill.
   c.   I see Bill being shot at by John.

However, the analysis of *see* and its complements is much less clear than the analysis of *appear* has generally been believed to be, so it is of no immediate help for (29) to suggest relating *appear* to *see*. But it is no doubt at least relevant that the verb *appear* is a psychological verb, so that the differences in (29) may be related to different perceptions leading to essentially the same assertion.

**3.2.3   *Certain.*** For contrast, consider the third set of examples with the nonpsychological sense of *certain*.

(31)   a.   Nobody is (absolutely) certain to pass the test.
   b.   It is (absolutely) certain that nobody will pass the test.
   c.   It is not (absolutely) certain that anybody will pass the test.

The problem here is that (31)a, which is sharply nonsynonymous with both (31)b and (31)c, would seem to be derivable from both of them on the classical analysis of *certain*.[13] *Certain* must allow subject-raising because of sentences like (32).

(32)   There is certain to be an argument over that.

And yet to allow subject-raising to apply to either (31)b or (31)c would lead to a change in meaning of a much more fundamental sort than that in either (27) or (29). (31)a can be paraphrased by (33).

(33)   There is nobody of whom it is (absolutely) certain that he will pass the test.

(Thus under a common kind of grading system, (31)b and (31)c are both false, while (31)a is true.) A logician would have no difficulty in representing the differences in the sentences of (31) in terms of differing "scopes" of three elements: negation, an existential quantifier, and a modal operator "certain"; and a linguist might be tempted to simply translate these scope differences into spatial configurations, with trees roughly as in (34).

[13] See Rosenbaum (1967) and Partee (1968).

(34)

a.

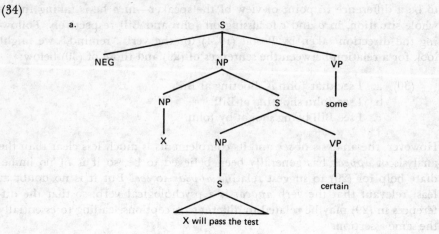

b.

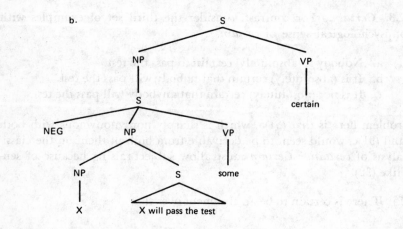

c.

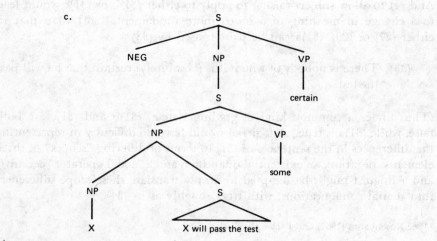

But the problem clearly does not end with the postulation of such deep structures, since it still remains to show how the syntactic rules would map such structures onto the right surface structures. A naive linguist might suppose, for instance, that a deep structure like (34)a would turn into something more like (35) or (36) below than (31)a, and it is incumbent upon the hypothetical proposers of (34)a to show in a non-*ad hoc* way why it can turn into (31)a.

(35)   Those who it is certain will pass the test are none.
(36)   There is no one who it is certain will pass the test.

If one were to maintain the classical syntactic analysis, allowing (31)a to be derived from (31)b or perhaps (31)c (or perhaps both), there would be both the particular problem of characterizing the semantic effect of subject-raising in such cases and the more general problem of stating constraints on how transformational rules (or more global properties of derivation) in general can affect semantic interpretation. The corresponding problem for the analysis suggested in (34) is to find constraints on the transformational rules (or on derivations) so that the rules never apply in cases where their application would change meaning. At the moment there seem to be no obvious solutions in either direction.

Examples (27), (29), and (31) all involve matrix subjects derived in some sense from embedded sentences. What is clear is that appearing in matrix subject position is of semantic relevance, and what is in dispute is how that fact iṣ to be captured. A second-order problem which faces any analysis is to explain why the three quite different semantic effects observed all are associated with the single phenomenon of raising to subject, and why, for instance, contrastive stress has a similar effect only in (27)a.

**3.2.4   *Loading the truck with hay.***   The last set of examples concerns the direct object position in simplex sentences. Partee (1965) and Fillmore (1968) consider pairs of sentences like (37)a and b:

(37)   a.   We loaded the truck with hay.
       b.   We loaded hay onto the truck.

Both authors argue that the distributional similarities between the *a* and *b* type sentences are striking enough that they must be transformationally related. The verbs which show this kind of relation, sometimes with different prepositions, include *spray (wall, paint), spatter, spread (bread, honey), sprinkle, smear, plant (garden, corn), splash, wrap (Johnny, towel)*. But as Fillmore notes (p. 48, footnote 49), there is often a slight semantic difference between the paired sentences. For instance, (37)a suggests that the truck was filled, but (37)b does not. Similar differences appear in (38) and (39).

(38) a. David planted his garden with corn.
    b. David planted corn in his garden.
(39) a. Wrap the baby with/in a soft towel.
    b. Wrap a soft towel around the baby.

Sentence (38)a, but not (38)b, indicates that the garden had only corn planted in it; sentence (39)a more than (39)b suggests that the baby should be entirely wrapped up.

The fact that the *a* sentences use *with* with most of these verbs may not be pure accident. Although the *with*-phrases in (37)a, (38)a, and (39)a do not seem to be instrumental adverbs, they are not far removed. If one's object is to get the truck loaded, get the garden planted, or get the baby wrapped up, one can use hay, corn, or a towel to accomplish the task. Such paraphrases with *use* are typical behavior for instrumental adverbs (see G. Lakoff, 1968a). The main argument against calling these *with*-phrases simply instrumental adverbs is that they co-occur with other *with*-phrases which are much more clearly instrumental.

(40) a. We loaded the truck with hay with pitchforks.
    b. David planted his garden with corn with a hoe.

In any case, the similarity to instrumental adverbs might suggest a direction to look for an explanation of the difference between the *a* and *b* sentences of (37)–(39).

## 4. Conclusions

The suggestion that transformations might be meaning-preserving has led to the investigation of a number of intriguing problems. The great majority of transformations can easily be stated so as to be meaning-preserving for the great majority of sentences; this fact alone strongly supports such a requirement on the theory, and undoubtedly constitutes the major argument of most of the defenders of such a requirement. However, the radical differences among alternative proposals for handling the recalcitrant minority of cases make it clear that the burden of semantic interpretation cannot simply be placed on the shoulders of the syntactic deep structure (no matter how deep) without some accompanying contortions and readjustments of the latter. In short, I would suggest that the hypothesis of meaning-preservingness of transformations has so far eluded both demonstration and refutation; that it is clearly worth pursuing as far as possible; and that further work on the sorts of apparent counterexamples discussed above may well be the key to a deeper understanding of the relation between semantics and syntax.

## REFERENCES FOR 'ON THE REQUIREMENT THAT TRANSFORMATIONS PRESERVE MEANING'

Carden, G. 1967. English quantifiers. Unpublished Master's thesis. Harvard University.

Chapin, P. 1967. On the syntax of word-derivation in English. Unpublished doctoral dissertation. MIT.

Chomsky, N. 1957. Syntactic structures. The Hague: Mouton.

Chomsky, N. 1964. Current issues in linguistic theory. In: The structure of language. Edited by J. A. Fodor and J. J. Katz. Englewood Cliffs, N.J.: Prentice-Hall.

Chomsky, N. 1965. Aspects of the theory of syntax. Cambridge, Mass.: The MIT Press.

Chomsky, N. 1966. Linguistic Institute lectures. Unpublished. MIT.

Chomsky, N. 1968. Remarks on nominalization. (Reprinted in Chapter 5 of this volume.)

Chomsky, N. 1969. Deep structure, surface structure, and semantic interpretation. [Published 1971, in: Semantics. Edited by D. Steinberg and L. Jakobovits. Cambridge: Cambridge University Press. 183-216.]

Dougherty, R. 1968. A transformational grammar of coordinate conjoined structures. Unpublished doctoral dissertation. MIT.

Dougherty, R. 1969. An interpretive theory of pronominal reference. Foundations of Language 5.488-519.

Fillmore, C. 1967. On the syntax of preverbs. Glossa 1.91-125.

Fillmore, C. 1968. The case for case. In: Universals in linguistic theory. Edited by E. Bach and R. Harms. New York: Holt, Rinehart and Winston. 1-90.

Fraser, B. 1970. Idioms within a transformational grammar. Foundations of Language 6.22-42.

Joos, M. 1957. Readings in linguistics. Washington, D.C.: American Council of Learned Societies.

Katz, J., and J. Fodor. 1963. The structure of a semantic theory. Lg. 39.170-210.

Katz, J., and P. Postal. 1964. An integrated theory of linguistic descriptions. Cambridge, Mass.: The MIT Press.

Kuroda, S.-Y. 1965. Generative grammatical studies in the Japanese language. Unpublished doctoral dissertation. MIT.

Lakoff, G. 1965. On the nature of syntactic irregularity. Doctoral dissertation. Indiana University. [Published 1970, as Irregularity in syntax. New York: Holt, Rinehart and Winston.]

Lakoff, G. 1968a. Instrumental adverbs and the concept of deep structure. Foundations of Language 4.4-29.

Lakoff, G. 1968b. Repartee, or a reply to 'Negation, conjunction and quantifiers'. [Published 1970, in: Foundations of Language 6.389-422.]

Lakoff, G. 1969a. On derivational constraints. CLS 5.117-139.

Lakoff, G. 1969b. On generative semantics. [Published 1971, in: Semantics. Edited by D. Steinberg and L. Jakobovits. Cambridge: Cambridge University Press. 232-296.]

Lakoff, R. 1969. Some reasons why there can't be any some-any rule. Lg. 45.608-615.

McCawley, J. 1968. The role of semantics in grammar. In: Universals in linguistic theory. Edited by E. Bach and R. Harms. New York: Holt, Rinehart and Winston. 125-169.

McCawley, J. 1969. Semantic representation. [To appear in: Garvin. Cognition and artificial intelligence.]

Partee, B. 1965. Subject and object in Modern English. Unpublished doctoral dissertation. MIT.

Partee, B. 1968. On some fundamental conflicts in the establishment of deep-structure subjects. Unpublished paper.

Partee, B. 1970. Negation, conjunction and quantifiers: Syntax vs. semantics. Foundations of Language 6.153-165.

Peters, S., and R. Ritchie. 1969. A note on the universal base hypothesis. Journal of Linguistics 5.150-152.

Postal, P. 1971. On the surface verb 'remind'. In: Studies in linguistic semantics. Edited by C. J. Fillmore and D. T. Langendoen. New York: Holt, Rinehart and Winston. 181-272.

Rosenbaum, P. 1967. The grammar of English predicate complement constructions. Cambridge, Mass.: The MIT Press.

Ross, J. R. 1967. Constraints on variables in syntax. Unpublished doctoral dissertation. MIT.

Stockwell, R., et al. 1969. Integration of transformational theories on English syntax. Los Angeles. [Published as: R. Stockwell, P. Schachter, and B. H. Partee. 1973. The major syntactic structures of English. New York: Holt, Rinehart and Winston.]

## QUESTIONS

Question 1. In Section 1, Partee discusses the history of the proposal that transformations preserve meaning, pointing out that at the time she wrote this article the two extremes on the position were (a) that transformations strictly preserved meaning--and, thus, deep structures of a very abstract nature were needed in order to represent all the meaning of an S in its underlying structure (i.e. the Generative Semantics position of McCawley and others), and (b) that transformations did not strictly preserve meaning, but rather both deep structure and derived structures contributed to the semantic interpretation of an S (the EST of Chomsky and others). Today the second position has changed further so that proponents of the EST claim that all semantic interpretation (including grammatical relations such as deep subject, etc.) is available from the surface structure enriched with traces, and access to deep structure is no longer necessary for semantics. (See Chomsky 1976 and Chomsky and Lasnik 1977.)

Consider Kuroda's claim, noted by Partee, that *even, only,* and *also* are limited to one occurrence per sentence node and are transformationally moved to their surface position. If Kuroda's claim were true, which theory would (i) through (iii) offer evidence for, Generative Semantics or the EST? Why?

(i) Only John can understand Martha.
(ii) John can only understand Martha.
(iii) John can understand only Martha.

Question 2. Partee's discussion of Chapin (toward the end of Section 1.2) suggests that all verbs to which *-able* is suffixed are to be understood as passive. That is, *breakable* means *able to be broken.* Why is the word *perishable* a problem for (Partee's interpretation of) Chapin? Can you think of any other words like *perishable?*

*Question 3. Partee points out that choosing the criteria for determining synonymy is not a simple matter. If we were to say that two Ss were synonymous if they would have the same truth value in all possible worlds, how would this criterion prove inadequate for questions? For imperatives? Can you offer some alternative approaches to the question of synonymy?

*Question 4. Partee mentions that Katz and Postal (1964) proposed abstract markers such as WH and NEG, which obligatorily triggered Question Formation and Negative Placement, respectively. In this way, questions and negative sentences do not provide evidence against the meaning-preserving hypothesis.

Imperative sentences such as (i) might be derived from either (ii) or (iii).

(i) Finish your homework before dinner.
(ii) You will finish your homework before dinner.
(iii) I order you to finish your homework before dinner.

Would you need to propose some sort of abstract marker such as IMP in either case? Why? If you can find independent syntactic motivation for such a marker, please give it.

*Question 5. It has been proposed by McCawley (1970) that passive and active sentences have different deep structures. Example (i) would be the deep structure of *John sees Susan* and (ii) would be the deep structure of *Susan is seen by John*.

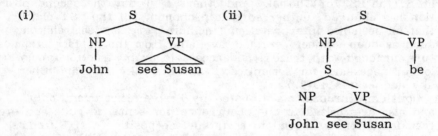

(Actually, McCawley has S branch to VP NP instead of NP VP. This detail is irrelevant to the question we want you to focus on, however.) Does this proposal amount to the same kind of 'trigger' as WH or IMP? Does it obscure the relationship between active and passive sentences? Do you see any problems with it?

*Question 6. Toward the end of Section 2.2, Partee discusses the same problem we dealt with in Fodor's article. Like Fodor, she argues against Lakoff's causative analysis, but on somewhat different grounds. Fodor says that if Lakoff derives *kill* from *cause to die*, the argument fails for syntactic reasons. Partee says that if Lakoff does not derive *kill* from *cause to die*, but instead from an abstract verb CAUSE plus *to die*, his claim is vacuous; it has no empirical content. His abstract verb CAUSE differs from the actual verb *cause* just enough to account for the syntactic and semantic difficulties, such as those raised by Fodor. Thinking back to Ross' performative verbs, which are deleted always and only when they are abstract, try to decide if Partee could make the same argument against Ross' proposal.

**Question 7. In Section 3, Partee discusses various syntactic phenomena that are relevant to the meaning-preserving hypothesis. She notes first that the interpretation of quantifiers in general causes problems--and gives examples with reflexivization, Equi NP Deletion, and relativization. We go into some possible solutions for the reflexivization phenomena in Homework Problem I. After you have completed the Homework Problem, consider what analogues the proposals for reflexivization might have for Equi NP Deletion. Discuss the analogues, if they exist, for relativization. If they do not exist, explain why.

*Question 8. What is the problem with deriving (ii) from (i) (as Chomsky does)?

(i) Each of the men hates his brothers.
(ii) *The men each hate his brothers.

Partee proposes instead to derive (iii) from (i). What new syntactic mechanism will she now need that Chomsky did not need?

(iii) The men each hate their brothers.

Chomsky will derive (iii) from (iv). What syntactic mechanism will Chomsky need that Partee does not need?

(iv) *Each of the men hates their brothers.
$\quad\quad\quad\quad\quad\quad$ i $\quad\quad\quad\quad\quad$ i

(Be sure to note the singular agreement on *hates*.)
How do (v) through (xi) give evidence that there is a rule of *Each*-Hopping?

(v) Each of the men has been seated.
(vi) The men each have been seated.
(vii) The men have each been seated.
(viii) *Each of the men each has been seated.
(ix) *Each of the men has each been seated.
(x) *The men each have each been seated.
(xi) *Each of the men each have each been seated.

**Question 9. Partee suggests that a rule turning *his* to *their* in *each*-hopped Ss receives independent support from conjunction-reduction. Following McCawley (1968), she would derive all conjunction-reduction from *respectively*-conjunction by an optional rule. Do you judge (i) acceptable?

(i) John and Bill hate himself$_1$ and himself$_2$, respectively.

Contrast (i) to (ii).

(ii) John and Bill hate Sue and Mary, respectively.

If you find (ii) much better than (i), try to come up with an explanation.

Partee wants to derive (iii) from (i) by way of a collapsing rule (which also deletes *respectively*).

(iii) John and Bill hate themselves.

Consider Partee's derivation and the alternative below for (iv).

(iv) John and Bill ate peas.  (not together)

Partee would derive (iv) as shown in (v) (with the asterisk reflecting our own acceptability judgment.)

(v) a. John ate peas and Bill ate peas.
(v) b. *John and Bill ate peas and peas respectively.
(v) c. John and Bill ate peas.

An alternative derivation would be to derive (iv) directly from (v-a) by a rule which conjoins different subjects and merely writes out the VP once.  This rule would consider two VPs as identical as long as they contained the same words.  Coreference (of the peas, in this case) would not be necessary--instead, only identity of VPs would be necessary for conjunction-reduction.  This alternative derivation would derive (iii) as shown in (vi).

(vi) a. John hates himself and Bill hates himself.
(vi) b. *John and Bill hates himself$_{i+j}$.
(vi) c. John and Bill hate themselves.

A feature changing rule sensitive to the features of subject and object in (vi-b) would apply to (vi-b) to give (vi-c). (Note that we are leaving aside the question of proper agreement on the predicate.)  This may be the same rule Partee would like to use to derive (vii) from (viii).

(vii) The men each hate themselves.
(viii) Each of the men hates himself.

In this alternative hypothesis, the difference between (ix) and (x), both deriving from (xi), would be that in (x) a rule changing *a book* to *books* has applied.

(ix) John and Bill read a book.
(x) John and Bill read books.
(xi) John read a book and Bill read a book.

One might object, asking how the feature changing rule is to know that *a book* stays *a book* in (ix) (where John and Bill read the same book), but *a book* changes to *books* in (x) (where John and Bill each read a different book).  The answer may well be that the feature changing rule does *not* know. Instead, the rule optionally applies to either reading (the coreferential one or the noncoreferential one). Then a surface rule of semantic interpretation which looks at the features of both subject and object tells us which reading we have ended up with.

How does (xii) show that we need such a surface rule of semantic interpretation independently of conjunction-reduction?

(xii) a. All the people in the world are reading books right now. (Cf. All the people in the world are reading a book right now.)

(xii) b. Everyone in the world is reading a book right now. (Cf. Everyone in the world is reading books right now.)

(Notice that the sentence in parentheses in (xii-a) is pragmatically unlikely, though not ungrammatical.)

Note that both (xiii) and (xiv) are good, but (xiv) cannot have the reading in which the subject is actually writing at the time of the utterance.

(xiii) I'm writing a book right now.

(xiv) I'm writing books right now. (That is, more than one is underway.)

Hence we have not asterisked the second sentence under (xii-b). (The distinction between Ss like (xiii) and (xiv) was brought to our attention by Frank Humphrey personal communication.)

Looking back then at the Ss with reflexives, we can see that this alternative hypothesis will generate Ss like (xv) by conjunction-reduction.

(xv) *John and Bill hate himself.

Since the feature changing rule is optional, we need some independent means for ruling out (xv). How does (xvi) show us that there is indeed a means for ruling out (xv) which is independent of conjunction-reduction?

(xvi) *All the people in the world hate himself.

For more reading on feature changing rules, see Fauconnier (1973) and Napoli (1975).

**Question 10. Discuss the problems which *respectively* conjunction-reduction presents for (i).

(i) John and Mary ate peas in the park and at the zoo respectively.

**Question 11. In Section 3.1.2, Partee gives examples of conjoined Ss and Ss with conjoined phrases (VPs and NPs) where the presence of a quantifier complicates a simple conjunction reduction from one to the other. She presents the very interesting example given in (i).

(i) Many airplanes stop at Dallas or Chicago.

She says that although (i) 'does not appear to involve phrasal conjunction, it has no obvious sentential source with either an *and* or an *or*'. It is generally accepted that we have to allow both sentential and phrasal conjunction in deep structure, as exemplified here.

(ii) John left and Mary left. (deep and surface S conjunction)
(iii) Red and green complement each other. (deep and surface phrasal conjunction)

A typical test (though not always applicable) for underlying S conjunction is the *both* test.

(iv) Both John and Mary left. (underlying S conjunction)
(v) *The child tried to mix both oil and water. (underlying phrasal conjunction)

A typical test (though not always applicable) for underlying phrasal conjunction is the *together* test.

(vi) *John and Mary are erudite together. (underlying S conjunction)
(vii) John and Mike paid my check together. (underlying phrasal conjunction)

Of course, *both* and *together* are mutually exclusive.

(viii) *Both Shakespeare and Marlowe wrote plays together.
(ix) *Both the company lawyer and the union lawyer hammered out the agreement together.

Do the following Ss involve underlying sentential or phrasal conjunction? Support your answer.

(x) John and Mary are fat.
(xi) The complex of Harvard and MIT corresponds to Berkeley.
(xii) John and Mary are alike.

(Examples (ii)-(xii) are adapted from Smith 1969 and Lakoff and Peters 1969.)

Now looking back at (i), we see *or* instead of *and*. Which of the examples in (xiii) through (xvi) involve underlying sentential disjunction and which involve underlying phrasal disjunction? Why?

(xiii) John left or Mary left.
(xiv) He'll do the one or the other.
(xv) John or Mary left.
(xvi) Ice cream or cake is a difficult choice.

Can you think of any tests to determine the kind of underlying disjunction? Why does Partee say (i) is a problem?

*Question 12. Partee says that a traditional subject raising analysis of *certain* might derive (i) from (ii) or (iii) or both, running into the problem of glaring lack of synonymy.

(i) Nobody is (absolutely) certain to pass the test.
(ii) It is (absolutely) certain that nobody will pass the test.
(iii) It is not (absolutely) certain that anybody will pass the test.

How are the following Ss relevant to a derivation of (i) from (iii)?

(iv) Homer didn't kiss anybody.
(v) Nobody was kissed by Homer.
(vi) *Anybody wasn't kissed by Homer.

(See Klima 1964.)

Question 13. In Section 3.2.4, Partee notes a difference in meaning between (i) and (ii).

(i) We loaded the truck with hay.
(ii) We loaded hay onto the truck.

In fact, there are some good syntactic arguments for not deriving one from the other. Consider (iii) through (v).

(iii) We loaded the truck full up with hay.
(iv) *We loaded hay onto the truck full up.
(v) *We loaded hay full up onto the truck.

How do (iii) through (v) supply an argument? Try to find other arguments against deriving (i) from (ii) or vice-versa.

**Question 14. It is important to remember that even when everyone believed that transformations did not change meaning, there was never any mechanism written into the grammar that made it impossible for transformations to change meaning--

neither a single rule nor a 'conspiracy' of all the other restrictions on transformations. How could the meaning-preserving rule be written into the grammar in a mechanistic way? (i.e. 'Transformations shall not change meaning' is the wrong answer.)

Assume now, with Chomsky, that transformations can change meaning, that in fact, all the nonsynonymous pairs that Partee discussed in this article should be related by transformations. Is it possible to allow these changes of meaning and still prevent the grammar, in principled ways, from changing (i) through (iii) into (iv) through (vi)?

(i) The snow slid off the side of the top of the barn.
(ii) Many people dislike vegetables.
(iii) A bachelor is an unmarried man.
(iv) The snow slid off the top of the side of the barn.
(v) People dislike many vegetables.
(vi) A bachelor is a bachelor.

## HOMEWORK PROBLEMS

I. One analysis of reflexive pronouns has them arising transformationally. That is, they replace full NPs.

An alternative analysis says that all reflexives originate in the deep structure. Let us call this the PS (Phrase Structure) analysis. There are many possible forms a PS analysis might take. We will consider one which claims that an NP of the form $[_{NP}$___self $_{NP}]$ is generated in the base, where the determiner of the noun *self* is left open. Then this determiner slot is transformationally filled by a possessive pronoun (*my* of *myself*, *her* of *herself*, etc., with the only problems being *him*, *it*, and *them* instead of *his, its,* and *theirs* in *himself, itself,* and *themselves*). This possessive pronoun is copied from some other NP in the same clause at some point in the derivation.

A. Consider the following Ss.

(1) The girl$_i$ hurt herself$_i$ /*her$_i$.
    The girl$_i$ lost her$_i$ /*his/*our/*your mind.
(2) *The girl's father hurt herself.
    *The girl's father lost her mind.
(3) *The girl and the boy hurt herself.
    *The girl and the boy lost her mind.
(4) The girl and the boy hurt themselves.
    The girl and the boy lost their minds.
(5) *The girl hopes that the boy won't hurt herself.
    *The girl hopes that the boy won't lose her mind.
(6) *The boy who found the girl hurt herself.
    *The boy who found the girl lost her mind.

(7) *The girl was hurt by herself.
 *Herself was hurt by the girl.
 *The girl's mind was lost by her.
 *Her mind was lost by the girl.

What would proponents of a T (transformational) analysis of reflexives have to say about (1) through (7)? What would proponents of the PS analysis outlined above have to say? (Please be brief. The major point to note is whether the restrictions on the $x$ in phrases like *lose $x$'s mind* tie in somehow (you figure out how) with the restriction on reflexives in one theory but not in the other.)

B. Consider,

(8) Only the devil pities himself.
(9) Only the devil pities the devil.

Note the meaning of (8) and (9). Which analysis of reflexives do (8) and (9) offer evidence for? Why?

C. Why is the existence of Ss such as (10) and (11) important for the PS analysis?

(10) The expression of self in 17th century literature was an overriding concern.
(11) I bought it for my own self--not for anyone else.

If you are interested in reading more on this particular PS analysis, see Helke (1973).

II. In Section 3.2.1, Partee discusses Ss which have traditionally been analyzed as having undergone *Tough* Movement. She assumes here that Ss like (1) and (2) are not synonymous.

(1) It is easy to please John.
(2) John is easy to please.

Try to find examples which make the lack of synonymy here more sharply discernible. How are the following pairs relevant to the two alternative analyses she offers for Ss such as (2)?

(3a) It's easy to keep tabs on Kissinger.
(3b) *Tabs are easy to keep on Kissinger.
(4a) *It's being easy to please John today.
(4b) John is being easy to please today.
(5a) *It's intentionally easy to please John.
(5b) John is intentionally easy to please.
(6a) It was a pleasure to eat a bunch of bananas; there are their skins.
(6b) *A bunch of bananas was a pleasure to eat; there are their skins.

(Examples (3) through (6) are adapted from Lasnik and Fiengo 1974.)

## SUGGESTED READINGS

Anderson, S. 1972. How to get *even*. Lg. 48:4.893-906. (For Question 1.)

Chomsky, N. 1976. Conditions on rules of grammar. Linguistic Analysis 2:4.303-351. (For Introduction and Question 1.)

Chomsky, N., and H. Lasnik. 1977. Filters and control. Linguistic Inquiry 8:3.425-504. (For Introduction and Question 1.)

Fauconnier, G. 1973. Cyclic attraction into networks of coreference. Lg. 49:1.1-18. (For Question 9.)

Helke, M. 1973. On reflexives in English. Linguistics 106. 5-23. (For Homework Problem I.)

Klima, E. 1964. Negation in English. In: The structure of language. Edited by J. A. Fodor and J. J. Katz. Englewood Cliffs, N.J.: Prentice-Hall. 246-323. (For Question 12.)

Lakoff, G., and S. Peters. 1969. Phrasal conjunction and symmetric predicates. In: Modern studies in English. Edited by D. Reibel and S. Schane. Englewood Cliffs, N.J.: Prentice-Hall. 113-142. (For Question 11.)

Lasnik, H., and R. Fiengo. 1974. Complement object deletion. Linguistic Inquiry 5:4.535-572. (For Homework Problem II.)

McCawley, J. 1970. English as a VSO language. Lg. 46.286-299. (For Question 5.)

Napoli, D. J. 1975. Consistency. Lg. 51:4.831-844. (For Question 9.)

Partee, B. H. 1970. Negation, conjunction and quantifiers: Syntax vs. semantics. Foundations of Language 6.153-165. (For an argument that not all the semantics can be read off the deep structure.)

Partee, B. H. 1975. Deletion and variable binding. In: The formal semantics of natural language. Edited by E. L. Keenan. Cambridge: Cambridge University Press. 16-34.

Smith, C. 1969. Ambiguous sentences with *and*. In: Modern studies in English. Edited by D. Reibel and S. Schane. Englewood Cliffs, N.J.: Prentice-Hall. 75-79. (For Question 11.)

# 10

## SUPER-EQUI AND THE INTERVENTION CONSTRAINT

George N. Clements

Introduction. In the 1960s one of the greatest preoccupations of syntacticians was the exploration of the usefulness of transformational accounts for various kinds of data. As the number of transformations proposed in the literature grew, the problem of properly constraining their power was addressed by many. Several different ideas emerged, with the two extremes consisting of those who sought to strictly limit the power of transformations and those who insisted their power needed to be much greater than previously expected. Those in the first group went on to devise alternative explanations for many phenomena; in particular, they proposed rules of semantic interpretation of surface structure (see Jackendoff 1972; Chomsky 1973, 1976; Chomsky and Lasnik 1977, among others). The second group went on to propose expansions of the formalism to include global rules and sometimes even transderivational rules (Lakoff 1970, Postal 1974, among others).

In the midst of this controversy Clements wrote 'Super-Equi and the Intervention Constraint'. He argues here that a transformational account of Super-Equi requires an intervention constraint which cannot be stated at the point at which Super-Equi is defined. Instead, the constraint operates if the intervening element appears at any point in the structural derivation of an S prior to the point at which Super-Equi is defined. The Intervention Constraint, therefore, cannot be stated locally, but rather constitutes an example of a global condition on the transformation Super-Equi. Clements then goes on to show that an interpretive account of Super-Equi does not require such an intervention constraint and can account for the data in question with a local rule. Since he takes the position that local accounts are preferable to global ones, he chooses the interpretive analysis.

Clements' article is important for its methodology as well as for the issues it handles. The process of elimination which he employs in arguing that Super-Equi is cyclic is widely used and should be mastered by the student. The range of data he examines to establish the global nature of the Intervention Constraint can serve as a model for the linguist faced with a phenomenon and setting out to determine whether or not the transformational and the interpretive approaches encounter the same problems and make the same predictions. And, finally, Clements states explicitly whatever assumptions are crucial to his arguments and ends with troublesome data for any analysis of Super-Equi, thereby leaving the reader with ideas for future research.

## SUPER-EQUI AND THE INTERVENTION CONSTRAINT

George N. Clements

1. Can rules of syntax make reference to semantic information? It has recently been suggested (e.g. by Jackendoff 1972) that they cannot. All rules of grammar which involve semantic properties in their description must, in this view, be formulated as rules of interpretation that impose the relevant semantic properties on phrase markers. This view makes an interesting empirical claim: given a linguistic phenomenon involving semantic properties, if the alternative transformational and interpretive approaches make different empirical predictions, it is the interpretive approach that will receive support.

An interesting case where this claim might in principle be tested is the rule of Super Equi-NP Deletion proposed by Grinder (1970, 1971). This is framed as an operation deleting the subject of a tenseless complement clause under identity with a NP which commands it in a higher clause. By the above hypothesis, since this rule involves semantic properties (coreference), it must be an interpretive rule. One may in consequence raise the question whether the interpretive reformulation makes distinct empirical predictions from the transformational approach, and if so, whether they are borne out.

Below, a number of facts are examined which show that the two theories do in fact make distinct empirical claims. It will be shown, in particular, that the deletion hypothesis is forced to introduce a condition on application known as the Intervention Constraint, in order to define 'islands' within which deletion is blocked. This condition seems distinctly ad hoc, as no other rule is known to be subject to this constraint. Furthermore, I will try to show that it is global in nature, since it must be satisfied by at least two points in a derivation; this conclusion, if true, casts some doubt on the correctness of the analysis which is forced to introduce it, since global conditions of this nature are not well motivated.

The examination of an interpretive reformulation of Super-Equi shows that the Intervention Constraint is not necessary. The range of deviant sentences it was designed to exclude are independently excluded by the principle of cyclic application. In the following discussion I will attempt to demonstrate this point by contrasting the properties of the two approaches. It will further be shown that the interpretive reformulation correctly handles a number of cases which proved intractable under the deletion approach, and allows a satisfactory single statement of complement subject phenomena in immediately subordinate clauses (the Equi cases) and in nonadjacent subordinate clauses (the Super-Equi cases).

2. In Grinder's formulation, Super Equi-NP Deletion applies to the (a) sentences below, yielding the (b) sentences:

(1a) $Mike_i$ thought that [it would be impolite [for $him_i$ to scratch himself]]
(1b) Mike thought that [it would be impolite [$\emptyset$ to scratch himself]]
(2a) $Lorenzo_i$ thought that [[$his_i$ holding his breath for ten minutes] would impress Sue]
(2b) Lorenzo thought that [[$\emptyset$ holding his breath for ten minutes] would impress Sue]

For convenience, let us refer to the commanding NP as the *controller*, and the complement clause subject as the *controllee*. An essential property of Super-Equi, as these examples reveal, is that it is not downwardbounded: the controller-controllee relation may be established between NPs in nonadjacent clauses. However, the application of Super-Equi need not be restricted to nonadjacent clauses: Grinder considered Super-Equi to be the generalized form of Equi, a position which I will assume here (see Section 5).

The unbounded nature of Super-Equi was contested by Kimball (1971), who proposed to reanalyze the data in such a way that complement subject deletion takes place only in adjacent clauses. In order to account for examples in which deletion appears to take place in nonadjacent clauses, a rule of Dative Deletion is introduced. This rule defines the deletion of a dative NP under identity with a commanding NP in a higher clause. Under this analysis, example (1b) would be derived as follows:

(3a) Mike thought that [it would be impolite for him [for him to scratch himself]] → EQUI
(3b) Mike thought that [it would be impolite for him [$\emptyset$ to scratch himself]] → DATIVE DELETION
(3c) Mike thought that [it would be impolite $\emptyset$ [$\emptyset$ to scratch himself]]

This analysis depends heavily on the plausibility of positing underlying datives in clauses commanding those in which deletion has taken place. While such an approach is plausible in the case of clauses with predicates such as *easy*, *fun*, *trivial*, etc., problems arise when we try to extend it to further cases.

An initial class of counterevidence, already pointed out by Grinder (1971), consists of examples such as (2b). By the Dative Deletion analysis, the underlying structure of (2b) must be (4a), below; however, a grammar capable of generating (4a) will also generate the deviant (4b):

(4a) Lorenzo thought that [[his holding his breath for ten minutes] would impress Sue for him]
(4b) *(His) holding his breath for ten minutes would impress Sue for Lorenzo

One might attempt to explain the deviance of (4b) on semantic, rather than grammatical grounds; nevertheless (2a) and (2b) are both semantically well-formed.

Further evidence damaging to the Dative Deletion hypothesis can be found in sentences constructed with predicates which never subcategorize datives. Examples of such predicates, consisting in part of adjectives expressing abstract concepts of time, history, logic, etc., include *premature, historical, epoch-making, early, late, (logically) inconsistent, (categorically) false, self-contradictory.* Compare the syntactic behavior of this class of adjectives with that of adjectives such as *easy:*

(5a) It would be logically inconsistent for non-persons to be persons.
(5b) For non-persons to be persons would be logically inconsistent.
(5c) *To be persons would be logically inconsistent for non-persons.
(5d) *It would be logically inconsistent to be persons, for non-persons.
(6a) It would be easy for doctors to increase their fees.
(6b) *For doctors to increase their fees would be easy.
(6c) To increase their fees would be easy for doctors.
(6d) It would be easy to increase their fees, for doctors.

These paradigms strongly suggest that sentences with *inconsistent* and sentences with *easy* are very different in underlying structure; the phrase *for nonpersons* in the sentences of (5) fails to show the properties of the dative complement to *easy* in (6). This follows from the semantic fact that concepts such as logical inconsistency, prematurity, etc. are not relative to individuals, but absolute. However, in spite of the fact that such predicates do not subcategorize datives, we find that Super-Equi is applicable:

(7a) Sophie believes it would be logically inconsistent for her to be taller than herself.
(7b) Sophie believes it would be logically inconsistent ∅ to be taller than herself.

(8a) The senators thought it would be premature for them
to vote themselves raises.
(8b) The senators thought it would be premature $\emptyset$ to vote
themselves raises.
(9a) Ted thought it was too late for him to declare himself a
candidate.
(9b) Ted thought it was too late $\emptyset$ to declare himself a
candidate.

It is difficult to see how a grammar that assigns underlying
datives to the predicates of (7)-(9) will be able to account for
the facts of (5)-(6), or for the semantic properties of the adjectives in question.

Another class of problems for the Dative Deletion analysis
comes from the consideration of predicates which only optionally
subcategorize datives. Sentences constructed with such predicates are ambiguous, depending on whether we interpret them
with an implicit dative or not. Thus the examples of (10), on
one reading, are synonymous with the corresponding sentences
of (11):

(10) Charles thought that the proposal was $\left\{\begin{array}{l}\text{unprecedented}\\\text{inappropriate}\\\text{unusual}\end{array}\right\}$

(11) Charles$_i$ thought that the proposal was $\left\{\begin{array}{l}\text{unprecedented}\\\text{inappropriate}\\\text{unusual}\end{array}\right\}$

for him$_i$.

In the other, absolute reading of (10), which is perhaps more
natural, the unprecedented (inappropriate, unusual) nature of
the proposal in question is understood in relation to the general
socio-historical context. These observations carry over into
examples where complement subject deletion has taken place.
The ambiguity of (12a), corresponding to that of the examples
of (10), depends on whether the adjective *unprecedented* is
construed as taking an implicit dative or not; (12b), on the
other hand, has only the absolute reading:

(12a) The President thought that it would be unprecedented
for him to offer his resignation on Bastille Day.
(12b) The President thought that it would be unprecedented
$\emptyset$ to offer his resignation on Bastille Day.

(12a), on the relative reading (where *for him* is construed as a
dative), is true even if the President recalls that a former
president offered his resignation on Bastille Day; (12b) does
not allow this reading. Thus, if Dative Deletion is to derive
(12b) from (12a), it will allow no natural way of accounting for
the extra reading of (12a). The Super-Equi analysis, on the
other hand, is consistent with the assignment of two underlying

structures to (12a), one containing a dative complement to *unprecedented* and the other containing no dative at all; in neither case is a rule of Dative Deletion required.

A further argument against the Dative Deletion analysis is offered by examples such as the following, where complement subject deletion takes place even in a case where the complement subject is not identical to the dative of the higher clause:

(13a) The General didn't agree that it would be good for the country for him to remove himself from office.

(13b) The General didn't agree that it would be good for the country $\emptyset$ to remove himself from office.

Here the Dative Deletion analysis faces an insoluble dilemma. If we assume that a given clause may contain at most one dative constituent, then Dative Deletion cannot be involved in the derivation of (13b). If on the other hand we allow two underlying dative constituents in single clauses, there is no non-ad hoc way of preventing the generation of (14):

(14) *(His) removing himself from office would be good for the country for the General.

From all these facts it must be concluded that a rule having the effect of Super-Equi, and quite distinct from Dative Deletion, must belong to English grammar.

3. Let us now consider the treatment of Super-Equi as a deletion rule. A problem immediately arises in attempting to account for the deviance of the starred examples in paradigms like the following.

(15a) Lorenzo thought that [[$\emptyset$ holding his breath for ten minutes] would impress Sue]

(15b) *Lorenzo thought that [it would impress Sue [$\emptyset$ to hold his breath for ten minutes]]

(15c) *Lorenzo thought that [Sue would be impressed by [$\emptyset$ holding his breath for ten minutes]]

(15d) *Lorenzo thought that [Sue believed that [it would be impressive [$\emptyset$ to hold his breath for ten minutes]]]

(15e) *That it impressed Sue [$\emptyset$ to hold his breath for ten minutes] gratified Lorenzo

(15f) Lorenzo asked Sue whether [[$\emptyset$ holding his breath for ten minutes] would impress Mary]

(15g) [That [$\emptyset$ holding his breath for ten minutes] impressed Sue] gratified Lorenzo

These examples show that not all NPs commanding the subject of tenseless complement clauses can act as Super-Equi controllers. In the above examples, some principle prevents *Lorenzo* from controlling complement subject deletion in (b)-(e).

Examples (b)-(d) suggest that this principle might be that another NP may not occur between a controller and a controllee, but (e) shows that this principle is too weak, and (f) shows that it is too strong.

The Intervention Constraint was proposed in order to account for the deviant examples. This constraint involved the notion *deletion path*, which was defined as follows.

(16) An element, $e_i$, is said to be in the *deletion path* of a deletion transformation, $T_i$, involving a controller, $C_i$, and a term to be deleted, $t_i$, if at the time of application of $T_i$

  (a) $e_i$ bears more primacy relations with respect to $t_i$ than does $C_i$, or

  (b) $C_i$ and $e_i$ bear the same primacy relations with respect to $t_i$ and $e_i$ lies between $C_i$ and $t_i$ in the linear order specified by precedence and $C_i$ and $e_i$ are not clause mates

(Grinder 1970:307). Given this definition, the Intervention Constraint can be formulated as follows.

(17) Super Equi-NP Deletion between $NP^a$ and $NP^b$ is blocked if there exists a possible controller $NP^c$ in the deletion path

(Grinder 1970:302). Let us call $e_i$ the 'intervening element'. Examination of the examples of (15) shows that in just the starred cases (as well as (g), to which we return below) an intervening element occurs in the deletion path. Case (b) of (16) accounts for the deviance of (15b), (15c), and (15d). In these examples, the controller *Lorenzo* and the intervening element *Sue* bear the same primacy relations with respect to the term to be deleted, that is, both of them precede and command, and they are not clause mates. Since *Sue* lies between the controller and the term to be deleted, it is in the deletion path of the deletion transformation, and the rule is blocked. Case (a) of (16) accounts for the remaining starred example, (15e). Since *Sue* both precedes and commands the term to be deleted, while *Lorenzo* only commands, *Sue* bears more primacy relations with respect to the term to be deleted, and therefore the rule is again blocked.

On the other hand, neither (15a) nor (15f) are deviant, since in neither case is an element in the deletion path. *Sue* is not in the deletion path in (15a) since it bears fewer primacy relations with respect to the term to be deleted than does Lorenzo. For the same reason, *Mary* is not in the deletion path in (15f). Finally, *Sue* is not in the deletion path in (15f) since it is exempted by the clause mate condition of (16b).

(15g) is a somewhat more problematical case. According to the definition of the deletion path, *Sue* is an interceptor, and the sentence is therefore marked ungrammatical. However, speakers do not consistently reject sentences constructed on this pattern. While (15g) strikes some (but not all) speakers as awkward, parallel examples such as those of (18) are generally found to be well formed.

(18a) That $\emptyset$ exiling himself might grieve the Queen never occurred to the minister
(18b) That $\emptyset$ offering his resignation might not upset the Senators worried Henry

It would appear that whatever contributes to the lower acceptability of examples like (15g) is independent of the constraints on Super-Equi. If this is true, and sentences like (18) are fully acceptable, then the Intervention Constraint would have to be modified accordingly. This would not appear to present a serious problem.[1]

Assuming, then, that there exists some descriptively adequate formulation of the Intervention Constraint, we may ask at what point in a derivation it applies. The obvious hypothesis would be that it applies when, and only when, Super-Equi is defined. Now, it can be shown, as I will argue below, that Super-Equi applies cyclically. One would therefore want to assume that the Intervention Constraint comes into play just at those points in the cycle where Super-Equi is defined, that is, when a potential Super-Equi controller comes into view for the first time. However, this is false, as we shall see.

I will argue that Super-Equi is a cyclic rule by a process of elimination, assuming three theoretical possibilities: precyclic application, cyclic application, and postcyclic application. Examples such as the following show that Super-Equi does not apply precyclically. (19a), though deviant, comes from underlying structures in which the deletion path is 'clear' (19b); and similarly for the examples of (20):

(19a) *Ted said that it would surprise Sue $\emptyset$ to declare himself a candidate.
(19b) Ted said that [[for him to declare himself a candidate] would surprise Sue]
(20a) *Dr. Lenz believed that Anne would be traumatized by $\emptyset$ analyzing his own dreams.
(20b) Dr. Lenz believed that [[his analyzing his own dreams] would traumatize Anne]

In (19), Extraposition, by moving the clause containing the element to be deleted to the right of *Sue*, brings an element into the deletion path. If the deletion were carried out precyclically, we would have to invent some means of preventing Extraposition from applying later. In (20) it is Passive that moves an element into the deletion path, and the same remarks apply.

To see that Super-Equi does not apply postcyclically, it is sufficient to observe that cyclic transformations may destroy the configuration upon which Super-Equi is defined, in which the controller commands the controllee. If Super-Equi were postcyclic, then, examples such as (21) and (22) should be deviant:

(21) ∅ Pardoning himself was generally thought to have been felt to be unwise by Mr. Nixon
(22) ∅ Pardoning himself was easy for me to imagine him capable of considering to be legal

However, though perhaps somewhat awkward, these examples are acceptable, and show that Super-Equi must have applied at a time when the controller still commanded the complement subject, that is, within the cycle.

We must therefore conclude that Super-Equi applies within the cycle. But this assumption is not yet sufficient to block the generation of further deviant sentences. Let us consider some cases. Under the deletion hypothesis, (23) comes from a source that can be represented as in (24):

(23) *Roger urged Sue [∅ to declare that [[∅ torturing himself] would be fun]]

(24)

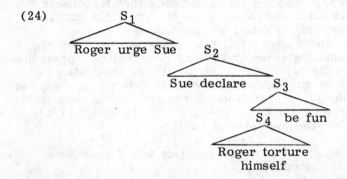

Recall that we have assumed that Super-Equi is simply the generalized form of Equi-NP Deletion, an assumption also made by Grinder and Jackendoff. Thus, Super-Equi will not be defined until the $S_1$ cycle, where it is defined twice, between the two occurrences of Roger and the two occurrences of Sue. The Intervention Constraint identifies the Sue of $S_2$ as an element in the deletion path, preventing deletion from applying to Roger; but deletion can be carried out on Sue of $S_2$. Now, however, the intervening element has been removed, so that the Intervention Constraint no longer blocks the deletion of Roger in $S_4$. Thus, Super-Equi is redefined, and (23) can be generated. Clearly, what is needed to block this undesirable consequence is a principle which prevents a rule from reapplying to its own output. However, until further cases are examined, it cannot simply be assumed that such a principle will give correct results elsewhere. Thus (23) poses at least a potential problem. Let us consider a more difficult case:

(25a) Mamie thought that [[∅ getting himself arrested on account of [her losing her temper]] would ruin Ike's career]

(25b) *Mamie thought that [[∅ getting himself arrested on account of [∅ losing her temper]] would ruin Ike's career]

In (25a), Super-Equi has applied once, yielding a well-formed sentence; in (25b) it has applied twice, yielding a deviant sentence. What explains the difference? Once again, let us examine the underlying structure assumed by the deletion hypothesis:

(26)

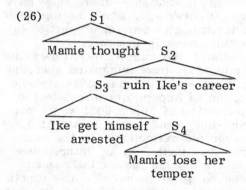

On the $S_4$ and $S_3$ cycles the relevant reflexivization rules, however they are to be formulated, will apply. On the $S_2$ cycle Super-Equi (the Equi subcase) is defined, and *Ike* in $S_3$ is deleted, giving (25a). Then on the $S_1$ cycle Super-Equi is defined on the lowest occurrence of *Mamie*, giving the deviant (25b). We observe that what has allowed deletion to take place, incorrectly, on the $S_1$ cycle is the fact that the potential intervening element *Ike* of $S_3$ has been removed on an earlier cycle.

A further problem is presented by examples involving the application of Passive:

(27) *Wilbur was afraid that ∅ misbehaving himself with Lola had been discovered by his wife

(28) *Salvador discovered that ∅ attempting to poison himself had been reported to the police by Thelma

Passive, applying on the next-to-last cycle, removes the potential intervening element; thus there is nothing to block the application of Super-Equi on the highest cycle.

These examples are sufficient to show that the Intervention Constraint, if it is to serve its purpose, cannot be restricted to the point at which Super-Equi is defined in the cycle. Rather, it appears to be the case that if an element ever appears in the deletion path prior to the point at which Super-Equi is defined, application is blocked.

This conclusion raises the question of whether statements of this sort can be admitted in grammatical description. Recent research has suggested that 'global' conditions of this type seem to be required only in the statement of rules involving the agreement of predicate elements with their end-of-cycle subjects (cf. Andrews 1971; Fauconnier 1973, 1974; Napoli 1973).[2] Other proposed cases of global conditioning of rules have been subjected to reanalysis within nonglobal frameworks (Baker and Brame 1972, Milsark 1972, Selkirk 1972, Emonds 1973). On theoretical grounds one would want to limit the use of global devices and global statements in grammar to just that set of cases--predicate agreement phenomena--where they have been shown to be necessary. Otherwise we would be unable to carry out the task of characterizing the general properties of the class (or classes) of possible rules in grammar.

In a recent paper, Jacobson and Neubauer (1974), observing examples like those of (23) and (25), have suggested that the device of the 'doom' marker, proposed in Postal (1970), would be sufficient to block application of Super-Equi to create the deviant cases. The first application of Super-Equi would not delete the complement subject, but would rather assign it a feature 'doom', marking it for eventual extinction. In the meantime, however, it would serve its function as an 'intervening' element, blocking Super-Equi. Whatever the intrinsic merits of this proposal, there can be no question but that the function of 'doom' marking is simply that of encoding global relationships that cannot be treated within the framework of nonglobal grammar. This has been recognized by Postal (1972), who suggests eliminating the doom feature for an overt global condition. Thus we are still led to the conclusion that the Intervention Constraint can only be formulated within a grammar that permits a relatively free use of global conditions, whether overtly stated or disguised as features.

4. The alternative proposal that I would like to suggest is that Super-Equi is a rule of interpretation which has the effect of defining the set of possible antecedents for phonologically null subjects. Each such null subject will be assigned a single antecedent in a given derivation, if a suitable candidate can be found. If an antecedent cannot be found in the sentence itself, independent discourse principles may succeed in locating one. If no antecedent can be found either in the sentence or in the discourse, the subject remains without interpretation, and the sentence is semantically deviant as a consequence.

In earlier discussions of Super-Equi, only examples containing possible antecedents within the sentence itself were considered. However, it is clear that sentences such as the following are acceptable, given appropriate discourse conditions:

(29) Giving myself a promotion would anger the press
(30) Helping yourself to seconds would shock the hostess
(31) Perjuring himself would be politically unwise

Such facts lend a certain amount of plausibility to the view that
at least some phonologically null subjects are directly generated
in underlying syntactic representations. Let us therefore consider the possibility of generalizing this analysis to all cases.

Super-Equi, applying cyclically, will define ties of antece-
dence between NPs and occurrences of the null NP $\Delta$ commanded
by them in lower cycles. In all cases, $\Delta$ must be the subject of
a tenseless clause. A further condition on application is the
following:

(32) Super-Equi is obligatory on a cycle in which $\Delta$ is
preceded by an (animate)[3] NP; otherwise it is optional.

It is assumed that cyclic rules are not extrinsically ordered,
and apply whenever their structural description is met. (32)
therefore applies to each configuration meeting the structural
description of Super-Equi.

For sample derivations, let us return to examples (15a) and
(15b), related by Extraposition. Both have the following underlying structure:

(33)

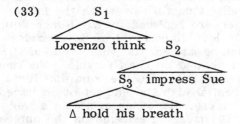

On the $S_2$ cycle, Super-Equi is optional, by (32). In order to
produce a well-formed reading, we must choose the option of
not applying it. In the derivation of (15a), nothing happens on
the $S_2$ cycle, and we proceed to $S_1$. As a NP (*Lorenzo*) occurs
to the left of $\Delta$, Super-Equi is obligatory. Since *Lorenzo* is
the only candidate, it becomes the antecedent of $\Delta$, giving the
correct interpretation.

In the derivation of (15b), however, Extraposition applies on
the $S_2$ cycle.[4] After the application of Extraposition, Super-
Equi is redefined, but now it is obligatory, by (32). Therefore *Sue* is identified as the antecedent of $\Delta$. But since *Sue*

cannot be the subject of *hold his breath*, the sentence is deviant. A parallel explanation accounts for the deviance of (15c).

The deviance of (15d) and (15e) follows also from (32), since *Sue* is encountered in the cycle before *Lorenzo*, and occurs to the left of $\Delta$. On the other hand, (15g) allows *Lorenzo* to become the antecedent of $\Delta$, since application of Super-Equi is optional on the intermediate cycle when *Sue* is first encountered.

Given the above formulation of Super-Equi, no special condition need be stated to explain the fact that clause mates of potential controllers do not block application. This can be seen by examining the derivation of (15f). On the $S_2$ cycle, *Mary* is a possible antecedent; but since no NP occurs to the left of $\Delta$ on this cycle, we may choose not to apply the rule. Passing to the $S_1$ cycle, the rule is obligatory by (32), and therefore it must assign an antecedent to $\Delta$. There are two possible candidates: *Lorenzo* and *Sue*. To derive (15f), we must choose *Lorenzo*. But choice of the subject is not obligatory: in the parallel example (34), below, the indirect object *Sue* has been chosen:

(34) Lorenzo told Sue that $\Delta$ holding her breath for ten minutes would impress Bill

As far as the paradigm of (15) is concerned, then, the deletion rule (as amended in footnote 1) and the interpretive rule give equivalent results. Let us now examine the examples that led us to the conclusion that the Intervention Constraint was global in nature. It can easily be seen that the problems that arose for the deletion rule do not arise for the interpretive rule.

In the interpretive approach, the structure underlying (23) will not be (24), but a parallel structure in which the lower occurrences of *Sue* and *Roger* are replaced by $\Delta$. Super-Equi is first defined on the $S_2$ cycle. Since the $\Delta$ of $S_2$ precedes the $\Delta$ of $S_4$, the former must be marked the antecedent of the latter. Super-Equi is again defined on the $S_1$ cycle. We know that verbs like *urge* independently impose the condition that their object must be coreferential with the subject of an immediately subordinate tenseless clause. In order to obtain a well-formed reading, therefore, *Sue* must be selected as the antecedent of the $S_2$ delta. But due to the transitivity of the coreference relation, *Sue* must be understood as the subject of $S_4$; hence the deviance of (23).

The deviance of (25b) is now simple to account for. Its underlying structure is parallel to (26), but deltas replace the lowest occurrences of *Ike* and *Mamie*. Super-Equi is first defined on the $S_3$ cycle; it is obligatory by (32), and the $S_3$ delta is selected as the antecedent of the $S_4$ delta. Thus the intended interpretation of (25b) is impossible.

The explanation for the deviance of (27) and (28) is also straightforward. Passive does not apply until the $S_2$ cycle. But before it applies, Super-Equi is defined under the obligatory case of (32). Assuming the principle that when an obligatory rule and an optional rule are simultaneously defined, the obligatory rule applies first, the underlying subject of the $S_2$ cycle in each case is marked as the antecedent of $\Delta$; hence the deviance of the examples.

From this discussion it must be concluded that the interpretive approach to the Super-Equi facts is not empirically equivalent to the deletion approach, but makes a very different theoretical claim. The deletion approach is consistent only with a theory of grammar which makes no claims, or only weak claims, about the nature of possible rules, since it permits the existence of rules whose structural description must be met twice, such as Super-Equi.[5] On the other hand, the interpretive approach is consistent with the strong position that structural conditions on rules need only be met once in a derivation, and that global conditioning of rules in general is restricted to a well-defined class of predicate modifier agreement rules. This position may conceivably prove to be false, but until contrary evidence appears it is the more interesting position to maintain.

5. We now have found reason to believe that Super-Equi is a rule of interpretation, rather than deletion. In the analysis presented above, Equi is simply a special case of Super-Equi, in accordance with Grinder's original insight. Let us therefore refer to them both as the Complement Subject Rule.

One might hesitate to accept an analysis in which Equi and Super-Equi are collapsed into a single rule. An apparent distinction between them is that Super-Equi is optional, while Equi is obligatory. However, the above analysis shows this to be untrue; both are optional if no NP appears to the left of $\Delta$ in a given cycle (for the Equi cases, the only cycle), but obligatory if one does. This has been demonstrated above for the Super-Equi cases; comparable Equi examples are given below:

(35a) $\Delta$ Giving myself a promotion would anger the press
(35b) *It would anger the press $\Delta$ to give myself a promotion
(35c) *The press would be angered by $\Delta$ giving myself a promotion
(36a) $\Delta$ Helping yourself to seconds would shock the hostess
(36b) *It would shock the hostess $\Delta$ to help yourself to seconds
(36c) *The hostess would be shocked by $\Delta$ helping yourself to seconds

Here, the (b) and (c) examples are deviant due to the fact that the Complement Subject rule obligatorily chooses an antecedent in the top cycle. This fact is predicted by the interpretive rule, but cannot be captured by the deletion approach, nor, needless to say, by any approach which refuses to identify the Equi and Super-Equi cases.

Another apparent distinction between Equi and Super-Equi was suggested by Neubauer (1972:290): 'while Equi is dependent solely on the verb of the controller's clause, Super-Equi is completely independent of any verb associated with the controller'. In the formulation given above, however, both Equi and Super-Equi are independent of the verb of the controller's clause, as the rule is ungoverned. What the verb of the controller's clause governs is not the application of the Complement Subject rule, but rather a coreference constraint on null subjects occurring in immediately subordinate clauses. This is a fact which is completely independent of the Complement Subject rule, and which does not require reference to it.

6. Grinder pointed out the existence of several examples which present special difficulties for his formulation of Super-Equi (Grinder 1970). One set of examples involves the Split Antecedents Phenomenon:

(37) Harry said that [Joan knew that [it was necessary [to report their own father to the authorities]]]

The problem which split antecedents present for a transformational approach to Super-Equi is quite parallel to that which they present for a transformational account of other rules involving anaphoric relations, such as pronominalization. Since neither antecedent, taken singly, is identical to the proform, an operation governed by identity should not in principle be able to be carried out. Thus, in (37), neither *Harry* nor *Joan* should singly be able to control the deletion of the underlying subject of *report*; furthermore, they occur on different cycles.

Split antecedents do not present a comparable problem for the interpretive approach to anaphoric relations. In the present case, *Joan* will obligatorily be associated with the null subject of *report* on the next-to-last cycle as its antecedent; however, Super-Equi is redefined on the final cycle, and as the rule was given earlier, nothing prevents it from reapplying to assign *Harry* to the null subject as a further antecedent. Since the null subject must be interpreted as plural in order to give a well-formed reading of the lowest clause, this derivation must be correct. Nevertheless, this account fails to explain the grammaticality of examples like (38):

(38) Harry said that [Joan knew that [it was necessary [to report her own father to the authorities]]]

This is because condition (32) defines Super-Equi as obligatory on the top cycle. In this case, that result would be incorrect; it must be possible for *Joan* to be the unique antecedent of the null subject of *report*, in order for the correct reading to be obtained. This suggests that (32) must be revised to state that if an antecedent has once been assigned to any given $\Delta$, all further applications of the rule to that $\Delta$ are optional.

A second set of problem sentences is exemplified by (39):

(39) John said that [Laura knew that [[torturing herself] would make [criticising himself] seem trivial]]

The problem for the deletion approach is that *Laura* meets the definition of an element in the deletion path, and therefore deletion of the subject of *criticising* under identity with *John* should be blocked. A formulation of a condition permitting deletion to take place introduces global relationships once again.

The problem is less severe for the interpretive approach. On the next-to-last cycle, *Laura* appears as a possible antecedent. Since *Laura* precedes both occurrences of $\Delta$, the rule is obligatory. But we must now specify in more detail what it means for a rule to be obligatory, in the case where more than one application is defined in nondisjoint domains. A priori, there are two possibilities: it either means that the rule must apply at least once, or it means that the rule must apply in each case where it is defined. Examples like (39) indicate that the first alternative must be the correct one. If this is true, then the obligatory condition is satisfied as soon as *Laura* is selected as the antecedent of the delta subject of *torturing*: the subject of *criticising* can remain uninterpreted until the top cycle.

## NOTES

For helpful discussions on various aspects of Super-Equi I would like to thank Richard Kayne, Susumu Kuno, David Perlmutter, Tanya Reinhart, Ivan Sag, and Scott Soames.

1. It would be sufficient to replace conditions (a) and (b) of (16) with the single condition: $e_i$ both precedes and commands $t_i$, and is not a clause mate of $C_i$.

2. Fauconnier, as well as Quicoli (1972), who reanalyzed the Greek case agreement data first extensively discussed in Andrews (1971), argue that the phenomena in question can be treated nonglobally within certain extensions of standard theory (see, respectively, Postal 1970 and Chomsky 1973).

3. I have not carefully studied the nature of the animacy condition suggested in this formulation. Some such condition is required in order to prevent sentences like (13b) from blocking.

4. Crucially, in this analysis, Extraposition must be a cyclic rule; otherwise, no general statement of the Super-Equi facts would be possible, under either the transformational or interpretive hypothesis. Super-Equi provides a strong argument for the cyclicity of Extraposition, as Jacobson and Neubauer have pointed out.

5. Although the Intervention Constraint was not presented as a part of the structural description of Super-Equi, it seems

fair to view it this way, since it is an ad hoc condition, not known to be involved in the application of other rules.

## REFERENCES FOR 'SUPER-EQUI AND THE INTERVENTION CONSTRAINT'

Andrews, A. 1971. Case agreement of predicate modifiers in Ancient Greek. Linguistic Inquiry 2.127-151.

Baker, C. L., and M. K. Brame. 1972. Global rules: A rejoinder. Lg. 48.51-75.

Chomsky, N. 1973. Conditions on transformations. In: A festschrift for Morris Halle. Edited by S. R. Anderson and P. Kiparsky. New York: Holt, Rinehart and Winston.

Emonds, J. 1973. Alternatives to global constraints. Glossa 7.39-62.

Fauconnier, G. 1973. Cyclic attraction into networks of coreference. Lg. 49.1-18.

Fauconnier, G. 1974. La coréférence: Syntaxe ou sémantique? Paris: Editions du Seuil.

Grinder, J. 1970. Super Equi-NP deletion. In: Papers from the Sixth Regional Meeting of the Chicago Linguistic Society. Department of Linguistics. Chicago: University of Chicago.

Grinder, J. 1971. A reply to 'Super Equi-NP deletion as dative deletion'. In: Papers from the Seventh Regional Meeting of the Chicago Linguistic Society. Department of Linguistics. Chicago: University of Chicago.

Jackendoff, R. 1972. Semantic interpretation in generative grammar. Cambridge, Mass.: The MIT Press.

Jacobson, P., and P. Neubauer. 1974. Extraposition rules and the cycle. Unpublished paper. University of California at Berkeley.

Kimball, J. 1971. Super Equi-NP deletion as dative deletion. In: Papers from the Seventh Regional Meeting of the Chicago Linguistic Society. Department of Linguistics. University of Chicago.

Milsark, G. 1972. Re: Doubl-ing. Linguistic Inquiry 3.542-549.

Napoli, D. 1973. Adverb agreement in Italian: A global rule. Paper presented at the LSA Winter Meeting, San Diego, California.

Neubauer, P. 1972. Super-Equi revisited. In: Papers from the Eighth Regional Meeting of the Chicago Linguistic Society. Department of Linguistics. University of Chicago.

Postal, P. 1970. On coreferential complement subject deletion. Linguistic Inquiry 1.439-500.

Postal, P. 1972. A global constraint on pronominalization. Linguistic Inquiry 3.35-60.

Quicoli, A. 1972. Aspects of Portuguese complementation. Unpublished doctoral dissertation. State University of New York. Buffalo, New York.

Selkirk, E. 1972. The phrase phonology of English and French. Unpublished doctoral dissertation. MIT.

QUESTIONS

Question 1. After reading Clements' first paragraph, give a statement of Jackendoff's restriction on transformations.

Question 2. Which of the following rules require access to semantic information: Reflexive, Raising into Object Position, Passive, Equi, Dative Movement? In each case what semantic information is necessary, if any?

Question 3. What is 'super' about Super-Equi? (See Clements' example (1).) How does it differ from Equi? Which of the rules listed in Question 2 are 'two story' and only apply to adjacent clauses?

Question 4. Define 'adjacent clauses' with a structural definition.

Question 5. How does Kimball's Dative Deletion rule purport to allow all cases of Equi to involve only adjacent clauses and never nonadjacent ones?

Question 6. Where is Kimball's dative in (i)?

(i) Lorenzo thought that his holding his breath for ten minutes would impress Sue for him.

Question 7. If (i) in Question 6 is a good deep structure, then (ii) here is an expected good surface S because (ii) is embedded in (i).

(ii) *(His) holding his breath for ten minutes would impress Sue for Lorenzo.

What is the source of the ungrammaticality of (ii)?

Question 8. In (i) and (ii), the key to the difference in the behavior of the *for* phrase is its constituency.

(i) a. It would be logically inconsistent for nonpersons to be persons.
(i) b. For nonpersons to be persons would be logically inconsistent.
(i) c. *To be persons would be logically inconsistent for nonpersons.
(i) d. *It would be logically inconsistent to be persons, for nonpersons.
(ii) a. It would be easy for doctors to increase their fees.
(ii) b. *For doctors to increase their fees would be easy.
(ii) c. To increase their fees would be easy for doctors.
(ii) d. It would be easy to increase their fees, for doctors.

In one case *for NP* forms a constituent with the other elements of the higher VP; in the other case *for NP* forms a constituent with the embedded infinitival VP. What constituency does *for nonpersons* have in (i)? What constituency does *for doctors* have in (ii)? Draw the deep trees. What movement rule has applied in (i-a)? Why is (ii-b) bad? Why is (i-c) bad? What rule has applied in (ii-c) that cannot apply to the Ss in (i)? (You do not have to name the rule; just describe what it does.) Why is (i-d) bad? What general constraint is violated? (Compare to *I hope to win, for John* meaning 'I hope for John to win'.) Why is (ii-d) good?

Question 9. Give the underlying structure for (i).

(i) Sophie believes it would be logically inconsistent to be taller than herself.

Number your NPs and Ss. What are the controller and the controllee of Super-Equi? How do examples like (i) supply evidence against Kimball's Dative Deletion proposal?

*Question 10. What are the two readings of (i)?

(i) The President thought that it would be unprecedented for him to offer his resignation on Bastille Day.

Which reading is not accounted for by Kimball's Dative Deletion? How does Clements account for both readings without any need for Dative Deletion? Which reading of (i) is the source for (ii)?

(ii) The President thought that it would be unprecedented to offer his resignation on Bastille Day.

How does this offer evidence against Kimball?

Question 11. Which *for* phrase in (i) is a dative? What is the other *for* phrase?

(i) The General didn't agree that it would be good for the country for him to remove himself from office.

Question 12. What would (i) be derived from?

(i) *(His) removing himself from office would be good for the country for the General.

Why does Clements give this example? What possible response on Kimball's part concerning (ii) is Clements trying to refute here?

(ii) The General didn't agree that it would be good for the country to remove himself from office.

How does (i) offer evidence against Kimball?

**Question 13.** Clements considers the possibility that Super-Equi is blocked when another NP intervenes between a controller and a controllee (as *Sue* does in (i-a) through (i-c)).

(i) a. *Lorenzo thought that it would impress Sue to hold his breath for ten minutes.
(i) b. *Lorenzo thought that Sue would be impressed by holding his breath for ten minutes.
(i) c. *Lorenzo thought that Sue believed that it would be impressive to hold his breath for ten minutes.

How does (ii) show that this proposal is too weak? (Note that Clements is assuming that inanimate NPs like *breath* and *minutes* are irrelevant and can be ignored.)

(ii) *That it impressed Sue to hold his breath for ten minutes gratified Lorenzo.

How does (iii) show that the proposal is too strong?

(iii) Lorenzo asked Sue whether holding his breath for ten minutes would impress Mary.

**Question 14.** The Intervention Constraint uses the term 'primacy relation'. There are two primacy relations: precede and command. Precede refers to the linear order of elements in a string. Thus in the string A B C D, we can say that A precedes B and C and D; B precedes C and D; C precedes D. Command refers to the tree structure. If the lowest S node that dominates A also dominates B, then we say A commands B. (See Langacker 1969 and Lasnik 1976 for further discussion.)

**\*Question 15.** Consider the Intervention Constraint (given as example (16) in Clements). Which of the two conditions of this constraint rules out (i-a) in Question 13? Which rules out (i-b)? (i-c)? (ii)? Why is (iii) not out? Does the Intervention Constraint predict that (iv) will be good or bad? Why? (You will have to do some of your own work here, since Clements' explanations are a bit sketchy.)

(iv) That holding his breath for ten minutes impressed Sue gratified Lorenzo.

**\*Question 16.** How do (i) and (ii) show that Super-Equi cannot apply precyclically? (Recall the Intervention Constraint.)

(i) a. *Ted said that it would surprise Sue to declare himself a candidate.

(i) b. Ted said that for him to declare himself a candidate would surprise Sue.

(ii) a. *Dr. Lenz believed that Anne would be traumatized by analyzing his own dreams.

(ii) b. Dr. Lenz believed that his analyzing his own dreams would traumatize Anne.

Question 17. What is Clements' strategy in his argument that Super-Equi is cyclic?

**Question 18. The deep structure for (i) is something like (ii).

(i) $\emptyset$ Pardoning himself was generally thought to have been felt to be unwise by Mr. Nixon.

(ii) $[_{S_1}$ Pro generally thought $[_{S_2}$ Mr. Nixon has felt $[_{S_3} [_{S_4}$ Mr. Nixon pardon himself$]_{S_4}$ be unwise$]_{S_3} ]_{S_2} ]_{S_1}$

What rule applies on $S_4$? No rules apply on $S_3$. What rules apply on $S_2$ and in what order? What rules apply on $S_1$ and in what order? In your derivation you should have included the rules Reflexive (whether transformational or interpretive), Raising into Object Position, and Passive. (Ignore Super-Equi for the moment.) Now go through the derivation first assuming Super-Equi is postcyclic. Give the surface structure resulting. Show what problem arises. Notice that in order to say that Nixon does not command $\emptyset$ in (i), we must not 'prune' Ss. That is,

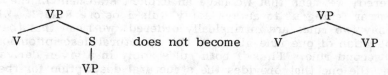

Now go through the derivation a second time assuming Super-Equi is cyclic. What cycle does it apply on? How does (i) show that Super-Equi cannot be postcyclic?

*Question 19. How does (i) differ crucially from (ii)?

(i) *Mamie thought that getting himself arrested on account of losing her temper would ruin Ike's career.

(ii) *Roger urged Sue to declare that torturing himself would be fun.

That is, why will Clements' proposed principle preventing a rule from applying to its own output prevent (ii) but not (i)?

**Question 20. Given (i), (ii), and (iii), what can you conclude about the Intervention Constraint?

   (i) *Mamie thought that getting himself arrested on account of losing her temper would ruin Ike's career.
  (ii) *Wilbur was afraid that misbehaving himself with Lola had been discovered by his wife.
 (iii) *Salvador discovered that attempting to poison himself had been reported to the police by Thelma.

Does the constraint apply at the point where Super-Equi is defined or at some other point? What is that other point?

Question 21. In the paragraph preceding Clements' example (32) he says that '$\Delta$ must be the subject of a tenseless clause'. He is adopting here a theory in which tenseless (i.e. infinitival) clauses are generated directly in the base.

Question 22. Consider footnote 3. Why is it necessary to have an animacy condition in order to prevent blocking (i)?

   (i) The General didn't agree that it would be good for the country to remove himself from office.

(What is the inanimate NP that intervenes between the real controller and the controllee but which cannot be taken as a controller?)

*Question 23. When we say two rules are extrinsically ordered, we mean that we have an explicit statement in the grammar telling us to always apply Rule 1 before Rule 2. When we say two rules are intrinsically ordered, we mean that the application of one rule gives us the structural description for the second rule. Thus if both rules apply in a given derivation, the one that provides the structural description for the other will automatically apply first. Consider the example, There was a demonstrator killed by a policeman. Do we have to explicitly state that Passive is ordered before There-Insertion?

**Question 24. Why is Super-Equi optional on $S_2$ in (i)?

(i)

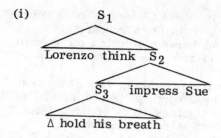

Why, since it is optional, must we choose not to apply Super-Equi on $S_2$? Which NPs control deletion in (ii) and (iii)?

(ii) Lorenzo thought that holding his breath would alarm Mike.

(iii) Lorenzo thought that it would alarm Mike to hold his breath for ten minutes.

*Question 25.   Given (i), why must *Lorenzo* be the antecedent for $\Delta$ in (ii)?   (What other considerations come in here?)

(i) Lorenzo told Sue that $\Delta$ holding her breath for ten minutes would impress Bill.

(ii) Lorenzo asked Sue whether $\Delta$ holding his breath for ten minutes would impress Mary.

Which NP controls deletion in (iii)?

(iii) Lorenzo asked Mike whether holding his breath for ten minutes would alarm Harry.

*Question 26.   What is the 'transitivity of the coreference relation' in (i) that Clements talks of in the second paragraph following his example (34)?

(i) *Roger urged Sue to declare that torturing himself would be fun.

Ultimately, why is (i) out, according to Clements? Which NP controls deletion in (ii)?

(ii) Roger urged Mike to declare that torturing himself would be fun.

*Question 27.   Ultimately, why is (i) out, according to Clements?

(i) *Mamie thought that getting himself arrested on account of losing her temper would ruin Ike's career.

Go through the derivations of (ii) and (iii).

(ii) Mamie thought that getting himself arrested on account of losing his temper would ruin Ike's career.
(iii) Mamie thought that getting herself arrested on account of losing her temper would ruin Ike's career.

Question 28. In the next to the last paragraph of Section 4, Clements proposed that when the structural description of more than one rule is met at once, obligatory rules apply before optional ones. What obligatory rules do you know of?

*Question 29. Why doesn't the split controller in (i) present a problem for Clements?

(i) Harry said that Joan knew that it was necessary to report their own father to the authorities.

How is (ii) parallel to (i)? How does it differ?

(ii) Harry said that Joan knew that it was necessary to report her own father to the authorities.

What modification of the application of Super-Equi (as given in Clements' example (32)) does Clements therefore propose?

**Question 30. Clements proposes that when the structural description for an obligatory rule is met in nondisjoint domains, the rule must apply at least once but not necessarily in every case where it is defined. Try to find Ss in which the structural description for an obligatory rule is met in two ways at the same point in the derivation. Does Clements' proposal work for your Ss?

## HOMEWORK PROBLEMS

I. In order to generate Clements' example (23) (*Roger urged Sue to declare that torturing himself would be fun) Super-Equi must apply twice: first between the Sues (the Equi subcase), then between the Rogers (since the intervening Sue is now out of the picture). Clements suggests that we can block example (23) by a principle which prevents a rule from reapplying to its own output.
Consider the following Ss.

(1a) Mary was given the ring by John.
(1b) *The ring was been given by John by Mary.
(2a) That John won seemed to be a surprise.
(2b) *John seemed to be a surprise to win.

A. What rule has applied to what immediately underlying structure to yield (1a)? (2a)?

B. What rule has applied to what immediately underlying structure to yield (1b)? (2b)?

C. What principle could we use to rule out (1b) and (2b)? Please try to be explicit in terms of exactly which kinds of rules this principle would apply to and exactly what the principle would block. Specifically, make sure your principle will not block (3) and (4).

(3) John is expected to be elected president by the whole nation.
(4) John seems to be certain to win.

Once you give your principle, show how it will not block (3) and (4).

D. Take the rule Raising into Object Position and give examples and discussion showing how your principle will or will not affect this rule.

II. Consider Clements' examples (29) through (31), repeated here for convenience.

(1) Giving myself a promotion would anger the press.
(2) Helping yourself to seconds would shock the hostess.
(3) Perjuring himself would be politically unwise.

What would Ross' performative analysis have to say about these examples? Be sure to consider each example separately, since the performative analysis would say different things about each one.

III. In Clements' analysis of Super-Equi, Δ subjects are generated in the deep structure, as schematized in Clements' examples (33) through (34). Consider (1) and (2).

(1) John wanted to be noticed by Sue.
(2) John tried to be easy to get along with.

Give a derivation of (1) and of (2) according to Clements. What new empty deep nodes do we now need?
How might Clements explain the fact that we do not get surface Ss like (3) through (6)?

(3) *Was noticed by Sue.
(4) *Was easy to get along with.
(5) *Mary put in the pocket. (Here the *put in* is that of *I put the paper in the drawer* and not the *put in* of *I put in the cat.*)
(6) *I stuffed Kleenex into.

## SUGGESTED READINGS

Chomsky, N. 1976. Conditions on rules of grammar. Linguistic Analysis 2:4.303-351. (For a general discussion of interpretive rules.)

Chomsky, N., and H. Lasnik. 1977. Filters and control. Linguistic Inquiry 8:3.425-504. (For more discussion of interpretive rules and other alternatives to transformations.)

Green, G. 1973. Some remarks on split controller phenomena. CLS 9.123-138. (For discussion of Ss such as Clements' example (37).)

Hankamer, J., and I. Sag. 1976. Deep and surface anaphora. Linguistic Inquiry 7:3.391-428. (For the paper topic: Exactly where can Equi look for an antecedent? This paper topic ties in with Homework Problem II.)

Hayes, B. 1976. The semantic nature of the intervention constraint. Linguistic Inquiry 7:2.371-376.

Jacobson, P., and P. Neubauer. 1976. Rule cyclicity: Evidence from the intervention constraint. Linguistic Inquiry 7:3.429-461.

Kimball, J. 1972. Cyclic and linear grammars. In: Syntax and semantics, Volume 1. Edited by J. Kimball. New York: Academic Press. 63-80. (For a discussion of rule ordering.)

Koutsoudas, A. 1972. The strict order fallacy. Lg. 48:1.88-96. (For further discussion of rule ordering.)

Kuno, S. 1974. Super Equi-NP deletion is a pseudo-transformation. NELS V. Cambridge, Mass.: Harvard University. 29-44.

Lakoff, G. 1970. Global rules. Lg. 46:3.627-639.

Langacker, R. 1969. On pronominalization and the chain of command. In: Modern studies in English. Edited by D. Reibel and S. Schane. Englewood Cliffs, N.J.: Prentice-Hall. 160-186. (For a discussion of the primacy relations.)

Lasnik, H. 1976. Remarks on coreference. Linguistic Analysis 2.1-22.

Lasnik, H., and R. Fiengo. 1974. Complement object deletion. Linguistic Inquiry 5:4.535-572. (For another analysis of *easy* type predicates, as in Homework Problem III.)

Postal, P. 1974. On raising. Cambridge, Mass.: The MIT Press. (See Chapters 5 and 8 of Postal's book in particular for examples of proposed global and transderivational conditions and rules.)

Wasow, T. 1972. Anaphoric relations in English. Unpublished doctoral dissertation. MIT.

# 11

FACT

## Paul Kiparsky and Carol Kiparsky

Introduction. Before Paul and Carol Kiparsky wrote 'Fact', the most systematic and complete work on the subject of English Complementation was Rosenbaum's 1967 book. Rosenbaum had every predicate marked arbitrarily as taking certain complementizers and not others. The predicates could be grouped semantically into groups that more or less coincided with groups having similar syntactic marking, but there was no formal way to express the coincidence.

'Fact' changed all that and by its elegance gave new hope at once, paradoxically, both to those who believed in an entirely autonomous syntax and to those who believed that syntax and semantics were one. Today, it is probably the latter group whose work owes most to this article, for the Kiparskys' head noun *fact* has not been taken nearly as far by other researchers as has their discussion of the role of logical presupposition in syntax. A great deal of very interesting work is now being done on the logical structure of language. However, as a study of this work requires familiarity with logical notation, we have included in this volume only the article which first gave new impetus to the perennial swing of the linguistic pendulum back toward the effort to relate syntactic and semantic regularities.

PAUL KIPARSKY AND CAROL KIPARSKY

# FACT*

The object of this paper is to explore the interrelationship of syntax and semantics in the English complement system. Our thesis is that the choice of complement type is in large measure predictable from a number of basic semantic factors. Among these we single out for special attention PRESUPPOSITION by the speaker that the complement of the sentence expresses a true proposition. It will be shown that whether the speaker presupposes the truth of a complement contributes in several important ways to determining the syntactic form in which the complement can appear in the surface structure. A possible explanation for these observations will be suggested.

## 1. TWO SYNTACTIC PARADIGMS

The following two lists both contain predicates which take sentences as their subjects. For reasons that will become apparent in a moment, we term them FACTIVE and NON-FACTIVE.

| FACTIVE | NON-FACTIVE |
|---|---|
| significant | likely |
| odd | sure |
| tragic | possible |
| exciting | true |
| relevant | false |
| matters | seems |
| counts | appears |
| makes sense | happens |
| suffices | chances |
| amuses | turns out |
| bothers | |

* This work was supported in part by the U.S. Air Force (ESD Contract AF19(628)-2487) and the National Institutes of Health (Grant MH-13390-01).

This paper developed through several revisions out of a paper read in 1967 at Bucharest. These revisions were largely prompted by helpful discussions with many colleagues, among whom we would especially like to thank John Kimball, George Lakoff, Robin Lakoff, Haj Ross, and Timothy Shopen.

We shall be concerned with the differences in structure between sentences constructed with factive and non-factive predicates, *e.g.*:

Factive:      *It is significant that he has been found guilty*
Non-factive: *It is likely that he has been found guilty*

On the surface, the two seem to be identically constructed. But as soon as we replace the *that*-clauses by other kinds of expressions, a series of systematic differences between the factive and non-factive predicates begins to appear.

(1) Only factive predicates allow the noun *fact* with a sentential complement consisting of a *that*-clause or a gerund to replace the simple *that*-clause. For example,

*The fact that the dog barked during the night*
*The fact of the dog's barking during the night*

can be continued by the factive predicates *is significant, bothers me,* but not by the non-factive predicates *is likely, seems to me.*

(2) Only factive predicates allow the full range of gerundial constructions, and adjectival nominalizations in *-ness,* to stand in place of the *that*-clause. For example, the expressions

*His being found guilty*
*John's having died of cancer last week*
*Their suddenly insisting on very detailed reports*
*The whiteness of the whale*

can be subjects of factive predicates such as *is tragic, makes sense, suffices,* but not of non-factive predicates such as is *sure, seems, turns out.*

(3) On the other hand, there are constructions which are permissible only with non-factive predicates. One such construction is obtained by turning the initial noun phrase of the subordinate clause into the subject of the main clause, and converting the remainder of the subordinate clause into an infinitive phrase. This operation converts structures of the form

*It is likely that he will accomplish even more*
*It seems that there has been a snowstorm*

into structures of the form

*He is likely to accomplish even more*
*There seems to have been a snowstorm*

We can do this with many non-factive predicates, although some, like *possible,* are exceptions:

*It is possible that he will accomplish even more*
*\*He is possible to accomplish even more*

However, none of the factive predicates can ever be used so:

> *He is relevant to accomplish even more
> *There is tragic to have been a snowstorm

(4) For the verbs in the factive group, extraposition[1] is optional, whereas it is obligatory for the verbs in the non-factive group. For example, the following two sentences are optional variants:

> That there are porcupines in our basement makes sense to me
> It makes sense to me that there are porcupines in our basement

But in the corresponding non-factive case the sentence with the initial that-clause is ungrammatical:

> *That there are porcupines in our basement seems to me
> It seems to me that there are porcupines in our basement

In the much more complex domain of object clauses, these syntactic criteria, and many additional ones, effect a similar division into factive and non-factive predicates. The following lists contain predicates of these two types.

| FACTIVE | NON-FACTIVE |
|---|---|
| regret | suppose |
| be aware (of) | assert |
| grasp | allege |
| comprehend | assume |
| take into consideration | claim |
| take into account | charge |
| bear in mind | maintain |
| ignore | believe |
| make clear | conclude |
| mind | conjecture |
| forget (about) | intimate |
| deplore | deem |
| resent | fancy |
| care (about) | figure |

(1) Only factive predicates can have as their objects the noun fact with a gerund or that-clause:

Factive:  *I want to make clear the fact that I don't intend to participate*
*You have to keep in mind the fact of his having proposed several alternatives*

---

[1] Extraposition is a term introduced by Jespersen for the placement of a complement at the end of a sentence. For recent transformational discussion of the complexities of this rule, see Ross (1967).

Non-factive: *I assert the fact that I don't intend to participate
              *We may conclude the fact of his having proposed several alternatives

(2) Gerunds can be objects of factive predicates, but not freely of non-factive predicates:

Factive:      Everyone ignored Joan's being completely drunk
              I regret having agreed to the proposal
              I don't mind your saying so

Non-factive: *Everyone supposed Joan's being completely drunk
              *I believe having agreed to the proposal
              *I maintain your saying so

The gerunds relevant here are what Lees (1960) has termed 'factive nominals'. They occur freely both in the present tense and in the past tense (having -En). They take direct accusative objects, and all kinds of adverbs and they occur without any identity restriction on their subject.[2] Other, non-factive, types of gerunds are subject to one or more of these restrictions. One type refers to actions or events:

He avoided getting caught
*He avoided having got caught
*He avoided John's getting caught

Gerunds also serve as substitutes for infinitives after prepositions:

I plan to enter the primary
I plan on entering the primary
*I plan on having entered the primary last week

Such gerunds are not at all restricted to factive predicates.
   (3) Only non-factive predicates allow the accusative and infinitive construction.

Non-factive: I believe Mary to have been the one who did it
              He fancies himself to be an expert in pottery
              I supposed there to have been a mistake somewhere

Factive:      *I resent Mary to have been the one who did it
              *He comprehends himself to be an expert in pottery
              *I took into consideration there to have been a mistake somewhere

As we earlier found in the case of subject complements, the infinitive construction is

---

[2] There is, however, one limitation on subjects of factive gerunds:

                *It's surprising me that he succeeded dismayed John
                *There's being a nut loose disguntles me

The restriction is that clauses cannot be subjects of gerunds, and that the gerund formation rule precedes extraposition and there-insertion.

excluded, for no apparent reason, even with some non-factive predicates, *e.g.*, *charge*. There is, furthermore, considerable variation from one speaker to another as to which predicates permit the accusative and infinitive construction, a fact which may be connected with its fairly bookish flavor. What is significant, however, is that the accusative and infinitive is not used with factive predicates.

## 2. PRESUPPOSITION

These syntactic differences are correlated with a semantic difference. The force of the *that*-clause is not the same in the two sentences

> *It is odd that it is raining* (factive)
> *It is likely that it is raining* (non-factive)

or in the two sentences

> *I regret that it is raining* (factive)
> *I suppose that it is raining* (non-factive)

The first sentence in each pair (the factive sentence) carries with it the presupposition 'it is raining'. The speaker presupposes that the embedded clause expresses a true proposition, and makes some assertion about that proposition. All predicates which behave syntactically as factives have this semantic property, and almost none of those which behave syntactically as non-factives have it.[3] This, we propose, is the basic difference between the two types of predicates. It is important that the following things should be clearly distinguished:

(1) Propositions the speaker asserts, directly or indirectly, to be true
(2) Propositions the speaker presupposes to be true

Factivity depends on presupposition and not on assertion. For instance, when someone says

> *It is true that John is ill*
> *John turns out to be ill*

he is ASSERTING that the proposition 'John is ill' is a true proposition, but he is not

---

[3] There are some exceptions to this second half of our generalization. Verbs like *know, realize*, though semantically factive, are syntactically non-factive, so that we cannot say *\*I know the fact that John is here*, *\*I know John's being here*, whereas the propositional constructions are acceptable: *I know him to be here*. There are speakers for whom many of the syntactic and semantic distinctions we bring up do not exist at all. Professor Archibald Hill has kindly informed us that for him factive and non-factive predicates behave in most respects alike and that even the word *fact* in his speech has lost its literal meaning and can head clauses for which no presupposition of truth is made. We have chosen to describe a rather restrictive type of speech (that of C.K.) because it yields more insight into the syntactic-semantic problems with which we are concerned.

PRESUPPOSING that it is a true proposition. Hence these sentences do not follow the factive paradigm:

> *John's being ill is true
> *John's being ill turns out
> *The fact of John's being ill is true
> *The fact of John's being ill turns out

The following sentences, on the other hand, are true instances of presupposition:

> It is odd that the door is closed
> I regret that the door is closed

The speaker of these sentences presupposes 'the door is closed' and furthermore asserts something else about that presupposed fact. It is this semantically more complex structure involving presupposition that has the syntactic properties we are dealing with here.

When factive predicates have first person subjects it can happen that the top sentence denies what the complement presupposes. Then the expected semantic anomaly results. Except in special situations where two egos are involved, as in the case of an actor describing his part, the following sentences are anomalous:

> *I don't realize that he has gone away
> *I have no inkling that a surprise is in store for me[4]

Factivity is only one instance of this very basic and consequential distinction. In formulating the semantic structure of sentences, or, what concerns us more directly here, the lexical entries for predicates, we must posit a special status for presuppositions, as opposed to what we are calling assertions. The speaker is said to 'assert' a sentence plus all those propositions which follow from it by virtue of its meaning,

---

[4] In some cases what at first sight looks like a strange meaning shift accompanies negation with first person subjects. The following sentences can be given a non-factive interpretation which prevents the above kind of anomaly in them:

> I'm not aware that he has gone away
> I don't know that this isn't our car

It will not do to view these non-factive that-clauses as indirect questions:

> *I don't know that he has gone away or not

We advance the hypothesis that they are deliberative clauses, representing the same construction as clauses introduced but that:

> I don't know but that this is our car

This accords well with their meaning, and especially with the fact that deliberative but that-clauses (in the dialects that permit them at all) are similarly restricted to negative sentences with first person subjects:

> *I know but that this is our car
> *John doesn't know but that this is our car

not, *e.g.*, through laws of mathematics or physics.[5] Presumably in a semantic theory assertions will be represented as the central or 'core' meaning of a sentence — typically a complex proposition involving semantic components like '$S_1$ *cause* $S_2$', '$S$ *become*', '$N$ *want* $S$' — plus the propositions that follow from it by redundancy rules involving those components. The formulation of a simple example should help clarify the concepts of assertion and presupposition.

*Mary cleaned the room*

The dictionary contains a mapping between the following structures:

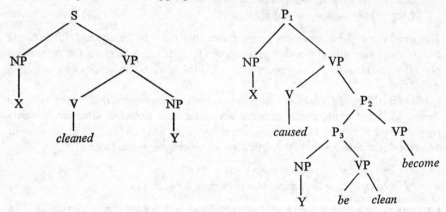

where S refers to the syntactic object 'Sentence' and P to the semantic object 'Proposition'.

A redundancy rule states that the object of *cause* is itself asserted:

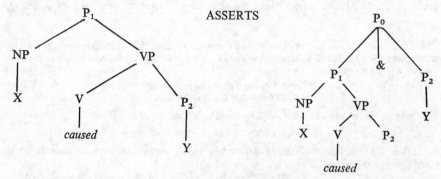

---

[5] We prefer 'assert' to 'imply' because the latter suggests consequences beyond those based on knowledge of the language. This is not at all to say that linguistic knowledge is disjoint from other knowledge. We are trying to draw a distinction between two statuses a defining proposition can be said to have in the definition of a predicate, or meaning of a sentence, and to describe some consequences of this distinction. This is a question of the semantic structure of words and can be discussed independently of the question of the relationship between the encyclopedia and the dictionary.

This rule yields the following set of assertions:

$X$ caused[6] $Y$ to become clean
$Y$ became clean

[Why the conjunction of $P_1$ and $P_2$ is subordinated to $P_0$ will become clear below, especially in (3) and (5)]

Furthermore, there is a presupposition to the effect that the room was dirty before the event described in the sentence. This follows from *become*, which presupposes that its complement has, up to the time of the change referred to by *become*, not been true. This may be expressed as a redundancy rule:

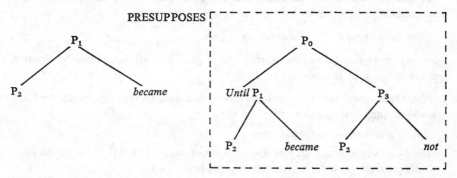

(Presuppositions will be enclosed in dotted lines. Within the context of a tree diagram representing the semantic structure of a sentence, presuppositions which follow from a specific semantic component will be connected to it by a dotted line).

That this, like the factive component in *regret* or *admit*, is a presupposition rather than an assertion can be seen by applying the criteria in the following paragraphs.

(1) Presuppositions are constant under negation. That is, when you negate a sentence you don't negate its presuppositions; rather, what is negated is what the positive sentence asserts. For example:

*Mary didn't clean the room*

unlike its positive counterpart does not assert either that the room became clean or, if it did, that it was through Mary's agency. On the other hand, negation does not affect the presupposition that it was or has been dirty. Similarly, these sentences with factive predicates

*It is not odd that the door is closed*
*John doesn't regret that the door is closed*

presuppose, exactly as do their positive counterparts, that the door is closed.

---

[6] Though we cannot go into the question here, it is clear that the tense of a sentence conveys information about the time of its presuppositions as well as of its assertions, direct and indirect. Thus tense (and likewise mood, cf. footnote 8) is not an 'operator' in the sense that negation and other topics discussed in this section are.

In fact, if you want to deny a presupposition, you must do it explicitly:

*Mary didn't clean the room; it wasn't dirty*
*Legree didn't force them to work; they were willing to*
*Abe didn't regret that he had forgotten; he had remembered*

The second clause casts the negative of the first into a different level; it's not the straightforward denial of an event or situation, but rather the denial of the appropriateness of the word in question (spaced out above). Such negations sound best with the inappropriate word stressed.

(2) Questioning, considered as an operation on a proposition P indicates 'I do not know whether P'. When I ask

*Are you dismayed that our money is gone?*

I do not convey that I don't know whether it is gone but rather take that for granted and ask about your reaction.

(Note that to see the relation between factivity and questioning only yes-no questions are revealing. A question like:

*Who is aware that Ram eats meat*

already by virtue of questioning an argument of *aware*, rather than the proposition itself, presupposes a corresponding statement:

*Someone is aware that Ram eats meat*

Thus, since the presupposition is transitive, the *who*-question presupposes all that the *someone*-statement does.)

Other presuppositions are likewise constantly under questioning. For instance, a verb might convey someone's evaluation of its complement as a presupposition. To say *they deprived him of a visit to his parents* presupposes that he wanted the visit (*vs. spare him a visit...*). The presupposition remains in *Have they deprived him of a...?* What the question indicates is 'I don't know whether they have kept him from...'

(3) It must be emphasized that it is the SET of assertions that is operated on by question and negation. To see this, compare —

*Mary didn't kiss John*
*Mary didn't clean the house*

They have certain ambiguities which, as has often been noted, are systematic under negation. The first may be equivalent to any of the following more precise sentences:

*Someone may have kissed John, but not Mary*
*Mary may have kissed someone, but not John*
*Mary may have done something, but not kiss John*
*Mary may have done something to John, but not kiss him*

And the second:

> *Someone may have cleaned the house, but not Mary*
> *Mary may have cleaned something, but not the house*
> *Mary may have done something, but not clean the house*
> *Mary may have done something to the house, but not clean it*

All of these readings can be predicted on the basis of the constituent structure:

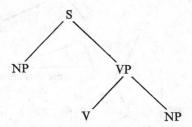

Roughly, each major constituent may be negated.

But the second sentence has still another reading:

> *Mary may have been cleaning the house, but it didn't get clean*

That extra reading has no counterpart in the other sentence. *Clean* is semantically more complex than *kiss* in that whereas *kiss* has only one assertion (press the lips against), *clean* has two, as we have seen above. How this affects the meaning of the negative sentence can be seen through a derivation:

(i)

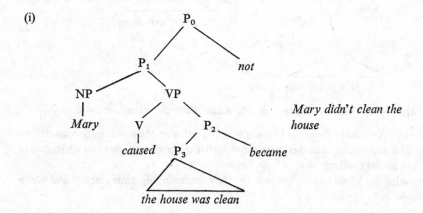

(ii) Application of redundancy rule on 'cause':

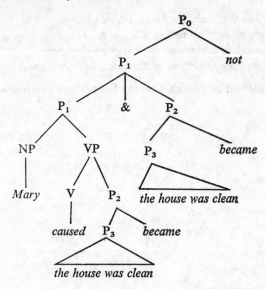

*It's not the case that both Mary cleaned the house and the house is clean.*

(iii) DeMorgan's Law yields

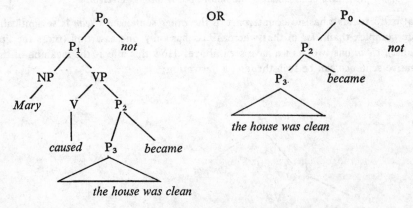

*Either 'Mary didn't clean the house' or 'the house didn't get clean'.*

Thus to say *Mary didn't clean the house* is to make either of the two negative assertions in (iii). The remaining readings arise from distribution of *not* over the constituents of the lexicalized sentence.

Presumably the same factors account for the corresponding ambiguity of *Did Mary clean the house?*

(4) If we take an imperative sentence like:

*(You) chase that thief!*

to indicate something like:

*I want (you chase that thief)*

then what 'I want' doesn't include the presuppositions of S. For example, S presupposes that

*That thief is evading you*

but that situation is hardly part of what 'I want'.

The factive complement in the following example is likewise presupposed independently of the demand:

*Point it out to 006 that the transmitter will function poorly in a cave*

Assume the dictionary contains this mapping:

From the causative redundancy rule, which adds the assertion $P_1$, the definition of *point out*, and the fact that *want* distributes over subordinate conjuncts, it follows that the above command indicates:

*I want 006 to become aware that the transmitter...*

However it doesn't in any way convey

*I want the transmitter to function poorly in a cave*

nor, of course, that

*I want 006 not to have been aware...*

(5) We have been treating negation, questioning, and imperative as operations on

propositions like implicit 'higher sentences'. Not surprisingly explicit 'higher sentences' also tend to leave presuppositions constant while operating on assertions. Our general claim is that the assertions of a proposition ($P_k$) are made relative to that proposition within its context of dominating propositions. Presuppositions, on the other hand, are relative to the speaker. This is shown in Figures 1 and 2. Fig. 1 shows that the presuppositions of $P_k$ are also presupposed by the whole proposition $P_0$. In Fig. 2 we see that whatever $P_0$ asserts about $P_k$ it also asserts about the SET (see (3) above) of propositions that $P_k$ asserts.

Figure 1:                                          Figure 2:

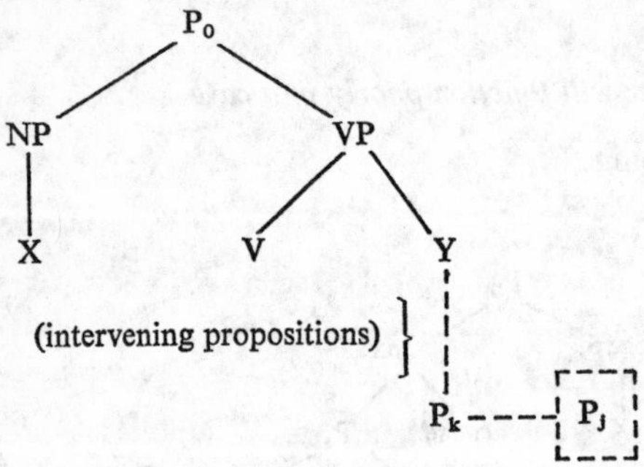

*Redundancy rule:*

$P_k$ presupposes $\boxed{P_J}$

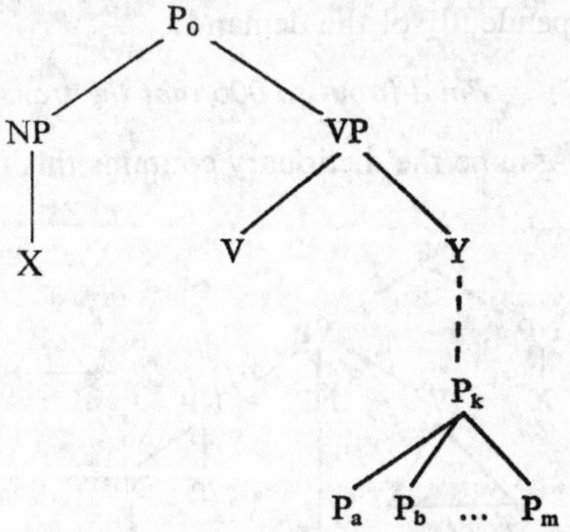

*Redundancy rule:*

$P_k$ asserts $\{P_a, P_b, ..., P_m\}$

Let us further exemplify this general claim:

> *John appears to regret evicting his grandmother*

Since *appear* is not factive this sentence neither asserts nor presupposes

> *John regrets evicting her*

However it does presuppose the complement of the embedded factive verb *regret*, as well as the presupposition of *evict* to the effect that he was her landlord.

It does not matter how deeply the factive complement (spaced out) is imbedded:

> *Abe thinks it is possible that Ben is becoming ready to encourage Carl to acknowledge that he had behaved churlishly*

This claim holds for presuppositions other than factivity. We are not obliged to conclude from

*John refuses to remain a bachelor all his life*

that he plans to undergo demasculating surgery, since *bachelor* asserts *unmarried*, but only presupposes *male* and *adult*. Thus it yields:

*John refuses to remain unmarried all his life*

but not

*John refuses to remain male (adult) all his life*

(6) A conjunction of the form $S_1$ *and* $S_2$ *too* serves to contrast an item in $S_1$ with one in $S_2$ by placing them in contexts which are in some sense not distinct from each other. For instance,

*Tigers are ferocious and panthers are (ferocious) too*
*\*Tigers are ferocious and panthers are mildmannered too*

Abstracting away from the contrasting items, $S_1$ might be said semantically to include $S_2$. The important thing for us to notice is that the relevant type of inclusion is *assertion*. Essentially, $S_2$ corresponds to an assertion of $S_1$. To see that presupposition is not sufficient, consider the following sentences. The second conjunct in each of the starred sentences corresponds to a presupposition of the first conjunct, while in the acceptable sentences there is an assertion relationship.

*John deprived the mice of food and the frogs didn't get any either*
*\*John deprived the mice of food and the frogs didn't want any either*
*John forced the rat to run a maze and the lizard did it too*
*\*John forced the rat to run a maze and the lizard didn't want to either*
*Mary's refusal flabbergasted Ron, and he was surprised at Betty's refusal too*
*\*Mary's refusal flabbergasted Ron and Betty refused too*

### 3. A HYPOTHESIS

So far, we have presented a set of syntactic-semantic correlations without considering how they might be accounted for. We shall continue by analyzing these facts and others to be pointed out in the course of the discussion, in terms of a tentative explanatory hypothesis, by which the semantic difference between the factive and non-factive complement paradigms can be related to their syntactic differences, and most of the syntactic characteristics of each paradigm can be explained. The hypothesis which we should like to introduce is that presupposition of complements is reflected in their syntactic deep structure. Specifically, we shall explore the possibility that factive and non-factive complements at a deeper level of representation differ as follows:[7]

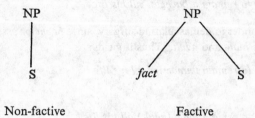

Non-factive                               Factive

[7] It is not quite as simple as this. Consider, for one thing, the sentences:

> John's eating them would amaze me
> I would like John's doing so

These sentences do not at all presuppose that the proposition in the complement is true. This indicates a further complexity of the FACT postulated in the deep structure of factive complements. Like verbs, or predicates in general, it appears to take various tenses or moods. Note that these correspond to the above sentences:

> If he were to eat them it would amaze me
> I would like it if John were to do so

These can also be constructed as

> If it were a fact that he ate them it would amaze me

A second over-simplification may be our assumption that sentences are embedded in their deep structure form. A case can be made for rejecting this customary approach in favor of one where different verbs take complements at different levels of representation. Consider direct quotation, which appears not to have been treated in generative grammar. The fundamental fact is that what one quotes are surface structures and not deep structures. That is, if John's words were 'Mary saw Bill', then we can correctly report

> John said: 'Mary saw Bill'

but we shall have misquoted him if we say

> John said: 'Bill was seen by Mary'

If we set up the deep structure of both sentences simply as

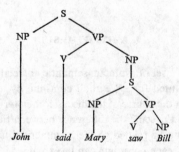

then we have not taken account of this fact. We should be forced to add to this deep structure the

If this interpretation is correct, then closest to the factive deep structure are sentences of the type

> *I regret the fact that John is ill*

The forms in the factive paradigm are derived by two optional transformations: formation of gerunds from *that*-clauses in position after nouns, and deletion of the head noun *fact*. (We do not pause to consider the general rules which take care of the details involving *that* and *of*.) By gerund-formation alone we get

> *I regret the fact of John's being ill*

---

specification that the complement either must or cannot undergo the passive, depending on which of the sentences we are quoting. Since sentences of any complexity can be quoted, to whose deep structures the passive and other optional transformations may be applicable an indefinite number of times, it is not enough simply to mark the embedded deep structure of the quoted sentence as a whole for applicability of transformations. What has to be indicated according to this solution is the whole transformational history of the quoted sentence.

A more natural alternative is to let the surface structure itself of the quoted sentence be embedded. This would be the case in general for verbs taking direct quotes. Other classes of verbs would take their complements in different form. We then notice that the initial form of a complement can in general be selected at a linguistically functional level of representation in such a way that the truth value of the whole sentence will not be altered by any rules which are applicable to the complement. Assuming a generative semantics, the complements of verbs of knowing and believing are then semantic representations. From

> *John thinks that the McCavitys are a quarrelsome bunch of people*

it follows that

> *John thinks that the McCavitys like to pick a fight*

That is, one believes propositions and not sentences. Believing a proposition in fact commits one to believing what it implies: if you believe that Mary cleaned the room you must believe that the room was cleaned. (Verbs like *regret*, although their objects are also propositions, differ in this respect. If you regret that Mary cleaned the room you do not necessarily regret that the room was cleaned).

At the other extreme would be cases of phonological complementation, illustrated by the context

> *John went '..........'*

The object here must be some actual noise or a conventional rendering thereof such as *ouch* or *plop*.

A good many verbs can take complements at several levels. A verb like *scream*, which basically takes phonological complements, can be promoted to take direct quotes. *Say* seems to take both of these and propositions as well.

Are there verbs which require their complement sentences to be inserted in deep structure form (in the sense of Chomsky)? Such a verb $X$ would have the property that

> *John Xed that Bill entered the house*

would imply that

> *John Xed that the house was entered by Bill*

but would not imply that

> *John Xed that Bill went into the house.*

That is, the truth value of the sentence would be preserved if the object clause underwent a different set of optional transformations, but not if it was replaced by a paraphrase with another deep structure source. It is an interesting question whether such verbs exist. We have not been able to find any. Unless further search turns up verbs of this kind, we shall have to conclude that, if the general idea proposed here is valid, the levels of semantics, surface structure, and phonology, but not the level of deep structure, can function as the initial representation of complements.

*Fact*-deletion can apply to this derived structure, giving

> *I regret John's being ill*

If *fact*-deletion applies directly to the basic form, then the simple *that*-clause is formed:

> *I regret that John is ill*

Although this last factive sentence has the same superficial form as the non-factive

> *I believe that John is ill*

according to our analysis it differs radically from it in syntactic form, and the two sentences have different deep structures as diagrammed above. Simple *that*-clauses are ambiguous and constitute the point of overlap (neutralization) of the factive and non-factive paradigms.

If factive clauses have the deep structures proposed by us, these various surface forms in which factive clauses can appear become very easy to derive. That is one piece of support for our hypothesis. The remaining evidence can be grouped under three general headings:

(1) syntactic insulation of factive clauses (Section 4)
(2) indifferent and ambiguous predicates (Section 5)
(3) pronominalization (Section 6)

### 4. SYNTACTIC INSULATION OF FACTIVE CLAUSES

Let us first return in somewhat more detail to infinitive constructions, examining first the derivation of infinitives in general and then of the class of infinitive constructions which we mentioned as being characteristic of non-factive predicates. Basic to our treatment of infinitives is the assumption that non-finite verb forms in all languages are the basic, unmarked forms. Finite verbs, then, are always the result of person and number agreement between subject and verb, and non-finite verbs, in particular

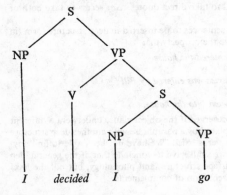
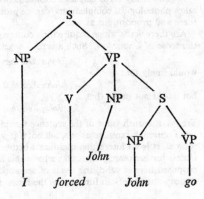

infinitives, come about when agreement does not apply. Infinitives arise regularly when the subject of an embedded sentence is removed by a transformation, or else placed into an oblique case, so that in either case agreement between subject and verb cannot take place. There are several ways in which the subject of an embedded sentence can be removed by a transformation. It can be deleted under identity with a noun phrase in the containing sentence, as in sentences like *I decided to go* and *I forced John to go* (cf., Rosenbaum, 1967).

After prepositions, infinitives are automatically converted to gerunds, *e.g.*, *I decided to go vs. I decided on going*; or *I forced John to do it vs. I forced John into doing it*. These infinitival gerunds should not be confused with the factive gerunds, with which they have in common nothing but their surface form.

A second way in which the subject of an embedded sentence can be removed by a transformation to yield infinitives is through raising of the subject of the embedded sentence into the containing sentence. The remaining verb phrase of the embedded sentence is then automatically left in infinitive form. This subject-raising transformation applies only to non-factive complements, and yields the accusative and infinitive, and nominative and infinitive constructions:

> *He believes Bacon to be the real author*
> *This seems to be Hoyle's best book*

The operation of the subject-raising rule in object clauses can be diagrammed as follows:

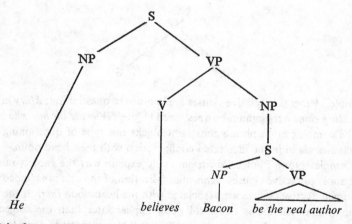

The italicized noun phrase is raised into the upper sentence and becomes the surface object of its verb.[8]

---

[8] This subject-raising rule has figured in recent work under at least three names: pronoun replacement (Rosenbaum 1967); expletive replacement (Langendoen 1966); and *it*-replacement (Ross 1967). Unfortunately we have had to invent still another, for none of the current names fit the rule as we have reformulated it.

We reject, then, as unsuccessful the traditional efforts to derive the uses of the infinitive from its being 'partly a noun, partly a verb', or, perhaps, from some 'basic meaning' supposedly shared by all occurrences of infinitives. We reject, also, the assumption of recent transformational work (*cf.*, Rosenbaum, 1967) that all infinitives are "*for-to*" constructions, and that they arise from a "complementizer placement" rule which inserts *for* and *to* before clauses on the basis of an arbitrary marking on their verbs. Instead, we claim that what infinitives share is only the single, relatively low-level syntactic property of having no surface subject.

Assuming that the subject-raising rule is the source of one particular type of infinitive complements, we return to the fact, mentioned earlier, that factive complements never yield these infinitive complements. We now press for an explanation. Why can one not say

> *He regrets Bacon to be the real author*
> *This makes sense to be Hoyle's best book*

although the corresponding *that*-clauses are perfectly acceptable? It is highly unlikely that this could be explained directly by the SEMANTIC fact that these sentences are constructed with factive predicates. However, the deep structure which we have posited for factive complements makes a syntactic explanation possible.

Ross (1967) has found that transformations are subject to a general constraint, termed by him the Complex Noun Phrase Constraint, which blocks them from taking constituents out of a sentence $S$ in the configuration

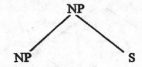

For example, elements in relative clauses are immune to questioning: *Mary* in *The boy who saw Mary came back* cannot be questioned to give *Who did the boy who saw come back?* The complex noun phrase constraint blocks this type of questioning because relative clauses stand in the illustrated configuration with their head noun.

This Complex Noun Phrase Constraint could explain why the subject-raising rule does not apply to factive clauses. This misapplication of the rule is excluded if, as we have assumed, factive clauses are associated with the head noun *fact*. If the optional transformation which drops this head noun applies later than the subject-raising transformation (and nothing seems to contradict that assumption), then the subjects of factive clauses cannot be raised. No special modification of the subject-raising rule is necessary to account for the limitation of infinitive complements to non-factive predicates.

Another movement transformation which is blocked in factive structures in the same way is NEG-raising (Klima, 1964), a rule which optionally moves the element

NEG(ATIVE) from an embedded sentence into the containing sentence, converting for example the sentences

*It's likely that he won't lift a finger until it's too late*
*I believe that he can't help doing things like that*

into the synonymous sentences

*It's not likely that he will lift a finger until it's too late*
*I don't believe that he can help doing things like that*

Since *lift a finger*, punctual *until*, and *can help* occur only in negative sentences, sentences like these prove that a rule of NEG-raising is necessary.

This rule of NEG-raising never applies in the factive cases. We do not get, for example:

*\*It doesn't bother me that he will lift a finger until it's too late*

from

*It bothers me that he won't lift a finger until it's too late*

or

*\*I don't regret that he can help doing things like that*

from

*I regret that he can't help doing things like that*

Given the factive deep structure which we have proposed, the absence of such sentences is explained by the complex noun phrase constraint, which exempts structures having the formal properties of these factive deep structures from undergoing movement transformations.[9]

Factivity also erects a barrier against insertions. It has often been noticed that subordinate clauses in German are not in the subjunctive mood if the truth of the clause is presupposed by the speaker, and that sequence of tenses in English and French also depends partly on this condition. The facts are rather complicated, and to formulate them one must distinguish several functions of the present tense and bring in other conditions which interact with sequence of tenses and subjunctive insertion. But it is sufficient for our purposes to look at minimal pairs which show that one of the elements involved in this phenomenon is factivity. Let us assume that Bill takes it for granted that the earth is round. Then Bill might say:

[9] We thought earlier that the oddity of questioning and relativization in some factive clauses was also due to the Complex Noun Phrase Constraint:

*\*How old is it strange than John is?*
*\*I climbed the mountain which it is interesting that Goethe tried to climb.*

Leroy Baker (1967) has shown that this idea was wrong, and that the oddity here is not due to the Complex Noun Phrase Constraint. Baker has been able to find a semantic formulation of the restriction on questioning which is fairly general and accurate. It appears now that questioning and relativization are rules which follow *fact*-deletion.

*John claimed that the earth was (\*is) flat*

with obligatory sequence of tenses, but

*John grasped that the earth is (was) round*

with optional sequence of tenses. The rule which changes a certain type of present tense into a past tense in an embedded sentence if the containing sentence is past, is obligatory in non-factives but optional in factives. The German subjunctive rule is one notch weaker; it is optional in non-factives and inapplicable in factives:

*Er behauptet, dass die Erde flach sei (ist)*
*Er versteht, dass die Erde rund ist (\*sei)*

The reason why these changes are in part optional is not clear. The exact way in which they are limited by factivity cannot be determined without a far more detailed investigation of the facts than we have been able to undertake. Nevertheless, it is fairly likely that factivity will play a role in an eventual explanation of these phenomena.[10]

## 5. INDIFFERENT AND AMBIGUOUS PREDICATES

So far, for clarity of exposition, only predicates which are either factive or non-factive have been examined. For this set of cases, the factive and non-factive complement paradigms are in complementary distribution. But there are numerous predicates that take complements of both types. This is analogous to the fact that there are not only verbs which take concrete objects and verbs which take abstract objects but also verbs which take either kind. For example, *hit* requires concrete objects (*boy, table*), *clarify* requires abstract objects (*ideas, fact*), and *like* occurs indifferently with both. Just so we find verbs which occur indifferently with factive and non-factive complements, *e.g., anticipate, acknowledge, suspect, report, remember, emphasize, announce, admit, deduce.* Such verbs have no specification in the lexicon as to whether their complements are factive. On a deeper level, their semantic representations include no specifications as to whether their complement sentences represent presuppositions by the

---

[10] This may be related to the fact that (factive) present gerunds can refer to a past state, but (non-factive) present infinitives can not. Thus,

*They resented his being away*

is ambiguous as to the time reference of the gerund, and on one prong of the ambiguity is synonymous with

*They resented his having been away.*

But in

*They supposed him to be away*

the infinitive can only be understood as contemporaneous with the main verb, and the sentence can never be interpreted as synonymous with

*They supposed him to have been away.*

speaker or not. Syntactically, these predicates participate in both complement paradigms.

It is striking evidence for our analysis that they provide minimal pairs for the subtle meaning difference between factive and non-factive complements. Compare, for example, the two sentences

*They reported the enemy to have suffered a decisive defeat*
*They reported the enemy's having suffered a decisive defeat*

The second implies that the report was true in the speaker's opinion, while the first leaves open the possibility that the report was false. This is explained by our derivation of infinitives from non-factives and gerunds from factives. Similarly compare

*I remembered him to be bald (so I was surprised to see him with long hair)*
*I remembered his being bald (so I brought along a wig and disguised him)*

Contrast *forget*, which differs from *remember* in that it necessarily presupposes the truth of its object. Although it is logically just as possible to forget a false notion as it is to remember one, language seems to allow for expressing only the latter. We cannot say

*\*I forgot that he was bald, which was a good thing since it turned out later that he wasn't after all*
*\*I forgot him to be bald*

There is another kind of case. Just as different meanings may accompany subjects or objects differing by a feature like concreteness, as in

*The boy struck₁ me*
*The idea struck₂ me*

so verbs may occur with factive and non-factive complements in different meanings. Compare

(a)  *I explained Adam's refusing to come to the phone*
(b)  *I explained that he was watching his favorite TV show*

In (a), the subordinate clause refers to a proposition regarded as a fact. *Explain*, in this case, means 'give reasons for'. When the object is a *that*-clause, as in (b), it can be read as non-factive, with *explain that S* understood as meaning 'say that S to explain X'. To account for the differences between (a) and (b), we might postulate two lexical entries for *explain* (not denying that they are related). In the entry appropriate to (a) there would be a presupposition that the subordinated proposition is true. This would require a factive complement (recall that the form of the complement has an associated interpretation) in the same way as the two verbs *strike₁* and *strike₂* would receive different kinds of subjects. The entry for (b) would have among its presuppositions that the speaker was not committing himself about the truth of the subordinated proposition, so that a factive complement would not fit. Thus, the meaning of the complement form is directly involved in explaining its occurrence with particular verbs.

## 6. PRONOMINALIZATION

The pronoun *it* serves as an optional reduction of *the fact*. It can stand directly before *that*-clauses in sentences with factive verbs:

> *Bill resents it that people are always comparing him to Mozart*
> *They didn't mind it that a crowd was beginning to gather in the street*

Although the difference is a delicate one, and not always clear cut, most speakers find *it* unacceptable in the comparable non-factive cases:

> *\*Bill claims it that people are always comparing him to Mozart*
> *\*They supposed it that a crowd was beginning to gather in the street*

This *it*, a reduced form of *the fact*, should be distinguished from the expletive *it*, a semantically empty prop which is automatically introduced in the place of extraposed complements in sentences like

> *It seems that both queens are trying to wriggle out of their commitments*
> *It is obvious that Muriel has lost her marbles*

Rosenbaum (1967) tried to identify the two and to derive both from an *it* which he postulated in the deep structure of all noun clauses. This was in our opinion a mistake. In the first place, the two *it*'s have different distributions. Expletive *it* comes in regardless of whether a factive or non-factive clause is extra-posed, and does not appear to be related to the lexical noun *fact*, as factive *it* is.

The relationship of factive *it* to the lexical noun *fact*, and its distinction from expletive *it*, is brought out rather clearly by a number of transformational processes. For example, the presence of factive *it* blocks the formation of relative clauses just as the lexical noun *fact* does:

> *\*This is the book which you reported it that John plagiarized*
> *\*This is the book which you reported the fact that John plagiarized*
> *This is the book which you reported that John plagiarized*

But expletive *it* differs in permitting relativization:

> *That's the one thing which it is obvious that he hadn't expected*
> *\*That's the one thing which the fact is obvious that he hadn't expected*

As Ross (1966) has shown, facts like these create seemingly insoluble problems for a system like Rosenbaum's, in which factive and expletive *it* are derived from the same source. We have not proposed an alternative in anything like sufficient detail, but it is fairly clear that a system of rules constructed along the general lines informally sketched out here, which makes exactly the required syntactic distinction, will not have inherent difficulties in dealing with these facts.

Direct comparison of factive *it* and expletive *it* shows the expected semantic difference. The comparison can be carried out with the verbs which are indifferent as to factivity:

> *I had expected that there would be a big turnout (but only three people came)*
> *I had expected it that there would be a big turnout (but this is ridiculous — get more chairs)*

The second sentence, with *it*, suggests that the expectation was fulfilled, whereas the first is neutral in that respect. On the other hand, expletive *it* adds no factive meaning, and the following sentence is ambiguous as between the factive and non-factive interpretation:

> *It was expected that there would be a big turnout*

This analysis makes the prediction that cases of *it* which cannot be derived from *fact* will present no obstacle to relativization. This is indeed the case:

> *Goldbach's conjecture, which I take it that you all know ...*
> *The report, which I will personally see to it that you get first thing in the morning ...*
> *This secret, which I would hate it if anyone ever revealed ...*

On the other hand, it is not too clear where these *it*'s do come from. Perhaps their source is the "vacuous extraposition" postulated by Rosenbaum (1967).[11]

The deep structures which we have posited for the two types of complements also explain the way in which they get pronominalized. In general, both factive and non-factive clauses take the pro-form *it*:

> *John supposed that Bill had done it, and Mary supposed it, too*
> *John regretted that Bill had done it, and Mary regretted it, too*

But the two differ in that only non-factive clauses are pronominalized by *so*:

> *John supposed that Bill had done it, and Mary supposed so, too*
> *\*John regretted that Bill had done it, and Mary regretted so, too*

These facts can be explained on the basis of the fairly plausible assumptions that *it* is the pro-form of noun phrases, and *so* is the pro-form of sentences. Referring back to the deep structures given in Section 3, we see that the only node which exhaustively dominates factive complements is the node NP. For this reason the only-pro-form for them is the pro-form for noun phrases, namely, *it*. But non-factive complements are exhaustively dominated by two nodes: NP and S. Accordingly, two pro-forms are available: the pro-form for noun phrases, *it*, and the pro-form for sentences, *so*.

---

[11] Dean (1967) has presented evidence from German and English that extraposition is the general source of expletive pronouns.

We have dealt with the syntactic repercussions of factivity in sentential complementation. This is really an artificially delimited topic (as almost all topics in linguistics necessarily are). Factivity is relevant to much else in syntax besides sentential complementation, and on the other hand, the structure of sentential complementation is naturally governed by different semantic factors which interact with factivity. That is one source of the painful gaps in the above presentation which the reader will surely have noticed. We conclude by listing summarily a couple of possible additional applications of factivity, and some additional semantic factors which determine the form of complements, in order at least to hint at some ways in which the gaps can be filled, and to suggest what seem to us promising extensions of the approach we have taken.

(1) There is a syntactic and semantic correspondence between TRUTH and SPECIFIC REFERENCE. The verbs which presuppose that their sentential object expresses a true proposition also presuppose that their non-sentential object refers to a specific thing. For example, in the sentences

> *I ignored an ant on my plate*
> *I imagined an ant on my plate*

the factive verb *ignore* presupposes that there was an ant on my plate, but the nonfactive verb *imagine* does not. Perhaps this indicates that at some sufficiently abstract level of semantics, truth and specific reference are reducible to the same concept. Frege's speculations that the reference of a sentence is its truth value would thereby receive some confirmation.

Another indication that there is a correspondence between truth of propositions and specific reference of noun phrases is the following. We noted in Section 1 that extraposition is obligatory for non-factive subject complements. Compare

> *That John has come makes sense* (factive)
> *\*That John has come seems* (non-factive)

where the second sentence must become

> *It seems that John has come*

unless it undergoes subject-raising. This circumstance appears to reflect a more general tendency for sentence-initial clauses to get understood factively. For example, in saying

> *The UPI reported that Smith had arrived*
> *It was reported by the UPI that Smith had arrived*

the speaker takes no stand on the truth of the report. But

> *That Smith had arrived was reported by the UPI*

normally conveys the meaning that the speaker assumes the report to be true. A non-factive interpretation of this sentence can be teased out in various ways, for example by laying contrastive stress on the agent phrase (*by the UPI, not the AP*). Still, the unforced sense is definitely factive. These examples are interesting because they suggest that the factive *vs.* non-factive senses of the complement do not really correspond to the application of any particular transformation, but rather to the position of the complement in the surface structure. The interpretation can be non-factive if both passive and extraposition have applied, or if neither of them has applied; if only the passive has applied, we get the factive interpretation. This is very hard to state in terms of a condition on transformations. It is much easier to say that the initial position itself of a clause is in such cases associated with a factive sense.

This is which the parallelism between truth and specific reference comes in. The problem with the well-known pairs like

> *Everyone in this room speaks two languages*
> *Two languages are spoken by everyone in this room*

is exactly that indefinite noun phrases such as *two languages* are understood as referring to specific objects when placed initially ('there are two languages such that ...'). Again, it is not on the passive itself that the meaning depends. In the sentence

> *Two languages are familiar to everyone in this room*

the passive has not applied, but *two languages* is again understood as specific because of its initial position.

(2) We also expect that factivity will clarify the structure of other types of subordinate clauses. We have in mind the difference between purpose clauses (non-factive) and result clauses (factive), and different types of conditional and concessive clauses.

(3) There are languages which distinguish factive and non-factive moods in declarative sentences. For example, in Hidatsa (Matthews, 1964) there is a factive mood whose use in a sentence implies that the speaker is certain that the sentence is true, and a range of other moods indicating hearsay, doubt, and other judgments of the speaker about the sentence. While this distinction is not overt in English, it seems to us that it may be sensed in an ambiguity of declarative sentences. Consider the statement

> *He's an idiot*

There is an ambiguity here which may be resolved in several ways. For example, the common question

> *Is that a fact or is that just your opinion?*

(presumably unnecessary in Hidatsa) is directed exactly at disambiguating the statement. The corresponding *why*-question

> *Why is he an idiot?*

may be answered in two different ways, *e.g.,*

(a) *Because his brain lacks oxygen*
(b) *Because he failed this simple test for the third time*

There are thus really two kinds of *why*-questions: requests for EXPLANATION, which presuppose the truth of the underlying sentence, and requests for EVIDENCE, which do not. The two may be paraphrased

(a) *Why is it a fact that he is an idiot?*
(b) *Why do you think that he is an idiot?*

### 8. EMOTIVES

In the above discussion we rejected Rosenbaum's derivation of infinitive complements like

> *I believe John to have liked Anselm*
> *I forced John to say* cheese

from hypothetical underlying forms with *for–to*

> *\*I believe for John to have liked Anselm*
> *\*I forced John for John to say* cheese

This leaves us with the onus of explaining the *for–to* complements which actually occur on the surface:

> *It bothers me for John to have hallucinations*
> *I regret for you to be in this fix*

But once the spurious *for–to*'s are stripped away, it becomes clear that the remaining real cases occur with a semantically natural class of predicates. Across the distinction of factivity there cuts orthogonally another semantic distinction, which we term EMOTIVITY. Emotive complements are those to which the speaker expresses a subjective, emotional, or evaluative reaction. The class of predicates taking emotive complements includes the verbs of emotion of classical grammar, and Klima's affective predicates (Klima, 1964), but is larger than either and includes in general all predicates which express the subjective value of a proposition rather than knowledge about it or its truth value. It is this class of predicates to which *for–to* complements are limited. The following list illustrates the wide range of meanings to be found and shows the cross-classification of emotivity and factivity.

| Factive examples | Emotive | Nonemotive |
|---|---|---|
| Subject Clauses | important | well-known |
| | crazy | clear |
| | odd | (self-evident) |

|                    | *Emotive*            | *Nonemotive*         |
|--------------------|----------------------|----------------------|
| *Subject Clauses*  | relevant             | goes without saying  |
|                    | instructive          |                      |
|                    | sad                  |                      |
|                    | suffice              |                      |
|                    | bother               |                      |
|                    | alarm                |                      |
|                    | fascinate            |                      |
|                    | nauseate             |                      |
|                    | exhilarate           |                      |
|                    | defy comment         |                      |
|                    | surpass belief       |                      |
|                    | a tragedy            |                      |
|                    | no laughing matter   |                      |
| *Object Clauses*   | regret               | be aware (of)        |
|                    | resent               | bear in mind         |
|                    | deplore              | make clear           |
|                    |                      | forget               |
|                    |                      | take into account    |

*Non-factive examples*

|                    | *Emotive*            | *Nonemotive*         |
|--------------------|----------------------|----------------------|
| *Subject Clauses*  | improbable           | probable             |
|                    | unlikely             | likely               |
|                    | a pipedream          | turn out             |
|                    | nonsense             | seem                 |
| *future* { | urgent            | imminent             |
|          { | vital             | in the works         |
| *Object Clauses* *future* { | intend   | predict              |
|          { | prefer            | anticipate           |
|          { | reluctant         | foresee              |
|          { | anxious           |                      |
|          { | willing           |                      |
|          { | eager             |                      |
|                    |                      | say                  |
|                    |                      | suppose              |
|                    |                      | conclude             |

We have proposed that infinitives are derived in complements whose verbs fail to undergo agreement with a subject. In the infinitives mentioned in Section 4, agreement did not take place because the subject was in one or another way eliminated by a transformation. There is a second possible reason for non-agreement. This is that the subject is marked with an oblique case. There seem to be no instances, at least in the Indo-European languages, of verbs agreeing in person and number with anything else than nominative noun phrases. Good illustrations of this point are the German pairs

*Ich werde betrogen* (I am cheated)
*Mir wird geschmeichelt* (I am flattered)
*Ich bin leicht zu betrügen* (I am easy to cheat)
*Mir ist leicht zu schmeicheln* (I am easy to flatter)

Presumably the same syntactic processes underlie both sentences in each pair. The accusative object of *betrügen* is changed into a nominative, whereas the dative object of *schmeicheln* stays in the dative. But from the viewpoint of agreement, only the nominative counts as a surface subject.

As the source of *for* with the infinitive we assume a transformation which marks the subjects in complements of emotive predicates with *for*, the non-finite verb form being a consequence of the oblique case of the subject.

We can here only list quickly some of the other syntactic properties which emotivity is connected to, giving an unfortunately oversimplified picture of a series of extremely complex and difficult problems. What follows are only suggestive remarks which we plan to pursue at a later time.

First of all, emotives may optionally contain the subjunctive marker *should*:

*It's interesting that you should have said so*
*\*It's well-known that you should have said so*

(We do not of course mean the *should* of obligation or the *should* of future expectation, which are not limited to emotives).

We assume that a future *should* is optionally deleted by a late rule, leaving a bare infinitive:

*I'm anxious that he (should) be found*
*It's urgent that he (should) be found*

Emotive complements can be identified by their ability to contain a class of exclamatory degree adverbs such as *at all* or (unstressed) *so, such*:

*It's interesting that he came at all*
*\*It's well-known that he came at all*

Finally, it seems that one of the conditions which must be placed on relativization by *as* is that the clause be non-emotive although many other factors are certainly involved:

*\*As is interesting, John is in India*
*As is well-known, John is in India*

Syntactic-semantic interrelationships of this kind form the basis of a system of deep structures and rules which account for the complement system of English, and other languages as well. The importance of a system successfully worked out along the general lines suggested above would lie in its ability to account not only for the syntactic structure of sentential complementation, but also for its semantic structure, and for the relationship between the two. Our analysis of presupposition in the complement system contributes a substantial instance of the relation between syntax and semantics, and enables us to correct an error which has been made in most past work on transformational syntax. The error is that different types of complements (*that*-clauses, gerunds, infinitives) have all been assumed to have the same deep structure, and hence to be semantically equivalent.[12] We have seen that there is good reason to posit a number of different base structures, each mapped by transformations into a syntactic paradigm of semantically equivalent surface structures. The base structures differ semantically along at least two independent dimensions, which express the judgment of the speaker about the content of the complement sentence.

This approach to a theory of complementation is not only more adequate from a semantic point of view. Its purely syntactic advantages are equally significant. It eliminates the need for marking each verb for compatibility with each surface complement type, that is, for treating complementation as basically irregular and unpredictable. We account for the selection of complement types quite naturally by our proposal that there are several meaningful base structures, whose choice is in large part predictable from the meaning of each predicate. These base structures are subject to various transformations which yield surface structures in which the relation between form and meaning is considerably obscured.

REFERENCES

Baker, Leroy,
    1967   "A Class of Semantically Deviant Questions" (unpublished).
Dean, Janet
    1967   "Noun Phrase Complementation in English and German" (unpublished).
Klima, Edward S.,
    1964   "Negation in English", in: Fodor and Katz, eds., *The Structure of Language* (Englewood Cliffs, N.J., Prentice-Hall).
Langendoen, D.T.,
    1966   "The Syntax of the English Expletive 'IT'", *Georgetown University Monograph Series on Languages and Linguistics*, No. 19: 207-216.
Lees, Robert B.,
    1960   *The Grammar of English Nominalizations* (The Hague, Mouton).

[12] The studies of Lees (1960) and Vendler (1964), however, contain many interesting semantic observations on sentential complementation and nominalization which still await formal description and explanation.

Matthews, G. H.,
   1964   *Hidatsa Syntax* (The Hague, Mouton).
Rosenbaum, P. S.,
   1967   *The Grammar of English Predicate Complement Constructions* (Cambridge, Mass., M.I.T.-
          Press).
Ross, John Robert
   1966   "Relativization in Extraposed Clauses (A Problem which Evidence is Presented that Help is
          Needed to Solve)" ($=$ *Mathematical Linguistics and Automatic Translation*, Report No. NSF-
          17 to the National Science Foundation, Harvard University, Computation Laboratory).
   1967   "Constraints on Variables in Syntax" (Unpublished dissertation, M.I.T.).
Vendler, Zeno,
   1964   "Nominalizations" (Mimeographed, University of Pennsylvania).

QUESTIONS

Question 1. Why is (i) a very strange sentence?

(i) *That fact is true.

Where is the problem? Consider Kiparsky and Kiparsky's first test for factives (the possibility of having *the fact that S*). Could we simply use the test *the fact* instead of *the fact that S*? Do all factives with sentential subjects allow *the fact that S*? Give examples.

*Question 2. Why are gerundial constructions and adjectival nominalizations in *-ness* incompatible with nonfactive predicates? Do all factives with sentential subjects allow these two constructions? Note that part of the problem is that nonfactive predicates more often require that their complements be Ss rather than simple NPs. Thus we have (i), but not (ii).

(i) Disasters are tragic.
(ii) *Disasters seem.

Some nonfactive predicates taking object complements take NP complements more easily than those taking subject complements, and do in fact allow some of the test NPs offered by the Kiparskys.

(iii) She imagined the whiteness of the whale.
(iv) She imagined his being found guilty.

Of course, the reading of *imagine* in Ss like (iii) and (iv) is more 'conjure up the image' than 'assume' or 'think'.
But in the main, the observation of Kiparsky and Kiparsky is correct and needs to be explained. One might reconsider their observation in the light of their Section 7.1.

*Question 3. Consider (i) and (ii).

(i) It seems that there has been a snowstorm.
(ii) There seems to have been a snowstorm.

What rule yields (ii)? Kiparsky and Kiparsky assume that (ii) derives directly from (i), rather than that (i) and (ii) are both derived from the same underlying source by the application of different rules. Do they give any evidence for this assumption? Can you think of any? Will any problems arise if we do not make this assumption?
How do the following data provide an argument for the rule the Kiparskys assume, Raising into Subject Position?

(iii) John seems to be liked by everyone.
(iv) Everyone seems to like John.

Note that (iii) and (iv) are synonymous. (Your discussion of (i) through (iv) should make you recall Perlmutter's article in this same volume.)

Question 4. Kiparsky and Kiparsky give three tests for factive/nonfactive predicates which can take sentential objects. Using these three tests, classify the following predicates as factive or nonfactive: *admire*, *expect*, and *think*.

Question 5. Consider (i).

(i) Terry has stopped beating her husband.

What are its presuppositions? What does it assert? Use the Kiparskys' two syntactic tests (negation and questioning) to determine the presuppositions.

Question 6. Consider Kiparsky and Kiparsky's example, repeated here, with their tree:

(i) Mary didn't kiss John.

(ii)

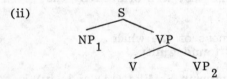

They give four readings for this sentence, differing by the placement of the negative. Give each reading and tell which major constituent is negated in each reading.

Question 7. The sentence (i) has a fifth reading besides the four corresponding to the negation of each major constituent in the apparent structure. The five readings are given in (ii) through (vi).

(i) Mary didn't clean the room.
(ii) Someone may have cleaned the room, but it wasn't Mary.
(iii) Mary may have done something, but not clean the room.
(iv) Mary may have cleaned something, but not the room.
(v) Mary may have done something to the room, but not clean it.
(vi) Mary may have performed the action of cleaning the room, but she didn't succeed in getting the room clean.

Where does the reading in (vi) come from? (Consider Kiparsky and Kiparsky's redundancy rule on the assertions of a 'cause' sentence.) Give proper intonation contours for each of the five readings.

Question 8. What is DeMorgan's Law with respect to $\sim(A \wedge B)$ (where "$\sim$" means 'not' and "$\wedge$" means 'and')? Give two synonymous example Ss corresponding to $\sim(A \wedge B)$ and $\sim A \vee \sim B$ (where "$\vee$" means 'or'), and give two more for $\sim(A \vee B)$ and $\sim A \wedge \sim B$.

Question 9. If an imperative sentence such as (i) indicates (ii), then what are the two propositions I want when I say (iii)? (See the Kiparskys' causative redundancy rule.)

(i) Chase that thief!
(ii) I want you to chase that thief.
(iii) Point it out to 006 that the transmitter will function poorly in a cave!

*Question 10. What semantic (syntactic?) property do negation, questioning, and imperatives, as syntactic operations, share?

**Question 11. The Kiparskys say that WH questions carry a positive presupposition, so that (i) presupposes (ii).

(i) Who wants the last cookie?
(ii) Someone wants the last cookie.

If this were the case, a negative answer to the question ('Nobody') should be a denial of the presupposition. However, there are WH questions (like (iii)) which seem to presuppose that their answer will be negative and to which a positive reply (like (v)) is felt to be a presupposition denial.

(iii) Who would ever want to marry him?
(iv) Nobody would ever want to marry him.
(v) I would.

How can Kiparsky and Kiparsky's assumptions about WH questions be revised to take such examples into account?

Question 12. The Kiparskys say that (i) neither asserts nor presupposes (ii).

(i) John appears to regret evicting his grandmother.
(ii) John regrets evicting his grandmother.

Give a sentence that asserts (ii) but does not presuppose (ii), and another that presupposes (ii) but does not assert (ii). Is it possible to have a sentence that both presupposes and asserts (ii)?

Question 13. What is the presupposition in (i)? What is the assertion?

(i) She regrets having left home.

Do (ii) through (iv) share (i)'s presupposition? Do they share (i)'s assertion?

(ii) I wonder if she regrets having left home.
(iii) If she regrets having left home, she isn't admitting it.
(iv) John says it's significant that she regrets having left home.

Question 14. What is contrasted in the structure '$S_1$ and $S_2$, too'? Give examples parallel to those the Kiparskys give.

Question 15. What is the syntactic difference that the Kiparskys propose to parallel (i.e. reflect) the presuppositional difference between factives and nonfactives?

Question 16. Footnote 7 raises two interesting if peripheral problems with which all studies of the truth value of related sentences must deal. One is the problem of quotation and opacity; the other is conditional sentences. Both arise when it is unclear how much responsibility the speaker will take for the content of the sentence. In the second clause of (i), is it presupposed that I have offended you?

(i) If I have offended you, I regret $\begin{Bmatrix} \text{having done so} \\ \text{that fact} \end{Bmatrix}$.

*Question 17. Kiparsky and Kiparsky claim that *the fact that S* and *that S* mean the same thing when used as the complement of factive predicates. Consider examples (i) and (ii).

(i) He confessed the fact that he had known her.
(ii) He confessed that he had known her.

Could both or either of them be followed by (iii)?

(iii) But it was a false confession.

Compare (i) and (ii) to (iv) and (v).

(iv) He admitted the fact that he had known her.
(v) He admitted that he had known her.

If you find any difference in meaning between these two pairs, discuss that difference as precisely as you can. (You will probably want to talk about presuppositions.) What significance do differences like these have for Kiparsky and Kiparsky's proposal? (These examples are due, with slight modification, to Bolinger 1976.)

*Question 18. What is the Complex NP Constraint (CNPC)? How could the CNPC block Raising into Subject Position and Raising into Object Position from factive complements but not from nonfactive ones? After reading the discussion of intrinsic and extrinsic ordering in the questions on Berman's article in this volume, recall that Kiparsky and Kiparsky require that raising of embedded subjects and negatives precede *fact* deletion. Is this intrinsic or extrinsic ordering?

Question 19. What is Neg-raising? (See Lakoff's article in this volume.) How is it blocked from factive complements? The Kiparskys mention 'punctual' *until*. Give an example of a non-punctual *until*.

**Question 20. Rosenbaum (1967) proposes that Extraposition may apply vacuously by changing the constituency of a sentence final sentential constituent without changing its linear position. Thus he would claim that in (i) the *it* arises because the sentential complement following it has been 'extraposed' to be a constituent of the VP, as in (ii).

(i) Bill resents it that people are always comparing him to Mozart.

(ii)

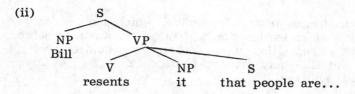

Kiparsky and Kiparsky claim that this *it* is reduced from *the fact* and is not an expletive *it* (i.e. it is not the result of Extraposition). Thus they give (i) the structure in (iii).

(iii)

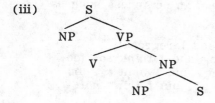

How are the following Ss relevant to choosing between the two proposed structures?

   (iv) Bill resents the fact that Sue left and the fact that John didn't.
   (v) *Bill resents it that Sue left and it that John didn't.
   (vi) Bill resents the fact that Sue left and John didn't.
   (vii) Bill resents it that Sue left and John didn't.

Try to give other evidence that bears on the question. (You might consider the placement of VP adverbs like *very much*, of negatives like *not at all*, of sentential adverbs like *obviously*, and of parentheticals like *I believe*.)

*Question 21. The Kiparskys claim that *it* is the proform for NPs and since factive complements are dominated exhaustively only by NPs, as shown in (i), *it* is the only possible proform for factives.

(i)

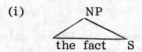

On the other hand, nonfactives are dominated exhaustively by both NP and S, as in (ii), so both *it* (the proform for NPs) and *so* (the proform for Ss) can replace nonfactives.

(ii)    NP
         |
         S

Find three predicates taking nonfactives which can use only *so*. Can you think of an explanation Kiparsky and Kiparsky might give for why extraposition of nonfactives from subject position either does not allow any proform or allows only the proform *so*, as in (iii) and (iv)?

   (iii) It's likely.
   (iv) It seems so/*it.

Question 22. A possible paper topic might be to describe the distribution of *it*, *so*, *to*, and *not* in sentences such as (i) through (iv).

   (i) I know that I did wrong and I regret *it*.
   (ii) You think that I did wrong and I think *so*, too.
   (iii) John wants to go swimming, and I want *to*, too.
   (iv) Sam believes we ought to go, but I think *not*.

**Question 23. Look at the Kiparskys' proposal about the correspondence between the truth of propositions and the specific reference of NPs. Consider sentences with generic NPs and see whether or not they fit into the Kiparskys' proposed schema. (See Pope 1976:13-22 for further discussion.)

*Question 24. Consider Kiparsky and Kiparsky's observation that propositions in sentence initial position are (usually) understood as factive and NPs in sentence initial position are (usually) understood as specific. It is a fact of English that we tend to put old information (information already present in the discourse or presumed to be common knowledge) early in the sentence and new information toward the end of the sentence. How do these two observations relate to each other?

Question 25. What is an 'emotive' predicate? Give your own examples of emotive factive predicates that take subject complements and object complements, and emotive nonfactive predicates that take subject complements and object complements. Can you think of any nonemotive predicates that can take *for...to* complements? Is *arrange* emotive?

Question 26. Do you know of any language where a verb may agree for person and number with an oblique (i.e. nonnominative) NP? Does this happen in main clauses, embedded clauses, or both? Does it have anything to do with factivity?

Question 27. What do you think of saying that (i) derives by a modal deletion rule from the same S with *should* present?

(i) I'm anxious that he be found.

Why does (ii) present a problem? Can you find other problems for the modal deletion proposal?

(ii) I demand that he be found.

**Question 28. For the student interested in logic, it might be worthwhile to consider some alternatives to the Kiparsky and Kiparsky approach.
The Kiparskys claim that factive verbs presuppose the truth of their complement. They do not give a definition of 'presupposition' but rather talk about what presuppositions we find in particular examples and the syntactic patterning of presuppositions (they are constant under negation; they are not questioned in a question). And at one point (immediately before Figure 1) they claim that presuppositions are 'relative to the speaker'. Bolinger (forthcoming) claims that factive verbs 'entail the factuality of their complements'. The usual definition of *entail* is as follows: proposition $P_1$ entails a proposition $P_2$ if for all worlds in which $P_1$ is true, $P_2$ must also be true.

Thus Bolinger's claim amounts to saying that a predicate is factive if the proposition in which it occurs entails the proposition of its complement.

Consider examples (i) through (iv).

(i) I regret that he broke his leg.
(ii) I don't regret that he broke his leg.  In fact, he never broke it.
(iii) Do you regret that he broke his leg?
(iv) She regrets that he broke his leg, but she's an idiot. She can't see that he's just faking.

Discuss the strengths and weaknesses of Bolinger's and Kiparsky and Kiparsky's views with respect to (i) through (iv). Try to find a solution of your own that is superior.

## HOMEWORK PROBLEMS

I. *know*

A. In footnote 3, Kiparsky and Kiparsky say that *know* is semantically factive but syntactically nonfactive.  Find three arguments with examples for saying *know* is syntactically nonfactive.  (Be sure to consider various tenses.)

B. Compare *know about* to *know*.  Is *know about* factive or nonfactive?  Give three arguments with examples for your answer.

II. *seem*

Consider sentences (1) through (6).

(1) It seemed that Pete would win.
(2) *That Pete would win seemed.
(3) It was unlikely that Pete would win.
(4) That Pete would win was unlikely.
(5) It seemed unlikely that Pete would win.
(6) That Pete would win seemed unlikely.

A. Give a derivation for (5) and (6).  (Note that the problem is how to explain (6) in light of (2).  Assume that the rules Extraposition and Raising into Subject Position exist.  What new rule must you propose in the derivation of (5) and (6)?

Now consider these examples.

(7a) *The fact that Pete would win seemed.
(7b) *The fact seemed that Pete would win.
(8) The fact that Pete would win was important.
(9) The fact that Pete would win seemed important.

B.  Give a derivation for (9).  (Here the problem is how to explain (9) in light of (7).)  Do you need the same rule you proposed for (6) or a new one?

C.  Give one semantic or syntactic argument of your own for the rule proposed to explain (6).  Be sure to make this an argument (with good and bad examples and a generalization that will be missed unless we propose the rule, or a set of data that cannot be explained unless we propose the rule, or some other form of argument) and not just a discussion.

D.  Give one semantic or syntactic argument of your own against the rule proposed to explain (6).  Again, be sure you give an argument and not just a discussion.

## SUGGESTED READINGS

Bolinger, D.  1976.  Gradience in entailment.  Language Sciences 41.1-13.  (For Question 17.)

Bolinger, D.  1978.  Free will and determinism in language: Or who does the choosing, the grammar or the speaker?  In: Contemporary studies in Romance linguistics.  Edited by M. Suñer.  Washington, D.C.:  Georgetown University Press. 1-17.  (For Homework Problem III.)

Bresnan, J.  1970.  On complementizers: Toward a syntactic theory of complement types.  Foundations of Language 6.297-321.  (For a discussion of complementizers and pre-suppositions.)

Bresnan, J.  1972.  Theory of complementation in English syntax.  Unpublished doctoral dissertation.  MIT.

Hooper, J.  1975.  On assertive predicates.  In:  Syntax and Semantics 4.91-124.  (For a discussion of assertions.)

Hooper, J., and S. A. Thompson.  1973.  On the applicability of root transformations.  Linguistic Inquiry 4:4.465-498. (For Question 12.)

Horn, L.  1972.  On the semantic properties of logical operators in English.  Unpublished doctoral dissertation.  University of California.

Karttunen, L.  1971a.  Implicative verbs.  Lg. 47.340-358. (For a discussion of predicates and presuppositions other than factives.)

Karttunen, L.  1971b.  Some observations on factivity.  Papers in Linguistics 4:1.55-69.

Karttunen, L.  1974.  Presupposition and linguistic context. Theoretical linguistics 1:1/2.181-194.  (For a pragmatic view of presuppositions.)

Karttunen, L., and S. Peters.  1977.  Requiem for presupposition.  Berkeley Linguistics Society 3.360-371.  (For Question 28.)

Kempson, R.  1977.  Semantic theory.  Cambridge:  Cambridge University Press.  (p. 145 and following.)

Lakoff, R. 1973. Review of: Progress in linguistics. Edited by M. Bierwisch and K. Heidolph. Lg. 49.685-696. (For a review of Kiparsky and Kiparsky's paper.)

Pope, E. 1976. Questions and answers in English. The Hague: Mouton. (Chapter 1 for Question 23.)

Rosenbaum, P. 1967. The grammar of English predicate complement constructions. Cambridge, Mass.: The MIT Press.

# 12

## ON THE VSO HYPOTHESIS

Arlene Berman

Introduction. One of the reasons linguists are so fascinated with the hierarchical structure of language is that it does not show itself plainly, for it is hidden by the fact that speech and hearing are inherently only linear. Yet even the apparently superficial linear order of words leads to interesting linguistic universals and speculations about the way the human brain necessarily structures experience.

One comprehensive study of word order that was the inspiration for many later studies was that of Greenberg (1966, cited in Berman's article). There many natural languages were classified by the respective order of their verb (V), subject (S), and object (O), and correlations were pointed out between the order of these major constituents and other syntactic structures such as the order of nouns and their modifiers and the structure of PPs. While Greenberg is not explicit about how he weighted the data in reaching his conclusions (for example, in English we have various word orders as exemplified by *John ate the peas, Have you a nickel?, Plums he buys on Tuesdays*), it seems reasonable to assume he took nonconjoined, noncomplex, nonnegative, nonemphatic surface declarative sentences as his basis. Certainly he never speculated about deep structure order.

Since every language offers variations on its basic surface word order (see the English examples in the preceding paragraph), a natural question for a transformationalist is: which order is the correct underlying one? Indeed, it is theoretically possible to posit an underlying order that corresponds to no good surface sentence. That is, as we discussed earlier with respect to Ross' Universal Base Hypothesis (in his article in this volume), it is theoretically possible to propose any order, say VSO, as the deep order for a language L. Then we could make

369

our first (or any later) transformation reorder the constituents, as say, SVO, and go on with the grammar from there. But a proposal for a given deep order demands serious consideration only if that order is kept long enough to allow us to simplify the grammar in other ways. The real question, then, is what order gives us the 'best' grammar for the language L. Here one might talk of various standards such as whether or not generalizations are captured, how much power is needed by the rules, how much 'cost' various rules and conditions add to the grammar, and, perhaps (though this is by no means a logically necessary criterion) the simplicity of the structural description and structural change of the rules. (Perlmutter 1971 (epilogue) offers suggestions about such types of considerations.)

English has been analyzed as underlyingly SVO, VSO, and SOV by various linguists at various times. In Berman's article, she takes McCawley's (1970) proposal that English is a VSO language and argues that this hypothesis fails, both in explanatory power and descriptive adequacy. Instead, she proposes that an SVO order is superior and points out that this is, indeed, the most frequent surface word order and this is the significant word order for English for the types of correlations made in Greenberg's study.

Berman's article is very clearly written and, like the other articles in this book, it has been chosen because it acquaints the student with types of argumentation that have become classic. Particular attention should be paid to the arguments based on ordering (with the exception of her Section 1.3, as pointed out in our Question 4) and ad hoc global conditions.

In reading this article, you encounter the terms 'intrinsic' and 'extrinsic' ordering many times, so a review of these notions may be helpful here. Two rules are intrinsically ordered if the structural description (SD) of the second is only met after the first has applied. That is, the first supplies or creates the SD for the second. As a hypothetical example, consider $R_1$ and $R_2$.

$$R_1: \quad X \quad V \quad P \quad NP \quad Y$$
$$\phantom{R_1:} \quad 1 \quad 2 \quad 3 \quad 4 \quad 5 \Longrightarrow 1\ 2\ 4\ 3\ 5$$

$$R_2: \quad X \quad V \quad NP \quad P \quad NP \quad Y$$
$$\phantom{R_2:} \quad 1 \quad 2 \quad 3 \quad 4 \quad 5 \quad 6 \Longrightarrow 1\ 2\ 3\ 5\ 4\ 6$$

Now even in an essentially unordered grammar that allows optional rules to apply whenever they can (i.e. whenever their SD is met) and requires obligatory rules to do so, $R_2$ will always follow $R_1$. $R_2$ cannot apply to the input for $R_1$ but it can apply to its output. (While in this particular case $R_1$ cannot apply to the output of either rule, this is not a necessary consequence of intrinsic ordering.)

As another example, consider $R_3$ and $R_4$.

$R_3$:  X  V  A  NP  NP  Y
       1  2  3  4   5   6 $\implies$ 1 2 4 3 5 6

$R_4$:  X  V  A  NP  NP  Y
       1  2  3  4   5   6 $\implies$ 1 2 3 5 4 6

Now if the SD for $R_4$ is met, the SD for $R_3$ is also met. Neither of these rules creates a structure to which the other can apply from an original structure to which the other could not apply. Thus they are not intrinsically ordered. In a given derivation we might have only $R_3$ apply or only $R_4$, or $R_4$ followed by $R_3$. (We can never have $R_3$ followed by $R_4$, since $R_3$ destroys the SD for $R_4$. But, once more, this is an accident of the particular case and is not relevant to the question of intrinsic ordering.)

As a third case, consider $R_5$ and $R_6$.

$R_5$:  X  V  A  PP  A  Y
       1  2  3  4   5  6 $\implies$ 1 2 5 4 3 6

$R_6$:  Z  NP  V  A  PP  A  Y
       1  2   3  4  5   6  7 $\implies$ 1 3 4 5 6 2 7

Again, if the SD of $R_6$ is met, the SD of $R_5$ is met. So neither rule creates a new environment for the other rule. In a given derivation we might have only $R_5$ apply or only $R_6$ apply, or $R_6$ followed by $R_5$, or $R_5$ followed by $R_6$ (in the case in which the X variable of $R_5$'s SD is analyzable as Z NP). Thus these rules are not intrinsically ordered.

On the other hand, two rules are extrinsically ordered if the grammar must explicitly state 'Rule$_a$ follows Rule$_b$'. This will be necessary if an ungrammatical S results from some other order and if there is no other mechanism in the grammar to block the ungrammatical result. For instance, suppose that $R_7$ and $R_8$ are as follows.

$R_7$:  X  V  NP  Y
       1  2  3   4 $\implies$ 1 3 2 4

$R_8$:  X  V  P  NP  Y
       1  2  3  4   5 $\implies$ 1 2 4 3 5

And suppose that NP V P is an ungrammatical string. Then we cannot allow $R_7$ to apply to the output of (i.e. follow) $R_8$. Therefore the two rules must be extrinsically ordered (in the absence of any other mechanism to rule out the bad output). Many linguists believe extrinsic (but not intrinsic) ordering statements add to the 'cost' of the grammar and are, furthermore, unnecessary. Berman and McCawley would agree with the former if not the latter opinion.

Notice that many rules are neither intrinsically nor extrinsically ordered with respect to each other. See the homework for more on intrinsic and extrinsic ordering.

*Arlene Berman* # On the VSO Hypothesis*

In this article, I will argue against McCawley's proposal (1970) that the underlying word order in English is VSO (Verb Subject Object), with the surface SVO pattern characteristic of English being produced by a late rule of Subject Formation (McCawley's V–NP Inversion, henceforth SF). McCawley's primary argument in favor of this hypothesis is that it simplifies the statement of a large number of syntactic transformations, at the same time giving syntactic structures that look more like the semantic representations of current logical notation.[1] While this latter result may be desirable, it is necessary, as McCawley recognized, that underlying VSO order reflect some generalization(s) about English syntax, i.e. that it be syntactically motivated.

With respect to such syntactic motivation, McCawley states: "Of the fifteen transformations of English that I can argue must be in the cycle, there are ten for which it makes no significant difference whether they apply to structures with predicate first or predicate second . . . For the remaining five cyclic transformations . . . the version of the transformation that assumes predicate-first order is significantly simpler in the sense of either involving fewer elementary operations or applying under conditions which can be stated without the use of the more exotic notational devices that have figured in transformational rules" (1970, 292). The five rules cited are Passive, *There* Insertion, Subject Raising, Predicate Raising, and Negative Raising. McCawley points out that, given predicate-first order, Passive can be represented as a simple operation which moves the subject to the end of the clause, instead of one which involves movement of two noun phrases: ". . .the object will then automatically be in 'subject position', i.e. it will directly follow the verb and thus will become surface subject by [SF]" (1970, 293).

* I would like to thank several people for reading and commenting on an earlier version of this paper, most notably Avery Andrews, C. L. Baker, Jorge Hankamer, Stanley Legum, David Perlmutter, Paul Postal, and Robert Wall. I would especially like to thank Susan Schmerling and Michael Szamosi for the time they spent discussing the topic with me and helping clarify the issues, and for reading numerous preliminary drafts and giving helpful comments on them. None of these people necessarily agree with the conclusions reached here, and remaining mistakes are all my own.

[1] McCawley claims that current logical notation, which customarily places the predicate first (or last), is in some way "natural" rather than a result of arbitrary convention. To my knowledge, logicians assign no significance to the shape of their formulae. While it may be true, as McCawley suggests, that the particular notational conventions used by most logicians reflect some deep-seated semantic generalization, no evidence exists that they are anything but arbitrary.

[1]

Similarly, in the case of *There* Insertion, predicate-first order permits a simple insertion of *there* immediately to the right of the verb, without an additional movement operation to displace the original subject. Thus inserted, *there* is again automatically eligible for fronting by SF.

As for the remaining three rules, McCawley points out that they all involve "pulling up" some item from an embedded clause into the matrix clause. The embedded clause may be either a subject or object complement and thus, in a verb-medial system, may either precede or follow the matrix verb. Therefore, the transformations in question must somehow manage to apply both left-to-right and right-to-left, depending on the position of the complement. However, under the VSO hypothesis these rules can be made to apply in a unidirectional fashion to structures of the form V (NP) S, where S represents an object or a subject complement according to whether the second term, NP, is present or not.

Of these arguments, by far the strongest is the case of Subject Raising,[2] and this is the rule most often cited in support of VSO (cf. in particular Postal (to appear)). On the strength of the Raising argument, Perlmutter (in preparation a) has claimed that Portuguese is underlyingly VSO. The same could be said for French, Spanish, Italian, and probably several other surface SVO languages (in any case, all those that have such a dual Raising process). However, this argument crucially depends on the assumption that Raising out of subject complements and Raising out of object complements are the same rule, an assumption that is, at best, moot (cf. Szamosi 1973 and section 1.6 of this article for arguments against this assumption). The syntactic evidence for VSO, then, is not overwhelming.

In addition to the arguments summarized above, McCawley conjectured that there are no languages that are underlyingly verb-medial: all languages are either VSO or SOV in underlying structure. Noting that all languages that are not verb-peripheral are verb-second languages and not, say, verb-penultimate languages, McCawley further suggested that all surface SVO languages be derived from an underlying VSO pattern. This assumption is supported by the fact that VSO and

---

[2] As for McCawley's other arguments, *There* Insertion seems to me to be so poorly understood that it cannot figure in arguments of this kind until we have some better idea of how it works. Similarly, the controversial status of Predicate Raising argues against considering it in this context. As for Negative Raising, McCawley gives the following examples to show that Negative Raising out of both subject and object embeddings is possible.

    (i)   I think that Harry won't be here until Friday. (his (11a))
    (ii)  I don't think that Harry will be here until Friday. (his (11b))
   (iii)  It's likely that Nixon won't send the marines to Botswana until 1972. (his (12a))
   (iv)  It's not likely that Nixon will send the marines to Botswana until 1972. (his (12b))

However, the above examples show only that Negative Raising out of the complements of both subject- and object-embedding predicates is possible; there is no evidence that Negative Raising can apply to a subject complement in subject position. In fact, (v) shows that the result of such an operation is unacceptable:

    (v)  *That Nixon will send the marines to Botswana until 1972 is unlikely.

This leaves the argument based on Passive. I will show below (section 1.1) that McCawley's simplification of the rule is achieved at the cost of descriptive adequacy.

SVO languages are typologically similar in many ways. As an example of this, McCawley cites a conjecture by Ross that all VSO and SVO languages have preposed conjunctions underlyingly, while SOV languages have postposed ones.

As noted, the syntactic evidence for the VSO hypothesis is not very strong, but impressive counterevidence to it has not been forthcoming either. Thus, typological considerations of the sort outlined above, coupled with the potential link between syntactic and logical structures that the hypothesis offers, have given it considerable appeal.

In this article, I will present syntactic arguments that the VSO hypothesis is incorrect. I will show that, for a large number of transformations, both cyclic and postcyclic, considerable complications result if they are stated in a predicate-first system. These transformations fall into distinct classes; I will show that for each class, the VSO hypothesis makes the wrong prediction about the way the rules in the class operate.

Given Perlmutter's extension of the VSO hypothesis to Portuguese (and potentially to at least French, Spanish, and Italian as well), processes from these languages that involve underlying word order are relevant to the evaluation of the VSO hypothesis. Most of the arguments given here come from English and French; in some cases, it is indicated that similar arguments could be given from other languages. On the basis of this evidence, I will argue that the VSO hypothesis is, in principle, unable to capture important generalizations about English and similar surface SVO languages and that it makes wrong predictions about the class of possible languages.

Before proceeding with the body of the article, a word on the ordering of SF is necessary. Citing an observation by John Kimball that cyclic rules do not radically change structure, McCawley postulated that SF is postcyclic. In addition, his particular analysis of *There* Insertion dictates that SF be postcyclic. Not all linguists have considered these arguments for postcyclic SF compelling.[3] Accordingly, I will present arguments against the VSO hypothesis both under the assumption that SF is postcyclic (section 2) and under the assumption that SF is cyclic (section 3). Section 1 deals with problems that would arise under either ordering. Section 4 is a summary.

**1.** In this section, six arguments are given against VSO that are essentially independent of the ordering of SF. The first deals with difficulties in deriving certain types of passive

---

[3] For example, Green (1972) describes SF as a cyclic rule. Postal (to appear) argues that SF must be postcyclic rather than last cyclic, because if it were last cyclic, on the final cycle it would have to be extrinsically ordered to follow Raising (his fn. 23). The same argument would hold if SF were cyclic.

Postal formulates the structural description of Raising as follows:

(i)  X  V  (NP)  [$_{NP}$[$_S$V NP Y]]  Z  (his (49))

If Raising is instead formulated as applying to (ii) it is, in effect, intrinsically ordered to precede SF on any cycle.

(ii)  X  [$_S$V  (NP)  [$_{NP}$[$_S$V NP Y]]]  Z

Under such a formulation, Postal's ordering argument no longer holds, and the cyclicity of SF remains an open question. If SF is cyclic, the only change in (ii) is that the V in the embedded S is removed.

sentences given underlying VSO order. The second argument involves an inversion process in French relative clauses. The third, fourth, and fifth relate to Particle Movement, Dative Movement, and Heavy NP Shift respectively and argue that stating these rules in a VSO system requires complication and not simplification of these rules. The last section deals with the Raising argument mentioned earlier.

*1.1.* Consider sentences like (1a–c):

(1) a. Someone took advantage of their innocence.
   b. Advantage was taken of their innocence.
   c. Their innocence was taken advantage of.

Given SVO order, there is a fairly natural way of deriving both (1b) and (1c) from the same underlying structure, as follows: assume that *take advantage* is a "complex verb", with internal structure like that shown in (2):[4]

(2)

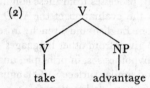

In underlying structure, then, (1a) is something like (3):

(3)

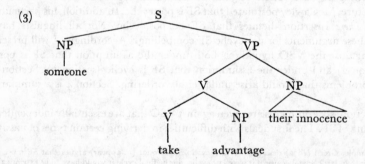

---

[4] The status of *of* in sentences like (1) is not entirely clear. The question is whether it originates as a verbal particle (a sister of *advantage*) or a preposition on *their innocence*. While it is totally governed by the verb complex, like a particle, it "feels" more like a preposition in (1a) and (1b). The behavior of Passive with respect to prepositions is far from straightforward; it seems in general to be able to ignore prepositions that are verb-governed (*Joe was harshly spoken to, the situation will be looked into*), but not in general able to ignore prepositions (but: *this bed was slept in*). The status of *of* does not seem to affect the argument here, and it is accordingly omitted from trees.

(3) meets the structural description (SD) of Passive in two ways: first, the entire complex *take advantage* satisfies the V in the SD of Passive, and its object, *their innocence*, satisfies the NP node. Passive produces (1c). Second, the dominated V, *take*, satisfies the V node in the SD of Passive, and *advantage* satisfies the NP node. The remainder of the sentence, in this case *of their innocence*, is subsumed by the end variable in the SD of Passive. The result is (1b). That is, given SVO order, the fact that we find pairs like (1b) and (1c) is due to the fact that the tree underlying these sentences has two proper analyses in terms of the Passive rule, and thus, two good outputs. This analysis of the sentences of (1) makes two claims, which seem intuitively to be correct: (i) that the sentences of (1) have the same underlying structure, and (ii) that *take advantage* is underlyingly a unit. In addition, it makes it possible to handle the fact that anarthrous *advantage* does not occur freely in NP slots.

However, if we start out with underlying VSO order, these results are lost. In order to derive (1c), *take advantage* must originate as a complex verb, as it does in (2). Then its two arguments, *someone* and *their innocence*, will be interchanged by Passive, as in the case of simple transitive verbs. But in order to derive (1b), *advantage* must be to the right of *someone*, so that Passive may leave it in (derived) subject position. That is, we must have (4) in order to derive (1b), but (5) in order to derive (1c).

(4)

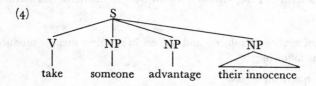

(5)

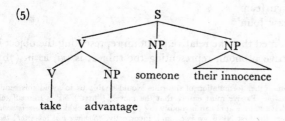

Given VSO order, then, (1b) and (1c) can no longer be derived from the same underlying structure, and (1a) is now structurally ambiguous, since it presumably has both (4) and (5) as a source. *Take advantage* is now a unit in some deep structures, but not others, and we have no way of accounting for the fact that anarthrous *advantage* cannot occur freely as an NP, since it appears to in the structure (4). Thus,

VSO word order forces us to derive (1b) and (1c) very differently, from totally different underlying structures.[5]

English has a small number of other idioms which behave the same way, with some variation from speaker to speaker. Other languages, like French and Portuguese, have similar constructions, but due to an independent constraint against stranding prepositions, double passives do not show up. That is, French and Portuguese equivalents of (1a) have passives corresponding to (1b) but not to (1c). Therefore, the same argument cannot be given in its entirety for these languages. However, consider the derivation of passives like (1b) in these languages, for example (6):

(6) a.  Tort    a été donné à la   police.
        wrong was   given  to the police
        'The police were blamed.'
    b.  Assistance a été prêtée aux victimes.
        aid        was lent    to the victims
    c.  Reforços       foram enviados à região.
        reinforcements were  sent       to the region

The idioms *donner tort* 'blame', *prêter assistance* 'lend assistance', and *enviar reforços* 'send reinforcements' cannot originate as underlying units, and there is no way of accounting for the occurrence of anarthrous *tort*, *assistance*, and *reforços* in idioms of this sort and nowhere else.

*1.2.*  In French, Relativization of subjects and objects in simple sentences produces relative clauses like the following:

(7) a.  l'homme que Jean a vu
        'the man that John saw'
    b.  l'homme qui a vu Jean
        'the man that saw John'

Traditionally, it has been claimed that the relative pronoun representing the object is *que*, as in (7a), and the relative pronoun representing the subject is *qui*, as in (7b).

---

[5] It might be claimed that some other formulation of the rules would enable us to avoid this result. Assuming that trees like (5) are possible, Passive must ensure that the moved ("first") NP is immediately dominated by S, for if one wished to have Passive apply ambiguously to (5), the results would be: *Their innocence was taken advantage of by someone* (where the first NP is *someone*), and, incorrectly, *\*Someone was taken (of) their innocence by advantage* (where the first NP chosen was *advantage*). In fact, assuming underlying trees like either (4) or (5), but not both, there is no way to have Passive apply ambiguously to either tree. One might then claim that the double passives arise not by ambiguous application of Passive, but rather by ambiguous application of SF. That is, we start with (5), and Passive moves *someone* to the right of *their innocence*. SF can then front either *their innocence* or *advantage*, since both are to the right of V. This works out all right in these cases, but there is a problem with allowing SF to behave "stupidly" in this manner. Suppose Passive does not apply. If SF works in this way, we will derive, incorrectly *\*Advantage took someone (of) their innocence*. I see no way around having different underlying structures for (1b) and (1c)—and consequently ambiguous underlying structures for (1a)—if Passive applies to verb-initial structures.

However, Perlmutter (in preparation c) argues that relativization of subjects and direct objects in French is accomplished by deletion, and that the *que/qui* that introduces relative clauses of this sort is, in all instances, the complementizer *que* that introduces other types of embedded sentences, as in (8):

(8) Je crois *que* Jean est malade.
'I believe that John is sick.'

The distribution of *que* and *qui* in relative clauses is accounted for by the following rule:[6]

(9) *MasQUErade*
*que* $\Rightarrow$ qui / ____ V

It is clear that this account of relativization will derive relative clauses like those of (7) without problems.

There are several arguments that support this approach, the most convincing of which is the following. Consider sentences like those in (10):

(10) Tu as dit que l'homme est venu.
'You said that the man came.'

If (10) is embedded in a relative clause whose head noun is *l'homme*, the result is (11):

(11) l'homme que tu as dit qui est venu
'the man that you said came'

Following the traditional account of relativization, (11) should be unacceptable on two counts: first, since a subject is being relativized, the relative pronoun should be *qui*; second, the *que* complementizer introducing the subordinate clause in (10) should be unaffected by relativization. The traditional account would thus predict (12):

(12) *l'homme qui tu as dit qu'est venu

The approach using MasQUErade, on the other hand, predicts (11). We start out with the structure shown in (13):

(13) [$_{NP}$l'homme [$_S$que tu as dit [$_S$que il est venu]]][7]

First, the embedded *il* is deleted by Relativization, under coreference to the head noun, and then the *que* $\Rightarrow$ *qui* rule operates. Since the first *que* in the string is followed

---

[6] The same analysis is proposed independently in Moreau (1971) and Gross (1968). The name, MasQUErade, is due to Perlmutter, but the formulation given in (9) is that of Moreau.

[7] I am using SVO order here, since at this point in the argument, the order makes no important difference. Also, I am using a pronoun, *il*, to represent the embedded occurrence of *l'homme*. Perlmutter (1972) has argued that the relevant deletion in French Relativization is deletion of a pronoun. Whether that pronoun is there underlying or is the result of some pronominalization rule is irrelevant to the argument.

by a noun phrase, the rule fails to apply. However, since the second *que* is followed by V the rule now applies, correctly producing (11).

An independent argument given by Perlmutter that the *qui* that "represents" the subject in relative clauses like (7b) is not a relative pronoun is the following. Compare (14) and (15):

(14)  les enfants, qui sont intelligents
      'the children, who are intelligent'
(15)  les linguistes, les enfants de qui sont intelligents
      'linguists, the children of whom are intelligent'

The *qui* of *de qui* in (15) is a real relative pronoun and not a complementizer (as are other relative pronouns inside prepositional phrases (cf. Perlmutter 1972)). If the *qui* in (14) were also a relative pronoun, we would predict that it would behave like *qui* in (15). However, consider (16) and (17):

(16)  les enfants, qui certainement sont intelligents
      'the children, who certainly are intelligent'
(17)  *les linguistes, les enfants de qui certainement sont intelligents
      'linguists, the children of whom certainly are intelligent'

There seems to be a constraint in French that adverbs cannot intervene between relative pronouns and verbs. This constraint rules out (17). But, if this is so, how could we explain the grammaticality of (16), if *qui* were a relative pronoun? On the other hand, if the *qui* in (16) is really the complementizer *que* which has undergone MASQUERADE, the constraint on adverbs does not apply, and we predict that (16) will be acceptable. (After this article was in press, I learned that (15), as well as (17), is ill-formed. Therefore, the argument based on the difference between (16) and (17) is faulty. (I am grateful to Nicolas Ruwet for pointing this out to me.) However, there are other arguments for a *que* ⇒ *qui* rule (cf. Moreau 1971 and Perlmutter in preparation c), and the remainder of the material in this section is still valid.)

I assume, then, that MASQUERADE is a real rule in French. Further, it is clear that it is a very late rule. It must at least follow Relativization and *Wh* Fronting, or, following Perlmutter (1972), Shadow Pronoun Deletion. Furthermore, if French is a VSO language, it must follow SF. That this is necessary is clear from noun phrases like those of (7). Prior to SF and MASQUERADE, these constructions are as shown in (18):

(18)  a.  [$_{NP}$l'homme [$_S$que a vu Jean ____]]
      b.  [$_{NP}$l'homme [$_S$que a vu ____ Jean]]

The deletion site is indicated by ____ here, but it is not structurally present.[8] If

---

[8] If SF follows Relativization, it can be seen from these relative clauses that SF must be formulated globally in order to block its application in (18b), since at the time SF applied, (18a) and (18b) would be structurally indistinguishable. This is discussed below in section 2.1.

MASQUERade preceded SF, it would apply to (18a) and (18b) alike, ultimately producing (19a, b) rather than the correct (7).

(19) a. *l'homme qui Jean a vu
b. l'homme qui a vu Jean

Thus, SF must apply first, then MASQUERade.[9]

However, French also has relative clauses like the following:

(20) l'homme qu'a vu Jean
'the man that John saw'

(20) is a stylistic variant of (7a); *Jean* is the subject of the relative clause. In order to derive (20), a rule of Subject Verb Inversion is needed. This rule must follow MASQUERade, so that the *que* in (20) is retained and so that (20) is differentiated from (7b), in which *Jean* is the object.

[9] Note that this is an extrinsic ordering forced on us by the VSO hypothesis. If French is SVO, MASQUERade, as stated in (9), is intrinsically ordered with respect to Relativization in just the appropriate way.

There is a related phenomenon that is worth mentioning here. One way of forming *Wh* questions in French is by *Wh* Fronting and Subject Verb Inversion (assuming for the moment underlying SVO order). The *Wh* forms are *qui* for animates and *que* for inanimates. We have, then, the patterns:

(i) a. Quelqu'un est ici.
'Someone is here.'
b. Qui est ici?
'Who is here?'
c. Il a vu quelqu'un.
'He saw someone.'
d. Qui a-t-il vu?
'Who did he see?'

(ii) a. Quelque chose est sur la table.
'Something is on the table.'
b. *Qu'est sur la table?
('What is on the table?')
c. Il a vu quelque chose.
'He saw something.'
d. Qu'a-t-il vu?
'What did he see?'

What is interesting here is that inanimate subjects cannot be questioned in the same manner as animate subjects and both types of objects. The reason for this cannot be a restriction on the *Wh* Fronting rule, since inanimate subjects in embedded clauses can be questioned in this way:

(iii) a. Il a dit que quelque chose est sur la table.
'He said that something is on the table.'
b. Qu'a-t-il dit qui est sur la table?
'What did he say is on the table?'

(Note the operation of MASQUERade in (iiib).) I suspect that a transderivational constraint is involved, as follows: note that in (iib), *Wh* Fronting leaves a *que* followed by V. MASQUERade wants to operate here, but if it did, the output would be the same as that in which an animate subject was being questioned (as in (ib)). Nonapplication of MASQUERade would produce a bad output, application of MASQUERade an ambiguous surface structure. Both derivations block.

Note, by the way, that in order for *que* to be retained in (iid), it must have an NP adjacent to it at the time MASQUERade applies. It is clear that it is the existence of a subject NP that prevents MASQUERade from applying. If MASQUERade has the formulation given in (9), and we have VSO structures, MASQUERade must follow SF, and then we must have a rule of Subject Verb Inversion after SF to produce (iid) (cf. also below).

(22) to (23) will give the wrong results, since at the time Particle Movement applies it will be the subject that is adjacent to the verb. To avoid this wrong result, Particle Movement must be stated as follows:

(24)  $X [_V V \text{ Part}] NP NP Y$
       1   2   3    4  5  6 $\Rightarrow$ 1 2 4 5 3 6

This will give the right results, but it is clearly a more complicated rule than (22). Further, there is something intuitively wrong with (24): since the rule of Particle Movement has nothing to do with subjects, the subject should not have to figure as an essential term in the statement of the rule. But with VSO order, postcyclic SF, and cyclic Particle Movement, the rule of Particle Movement must explicitly mention the subject.

Is the situation changed if SF is cyclic? Particle Movement, as given in (22), will still apply to the tree given in (23), producing the wrong result. The formulation of (24) is still necessary. We can retain (22) only by extrinsically ordering SF before Particle Movement, thereby ensuring that Particle Movement applies to SVO structures.

Similarly, if Particle Movement is postcyclic, (24) is necessary unless SF is cyclic (or, if SF too is postcyclic, it must be extrinsically ordered before Particle Movement). The VSO hypothesis, then, forces us either to accept (24) or to posit otherwise unnecessary ordering statements—a complication over an SVO system either way.

*1.4.* Dative Movement is a cyclic rule that relates sentences like (25a) and (25b):

(25) a.  Mary gave a book to John.
     b.  Mary gave John a book.

Based on the interaction between Dative Movement and action nominalizations, I assume that (25a) is more basic and that (25b) is derived from it, although this assumption will not affect the argument here. McCawley has indicated that given underlying VSO order, it might not be necessary for Dative to be cyclic (because with VSO order Dative need not precede Passive, as it must in an SVO system). However, Dative Movement must be cyclic, regardless of its interaction with Passive and regardless of one's assumptions concerning underlying order. In order for Raising (which can be shown to be a cyclic rule) to derive both (26) and (27), both *a book* and *John* must be able to become cyclical subjects;[12] if Dative were postcyclic, (27) could not be derived.

(26)  A book seems to have been given to John.
(27)  John seems to have been given a book.

[12] Jackendoff (1972) gives the same argument for the cyclicity of Dative Movement.

It has been claimed for English that given VSO order, rules like the stylistic inversion discussed above are not needed, since the environments in which they apply may be described as the environments in which SF does not apply. This cannot be the case here (cf. also section 3 below). It cannot be that (20) is derived through the failure of SF to apply—if SF had not applied, MasQUErade would have, yielding (7b). Thus, given underlying VSO order, the derivation of (20) must involve both Verb Subject Inversion (SF) and Subject Verb Inversion, with MasQUErade intervening between them. Clearly this is a more complicated derivation than that required given underlying SVO order.

*1.3.* Particle Movement is the rule which relates sentences like the following:

(21) a.  John looked up the information.
     b.  John looked the information up.

There are many arguments that the particle, in this case *up*, originates as part of the verb,[10] i.e. that (21a) is more basic than (21b). The standard formulation for Particle Movement is as follows:

(22)  X [$_V$V Part] NP Y
      1   2    3    4 5 $\Rightarrow$ 1 2 4 3 5

That is, the particle is moved out from under the V node to the right of the adjacent NP.

In a VSO system, the structure of (21) is (23):

(23)

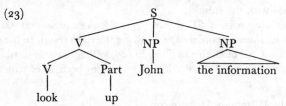

If Particle Movement is a cyclic rule[11] and SF a postcyclic one, the application of

---

[10] Cf. Fraser (1965) and Legum (1968).

[11] Ross (1967a) claims that Particle Movement must be postcyclic in order to account for the fact that it cannot apply in action nominalizations, i.e. for the fact that we find (i) but not (ii):

(i)  Her efficient looking up of the information pleased her boss.
(ii) *Her efficient looking of the information up pleased her boss.

However, this argument is not convincing, since Dative Movement, which must be cyclical (cf. section 1.4), shows the same behavior with respect to action nominalizations. That is, we have (iii) but not (iv):

(iii) Her giving of a present to John surprised us.
(iv) *Her giving of John a present surprised us.

The fact that a clearly cyclic transformation like Dative Movement has the same restriction as Particle Movement vitiates the force of Ross's argument that Particle Movement is postcyclic.

The standard formulation of Dative Movement is something like (28):

(28)  X V NP to NP Y
      1  2  3  4  5  6 $\Rightarrow$ 1 2 5 $\phi$ 3 6

That is, Dative Movement interchanges the NP immediately adjacent to V (the direct object) with a *to* + *NP* immediately to the right of it.

If English were underlyingly VSO, (25) would start out with the following structure:

(29)

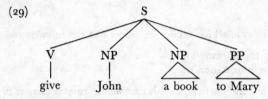

Suppose SF were postcyclic. In that case, (28) could not apply to (29), since the second NP to the right of V is not preceded by *to*. Thus, Dative Movement must be restated as (30):

(30)  X V NP NP to NP Y
      1  2  3  4  5  6  7 $\Rightarrow$ 1 2 3 6 $\phi$ 4 7

But (30) is unsatisfactory for the same reason (24) was: not only is it a "more complicated" rule than (28), but also it must explicitly mention the subject, although the rule itself has nothing to do with the subject.

The situation does not improve if SF is a cyclic rule. Assuming that Dative Movement and SF are not extrinsically ordered, we will get the right results in the case of structures like (29), since the SD of Dative as given in (28) will not be met until after SF has applied. However, we still need the version given in (30) because of sentences like (31):

(31)  John gave to the Watergate Defense Fund.

The rule in (28), applied to (31), would ultimately produce (32):

(32)  *The Watergate Defense Fund gave John.[13]

---

[13] It may be thought that this difficulty can be avoided by generating a dummy direct object, PRO, to serve as a "place holder" until after SF has applied. This, however, will introduce unwanted complications. In either system (VSO or SVO), the putative PRO does not interact with any known syntactic rule. It must be deleted before Dative, to avoid sentences like *John gave the WDF (PRO). If Dative and Passive are not extrinsically ordered, which they need not be, PRO must be deleted before Passive, to avoid *(PRO) was given to the WDF by John. For all practical purposes, then, PRO behaves as if it had never been there. The sole motivation for generating it is that, in a VSO system with cyclical SF and a "natural" formulation of Dative, it can be used to prevent (32), provided that PRO Deletion is extrinsically ordered after SF. This is a considerable complication over a system which directly generates the sentences in an SVO order, without a dummy direct object.

Thus, even if SF and Dative Movement are both cyclic, it is necessary to state Dative Movement as (30), which, as noted, is intuitively wrong as well as being more complicated than (28). The other alternative is to extrinsically order Dative after SF and to retain (28). This would simply ensure that Dative always applied to SVO structures—hardly an argument for VSO and, in any case, a complication.

*1.5.* Heavy NP Shift was first discussed by Ross (1967a). It derives sentences like (33a–c) from sentences like (34a–c):

(33) a. John gave to Mary a book that his father had recommended to him as being worth reading.

b. John spoke yesterday about the problems that are involved in developing a way to ease air pollution.

c. John loaded with hay the wagon that had been a part of the farm for as long as he could remember.

(34) a. ?*John gave a book that his father had recommended to him as being worth reading to Mary.

b. ?*John spoke about the problems that are involved in developing a way to ease air pollution yesterday.

c. ?*John loaded the wagon that had been a part of the farm for as long as he could remember with hay.

Heavy NP Shift thus moves direct objects and prepositional phrases to the right over adverbs and prepositional phrases. It cannot move subjects:

(35) a. The problems that are involved in developing a way to ease air pollution that will not be offensive to automobile manufacturers were discussed yesterday.

b. *Were discussed yesterday the problems that are involved in developing a way to ease air pollution that will not be offensive to automobile manufacturers.

The formulation of Heavy NP Shift is roughly that shown in (36):[14]

(36)   X V Y (prep) NP Z

    1 2 3    4     5 ⇒ 1 2 3 5 4

---

[14] The variables Y and Z in the statement of the rule cannot refer to unlimited domains. It is clear that Heavy NP Shift is bounded (in the sense of Ross (1967a))—it cannot move material "outside its own S". Similarly, Y subsumes prepositional phrases, adverbs, adjectives (as in *He considers beautiful any girl with blonde hair and blue eyes*), and perhaps some other things. The reader should interpret (36) in the obvious way.

If English is underlyingly VSO, Heavy NP Shift a cyclic rule, and SF a postcyclic rule, it is clear that the rule cannot be stated as (36), where any NP or PP to the right of the verb is permitted to be moved. Given these assumptions, there is no way to prevent Heavy NP Shift from moving subjects and thus producing sentences like (35b). Here again, (36) must be reformulated to mention the subject explicitly, despite the fact that the rule does not apply to subjects.[15]

If Heavy NP Shift and SF are both cyclic, in order to retain the simpler formulation of Heavy NP Shift it is necessary for the two rules to be extrinsically ordered so that SF precedes Heavy NP Shift. If both SF and Heavy NP Shift are postcyclic, (36) can be retained only by extrinsically ordering SF before it. (If SF is cyclic and Heavy NP Shift postcyclic, the problem does not arise.) All of the above cases require otherwise unnecessary ordering statements ensuring that Heavy NP Shift applies to SVO structures.

The feature common to the three rules just discussed—Particle Movement, Dative Movement, and Heavy NP Shift—is that they apply to nonsubjects. Given underlying VSO order, nonsubjects are structurally identifiable only by virtue of the fact that they follow subjects. If, in the course of a derivation, the subject is moved or deleted, structural identification is lost (cf. sections 2 and 4 below for further discussion of this). Since SF is a rule that displaces subjects, it is clear that the rules in question are not freely ordered with it and that ordering, whether extrinsic or intrinsic, is necessary. If they are to apply before SF, i.e. to VSO structures, these rules must explicitly mention the subject in the ways indicated above (note that this is necessarily the case if SF is postcyclic). Structural identification of nonsubjects is thus ensured and extrinsic ordering avoided, since the rules themselves are formulated in such a way as to "intrinsically" precede SF. If these rules are to follow SF (SF is necessarily cyclic in this case), the question of how to guarantee this remains. (There are at least two options available: extrinsic ordering statements, which allow us to retain the simpler formulation of these rules, or again having the rules explicitly mention the subject, this time to the left of the verb, thereby making the ordering "intrinsic".) However, any rule that follows SF is applying to SVO structures and provides no support for underlying VSO order.

Summing up then, if these rules are to apply to VSO structures, they must explicitly mention the subject and thus be stated in a pointlessly complicated (and highly counterintuitive) way. Note the suspicious fact that the complication of the rules is the same in each case. To avoid complicating the rules, we must use extrinsic ordering, which allows them to be stated on SVO structures. To the extent that several basic rules are most simply formulated in an SVO system, the claim that English is underlyingly VSO is wrong.

[15] Jerry Morgan has suggested (personal communication) that Heavy NP Shift should be allowed to apply freely to subjects as well as objects, with something like Perlmutter's Surface Subject Constraint ruling out sentences like (35b). If this is correct, Heavy NP Shift is not relevant to the evaluation of the VSO hypothesis.

*1.6.* As noted above, the only important syntactic argument that exists in favor of VSO order is that it makes it possible to state Raising into subject position (henceforth RS) and Raising into object position (henceforth RO) as a single rule in a very elegant fashion. Of course, this argument is at best as strong as the claim that RS and RO are, in fact, the same rule. While this has generally been assumed since the earliest discussion of Raising in transformational grammar,[16] it is far from clear that the collapsing of RO and RS into a single rule is not a spurious generalization. Szamosi (1973) provides some particularly telling evidence against this claim for languages like French and Hungarian (possibly also Spanish and Italian), concerning differences between when RS and RO can apply.

In these languages, it is the case that RO is possible only when the embedded predicate lacks a verb. There are no sentences in which RO has applied and the raised NP is followed by an infinitive. That is, using French as an example, we find that sentences like (37a, b) are acceptable but that sentences like (38a–c) are not.

(37) a.  Je considère Jean intelligent.
         'I consider John intelligent.

     b.  Je crois Jean drôle.
         'I believe John funny.'

(38) a.  *Je considère Jean être intelligent.
         'I consider John to be intelligent.'

     b.  *Je crois Jean être drôle.
         'I believe John to be funny.'

     c.  *Je considère Jean avoir fini ses devoirs.
         'I consider John to have finished his work.'

---

[16] A notable exception is Stockwell, Schachter, and Partee (1968), who do not, however, justify this separation. Rosenbaum (1967) first proposed that RO and RS be a single rule (his *It*-replacement), and this notion has been accepted by subsequent linguists who have dealt with Raising. It is clear that both processes are similar in many ways. However, this is also true of, say, Relativization and Question Formation, which are generally considered to be separate rules. The same thing holds for Extraposition and Extraposition from NP. Striking formal similarities between such pairs of rules have been recognized and used to class the rules together. No real evidence has ever been offered for conflating RO and RS into a single rule. Given the centrality of this assumption in the controversy over underlying word order, this question cannot be ignored.

One may note that RS has a good deal in common with Tough Movement, since both involve movement of an element of an embedded clause into matrix subject position. Looked at from this point of view, RO stands separate. Moreover, there are interrelations between RS and subject-controlled Equi, on the one hand, and RO and object-controlled Equi on the other, in that the former two produce surface object + infinitive constructions and the latter two verb + infinitive constructions. All of these rules are related in certain ways, and it is clear that these relations must be accounted for by an adequate grammar. It is equally clear that all of these processes cannot be manifestations of the same rule. At the moment, one can look at the grouping together of RO and RS into a single rule as a historical accident—no more justified than, say, a grouping together of RS and Tough Movement would be.

Postal (to appear) studies both RO and RS in considerable detail and gives ample evidence that both processes exist. However, the most he has to say about this question is that ". . . intuitively it seems that Rosenbaum's idea that the same rule is functioning in both (3) [RS] and (5) [RO] is correct . . ." (p. 4). None of Postal's data point to this as an inescapable conclusion.

This restriction holds only for RO; there are no predicates that allow RS that have such a restriction.[17]

There are two possible derivations for sentences like (39) in these languages, as well as in English:

(39)  John is considered (to be) intelligent.

We can apply first Raising and then Passive, so that an intermediate stage of (39) is (40):

(40)  PRO considers John (to be) intelligent.

In this derivation, we are using RO. Another possible derivation of (39) is that in which Passive precedes Raising. In this case, (39) is derived through an intermediate stage (41) and the type of Raising involved is RS.

(41)  [s[sJohn (to be) intelligent] is considered]

Returning now to French, this predicts that despite the ungrammaticality of (38), (42a) and (42b) will be as acceptable as (42c):[18]

(42)  a.  *Jean est considéré être intelligent.
          'John is considered to be intelligent.'
      b.  *Jean est considéré avoir fini ses devoirs.
          'John is considered to have finished his work.'
      c.  Jean est considéré intelligent.
          'John is considered intelligent.'

This is because there is a possible derivation for them in which RS applies, and since RS has no restriction on embedded infinitives, there should be nothing ruling out such sentences. However, as noted, they are bad.

At this point, there are several alternatives:

(43)  a.  Assume that Raising and Passive are extrinsically ordered, such that Raising precedes Passive. This will work, since in the derivation of (42), it will always be the case that RO is involved, never RS. But this requires a wholly unmotivated extrinsic ordering, and one that is language-particular (cf. Szamosi (1973) for evidence that English must allow the opposite ordering).

[17] Although sentences like (i) exist, there are also sentences like (ii):

(i)  Jean semble intelligent.
     'John seems intelligent.'
(ii) Jean semble être intelligent.
     'John seems to be intelligent.'

All RS verbs allow the pattern illustrated in (ii) (some allow that of (i) as well). The fact that sentences like (i) are possible with some RS verbs does not affect the argument.

[18] There is independent evidence that *croire* 'believe' does not permit Passive, so the sentence corresponding to (38b) in which Passive has applied can be ruled out independently.

b. Assume that the restriction on embedded infinitives is not a restriction on RO, but rather a restriction on specific predicates. Thus verbs like *considérer, croire,* and *juger* will have a specific restriction placed on them that Raising is unacceptable if an embedded infinitive results, regardless of whether RO or RS is involved. This, however, leaves it an accident that in these languages this restriction holds for all verbs for which RO is possible and for no verbs for which only RS is possible. It misses the generalization that the unacceptability of sentences like (42a, b) follows from the unacceptability of sentences like (38).

c. Assume that RO and RS are not the same rule. Then the restriction on embedded infinitives can be placed on RO and verbs like *considérer* can be marked for RO but not RS. RS can be left unconstrained.

Of these, (43c) seems to me to be the most reasonable alternative,[19] despite the fact that it involves giving up the claim that RO and RS are the same rule. And if (43c) is accepted, the prime syntactic motivation for VSO is lost.

The argument given above cannot be made for English. However, if RO and RS are different rules in French and Hungarian, the case for their being a single rule in English is considerably weakened. See Szamosi (1973) for an argument that RO and RS should be separate rules in English.

**2.** The arguments given above are all essentially independent of the cyclicity of SF; there are various other objections to the VSO hypothesis that depend on whether SF is cyclic or postcyclic. In this section, I will consider objections to a VSO system in which SF is postcyclic. These arguments consist in showing that if SF is postcyclic, a large number of rules must be stated with a totally ad hoc global condition. Giving arguments of this sort is not equivalent to arguing against global rules in general; what is challenged here is not the existence of global rules but rather the specific use of globality that is necessary in these cases.

Sections 2.2, 2.3, and 2.4 deal with Raising, Equi, and Tough Movement, respectively—cyclic rules whose structural descriptions require reference to more than one sentence. In these cases the problem we examined above for rules whose domain is a single sentence—that of structural identification for subject and object—cannot be resolved by formulating rules with an extra term. Here the rules must be stated globally.

---

[19] This, in effect, claims that derivations involving Passive/RS order are impossible in French. There may be an independent reason for this: passive forms in French, as in English, involve the copula; French has no postcopula elements (i.e. adjectives, like English *likely*) that trigger RS.

A case for RO and RS being separate rules can be made on the basis of Thai as well (I am indebted to Sarinee Anivan for this information). It can be shown that Thai has both RS and RO by arguments equivalent to those given in Postal (to appear) for English. However, in Thai, a special passive morpheme is used when a sentential object is passivized. Thai sentences equivalent to (39) never have this special marker, indicating that the RO/Passive derivation is the only one possible in these cases. Here too, a unitary rule of Raising is possible only if Raising is extrinsically ordered to precede Passive.

Section 2.1 deals with the rule of SF itself. Sections 2.5, 2.6, and 2.7 deal with certain postcyclic rules in languages other than English.

*2.1.* First, it is clear that a postcyclic SF must be formulated globally. This is evident from its interaction with Raising and Equi NP Deletion. Both of these cyclic rules move subjects out of embedded clauses, the first by moving them into a higher clause, the second by deleting them. Thus, at the time SF gets to apply, the structures underlying sentences like (44a, b) are (45a, b):

(44) a. Joe expects Mary to finish her work.
    b. Joe expects to finish his work.

(45) a.

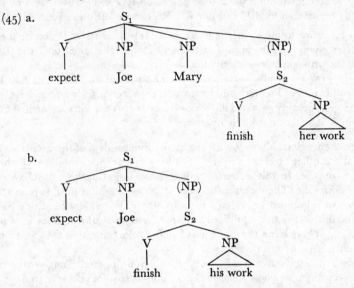

b.

What is to prevent SF from applying to the embedded sentence ($S_2$) of both of these trees, incorrectly producing (46a, b)?

(46) a. *Joe expects Mary her work to finish.
    b. *Joe expects his work to finish.

In order to block these sentences, SF must ensure that the NP it applies to was a subject at the end of the $S_2$ cycle. However, since this information will not be available at the time SF applies, the lack of structural differentiation of subjects and objects during the derivation makes it necessary that this rule be global.[20]

[20] The same argument that SF must be global is given in Postal (to appear), footnote 23.

The same argument can be made with respect to the interaction of SF with Question Formation and Relativization. Both of these rules move either subjects or objects to the left of the verb. If these rules precede SF, then, at the time SF applies, it will not be possible to tell whether a subject or object had been moved. Thus, for example, at the time SF applies, the relative clauses (47a, b) both have the structure (48), and to produce (47a) SF must check back to verify that *John* was a subject.

(47) a.   The man who John saw.
     b.   The man who saw John.

(48)   [$_{NP}$the man [$_S$who [$_S$saw John]]]

In order to ensure that these rules follow SF, an unmotivated extrinsic ordering is required. (Also, in order for this even to be possible, it must be stipulated that both Relativization and Question Formation are postcyclic rules, although there is no evidence against their being cyclic.[21])

*2.3.*   If SF is postcyclic, Raising (in any case, Raising into object position) must be stated globally. That this is true can be seen from sentences like (49) and (50):

(49)   I expect myself to win the election.
(50)   I expect to win the election.

Sentences like these are acceptable to most people, and they show that for verbs like *expect*, Equi NP Deletion is optional. Given, then, a structure like (51)

(51)

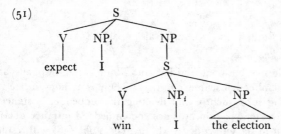

there is a good derivation in which the embedded instance of NP$_i$ is deleted by Equi and a good derivation in which the embedded instance of NP$_i$ is Raised. The former derivation gives (50), the latter (49). Note that in an SVO system, Raising and Equi need not be ordered with respect to each other, since the application of either automatically precludes application of the other. However, assuming that Equi and Raising are not extrinsically ordered in a VSO system leads to trouble; for, after Equi

---

[21] I do not mean "successive cyclic"; this notion is convincingly argued against in Postal (1972), to whom this term is due. Rather, I mean cyclic in the sense that both rules have a specific trigger and apply cyclically on the cycle in which the trigger is reached. For relative clauses, the trigger is the head noun. For questions, depending on other theoretical assumptions, the trigger may be either a higher verb (an abstract performative in the case of nonembedded questions) or a WH–COMP node in a higher sentence.

has deleted the embedded $NP_i$, what is to prevent Raising from applying and moving the NP adjacent to the embedded verb (at this point, *the election*) into the matrix? The result is (52):

(52)  *I expect the election to win.

Thus, unless Raising and Equi are extrinsically ordered, so that Raising precedes Equi, underlying VSO order requires that Raising be stated globally in order to block sentences like (52). It will be seen in the next section that even allowing this ad hoc ordering statement is inadequate.

*2.4.*  If SF is postcyclic, Equi NP Deletion must be stated globally. The argument here again concerns the interaction of Equi and Raising. Consider the tree (54) that would underlie a sentence like (53):

(53)  Mary expects Max to kiss her.

(54)

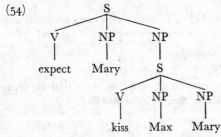

Verbs like *expect* allow both Equi, as in (55), and Raising, as in (53).

(55)  Mary expects to kiss Max.

Assuming no extrinsic ordering between Raising and Equi, what happens after Raising lifts *Max* out of the embedded sentence in (54)? There is no non-ad hoc way to block Equi from applying subsequently and deleting the embedded instance of *Mary* under coreference to the matrix subject, since the embedded instance of *Mary* is now immediately adjacent to the embedded verb. Sentences like (56) will result.[22]

(56)  *Mary expects Max to kiss.

It was noted in the previous section that ungrammatical sentences like (52) could be blocked if Raising and Equi are extrinsically ordered so that Raising precedes Equi. Given VSO order and a postcyclic rule of SF, in order to block unacceptable sentences like (56) by rule ordering, we would need to order Raising and Equi extrinsically so that Equi precedes Raising. Thus, statements of extrinsic rule ordering cannot be used in both of these cases. Given VSO order and postcyclic SF, Equi must be stated globally, again, to ensure that Equi deletes only cyclic subjects.

[22] Subject-controlled Equi cannot be prevented from applying across matrix objects, because of cases like *I promised Joe to behave myself.*

2.5. Given VSO order and a postcyclic rule of SF, Tough Movement must be stated globally. Tough Movement moves objects (direct objects, indirect objects, and objects of prepositions) out of embedded predicates to become derived matrix subjects. It cannot move embedded subjects. Thus, sentences like (58) below derive from the same structures as those underlying sentences like (57).

(57) a. $[_S[_S$to read this book] is impossible]
b. $[_S[_S$to give presents to Mary] is impossible]
c. $[_S[_S$to study by candlelight] is impossible]
d. $[_S[_S$that argument to be wrong] is impossible]

(58) a. This book is impossible to read.
b. Mary is impossible to give presents to.
c. Candlelight is impossible to study by.
d. *That argument is impossible to be wrong.

Not only can Tough Movement not move subjects (cf. (58d)), it cannot move an object across the subject of the sentential subject of *tough* predicates.[23] Thus, corresponding to sentences like (59a, b) we have no sentences like (60a, b).

(59) a. It would be impossible for Max for his children to go to that school.
b. It is impossible for your letter to be under the bed.

(60) a. *That school would be impossible for Max for his children to go to.
b. *The bed is impossible for your letter to be under.

There is convincing evidence (cf. the references in footnote 23) that in sentences like (61) the *for me* originates in the matrix as a prepositional phrase and acts as a controller to delete the embedded subject.

(61) That school would be impossible for me to go to.

Thus the structure underlying (61), in a VSO system, is (62):

(62)

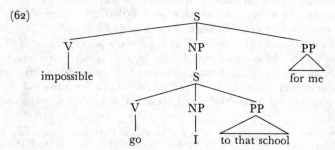

[23] Cf. Berman and Szamosi (1972), Appendix, and Berman (1973) for evidence for this.

There are also well-formed sentences having the underlying structure (62) in which the embedded subject is not coreferential to the object of *for* in the matrix. An example is (59a), which most people accept. This means that the SD for Equi between the matrix prepositional phrase and the embedded subject need not be met.[24] However, in order for Tough Movement to apply, the embedded subject must have been deleted, as noted above. That is, we start out with an embedded sentence containing a verb followed by any number of arguments, as in (63):

(63)   $V\ NP_1\ X\ NP_2\ X\ NP_3\ X \ldots$

At the time Tough Movement applies, the first of these arguments, the embedded subject, must have been deleted by Equi. However, unless it is stated globally, Tough Movement does not have access to the information it needs; all it sees is a verb followed by some number of noun phrases, i.e. (63). It cannot tell, on the basis of (63), whether or not it may move $NP_1$: it may if in an earlier stage of the derivation, there was an NP to the left of it. Nor does it know if it can move $NP_2$; it cannot, if $NP_1$ is a subject. And so on for $NP_3$, etc. What is needed is a global condition that checks and ensures that for any $NP_i$ to be moved, that NP at the end of the embedded S cycle was $NP_{i+1}$.

Again, this global condition is necessitated solely by the fact that subjects and nonsubjects cannot be structurally identified at the relevant stage of a derivation in a VSO system.

It might be claimed that the global conditions we have just been discussing all refer to cyclic subjects and that this is perfectly natural, since well-attested global rules make use of the very same notion.[25] This is not the case, however. Note that making SF, Raising, Equi, and Tough Movement global neither explains anything nor captures any generalizations. It serves the same function as the "extra NP" term in the rules discussed in section 1; it ensures that the distinction between subjects and nonsubjects is maintained. Hence, the fact that the condition on the rules just discussed must be global is purely accidental; the global statement of them is necessary only because these rules apply to domains which have already been cycled on. What is at issue here is more significant than the question of whether these rules should be stated globally or not, or whether the globality in question can be described in the same "natural" terms as that of independently motivated global rules.

A theory which postulates underlying VSO order and a postcyclic rule of SF can be regarded as making the following empirical claim: given a $[_S V\ NP]$ structure, transformations (cyclic and postcyclic, up to and including SF) are indifferent to whether the NP is the subject of an intransitive verb or the object of a transitive one (whose subject has disappeared). It makes this claim because it is implicit in the structure

---

[24] For most predicates of this type, if the SD of Equi is met the rule is obligatory. That is, most people reject sentences like *It would be impossible for me for me to go to that school*, while accepting sentences like (59). Cf. Berman (1973) for further discussion of this.

[25] E.g. the rule of Case Agreement in Classical Greek discussed in Andrews (1970).

$[_s$V NP (NP)] that identification of subject versus object is possible only when both are present. This claim, however, is quite clearly wrong. It has always been known that there are rules which require precisely this information; those we have just been considering are cases in point. The generalization that we want our theory to capture is this: rules need to know whether the constituent they are to apply to is a subject or not.

In considering the VSO hypothesis seriously, we found that in order to make this required information available to transformations, we had to include specific (global) conditions on several rules. It is not the globality of the rules that is at issue. Rather, it is the fact that the conditions are totally ad hoc. Assuming that global rules exist and granting even that their use in the grammar is "free", it is still clear that to state these particular global conditions is to miss a significant generalization. The ad hoc nature of this is shown clearly by the fact that we have to state the same global condition on every rule of a given type and that its effect, in every instance, is to get around the claim, implicit in the VSO hypothesis, that structural identification of subjects versus nonsubjects is irrelevant.

This line of reasoning carries over to the cases discussed in section 1. There, instead of global conditions, we had to make use of a complication in the statement of the rules, again, in order to preserve the subject/nonsubject distinction.

To claim that the complications (global or not) in the statements of the rules under discussion are perfectly in order is to claim that it is an accident that the same complication has to be introduced in the rules of section 1 and the same global condition attached in the rules discussed above in this section. When we realize, further, that the effect of the devices of section 1 and of section 2 is exactly the same, that the VSO hypothesis has to be patched up in every instance for exactly the same reason, it becomes clear that the hypothesis is empirically wrong.

*2.6.* Another rule that must be global if it applies to VSO structures is Cliticization. In many languages, pronominal objects are cliticized and moved either to second position in the sentence or to the verb. Thus, in French, for example, we have cases such as those in (64) where a nonpronominal direct object must show up to the right of the verb, but a pronominal direct object is cliticized and moves to the left of the verb.

(64) a. Je vois l'homme.
   I see the man
   b. Je le vois.
   I him see
   'I see him'.
   c. *Je l'homme vois
   d. *Je vois le

Kayne (to appear) argues that Cliticization must be a postcyclic rule, and his most convincing argument concerns the interaction of Cliticization and Tough Movement. (Perlmutter (in preparation b) also argues for the postcyclicity of Cliticization.)

Cliticization is an obligatory rule, and its effect is to adjoin the cliticized object to the verb, making it a single phonological word with the verb. Given, then, a sentence like (65)

(65)   Il est difficile à convaincre.
       'He is hard to convince.'

we start out with (66) (I use SVO order here, as the order is not relevant to his argument):

(66)   $[_S[_S$convaincre il] est difficile]

If Cliticization were cyclic, it would have to apply on the embedded S cycle, turning *il* into a clitic pronoun and attaching it to the verb. Then, when Tough Movement was able to apply on the matrix S cycle, *il* would not be able to be moved. However, (65) is a perfectly good sentence, and it shows that Cliticization must follow Tough Movement. If Tough Movement is a cyclic rule, it is necessary that Cliticization be postcyclic, if sentences like (65) are to be derived.

I assume then that Cliticization, as well as SF, is a postcyclical rule. Now, unless Cliticization is extrinsically ordered to follow SF, there will be derivations in which Cliticization precedes SF. Consider the two relative clauses (67a, b):

(67) a.   l'homme qu'il voit
          'the man that he sees'
     b.   l'homme qui le voit
          'the man that sees him'

After Relativization, but prior to both SF and Cliticization, they have the following structures:

(68) a.   $[_{NP}$l'homme $[_S$que voit il ____]
     b.   $[_{NP}$l'homme $[_S$que voit ____ il]

In (68), the deletion site is indicated by ____, but at the time it applies, Cliticization cannot see the deletion site unless it is stated globally. In order for Cliticization not to apply to (68a) it must be able to check back and distinguish the *il* in the embedded sentence of (68a) from the *il* of the embedded sentence of (68b).

The global condition on Cliticization is not necessary if SF precedes Cliticization in all derivations. However, to do that, an otherwise unnecessary extrinsic ordering becomes necessary. And, as in other cases where extrinsic ordering could be used to avoid complicating a rule, the effect of extrinsic ordering is to enable us to state the second transformation in an SVO system.

2.7. A large number of languages, including Spanish and Italian, have a rule deleting unstressed subject pronouns. Thus, using Italian as an example, we have sentences like (69a–c) where in each case the subject pronouns, *io, tu, lui*, respectively, are missing.

(69) a.  Vedo Giovanni.
         '(I) see John.'
     b.  Vedi Giovanni.
         '(You) see John.'
     c.  Vede Giovanni.
         '(He) sees John.'

Subject Pronoun Drop is a very late rule, and it is clearly postcyclic (cf. Perlmutter (in preparation a) for evidence for this in Portuguese—the same arguments hold for the other languages mentioned).

Given VSO order and a postcyclic rule of SF, without extrinsic ordering statements, there will be derivations in which Subject Pronoun Drop precedes SF. Consider then relative clauses like (70a, b):

(70) a.  l'uomo che vedo
         'the man that I see'
     b.  l'uomo che mi vede
         'the man that sees me'

Before any relevant rules apply, these have structures like (71a, b):

(71) a.  $[_{NP}$l'uomo $[_S$che vedo io lui]]
     b.  $[_{NP}$l'uomo $[_S$che vede lui io]]

The derivation of (70a) involves deletion (or movement) of *lui* (Relativization) and Subject Pronoun Drop, to delete *io*. Assuming that SF and Subject Pronoun Drop are not extrinsically ordered, there are two possible derivations: (a) SF followed by Subject Pronoun Drop and (b) Subject Pronoun Drop with no SF.

The derivation of (70b) involves deletion (or movement) of *lui* (Relativization), and Cliticization (*io* cliticizes to *mi*). However, after Relativization, (71a) and (71b) look identical. How can Subject Pronoun Drop be prevented from applying to (71b) at this point and producing (72)?

(72) *l'uomo che vede
      'the man who sees me'

((72) is a perfectly good relative clause, but cannot mean 'the man who sees me'. It means only 'the man who he sees'.) Unless Cliticization and Subject Pronoun Drop are extrinsically ordered, it cannot, given underlying VSO order. Thus, without extrinsic ordering, Subject Pronoun Drop (as well as Cliticization) must be made global, so that it can distinguish subjects from objects.

In languages with both rules (like Italian and Spanish), Cliticization and Subject Pronoun Drop apply in complementary environments: the former applies to non-subjects and the latter to subjects. In an SVO system, subjects and nonsubjects are always structurally distinguished; these rules, therefore, pose no problems and need not be ordered with respect to one another. Neither need be global. In a VSO system, without extrinsic ordering, there will be derivations in which both Cliticization and Subject Pronoun Drop follow Relativization but precede SF. Since Subject Pronoun Drop and Cliticization can apply in either order under this assumption, both must be global. If we allow Subject Pronoun Drop and Cliticization to be extrinsically ordered with respect to each other, only one of them need be global, namely the first (in either ordering), since once the first rule has applied, the second one may be stated so as to apply to any pronoun(s) remaining to the right of the verb. (This is because, as noted above, the rules apply in complementary environments.) Thus, if these rules are to apply to VSO structures (i.e. before SF), one of them must be global even with extrinsic ordering between them. If they follow SF, they are being stated in an SVO system, without globality, but, again, otherwise unnecessary extrinsic ordering statements must be made. Any one of these alternatives represents a complication over the treatment of pronominal subjects and objects in an SVO system.

2.8. Portuguese has two types of infinitives, traditionally called the Personal or Inflected Infinitive and the Impersonal or Uninflected Infinitive. Thus, for example, we find the following contrast:

(73) a.  Mandou os meninos brincar lá fora.
          'He ordered the children to play outside.'
     b.  Mandou os meninos brincarem lá fora.
          'He ordered that the children play outside.'

In (73a), the embedded infinitive *brincar* is uninflected; in (73b), *brincarem* has a third person plural ending, agreeing with *os meninos*. Perini (1972) argues that *mandar* 'to order' takes an object complement (like English *expect*) and optionally allows Raising. The difference between (73a) and (73b) is that Raising has applied in the former but not the latter. We can see this more clearly in cases where we have a pronoun instead of *os meninos*. Consider the following:

(74) a.  Mandou-os brincar lá fora.
          'He ordered them to play outside.'
     b.  *Mandou-os brincarem lá fora.
     c.  Mandou êles brincarem lá fora.
          'He ordered that they play outside.'
     d.  *Mandou êles brincar lá fora.

In (74a) and (74b), *êles* has been cliticized and attached to *mandou*. In order for this to have happened, *êles* must have been raised into the matrix sentence. Only the uninflected infinitive is possible. Cliticization of pronominal objects is obligatory; the fact that we have noncliticized pronouns in (74c) and (74d) indicates that these pronouns have remained subjects in the embedded sentence. Here only the inflected infinitive is possible. Similarly, note that a passive version of (73) is (75):

(75) a.  Os meninos foram mandados brincar lá fora.
         'The children were ordered to play outside.'
     b.  *Os meninos foram mandados brincarem lá fora.

Passive is possible only when the subject and object are clausemates; the fact that an inflected infinitive is impossible indicates that in (73a) Raising has moved *os meninos* into the matrix while in (73b) *os meninos* has remained in the embedded sentence.

The generalization, then, is that infinitives are inflected to agree with their subject; if the subject is removed by Raising (or Equi), no inflected infinitive results. It follows, then, that Infinitive Agreement must be postcyclic, since both Raising and Equi block its application. If Infinitive Agreement were cyclic, it would apply on the embedded S cycle, before Raising or Equi had a chance to remove the embedded subject, and contrasts like those in (73)–(75) would never arise.

Consider then a sentence like (76):

(76)  Mandou-os visitar-nos.
      'He ordered them to visit us.'

In a VSO system, (76) has an underlying structure like (77):

(77)  [$_S$mandar êle [$_S$visitar êles nos]]
       order    he    visit   they us

On the matrix S cycle, the subject of the embedded S, *êles*, is raised to be the object of *mandou*. Postcyclically, the matrix subject *êle* 'he' will be deleted by Subject Pronoun Drop, the raised object *êles* 'them' will cliticize onto *mandou* giving *mandou-os*, and the embedded object *nos* 'us' will cliticize onto *visitar*. At the end of the cyclic rules, however, we have (78):

(78)  [$_S$mandou (êle) êles [$_S$visitar _____ nos]]

If rules of this sort are not extrinsically ordered, Infinitive Agreement can precede Cliticization. What is to prevent Infinitive Agreement, then, from applying to the embedded S of (78) and making *visitar* agree with *nos*, ultimately producing (79) (where the elements in parentheses are to be deleted by Subject Pronoun Deletion)?

(79)  *(Êle) mandou-os (nos) visitarmos.

Thus, here again, without wholly ad hoc statements about the ordering of these rules, a global condition must be placed on Infinitive Agreement to ensure that it is triggered only by subjects.

The last three rules discussed are all postcyclic, and it might be claimed that, given a postcyclic rule of SF, there may be a "natural" way to (intrinsically) order these rules after SF, such that they apply to SVO structures. This proposed solution, which avoids the complications outlined above, seems reasonable for Subject Pronoun Drop and Infinitive Agreement. They are most naturally stated on SVO structures, and, by stating them that way, we can ensure that their application follows SF. The complications discussed above arose because we tried to force these rules to apply to VSO structures. I assume that no proponent of the VSO system would claim that all rules can be stated more simply on VSO structures.

The situation is different, however, with Cliticization. Here, as with the rules discussed in section 1, Cliticization must either follow or precede SF in all derivations. If it is to precede SF, it must be stated globally; the situation in this case is the same as that of Tough Movement (cf. section 2.4), where the rule applies to a string of the form V–X–NP–X–NP–X . . . and must know if the NP to be moved is a subject or nonsubject. If Cliticization is to follow SF, it again must be stated globally. The rule cannot be made to explicitly include the subject (to the left of V), since it applies to domains which have already been cycled on (in particular, to embedded clauses which may have lost their subjects through the application of rules like Raising and Equi).

At best, then, it might be claimed that while Cliticization remains a problem, Subject Pronoun Drop and Infinitive Agreement are as simply handled in a VSO system as in an SVO system, and therefore provide no evidence for either hypothesis. Such a claim, however, would be misleading. It obscures the fact that the only significant difference between Cliticization and the other two rules is that the latter apply to subjects and the former to nonsubjects.

Note that these three rules serve very similar and interrelated functions. Cliticization is essentially the equivalent of object incorporation or object agreement in other languages; Subject Pronoun Drop serves to get rid of information made redundant by Agreement. They are all postcyclic and rather "surfacy" rules—they neither alter structures significantly nor provide the input to rules that do. In a VSO system, even with "intrinsic" ordering of SF, Subject Pronoun Drop, and Infinitive Agreement (along the lines suggested above), it must be claimed that Cliticization is a rule different in kind from the latter two, requiring "special" information from earlier stages of the derivation. The generalization about the "surfacy" character and functional similarity of these rules comes closer to being captured, and the rules themselves are most naturally stated, in an SVO system.

3. In this section we will turn our attention to the possibility of underlying VSO order with a cyclic rule of SF. If SF is cyclic, it follows that all postcyclic rules will be defined on SVO structures, and therefore, no such rules are relevant. Nor are the cases of Equi, Raising, and Tough Movement discussed above, since in all of these

cases, the embedded sentence has SVO order at the time the rule applies. The problems that arise when SF is cyclic are of another sort. The claim I will make here is that if SF is cyclic, almost all sentences with surface VS order must go through a stage in which SV order is present. That is, I will argue that if SF is cyclic, McCawley's claim that a grammar with a rule of SF does not need a rule of Subject Verb Inversion is wrong. This was shown to be true above in the case of certain types of French relative clauses (section 1.2), independently of the ordering of SF. Here, we will assume simply that SF is cyclic and examine other cases of surface VS order.

*3.1.* Consider first simple yes–no questions like (80a, b):

(80) a. Has John come?
     b. Will John stay?

There are major differences among linguists on how such sentences are derived, involving the status of the auxiliaries *have* and *will*, the question of whether such sentences are themselves embedded under performatives or whether they are underlying "highest sentences", and probably other points as well. However, the consensus today seems to be that questions are formed with reference to some trigger, which I will call Q for convenience, and that this trigger is found in a sentence higher than the one which shows up as a question (cf. footnote (21)). The underlying structure of (80a) is thus (81):[26]

(81)

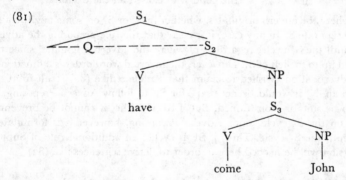

SF applies cyclically in $S_3$; on the $S_2$ cycle, Raising then moves *John* to follow *have*. Since SF is cyclic it applies again on the $S_2$ cycle. Thus, by the time the Q is reached on the $S_1$ cycle, SF has already applied, and a rule of Subject Verb Inversion is needed to produce (80a). Subject Verb Inversion is needed in an SVO system, but not SF. And, in an SVO system, it is not the case that sentences with surface SV order

---

[26] I assume here that auxiliaries are higher verbs, as proposed in Ross (1967b). The arguments given in this section are not changed if tense is also analysed as a higher verb (as proposed in McCawley 1971), so tense has not been indicated in trees.

in general go through a stage in which VS order is present. However, in order to derive VS sentences like (80) in a VSO system, a stage of the derivation in which SV order is present cannot be avoided.

*3.2.* Consider sentences like (82a, b):[27]

(82) a.  On the bed is sitting the child who caused all the trouble.
b.  Somewhere on this island is hidden an old chest full of gold doubloons.

In these sentences, Adverb Preposing is followed by a rule of Subject Predicate Inversion that is different from the Subject Verb (or Subject Aux) Inversion discussed above in that the subject is interchanged with more than just the first verb. Leaving out the adverb for the present, the structure underlying (82a) is something like (83):

(83)

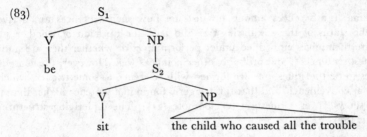

It is not clear where the adverb originates, whether in $S_2$ or $S_1$ or, some might claim, in a completely separate S. In any case, it is clear that the rule preposing the adverb cannot apply until the $S_1$ cycle, regardless of where the adverb originates, since the adverb must end up to the left of $S_1$. However, the inverted word order is a function of the preposed adverb: if one wished to claim that sentences like (82) result from the failure of SF to apply, it would be necessary for SF to follow Adverb Preposing, in order for SF to be suitably constrained. But if SF is cyclic, it cannot be prevented from applying on the $S_2$ cycle, since Adverb Preposing, however it is formulated, cannot apply until the $S_1$ cycle. Thus, if SF is cyclic, an additional rule of Subject Predicate Inversion will be needed here in order to derive sentences like (82).

*3.3.* It is probable that cases of Subject Aux Inversion triggered by the preposing of "negative containing" constituents will also pose a problem for a VSO system in which SF is cyclic. Consider sentences like (84a–c):

(84) a.  Never have I seen such a sight in my life . . .
b.  Under no circumstances is it possible to get into that room.
c.  In no way can he claim to have been original.

---

[27] Such sentences are discussed in Aissen and Hankamer (1972).

Under the assumption that Negative Preposing is postcyclic and SF cyclic, SF will apply before Negative Preposing, since the environment for the nonapplication of SF will not be available until after Negative Preposing has applied. Thus, in order to generate sentences like (84), Subject Aux Inversion will be needed, despite the existence of SF.

If Negative Preposing is a cyclic rule, the situation does not change appreciably. An unmotivated extrinsic ordering statement, insuring that SF always follows Negative Preposing, will be necessary, or the situation will be the same as if Negative Preposing were postcyclic. In either case, the situation is more complicated than in an SVO system.

The same argument can be made for the Directional Adverb Preposing rule that produces sentences like (85a, b):

(85) a. Out went John.
　　　b. Up soared the kite.

If the rule preposing directional adverbs like *out* and *up* is postcyclic, SF will apply before the adverbs are preposed and an additional rule will be needed to produce sentences like (85). If the adverb preposing rule is cyclic, it will have to be extrinsically ordered with SF in order to prevent the same situation from arising. Again, in an SVO system, none of these problems arise.

*3.4.* Consider (86):

(86) John likes blondes and so does Harry.

Arguments parallel to those in Grinder and Postal (1971) can be given that show that such sentences are derived by a deletion rule from conjunctions of full sentences. That is, (86) has (87) in its underlying structure:

(87) John likes blondes and Harry likes blondes.

The inversion that shows up in the second conjunct of sentences like (86) is triggered by the deletion of *likes blondes* under identity to the first conjunct. It is clear that the relevant deletion cannot be effected until the cycle of the S dominating both conjuncts. That means that all cyclic rules will apply to each of the conjuncts independently, before the deletion rule can apply. If SF is cyclic, it will apply to both the first and second conjuncts, producing SVO order. Then, on the top S cycle, the deletion rule applies. Only then is the environment for inversion of subject and auxiliary met. A rule of Subject Aux Inversion is needed to produce (86).

The identical argument can be made for sentences like (88):

(88) Joe likes blondes, as does Harry.

Here again, SF will apply to the *as* clause, before the deletion of *likes blondes* in that clause can be effected. An additional inversion rule is needed to produce the VS pattern that occurs.

A third type of VS construction of this sort is that found in sentences like (89):

(89)  John dates more girls than does Harry.

Here again, the clause following *than* begins as a full sentence and is reduced under identity to the main clause. Since it is this deletion that provides the environment for the inversion in the *than* clause, cyclic SF will have applied in that clause before the reduction. An additional inversion rule is needed to produce (89).

We see then that the conditions requiring VS surface order are defined either postcyclically or, if cyclically, then on a cycle which is always "higher up" than the one which actually shows up as VS. Hence, if SF is cyclic, the conditions for surface VS order cannot be stated as conditions on when SF is not to apply. Cyclic SF cannot be prevented from producing SV structures (strings) by the end of the relevant cycle; these structures will later be converted to VS structures by inversion rules. Thus, none of the various types of inversion rules needed in an SVO system can be dispensed with, and SF is needed in addition to them.

The problem is not only that having SF as well as the various inversion rules complicates the grammar in terms of rule count. One reason for setting up SVO structures and producing inverted patterns transformationally was that, intuitively, it was felt that VS constructions were in some way "marked", deviant from the norm. With the possible exception of yes–no questions, all cases of VS order are dependent on other transformations' (*Wh* Fronting, Adverb Preposing, etc.) having applied. In other words, the inversion rules are secondary processes, optional and/or obligatory under differing circumstances. The decision to derive VS order transformationally accorded with the transform-dependent nature of this order.

Intuitions, of course, are not an argument. But when, given certain theoretical assumptions, it turns out that every VS sentence must go through a stage of being SV (and every SV sentence must go through a stage of being VS) it seems that those assumptions are missing something.

4.  In proposing VSO order, McCawley was concerned with showing that there is syntactic justification for assuming that English is underlyingly verb-initial. The arguments against VSO that I have presented here are syntactic arguments—I have tried to show that syntactic rules in English and other surface SVO languages are most naturally stated on SVO structures. I have made no claims about semantic structures. Whether the linear order of predicates and arguments in semantic representation is significant, and whether predicate-initial semantic representations are correct, are questions which are beyond the scope of this article.

The hypothesis that English (or French, or Italian, etc.) has underlying VSO word order is nonvacuous only if it can be demonstrated that there exist syntactic rules that have to apply to constituents stated in VSO terms, or whose statement on VSO structures (at least) represents an advantage over the statement of the same rule in an SVO system. In the preceding sections, we have explored whether the VSO hypothesis has empirical content in just this sense. We found that cyclic clausemate rules (e.g. Dative Movement, Particle Movement, and Heavy NP Shift) require a special, more complicated, formulation if they are to apply to verb-initial trees. Under the generally accepted assumption that SF is postcyclic, two-story rules like Raising, Equi, and Tough Movement and postcyclic rules like SF, Cliticization, and Subject Pronoun Drop have to be stated globally, although the globality has no explanatory value. For each of the above cases, the complication in the statement of the rules does not capture anything about the nature of the rule involved; it is simply a consequence of its being stated on VSO structures, i.e. an artifact of the VSO hypothesis. Under the assumption that SF is a cyclic rule, it can be seen that the rule itself proves to be a complication, because in this case, all cases of inverted word order go through a sequence of VS–SV–VS order. Underlying VSO order prevents the passive sentences of section 1.1 from being derived adequately and forces the grammar to miss rather than capture generalizations about these sentences. The cases of stylistic inversion in French and Subject Predicate Inversion are more complicated in VSO regardless of the cyclicity of SF. The questions raised in section 1.6 regarding the unity of Raising render dubious the advantage of being able to state Raising as one rule. Based on the sample of rules surveyed here, it seems that the VSO hypothesis comes out inferior in terms of symbol count alone.

However, symbol count is, at best, a side issue. As McCawley (who explicitly denied accepting "evaluation measures" of this sort) recognized, the issue of SVO versus VSO is not one of "mine has ten, yours has twelve—I win!" The real defect of the VSO hypothesis is its failure to capture generalizations about English and similar surface SVO languages. What has emerged from this investigation is that for a large number of well-motivated syntactic transformations, there is a relevant distinction between subjects and nonsubjects. That is, while there do not seem to be rules which refer to, say, indirect objects or their complement class of nonindirect objects, or that apply to prepositional phrases beginning with *on*, or that differentiate between the fourth and fifth noun phrase after V, there are rules which refer solely to subjects and rules which refer only to nonsubjects. The "property" of being a subject or nonsubject cannot refer to a semantic notion, since subjecthood is shared by semantically empty noun phrases like *there* and expletive *it*, and every rule that applies to subjects applies to these. It has generally been assumed that grammatical relations can be adequately defined in terms of tree configurations, and both McCawley (1970) and the present article share this assumption.[28] While SVO trees implicitly allow us to characterize the subject/nonsubject distinction, verb-initial structures provide instead for defining

[28] Paul Postal and David Perlmutter (personal communication) have suggested that rules like Passive and Raising (and other rules as well) are defined in terms of grammatical relations rather than on tree structures and that grammatical relations themselves are defined structure-independently. Given such an approach, which still needs to be investigated, the issue at hand disappears.

such relations as "NP immediately to the right of V", "second NP from V", etc. It seems, however, that transformations do not make use of relations of this sort. While such relations can adequately distinguish subjects from nonsubjects in underlying structures (i.e. in structures which have undergone no deletion or reordering rules), they cannot adequately do this in trees in which deletions and reorderings have taken place. VSO erroneously predicts that in such cases, relations like "second NP from V" will continue to be useful in stating transformations.

If SF is postcyclic, the problem with the relations defined by VSO is immediately obvious. If more than one NP follows V, the displacement of the NP immediately adjacent to the V results in a tree in which V is still immediately followed by an NP. While transformations such as Passive reorder NPs to the right of V in such a way that the new NP adjacent to V is "equivalent" to the displaced NP, the NP left adjacent to V as a result of rules like Raising is not "equivalent" to the displaced NP in a linguistic-ally significant way. That is, the new "first NP" after Passive applies is also the new subject, the new "first NP" after Raising applies is not the new subject. The relations defined by VSO fail to distinguish between such transformations. Thus, if SF (or Raising, or Equi, etc.) is stated to apply to the NP immediately to the right of V, problems arise precisely because of the functional nonequivalence of NPs adjacent to V as a result of Passive and NPs adjacent to V as a result of Raising. These two rules are merely illustrative; the same problem, perhaps in slightly different guises, pervades the whole system.

If SF is cyclic, the same problem crops up in a slightly different way. The clausemate rules that need to distinguish between subjects and nonsubjects cannot be stated to apply to both VSO and SVO structures. It is obvious that allowing such rules to precede SF in some derivations and follow it in others is unworkable. If they always precede SF, the subject figures as an obligatory extra term to the right of the verb in order to make use of the notion "NP nonadjacent to V". If they follow SF, they are applying to SVO structures, but even here the situation is not parallel to what would happen if VSO structures had never existed. Here, the subject must still figure as an extra term, this time to the left of V, so that the relation of "first NP to the right of V" can be made to work without extrinsic ordering, as obtaining in an SVO string.

Thus, regardless of the ordering of SF, which we can think of as the mediating point between transformations applying to VSO structures and transformations applying to SVO structures, we must still define rules in terms of the type of relation described above. In the case of rules applying to VSO structures that apply (in whole or in part) to sentences already cycled on, we need to reconstruct the subject by global conditions. In the case of cyclic clausemate rules, we need to use extra terms to retain the subject/nonsubject distinction that these relations describe on underlying struc-tures. In either case, in order to make the syntax work, we must, in an ad hoc fashion, both circumvent the predictions made by VSO and reintroduce notions that are naturally definable if we start with SVO order. The VSO hypothesis is therefore defective in two ways: first, because it implicitly defines a set of relations that are unnecessary in characterizing syntactic phenomena, and second, because it does not adequately define those relations that are necessary. The situation is like "simplifying" the game of Chinese checkers by having all pieces of the same color, and then referring back to where each piece started in order to know what direction to move it in.[29]

The case against VSO was stated above in terms of generalizations missed if rules apply to verb-initial structures. It can also be stated in terms of what the VSO hypothesis implies about universal grammar.[30] The assumption that languages like English and French have underlying VSO order with a rule of SF requires, as we have seen, severe complications in the grammars of these languages. One would therefore predict that languages with underlying VSO and surface SVO order, but without these complications, would be quite common; i.e. that the complications, being unmotivated, would be accidental and language-particular. In other words, one would predict that there would be a number of languages in which sentences equivalent to the ungrammatical sentences given in this article would be grammatical. This prediction appears to be wrong, since no known SVO languages manifest phenomena even remotely resembling what the simpler formulations of the rules would produce. Hence, the VSO hypothesis makes a wrong prediction about the range of possible languages.

In order to make the absence of such languages nonaccidental, universal grammar (the metatheory) would have to be revised in such a way that the complications of the individual grammars considered above become an automatic consequence. In other words, the complexities of the individual grammars must have a counterpart in universal grammar; otherwise the theory predicts the existence of a large number of impossible languages. On the other hand, excluding from universal grammar the possibility that surface SVO languages are derived from underlying VSO structures would make the impossible languages impossible (or at least very difficult) and the possible ones comparatively natural.

The arguments given here do not bear on the question of whether or not there is a VP node. That is, I have argued for NP–V–NP rather than for NP–VP. While it seems to me that a good case for a VP or predicate node can be made, this issue has not been considered here at all.

Another interesting question which has not been considered here is the status of word order in general. Traditional typological studies have distinguished among three types of (surface) word order: VSO, SVO, and SOV. While there are real problems with the precise status of the terms S and O (especially for surface VSO languages), this three-way distinction has proved relevant to various fairly consistent differences among languages. For example, SOV languages typically have postpositions and not

---

[29] I am indebted to Robert Wall for this analogy.
[30] The observations in these two paragraphs are due to Avery Andrews.

prepositions and relative clauses in which the head noun follows the embedded clause, while SVO languages are predominantly prepositional, with relative clauses to the right of the head noun (cf. Greenberg 1966). Certain types of rules differ consistently depending on the (surface) word order. These differences must be accounted for, and the fact that they seem to be rather pervasive differences suggests that differences in surface word order are not purely superficial.

It should be noted that in arguing that English is not VSO, certain claims are being made about languages that are VSO. For example, if VSO languages truly have no structure beyond V–NP–NP, we might expect that notions like "first NP from V" will be relevant in defining transformations in these languages. I do not know whether or not this is the case, and it would seem that a prerequisite for answering this question is more work of a typological nature.[31]

### References

Aissen, J. and J. Hankamer (1972) "Shifty Subjects: A Conspiracy in Syntax," *Linguistic Inquiry* III, 501–504.

Andrews, A. (1971) "Case Agreement of Predicate Modifiers in Ancient Greek," *Linguistic Inquiry* II, 127–151.

Berman, A. (1973) *Adjectives and Adjective Complement Constructions in English*, unpublished Doctoral dissertation, Harvard University, Cambridge, Mass.

Berman, A. and M. Szamosi (1972) "Observations on Sentential Stress," *Language* 48, 304–325.

Fraser, B. (1965) *An Examination of the Verb Particle Construction in English*, unpublished Doctoral dissertation, MIT, Cambridge, Mass.

Green, G. (1972) "Some Observations on the Syntax and Semantics of Instrumental Verbs," in P. Peranteau, J. Levi, and G. Phares, eds., *Papers from the Eighth Regional Meeting of the Chicago Linguistic Society*, Chicago, Illinois.

Greenberg, J. (1966) "Some Universals of Grammar with Particular Reference to the Order of Meaningful Elements," in J. Greenberg, ed., *Universals of Language*, MIT Press, Cambridge, Mass.

Grinder, J. and P. Postal (1971) "Missing Antecedents," *Linguistic Inquiry* II, 269–312.

Gross, M. (1968) *Grammaire transformationnelle du Français, Syntaxe du Verbe*, Larousse, Paris.

Jackendoff, R. (1972) *Semantic Interpretation in Generative Grammar*, MIT Press, Cambridge, Mass.

---

[31] If it should turn out to be the case that some surface verb-initial languages have rules like English, French, etc., we would be at least as justified in claiming that these verb-initial languages are underlying verb-medial as the other way around. More justified, in fact, since we would avoid the type of undesirable complications discussed in the foregoing pages. Further, we would, in effect, be claiming that natural languages are characterized by a primary division of sentences into subject and predicate, with the main typological distinction being between those languages which have the verb rightmost in the predicate and those which have the verb leftmost in the predicate. In this fashion, we could maintain the claim that the subject/nonsubject distinction would have a universal structural correlate.

(I do not mean to advance this as a hypothesis, since the facts about VSO languages necessary to deciding questions of this sort are unknown to me and since the question of whether grammatical relations are to be structurally defined remains open.)

Kayne, R. (to appear) *The Transformational Cycle in French Syntax*, MIT Press, Cambridge, Mass.

Legum, S. (1968) "The Verb-Particle Construction in English, Basic or Derived?" in B. Darden, C. Bailey, and A. Davison, eds., *Papers from the Fourth Regional Meeting of the Chicago Linguistic Society*, Chicago, Illinois.

McCawley, J. (1970) "English as a VSO Language," *Language* 46, 286–299.

McCawley, J. (1971) "Tense and Time Reference in English," in C. Fillmore and D. T. Langendoen, eds., *Studies in Linguistic Semantics*, Holt, Rinehart and Winston, New York.

Moreau, M.–L. (1971) "L'homme que je crois qui est venu; qui, que: relatifs et conjonctions," *Langue Française* 11.

Perini, M. (1972) "On the Infinitive Clause in Portuguese," unpublished paper, University of Texas, Austin.

Perlmutter, D. (1972) "Evidence for Shadow Pronouns in French Relativization," in P. Peranteau, J. Levi, and G. Phares, eds., *The Chicago Which Hunt*, Chicago Linguistic Society, Chicago, Illinois.

Perlmutter, D. (in preparation a) "Object-Raising in Portuguese."

Perlmutter, D. (in preparation b) "Evidence for a Post-Cycle in Syntax."

Perlmutter, D. (in preparation c) "MasquErade in French."

Postal, P. (1972) "On Some Rules that are not Successive Cyclic," *Linguistic Inquiry* III, 211–222.

Postal, P. (to appear) *On Raising*, MIT Press, Cambridge, Mass.

Rosenbaum, P. (1967) *The Grammar of English Predicate Complement Constructions*, MIT Press, Cambridge, Mass.

Ross, J. R. (1967a) *Constraints on Variables in Syntax*, unpublished Doctoral dissertation, MIT, Cambridge, Mass.

Ross, J. R. (1967b) "Auxiliaries as Main Verbs," *Journal of Philosophical Linguistics* 1.1.

Stockwell, R., P. Schachter, and B. Partee (1968) *Integration of Transformational Theories of English Syntax*, Volume II. U.S. Air Force, ESD-TR-68-419.

Szamosi, M. (1973) "On the Unity of Subject Raising," in C. Corum, T. Smith-Stark, and A. Weiser, eds., *Papers from the Ninth Regional Meeting of the Chicago Linguistic Society*, Chicago, Illinois.

## QUESTIONS

**Question 1.** In Section 1.1, Berman discusses 'complex verbs' like *take advantage*. She claims that an underlying structure such as (i-a) nicely allows both the two passive sentences (i-b) and (i-c) to be generated.

(i) a.

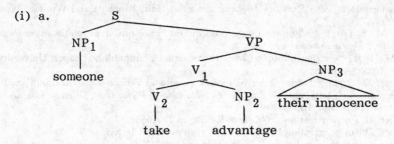

(i) b. Advantage was taken of their innocence.
(i) c. Their innocence was taken advantage of.

To get (i-b), Passive would apply to the string $NP_1$ $V_2$ $NP_2$. To get (i-c), Passive would apply to the string $NP_1$ $V_1$ $NP_3$.

There is a principle in syntax, however, called the A/A ('A over A') principle that the student should examine here. Chomsky (1964) proposed that in a structure such as (ii), where the node A is embedded within a larger phrase also dominated by the categorial node A, if a transformation is written to apply ambiguously to the lower or topmost A, it must apply to the top A.

(ii)

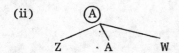

Thus the A/A Principle requires that a transformation applying to A in (ii) must apply to the circled (topmost) A unless the structural description of the rule makes it apply unambiguously to the lower A. Others (including Kayne 1975:115-116, in particular) have argued that the A/A Principle is better formulated so as to prohibit a transformation's applying to the lower A in (ii) (this is called the 'absolute' form of the principle). (See Chomsky 1973 for some discussion of these two formulations of the A/A Principle.) An example of the type of problem the A/A Principle was intended to handle is seen in (iii).

(iii) a. My brother ate the bagels in the box.
(iii) b. The bagels in the box were eaten by my brother.
(iii) c. *The bagels were eaten in the box by my brother.

(Sentence (iii-c) is good with the bizarre reading in which my brother was in the box as he ate the bagels. It is not good with the reading in which the bagels but not my brother were in the box. Only the second reading, the more usual reading, is at issue here.) The underlying structure for (iii-a) at the point just before Passive applies is given in (iv).

(iv)

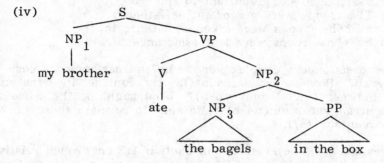

The SD for Passive is met by the string $NP_1$ V $NP_2$ as well as by the string $NP_1$ V $NP_3$ PP. But Passive applies only to the first string, just as the A/A Principle would demand.

If the A/A Principle is taken in its absolute form, should Passive be able to give us both (i-b) and (i-c) from (i-a)? If the A/A Principle is taken in its original form, should Passive be able to give us both (i-b) and (i-c) from (i-a)? In considering these questions, take the SD and SC of Passive to be as follows.

(v) SD   X   NP   V   NP   Y
     SC   1   2    3   4    5   $\Longrightarrow$   1   4   be+3   5   by+2

Note that the position of the NPs is affected by the SC but that of the V is not. If you decide that the A/A Principle should block the derivation of (i-b) from (i-a), how can you account for the fact that (i-b) is grammatical? If you propose that (i-b) and (i-c) derive from different underlying structures, how can you account for the fact that (i-b) and (i-c) are synonymous and (vi) is not ambiguous?

(vi) Someone took advantage of their innocence.

Question 2. 'Anarthrous' *advantage* means *advantage* with no article. Often idiom chunks (as discussed in Perlmutter's article in this volume) involve anarthrous NPs. For example, *keep tabs* has anarthrous *tabs*. In general, these NPs resist having any sort of modification although a few adjectives are acceptable.

(i) take unfair/*fair/great/little/*modest/??extreme advantage
(ii) keep careful/*careless/daily/??weekly/*annoying tabs

Does *keep tabs* behave like a complex verb with respect to Passive? Can you find other complex verbs? Are all idiom chunks complex verbs? Consider the following examples.

(iii) We gave/lent assistance to the troops.
(iv) We gave/lent the troops assistance.
(v) Assistance was given/lent to the troops.
(vi) The troops were given/lent assistance.
(vii) a. ?The troops were given assistance to.
(vii) b. *The troops were lent assistance to.

Is *give assistance* a complex verb? Is *lend assistance* a complex verb? How can you account for the contrast in grammaticality between (vii-a) and (vii-b)? What might be the cause(s) of the strangeness of (vii-a)? Be sure to compare these to *take advantage (of)*.

*Question 3. The argument in Section 1.2 on French relativization goes, basically, as follows. It has been claimed that one advantage of the VSO hypothesis is that rules such as stylistic inversion of a verb and its subject would not be needed. Instead, SF (subject formation) would simply not apply, leaving the surface having verb first. But with data from French relativization one can show that given an underlying VSO order we must apply the rules SF, MasQUErade, and Subject Verb Inversion in that order, in order to derive (i).

(i) l'homme qu'a vu Jean
    'the man that John saw'

With an underlying SVO order instead we find that Subject Verb Inversion and MasQUErade must apply in that order. Thus underlying VSO order not only does not have the claimed advantage (since both SF and SV Inversion take place here), but also requires a more complicated derivation of (i).

The two derivations of (i) are given here.

(ii) VSO         l'homme [que a vu Jean ___ ]
     SF    : l'homme [que Jean a vu ___ ]
     Mas   : DNA
     SVI   : l'homme [qu'a vu Jean ___ ]

(iii) SVO        l'homme [que Jean a vu ___ ]
      Mas   : DNA
      SVI   : l'homme [qu'a vu Jean ___ ]

In Berman's footnote 9, she remarks that a further disadvantage of the VSO hypothesis in contrast to the SVO hypothesis is that the former forces the extrinsic ordering of SF before Mas while with SVO, Mas and Relativization (the deletion part of relative clause formation) are intrinsically ordered in 'the appropriate way'. How does (iv) show that SF and Mas must be extrinsically ordered in the VSO hypothesis?

(iv) *l'homme qui Jean a vu
l'homme que Jean a vu
'the man that John saw'

Given the SVO hypothesis, why are Mas and Relativization intrinsically ordered? (Does one feed the other?) Consider example (v).

(v) l'homme qui a vu Jean
'the man who saw John' (and not 'the man who John saw'!)

Now consider the interaction of Mas and SVI in both hypotheses. Are they extrinsically or intrinsically ordered in either or both hypotheses? Consider (i) and (v) in your answer. Does your answer affect the effectiveness of Berman's argument based on French relativization?

**Question 4. In Section 1.3, Berman argues that, given 'the standard formulation for Particle Movement', a VSO underlying order calls for a more complicated account of particle behavior than an SVO analysis, regardless of the assumptions one makes about the cyclicity of the rules involved. Let us go through some derivations taking the standard formulation for PM to be (i) (as Berman offers).

(i) X [ V Part] NP Y
$\phantom{(i) X [}$ V
$\phantom{(i) }$ 1 $\phantom{[}$ 2 $\phantom{V}$ 3 $\phantom{Pa}$ 4 $\phantom{}$ 5 $\Longrightarrow$ 1 2 4 3 5

Answer the following questions assuming the VSO hypothesis. If PM is cyclic and SF postcyclic, we can never generate (ii). Why not?

(ii) John looked the information up.

If PM is postcyclic and SF is cyclic, we can generate both (ii) and (iii). How?

(iii) John looked up the information.

If both rules are cyclic and unordered with respect to each other, in what order do they apply to give (ii)? How would (iii) be derived? Berman's claim that (i) can be retained only 'by extrinsically ordering SF before Particle Movement' is an example of the strict order fallacy (studied by Koutsoudas 1972). In fact, no extrinsic ordering is called for here if we start from the assumption that rules need not be ordered and that a given rule can apply (or try to apply) both before and after any other rule. Likewise, if both rules are postcyclic and unordered, we can derive both (ii) and (iii). How? Here again, no extrinsic ordering statement is needed if we allow rules to be unordered. In each case the only problem will be that (iii) will have two derivations and two structures: if PM applies before SF, the Prt will still follow the V but it will no longer be in V.

But just to get both (ii) and (iii), the only problem for the VSO hypothesis is if PM is cyclic and SF is last- or postcyclic, or is extrinsically ordered to follow PM. However, since this situation is the most likely one (given that PM is probably cyclic and that the proposal of VSO underlying order really only has serious consequences if the SF rule is a very late rule), it is indeed a real problem for the VSO hypothesis.

Emonds (in the article in this volume) offers a different formulation for PM, repeated here.

$$\text{(iv) } X + V - NP - [P] - Y \Longrightarrow 1 - 3 - 2 - 4, \text{ where}$$
$$1 - 2 - 3 - 4 \text{ is a VP}$$

Under his analysis, particles are generated in post direct object position (i.e. normal PP position) and are optionally moved leftward to the V by the rule given in (iv). Emonds, of course, proposed his rule assuming the underlying order SVO. If, instead, we assume the underlying order VSO, (iv) might be rewritten as (something similar to) (v).

$$\text{(v) } X + V - (NP) - NP - [P] - Y \Longrightarrow 1 - 4 - 2 - 3 - 5$$
$$\phantom{\text{(v) } X + V - } 1 \phantom{()} 2 \phantom{(NP)} 3 \phantom{NP} 4 \phantom{[P]} 5$$

Given the VSO hypothesis, there is no underlying VP node-- thus the condition on (iv) that the string be a VP cannot be easily adjusted to fit (v). Still, let us assume for illustrative purposes that the safeguards behind the condition in (iv) could somehow be rewritten for (v). Now go through all the possible orderings of PM (with the rule in (v)) and SF, to see whether both (ii) and (iii) can be generated.

*Question 5. Notice Berman's footnote 11. After reading Chomsky's article in this volume and doing the homework assignment there, you can see that the nominalizations in this footnote could be argued to be derived from deep NPs. What explanation(s) can you offer for the failure of PM and Indirect Object Movement to apply here if these are deep NPs? Do you think Berman is right to suggest that the same reason is responsible for the inapplicability to these nominalizations of both PM and Indirect Object Movement?

**Question 6. In Section 1.4, Berman argues that regardless of the orderings of SF and Dative Movement (DM), the formulation of DM under the VSO hypothesis would have to be as in (i).

(i) X V NP NP *to* NP Y
   1  2  3   4   5   6   7 $\Longrightarrow$ 1 2 3 6 Ø 4 7

The formulation in (i) is not only more complicated (having more terms in it) than the standard formulation for DM; it is also 'intuitively wrong' since it needs to mention the subject NP (3 in this SD) in a rule which has 'nothing to do with the subject'. Furthermore, Berman argues, specific orderings of SF and DM call for other complications. Thus she concludes that the SVO hypothesis better accounts for DM.

Berman just briefly mentions that McCawley argued that DM need not be cyclic in the VSO hypothesis since it need not precede Passive. As you answer the following questions, use (i) and (ii) as the formulations of DM and Passive in the VSO hypothesis.

(ii) Passive: X V NP NP Y
            1  2  3   4  5 $\Longrightarrow$ 1 2 4 5 3

(McCawley does not give a SD or SC for Passive. However, he does state that the subject moves to the 'end of the clause' and that Passive is a cyclic rule. On this information, then, we have written the rule as in (ii).)

Use (iii) and (iv) as the formulations of DM and Passive in the SVO hypothesis.

(iii) X V NP *to* NP Y
    1  2  3   4   5   6 $\Longrightarrow$ 1 2 5 Ø 3 6

(iv) X NP V NP Y
    1  2  3  4  5 $\Longrightarrow$ 1 4 3 5 *by* + 2

Show that DM must be allowed to apply before Passive under the SVO hypothesis. Must DM be allowed to apply before Passive under the VSO hypothesis? Give a derivation of (v) under the VSO hypothesis.

(v) John was given the ring by Mary.

Could DM not be cyclic under the VSO hypothesis if Passive were cyclic and if (i) is the proper formulation of DM?

In the foregoing discussion, we took (i) as the proper formulation of DM in the VSO hypothesis. This formulation, however, contrasts with the one McCawley would offer in that none of the NPs are optional according to Berman, while one of them (term 3) is optional according to McCawley. Berman argues for the nonoptionality of these NPs on the basis of the starred (vi).

(vi) *The United Fund gave John.

With McCawley's formulation, (vi) could be derived from (vii) by DM followed by SF.

(vii) give John to the United Fund

Take (viii) as McCawley's alternative formulation of DM in the VSO hypothesis.

(viii) X V (NP) NP $to$ NP Y
$\phantom{(viii)}$ 1 2 3 $\phantom{X}$ 4 5 6 7 $\Longrightarrow$ 1 2 3 6 $\emptyset$ 4 7

Must DM in (viii) be allowed to apply before Passive?

**Question 7. In Section 1.5, Berman shows that Heavy NP Shift raises the same kinds of problems for the VSO hypothesis as PM and DM did. She gives a very nice, clear discussion, pulling all three cases together with their common point being that they are all rules that involve elements of the VP, but underlying VSO order brings in the problem of how to exclude a subject NP from being affected by the rules.

There is a new issue in this section, however: that just lightly touched on in footnote 15. Berman notes a suggestion of Jerry Morgan's that Heavy NP Shift 'be allowed to apply freely to subjects as well as object', producing sentences such as (ii) from (i).

(i) The problems that are involved in developing a way to ease air pollution that will not be offensive to automobile manufacturers were discussed yesterday.

(ii) *Were discussed yesterday the problems that are involved in developing a way to ease air pollution that will not be offensive to automobile manufacturers.

Then a constraint like Perlmutter's (1971: Chapter 3) Surface Subject Constraint, which, briefly, says that every surface sentence in English must have a subject for each S embedded in it (although there are wrinkles involving tensed embedded clauses not introduced by $that$), would mark (ii) as ungrammatical. Discuss the theoretical issues involved in the choice between (a) writing a rule in such a way as to apply to only those structures which will give a grammatical output upon application of the rule, and (b) writing a rule to apply to a variety of structures, only some of which will give grammatical outputs upon application of the rule and proposing surface filters to account for the ungrammatical outputs. Here you should recall the article by Partee in this volume. Why is it reasonable to consider a surface filter for blocking (ii), whereas one would most probably never have considered using a surface filter to block (iv-b) (where (iv-b) is the output of DM followed by SF on the underlying (iv-a) in the VSO hypothesis, using the standard formulation of DM given in (iii))?

(iii) X  V  NP  *to*  NP  Y
　　　 1  2  3　　4　 5　 6 $\Longrightarrow$ 1  2  5  $\emptyset$  3  6

(iv) a. gave John to the Watergate Defense Fund
(iv) b. *The Watergate Defense Fund gave John.

8 [Editor's Note]. In footnote 16, there is a misprint in lines 12 and 13. The words *former* and *latter* should be reversed in order.

*Question 9. In footnote 16, Berman mentions that Extraposition (Ex) and Extraposition from NP (Ex NP) might be just one rule. These rules apply in both subject and object positions. Consider the similarity of these rules in other respects to Heavy NP Shift (Heavy).

Ex from　　　 That he left annoyed me.
S Position　　 It annoyed me that he left.

Ex from　　　 I resented (it) that he left.
0 Position　　 I resented it very much that he left.

Ex NP from　 The man who talked so much just left.
S Position　　 The man just left who talked so much.

Ex NP from　 I liked the man who talked all night very much.
0 Position　　 I liked the man very much who talked all night.

Heavy　　　　 The man who talked so much just left.
S Position　　 (x)*Just left the man who talked so much.

Heavy　　　　 I liked the man who talked all night very much.
0 Position　　 I liked very much the man who talked all night.

Could the foregoing data be used to make an argument for ruling out (x) with a surface filter?

*Question 10. Assuming the VSO hypothesis, try to state Raising into Subject Position and Raising into Object Position as one rule 'in a very elegant fashion', as Berman says McCawley has done.

Question 11. Before beginning Section 2, it may be helpful to review the cycle. As the terms suggest, 'precyclic' rules apply before cyclic rules; 'cyclic' rules apply first to the lowest S, then to the next S up, and so on, ignoring all material not dominated by the S in question; 'last cyclic' rules are ordered among the cyclic rules but apply only on the topmost cycle; and 'postcyclic' rules apply after the topmost cycle is completed. There are many smaller issues as well, such as:

(1) Can a rule operating on the $S_1$ cycle mention elements in $S_1$ but physically affect only elements contained in $S_2$ in a structure such as:

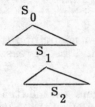

(2) Do pre- and postcyclic rules themselves apply to first $S_2$, then $S_1$, then $S_0$, or only to $S_0$? Also, while these terms are widely used, there remain many questions as to whether precyclic rules even exist and whether we do, indeed, have both last cyclic and postcyclic rules.

Finally, global constraints or rules refer not just to two structures adjacent in derivational history, but to two or more non-adjacent structures. They may even require access to entire derivations. Non-global or local rules apply indiscriminately to any structure which meets their SD at the time of application, regardless of what has preceded or what is to follow in the derivation.

Question 12.   Consider the argument in Section 2.5 for the globality of *Tough* Movement under the VSO hypothesis. In an S such as (i), Berman would have to claim that *(for) his children* is a matrix argument and not the subject of the lower clause. Why?

(i) This book is impossible for his children to read.

Now how do the Ss in (iii) and (iv) show that *(for) his children* in (i) is a matrix dative while *(for) his children* in (ii) is an embedded clause subject?

(ii) It would be impossible for Max for his children to go to that school.
(iii) a. For his children this book is impossible to read.
(iii) b. *For his children it would be impossible for Max to go to that school.
(iv) a. To read this book is impossible for his children.
(iv) b. *To go to that school would be impossible for Max for his children.

(Note that (iii-b) does have a good reading, but not that of (ii). Also, these sentences should make you recall the kind of data and argumentation presented by Clements in this volume with regard to questions of constituency of similar NPs.)

**Question 13. In Sections 2.1 through 2.5, Berman assumes that SF is postcyclic and argues that the VSO hypothesis forces us into global conditions on Raising into Object Position (RO), Equi, and *Tough* Movement. Even if one accepts global rules as a necessary extension of the theory, she shows that these particular global conditions are meant specifically to get 'around the claim, implicit in the VSO hypothesis, that structural identification of subjects versus nonsubjects is irrelevant'. Thus they are undesirable conditions and really help to point out the inadequacies of the VSO hypothesis.

Imagine a language with surface VSO order that has two story rules (similar to RO, Equi, or *Tough* Movement) which distinguish between subject NPs and nonsubject NPs. Test to see if global conditions would be needed in that language to prevent the misapplication of the rules. That is, imagine a language that has surface order as in (i) (where we use English words just as illustration).

(i) buy Mary a book

Now consider the situation of two story rules, such as RO and Equi, illustrated in (ii) and (iii).

(ii) expect Mary John to buy a book
(iii) expect Mary to win

Now suppose that in your imaginary language an S such as (iv-c) (or the analogue of it, given the language's two story rules) is ungrammatical. Would the language need a global condition to block Equi's following RO in (iv)?

(iv) a. expect Mary [kiss John Mary]
(iv) b. RO: expect Mary John [to kiss Mary]
(iv) c. Equi: expect Mary John to kiss

If (iv-c) (or its analogue) were bad and if the solution called for a global condition, how would this affect Berman's argument for English?

*Question 14. In Sections 2.6 through 2.8, Berman gives more cases of phenomena that need to distinguish between subjects and nonsubjects and that, accordingly, require either global conditions or, alternatively, extrinsic ordering statements under the VSO hypothesis. There may be a way around these complications, however, with Chomsky's (1973, 1975, 1976) trace theory. Chomsky proposes that whenever an NP is moved, a trace (t) is left behind. And these traces remain throughout the derivation, even appearing in surface structure. Consider, then, Berman's cliticization argument within trace theory. Underlying (i) would be (ii) after Relativization but before SF and Cliticization.

(i) a. l'homme qu'il voit 'the man who he sees'
(i) b. l'homme qui le voit 'the man who sees him'
(ii) a. $[_{NP}$l'homme $[_S$ que voit il t]]

(ii) b. $[_{NP}$l'homme $[_S$ que voit t il]]

(Of course, the assumption here must be that Relativization is a movement rather than deletion rule, since movement leaves a trace while deletion does not. If it should be shown that Relativization in French is a deletion rule, then trace theory has nothing new to say about the data in Sections 2.6 through 2.8 which involve relativization.)

But now Cliticization can easily distinguish between the il in (ii-a), which directly follows the V (i.e. is a subject), and the il in (ii-b), which is separated from the V by a t (i.e. is an object). Thus there is no need to extrinsically order SF before Cliticization.

Will trace theory also disarm Berman's argument in Section 2.7 involving Subject Pronoun Drop? What about that involving Portuguese Infinitive Agreement? The interested student should read the Chomsky works cited earlier, paying particular attention to his discussion of Equi phenomena (where he distinguishes two rules--one of deletion and one of interpretation), and then see if trace theory will disarm Berman's arguments involving RO and Equi. Those who are familiar with relational grammar and/or arc-pair grammar might try these alternatives, too.

*Question 15. In Section 3, Berman assumes SF is cyclic and claims that 'almost all sentences with surface VS order must go through a stage in which SV order is present'. Thus the derivation of such sentences involves both SF and inversion under the VSO hypothesis but involves only inversion under the SVO hypothesis.

In her examples she assumes that auxiliaries are main verbs. None of her arguments in this section except that in Section 3.2 would be affected at all if she assumed auxiliaries were not main verbs. Go through the argument in Section 3.2, modifying it as necessary, with the assumption that auxiliaries are not main verbs. This particular inversion rule will still provide an argument against the VSO hypothesis. How?

*Question 16. Berman does not discuss McCawley's claim that Predicate Raising and Neg Raising are more elegantly stated in the VSO hypothesis. Formulate those rules as needed for (i) and (ii) in both the VSO and the SVO hypotheses.

(i) a. John caused Sam to die.
(i) b. John killed Sam.
(ii) a. John thinks Sam isn't happy.
(ii) b. John doesn't think Sam is happy.

HOMEWORK PROBLEMS

I. Consider the following two derivations given in (2) and (3) for (1).

(1) Mary is expected to win the election.
(2)  someone expect [Mary win the election]
 RO: someone expect Mary [to win the election]
 Passive: Mary is expected to win the election.
(3)  someone expect [Mary win the election]
 Passive: [Mary win the election] is expected
 RS: Mary is expected to win the election.

(We have assumed here that the loss of the unspecified agent is either a part of the Passive rule or immediately follows it.)

Give arguments for choosing one derivation over the other for Ss such as (1). In making your arguments consider Ss such as:

(4a) Someone considered Mary to be intelligent.
(4b) Mary was considered to be intelligent.
(5a) *Someone decided Mary to be intelligent.
(5b) *Mary was decided to be intelligent.

(Before doing this problem, review the arguments in Section 1.6 of Berman's article very carefully.)

II. Are the following pairs of rules intrinsically ordered, and if so, which member of the pair comes first? (All rules here are optional. Also, the rules here are written in a simplified fashion with attention drawn to only those factors which are relevant to the question. In particular, we have eliminated variables that 'cover the tree')

(1a) V [NP VP] $\Longrightarrow$ V NP [VP]
   S        S
(1b) V Comp S $\Longrightarrow$ V S
(2a) V [NP VP] $\Longrightarrow$ V NP [VP]
   S        S
(2b) V [NP VP] $\Longrightarrow$ V [VP]
   S       S
(3a) V $NP_1$ $to$ $NP_2$ $\Longrightarrow$ V $NP_2$ $NP_1$
(3b) V NP $\Longrightarrow$ NP V
(4a) V NP $\Longrightarrow$ NP V
(4b) V [NP VP] $\Longrightarrow$ V NP [VP]
   S        S

III. Can you give an argument based on the Ss in (1) through (4) for an SV order stage in *there* sentences?

(1a) Three pigs were in the house.
(1b) There were three pigs in the house.
(2a) A little pig was in the house.
(2b) There was a little pig in the house.

How do (3b) and (4b) affect your argument?

(3a) Three pigs seem to be in the house.
(3b) There seem to be three pigs in the house
(4a) A little pig seems to be in the house.
(4b) There seems to be a little pig in the house.

(We credit examples like (3) and (4) and their significance to David Perlmutter, class lectures, MIT, 1973.)

## SUGGESTED READINGS

Chomsky, N. 1964. The logical basis of linguistic theory. In: Proceedings of the Ninth International Congress of Linguists, Cambridge, Mass., 1962. Edited by H. Lunt. The Hague: Mouton. (For Question 1.)

Chomsky, N. 1973. Conditions on transformations. In: A festschrift for Morris Halle. Edited by S. A. Anderson and P. Kiparsky. New York: Holt, Rinehart and Winston. 232-286. (For Question 11.)

Chomsky, N. 1975. Reflections on language. New York: Pantheon. (Especially Chapter 3, for Question 11.)

Chomsky, N. 1976. Conditions on rules of grammar. Linguistic Analysis 2:4.303-351. (For Question 11.)

Hudson, G. 1972. Is deep structure linear? In: Explorations in syntactic theory: UCLA Papers in Syntax 2. Los Angeles: University of California. 51-77.

Kayne, R. 1975. French syntax: The transformational cycle. Cambridge, Mass.: The MIT Press. (For Question 1.)

Koutsoudas, A. 1972. The strict order fallacy. Lg. 48:1.88-96. (For Question 4.)

Perlmutter, D. 1971. Deep and surface structure constraints in syntax. New York: Holt, Rinehart and Winston. (For the introduction and for Question 7.)

Ross, J. R. 1973. The penthouse principle and the order of constituents. In: You take the high node and I'll take the low node. Chicago: Chicago Linguistic Society. 397-422.

Schmerling, S. 1973. Subjectless sentences and the notion of surface structure. CLS 9.577-586. (For Question 9.)